My Leukaemia Fight

By Jake Andrade

To Diane

First published in Great Britain in 2023

Copyright © Text Jake Andrade 2023

ISBN 978-1-3999-4183-9

Printed and bound in Great Britain by TJ Books
Cover design and formatting by Softwood Self Publishing

Contents

Family photo on Christmas Day, 2015.

Introduction

Life can be turned upside down at any moment, often at times when you least expect it. Sometimes one is forced to go down a certain path in life, with a choice of only two options. One option is to fight for your life with no guarantee of survival. The alternative is certain death. Twice in my life, I was in this very situation, when I was diagnosed with Acute Myeloid Leukaemia (AML), and the experience transformed the future years of my life.

My name is Jake, and I was born on August 29th, 2002, at West Suffolk Hospital, located in a town named Bury St. Edmunds, in Suffolk, England. Since this was the hospital where my life journey began, it is unfortunate that I have had to associate it with anything else. Since my birth, I have lived in a nearby town, Stowmarket, with my parents and older sister, Kristy.

Growing up, I was always quite sick. I suffered with asthma when I was young, and Mum tells me I used to suffer from frequent chest infections. Luckily, I grew out of both of these. I have always had a weak immune system, describing myself as a 'cold magnet' as I seem to have this unfortunate ability of being able to catch every cough or cold going round. I used to – and still do – suffer quite badly with coughs and colds, an ordinary sniffle for most people giving me flu-like symptoms. Despite minor health problems here and there, I had no indication of what was to come. I had always got through my challenges and, despite being frequently ill, when I was well, I was *really* well. I describe myself as active but not healthy. While my diet could have – and should be – improved, in addition to always being slightly overweight, I still remained active. Never really into football, I instead spent my younger years as a child swimming, and up until I was thirteen, I attended tennis club every Thursday evening. I showed up at school and remained active outside it. This came to a halt when I was thirteen years old, when the next six months of my life would be spent in and out of hospital.

My story begins in 2016. After spending 2015 stress-free (I would say it was one of the greatest years of my life so far), with amazing experiences with friends and family, I was set on 2016 being an even better year. Now in Year 9 at high school, things were getting serious in terms of my education, with my GCSEs starting the next academic year, September 2016. In March 2016, I was lucky enough to have finalised my GCSE options. The day after submitting my options, who could have known that I had left school for the unforeseeable future? A week later, my life would be turned upside down, and my entire world would be shattered.

Fast forward to six months later, I survived the major obstacle that stood in my way: cancer. Very quickly I returned back to normal life, full of many amazing opportunities and experiences, and had, quite possibly, the best five years of my life! I was beginning to really make something of my life by starting the process of becoming an independent adult, where I learned to drive, finished school, went to university, and got a job. By the summer of 2021, I began to turn my negative experience with cancer into a positive by sharing my story to help others similar to me. I had worked on this book for five years and decided that my five years in remission would be a great celebratory marker to get this book published, and the publishing process was officially underway. Had I published this book then, it would only be half the length it is now.

Then came the absolute shock of December 2021, where the nasty cells that had been hiding in my bone marrow for five years while I was claiming to be in 'remission' – the cells that I was certain had been eradicated for good – suddenly started to show their faces again. After building a success story over five years, it was back to square one. All the progress I had made over five years all crashed down in only a few weeks. This time I would be going through the exact same thing again, though not as a paediatric, but an adult.

***

Mum gave me the idea to write this, and I have worked on this for almost six years. I started writing 'my journal', as I call it, a few days into my first stay in hospital. It started off as an actual diary, giving my first-hand account of each day's events, illustrated by some pretty awful cartoons drawn by myself. The idea to write a diary emerged when I was upset about losing my hair, so Mum suggested I cut some of my hair off and stick it in my diary as something to remember the 'old me' by. Regrettably, I have since lost the rough notebook that my diary was contained in, and I never did save a piece of my old hair. However, although this has turned more into a memoir, I believe that I remember enough about what I have experienced to give an accurate account of my story with Acute Myeloid Leukaemia.

My memory can be patchy at times, but I hope, with the help of my parents and the massive blue folder overflowing with my complex medical records, I can provide an accurate chronological account of my journey. Also helping me write this is my 'special box' dedicated to my cancer journey, which contains my scrapbook of cards, information booklets, letters, and newspaper articles during my hospital years. Of course, the internet has also helped me out when I have needed to define specific medical terms. My aim is for all of these resources to combine in linear order to successfully put you in my shoes as a cancer patient and survivor.

Because my first experience with cancer was as a paediatric, this book was originally aimed at children, teenagers, and their parents to use as a tool to help them through something similar, in addition to hopefully providing something of interest to the general reader. My relapse allowed this book to appeal to many more cancer patients, and while I acknowledge that all cancer journeys are different, I hope there is something here for everyone. I've stayed on paediatric wards and teenage wards and have attended adult clinics. I've been treated both as an inpatient and outpatient, with chemotherapy and radiotherapy, and have had two bone marrow transplants, each quite different from the other. I've been treated under three different hospitals and have had to relocate to a different city just to be treated. I've had countless blood and platelet transfusions, blood tests, antibiotics, infections, scans, biopsies, and much more. I know what life is like recovering from cancer and being in long-term remission, and I've also had to cope with the devastating news of relapse. I've even had to face cancer treatment through a global pandemic!

Because I was an adult when I relapsed, I had a lot more independence and understanding regarding my care and condition. This book covers all aspects of my cancer journey, from the health side to the social side and eventually my recovery. You may notice that in Part III of this book, I include a lot more technical medical terms; this is because more information was available to me as an adult than a paediatric.

I still try my best to make this approachable to the general reader, and I hope that this additional detail helps to put things into perspective about what it is actually like to be a cancer patient.

I try to keep to my experiences only, although I will mention a few other names here and there, as fellow patients were very important to my journey.

Part One

The First Battle

Chapter 1

A Really Bad Cold

Signs and symptoms before and during March 2016

Wednesday 16th March 2016. It was 9:10am, the very start of the school day. My friend, Liam, and I met about seven other classmates and the course leaders in the congregating classroom, where we were all set to meet for the day's adventure. Today wasn't going to be a normal school day. Only a few weeks into the course, we were set for our first school trip – a nine-mile walk.

I was in Year 9 – my first year of high school, having just finished middle school – and as a way of building confidence and making friends, Liam and I were put forward to take part in a CVQO course, which aimed to provide us with a vocational qualification once completed. Being on the course was very much like being in the army since we performed army rituals and the course leaders had actually previously been in the army. We were taught a number of life skills, including teamwork and navigation, hence the nine-mile walk.

Us classmates were all stood in the classroom, along with the course leaders, Mr Head and Mr Knight, waiting for the accompanying member of staff, Mrs Hamilton. I had spent the weekend preparing for the walk, having bought a new raincoat and walking boots. We were required to bring a lot – two coats, two-litres of water, lunch and snacks, a change of socks, boots, and the list goes on. A map and compass were provided. This wasn't any ordinary walk. This was a walk which was to be navigated by us, the students. We weren't going to get any help if we got lost; the concept was survival.

Like I said, I spent the weekend preparing. But as soon as Liam and I entered the classroom to meet the others, we were automatically told off for not being prepared.

"Why are you two in school uniform?" asked Mr Head.

In our defence, no one had told us *not* to wear school uniform. At least we had our walking boots on and a change of coats.

For me, not being prepared went beyond being in school uniform. I was feeling really unwell and had been for a few months. I was suffering from a cold and was constantly tired and breathless. Since January, my health had been deteriorating, but, believing it was something that would just blow over once we were out of the cold weather, I continued life as best I could into February and March. I never could have known that a week after this walk, I would be in a completely different place regarding both my health and where I'd be staying.

Mrs Hamilton finally arrived, and we set off on the walk. We were scheduled to finish at 3:30pm, just in time for the final school bell.

The first ten seconds of the walk were the best of the whole day; it rapidly got worse from there. The only thing that was bothering me was my nose – I'd had a cold for three months that wasn't going away. Then the cough started. It was the fresh air that sparked it. I choked and spluttered throughout the day.

I would have been lucky if that was the only thing I had to endure on this walk – but no, it got worse. About a minute in, 200 metres from the school gates, the slowest walk was overworking me, and I was becoming tired.

"The number one rule is that we all go the pace of the slowest person," Mr Head strictly stated.

I did feel a little bit guilty. The slowest person was me. I was walking so slow, but I was so tired, breathing heavily and gasping for breath. I felt as if I had finished running a marathon and my brain was pumping out of my head, as if it was trying to tell me to take it easy. *Badum badum badum* went the pulse in my brain, which made it seem as if my heart was stuck in my head and couldn't escape.

I was determined to power through. Anyway, I was only two minutes in; I didn't want to embarrass myself by quitting already. My parents had also spent lots of money on the equipment I required for this walk, so I had to at least try and complete it. Completing a nine-mile walk was something I was going to be proud of, and I wanted to keep going, no matter how bad I was feeling. After all, it was just a really bad cold, right?

Walking at a snail's pace, three minutes into the walk, my eyes started to go blurry. I felt dizzy and breathless. Feeling lightheaded was something I was used to by then, but it still bothered me. Every step I took felt like I was going to collapse and pass out.

Luckily for me, it wasn't my turn to navigate just yet, so I didn't really have to pay attention to anything. For the next hour, I tried as best as I could to view the scenery, having come off the busy roads and into the beautiful fields. It was a bit of a dull day. It wasn't raining but the clouds were dark and gloomy, and any chance the sun did have to shine through was undermined by the fast-blowing wind.

Choking and spluttering, an hour in and now on the fields bordering the dual-carriageway, Mr Head stopped and turned around. "You're not going to die on us, are you Jake?"

"No," I replied.

I tried to show my strength and continue to power through. The constant strain of coughing hurt my stomach muscles and caused some painful headaches. Mr Head recommended that I have a quick snack in order to boost my energy. I managed half a sausage roll, but after that I felt like throwing up.

Dragging my feet the entire way, we ended up at a church roughly around noon. It was lunchtime, so we decided to stop by a bench, near the church, to eat lunch. I was fortunate enough to be with a team that did not get frustrated with me. In a typical school hierarchal fashion, at lunchtime, the staff members got the bench and the students sat on the cold, muddy floor. Mrs Hamilton, who could tell I wasn't well, kindly gave up her seat for me. Mr Head kept asking if I had eaten all my lunch, but the thought of any food was making me feel sick. After half an hour, it was time to complete the second half of the walk.

My body temperature didn't reflect the weather. About three quarters through the walk, I began to feel very hot. Hotter than normal. I was sweating when no one else was, and so I stopped, took my winter coat off, and put my raincoat on instead. As soon as I did that, my sweating turned into constant shivering. My teeth were chattering and cold chills ran up my spine. So I took my raincoat off and put my winter coat back on. This went back and forth for a while, and the change in temperature was quick — it happened as soon as I changed coats. It was annoying but I was glad I had brought both coats with me, despite the heavy backpack, which worsened the back and shoulder pain that I had been suffering from for months.

Eventually, I just sat down on the floor, declaring that I needed a break. Mrs Hamilton asked if I needed to stop the walk and if I wanted anyone to come pick me up. I refused; I was going to do everything I could to complete this walk, even if it killed me. It wasn't a smart decision, and by this point, it was clear that in my condition, I had no business being out there. But I wanted to feel proud of myself.

The walk itself was a challenge, whether I was seriously ill or not. I recall getting stuck in the mud on at least one occasion, having to wrestle myself through bushes, and even having to be pulled out of a ditch. The weather from the previous day didn't help either, as walking in the fields of sludge made things very slippery.

There was a sigh of relief towards the end of the walk when I reached familiar territory. By now we were back in Stowmarket, albeit in the middle of a field I had never been in.

Mr Head kept giving words of encouragement. "Come on, Jake!" and "Almost there!"

Tired, breathless, choking, and spluttering, with *badum badum badum* in my head and a tissue up my nose, I completed the final hurdle up the steep hill, and by 3:30pm, I was back at the school gates. We all took a group photo, and Mrs Hamilton congratulated me for completing the walk when I knew I wasn't well.

I was so happy and proud of myself. I wasn't so happy to discover that I had to walk home from school, which was another two miles, but nonetheless, I felt a sense of accomplishment. I decided that I would take the next day off school, planning to be back on the Friday.

When I returned home, my feet froze and stiffened as I passed out on the sofa.

My sister, Kristy, wasn't very sympathetic when she saw me and bitterly grumbled, "Nine miles isn't that far."

Shortly after, I threw up the contents of my empty stomach, which resembled a watery bile. I slept most of the evening, which at this point was all I wanted to do, and ate very little of my dinner.

Little did I know, I had just had my last day as a Year 9 in school and an evil monster was tearing me apart, slowly growing and killing me on the inside. Exactly a week later, it would be killing me rapidly and my world would be shattered and changed forever. Life as I once knew it was about to be turned upside down. If I wanted to live, I was going to have to show more strength and courage than ever before.

***

The truth is that I had been feeling this bad for at least three months. Dad reckons it's even earlier than that, dating back to September 2015. He says the downfall was when I was on the traditional family weekend away. Despite actually feeling well then, there is a picture of me that he finds difficult to look at because I look really unwell. My hair had grown so much, and I was just passed out on an armchair. Apparently, after that holiday, I was never the same again.

This may seem strange, but I recall my first symptom occurring on New Year's Day in 2016, when we were having a family dinner at Grandma's. I say 'strange' because after such an amazing 2015, 2016 was doomed from the start. I wasn't very ill, but I was far from good. This symptom was a headache, which may seem minor to pretty much everyone, but it is significant for me for two reasons: it was unusual for me to have headaches, and with it came an unusual drowsiness. All the energy had been drained out of me. I had been on Christmas break, so it wasn't like I had been overworking myself. After this day, headaches began to appear more often, although they were not frequent, just more than I had been used to. I didn't question or worry about it. The same cannot be said for the drowsiness, however, and that seemed to remain with me 24/7. I just hoped that it would go on its own.

Late January was when things became considerably worse for me. My health really started deteriorating at this point, although, back then, I thought it would all blow over. I have always been one to catch every cough or cold going. The majority of people would always have a little sniffle or just a light cough when they catch the virus. I, however, would get it more like the flu 99% of the time and more often than most people. I think I was catching colds every month, at least. I'd go as far to say that I was catching a cold every three weeks, and that is not me exaggerating. I was always ill, and to some extent, I still am. Towards the end of January, I caught a cold, but unlike all of those previously, this cold did not go away. It got worse as time progressed. This cold would stay with me until late March, when something much stronger than my own immune system would be needed to end it.

A third symptom I suffered, starting in January 2016, was one I cannot explain very well. Even after Googling these symptoms, I cannot find any explanation related to my diagnosis five years later. I kept hearing my pulse in my head. To begin with, it was when I was doing exercise; in PE at school it was particularly annoying. As time went on, it was not only heard during intense exercise, but during light exercise, such as walking to and from school. I suffered it at home too; I couldn't walk up the stairs without hearing my pulse. As time progressed further, just sitting down watching the TV would cause the *badum badum badum* heartbeat in my head. It was more annoying than anything serious, but going into late February and early March, it was getting to the point where I could feel my brain pumping out of my head as if it was about to explode. It was like my body was trying to tell me something, doing everything it could to get my attention, shouting at me to get help. Why I was feeling like this seemed like such a mystery, but in January or early February, I wasn't too worried and continued to put off going to the doctor. I just tried to power through life. Things will get better on their own, I thought. How wrong I was.

In late January, the fourth symptom I began to suffer was dizziness and temporary partial sight loss. This scared me because as soon as I got up from a chair or sofa and was on my feet, the room would start spinning and my sight would turn grey like a TV screen. Once I rested my head on the wall for a few seconds, my balance and eyesight would return. January wasn't too bad as I was only a little bit dizzy and the sight loss was in the bottom of my eyes, but by February and March, the dizzy spells lasted longer and so did the sight loss, covering my entire vision. The longer it lasted, the more worrying it became, because I feared that it would be permanent. Before going to the doctor, I thought I would wait and see if it passed.

Going into February, things were continuing to go wrong. Still, I didn't really question it. I just thought all of this was caused by this never-ending cold and all of these problems were working in combination as a result of that. A new symptom developed in February, which was probably the worst of them all because of how it affected me in everyday life. All the symptoms I'd experienced so far were horrible, but I was able to cope with them. They were just on the sidelines, prominent in everyday life but not interfering. This one destroyed me. This one was tiredness. Severe fatigue. I could get eleven hours of sleep at night, uninterrupted, and wake up feeling like I hadn't slept for ten days. All my energy had been drained out of me. I only just managed to drag myself to school, except by this point, back and shoulder pain meant that carrying my school bag hurt like hell and Mum had to give me lifts every morning. I had no energy for anything else – school was the only thing I could handle, and even that was a challenge. I remember one weekend, when I was round Auntie Karen's for dinner, I had to lie down to have a nap during the dinner because I was so tired. Taking naps during dinner was not normal, especially for me, considering I love food. Bedtime became earlier and earlier, and every morning I was pressing the snooze button on my alarm more and more. But no matter how much sleep I got, the fatigue never disappeared and only seemed to worsen.

With the tiredness also came breathlessness. I was short of breath by doing any activity. Like the previous symptoms, it gradually became worse, starting during intense exercise and then when just carrying out simple and easy activities. I don't remember being severely out of breath. It wasn't like I was fighting for my life, but I was breathing quite heavily, and intense exercise made me out of breath much quicker than it would for a healthy person.

My sleep was disrupted occasionally, and I experienced a number of night sweats and weird dreams. One dream I recall is flying around on a giant chessboard. That being said, I remember being able to sleep really well, since that was all my body really wanted to do.

My temperature was also very unstable. At night, I was always hot. It could be cold outside with my bedroom windows wide open and the fan blowing, but I would still be boiling. During the day, my temperature was very unstable but predictable. I was rarely warm in the daytime. Going outside made me freezing cold, and while inside was a lot better, I was still cold. It was particularly difficult at school because the rules stated that students were not allowed in the corridors at break and lunch time, so to avoid me suffering, Liam and I had to hide under the stairs to avoid being caught by a teacher. Whether it was fevers I was suffering from, I don't know, because I never had my temperature taken during this period, but I can tell you it was a very similar feeling.

By March 2016, my health was rapidly deteriorating, and it was affecting my everyday functioning. I was in so much pain, suffering from back and shoulder ache, which was worsening. At first, I thought this was because I was carrying heavy bags to school with me, which was true, but then I realised my body was just shutting down. My cold got worse and worse, and my cough had got to the point where I was choking and spluttering everywhere, which gave me a red bloodshot eye and pain in my stomach. I was boiling at night, freezing by day. I was getting ten to twelve hours sleep but constantly felt I had not slept in days, and the easiest of activities made me out of breath. I was drowsy and dizzy all the time and was losing my sight more often and for longer. And on top of that, badum badum badum was what I heard all day every day, whether in a quiet or a noisy setting, which, along with the dizziness and drowsiness, made me feel very spaced-out. As the month of March continued, I noticed the sick days at school were becoming more frequent, and I also had to give up tennis club. It was bad enough having to go to school with the condition I was in, and as soon as I had returned home from a day at school, it was straight to the sofa. It was sad to see myself go from someone who was very much active to someone who was really unhealthy and whose life involved just going to school, watching TV, and sleeping. I don't think I was aware of how serious the situation was, despite feeling like this.

***

I used to walk to school with my friend, Ryan, and once on the way home, he told me that if I was feeling that bad, I should go to the doctor about it. I brushed it aside, although deep down I knew that my health was deteriorating and I really did need to go. This conversation was in mid-March. Before that, my parents and I seemed to have the perfect explanation for what was going on with me. Thinking back, rather than being explanations for what was going on with me, they were probably more likely reasons to dodge the problem ...

The cold was easy to explain. For my entire life I have been slightly overweight and getting me to eat vegetables is a challenge. Because I wasn't eating enough nutritious foods, I wasn't getting enough nutrients, so I couldn't get rid of the cold because my immune system couldn't fight it. That was probably the reason why I caught so many of them in the first place. It sounds silly but that is what a doctor would tell you – fruits and vegetables are good for the immune system. Therefore, to combat this, Mum put extra cucumber and lettuce on my plate every dinner time and I was encouraged to eat more fruit. I genuinely believed this would make all the difference, and my parents believed it too!

My explanation for the tiredness made perfect sense to me at the time. Back in January, I had started a Sunday paper round, and I had to get up at around 6:00am every morning. For school, I woke up at 7:00am every morning. My only lay-in day was Saturday, and I didn't have the full weekend of complete rest. At the time, I genuinely believed the busy weekend as the cause for my tiredness and I just had to keep going and get used to my new routine. Therefore, despite feeling so tired, it was just best to carry on and get through life.

I was in a lot of pain. That being said, I'm not one to complain about pain. I did my best to cover up as much as I could so I could function properly and continue everyday life. My parents only knew so much to the point that they weren't really concerned either. Of course, they knew the visible issues I was suffering from, most notably my cold and my tiredness, but they couldn't see the pulse in my head or my dizziness. All they could really tell was that I was looking paler than usual, but didn't really suspect anything major, and to begin with, like myself, they were not too concerned.

The most prominent reason I could think of for not seeing a doctor was because I feared that I would get turned away. I thought this was a bad cold and a doctor can't treat a cold. As I was young, I wasn't aware of the seriousness of the situation. Being young, I was not educated in symptoms of diseases. If I was gravely ill, then surely I'd have more serious symptoms, right? These all seemed like minor symptoms to me at the time, which were working in combination to make my life torture. Like I said, I thought this was all happening as a result of a really bad cold and thus my entire body was suffering as a result. Things like dizziness and tiredness can be signs of curable conditions too. I knew that if I went to the doctor with a cold, I'd get turned away because there's no cure for a cold and unnecessary appointments waste NHS money. Therefore, I was willing to try everything I could to make myself better before going to the doctor as a last resort. As you can imagine, and I'm sure you're not surprised to hear, all of my attempts to make myself better failed.

***

Thursday 17th March was my first of many consecutive days off. Nausea was a newly developed symptom, and that was in combination with all the other symptoms. I had planned to take just the Thursday off; the next days to come were not planned, and as the days went by, the worse my situation seemed to get.

For the next few days or so, I got up believing I would attend school that day. I'd get up, have breakfast, and then get in the shower, and that was where everything stopped going to plan. As soon as I got out of the shower, I would feel so sick, I'd get dizzy, and then I'd throw up in the toilet. Sometimes there was blood in my vomit. This seemed to go on for weeks, but looking at it now, it wasn't that long as this was all within a one-week period. I was so ill that the time seemed to drag.

One morning, I was able to get past shower time and start walking to school. But I forgot my house keys and had to turn back once I got to the end of the road, returning home in tears because I was feeling so unwell and was going to be late. Never had feeling unwell reduced me to tears. Mum didn't believe that anything severe was really going on and she wasn't happy that I was missing yet another day of school. I did get told off quite badly that morning; she thought I was trying to get out of going to school. I don't blame her if I'm honest; none of this was visible. The only thing she knew was that I was suffering from a cold which was making me unwell in other ways. Nobody, including myself, thought to question why it was making me ill in other ways, and I think that was where the problem lay. To everyone and I, it was just a really bad cold.

I think I frustrated my friends a bit as well by not turning up to school. My friend, Zoe, who I walked some of the way to school with every morning, knocked on my door only for me to tell her I wasn't going to school again, but I always promised I'd be in the next day. Liam was really the only person I hung around with at break and lunch, so when I was gone, he was all on his own – I did encourage him to hang out with others in my absence. After a while, it became very hard for him too. Little did he or I know, he was going to have to put up with that feeling of loneliness for a very long time.

The weekend of Saturday 19th and Sunday 20th March was a tough one. If the nine-mile walk itself was bad – which had taken place on March 16th – then the effects were much worse. An insect bite had developed on my leg. It was larger than average and seemed to get bigger – a large red spot. The excruciating pain it caused severely disrupted my walking, and it only got worse. It was so painful that my legs collapsed on me that Saturday night. I was now losing my mobility. Most of my weekend was spent obsessively rubbing cream up and down my leg to make the bite go down and relieve the pain and itching, with little success. My parents had to do my paper round for me that Sunday morning, and while I had to make the painful walk to sort the newspapers, I sat in the car while they delivered them. By this weekend, it was very clear to everyone that my health had rapidly deteriorated, and Dad had no choice but to get me an appointment to see the doctor the next day. Something really wasn't right, and it was time the problem was solved.

Monday 21st March was the first doctor's appointment I'd had in a while. Although I've always been one to catch everything going, up until this point, I had avoided going to the see the GP for most things. To some extent, I was right about fearing being turned away by the doctor; it was difficult for me to get an appointment because the first reaction Dad got over the phone from the receptionist was "We don't treat colds". It was like we had to fight and plead for the appointment. But it was clear this cold had lasted way too long and everything else I was experiencing was a clear sign that something was wrong. We didn't think to bring that up though. The main concern for this appointment was not all of the previous symptoms

I'd experienced, but the new ones: the bite on my leg and the bloodshot eye that my cough had given me. Three months of worsening health and this was all I thought to bring up in the consultation!

The doctor told me that the bloodshot eye would clear up on its own and was nothing to worry about, although he described the bite as 'nasty'. He asked if I was allergic to penicillin, something I didn't know the answer to because I had never needed it before. We were asked if anyone in our family history was allergic to it, and as far as we knew, only Grandma was. Perhaps the bite was infected, so he prescribed the penicillin anyway as a trial, which would hopefully help decrease the swelling and relieve the pain.

Tuesday 22nd March was a day spent at home. By this point, Dad was taking time off work to take care of me because it was clear I was really ill, but we were all hopeful that the penicillin prescribed would cure all my problems. Was penicillin going to be the magic drug that would help repair me and get me back to my normal self? The doctor didn't seem too concerned with anything else. As far as he was concerned, the bite was the only issue he could see.

The Easter holidays were approaching, so I decided I would stop saying I was coming into school the next day and just take the week off, giving me three weeks off to rest and recover and return to school fit and healthy. However, that night, my health continued to deteriorate as I had a high temperature and my heart began to beat abnormally strong and fast. At this point, I was scared because Dad was reading me a list of everything that I could have wrong with me, while Mum tried to calm me down and shut him up. Dad went on a late-night trip to Tesco to get a thermometer, while Mum tried to calm me down and give me paracetamol to combat my fever. Dad was really worried and was on the verge of either taking me to the hospital or calling 999, but the paracetamol calmed me down and my heartbeat and temperature relaxed. This was only temporary, and my condition would get much worse from then on. That being said, we were still optimistic. We were hopeful it was just a reaction to the penicillin. I was going to be monitored in the morning to see if I needed another appointment with the GP.

Chapter 2

The Darkest Days

My diagnosis: Wednesday 23rd March and Thursday 24th March 2016

Wednesday 23rd March 2016. Only the night before, I was sent to sleep with a fever, and luckily the paracetamol successfully brought my temperature down. I recall sleeping well for the night – albeit with an awful cold and cough – but the Wednesday morning was an unexpectedly early start. I woke up very thirsty at about 5:00am, so I got out of bed to get a drink of water. But when I took a sip, I felt a feeling of great discomfort. It was like I had swallowed my tongue, and with it came an excruciating sharp pain in my ear. My throat had also swelled up rapidly, and as the hours of the day went by, the size of my throat increased to the point where I looked like a bullfrog.

I went into my parent's room to talk to Dad about this. I tried to tell him as clearly as I could, but when I began talking, I discovered that I had lost my voice. Therefore, I was speaking with a very croaky voice and dry throat, and if I did try to talk, it brought on the pain in my ear. My communication for the day was brought down to a quiet whisper, and even then, it was still painful.

As soon as Combs Ford Surgery opened, Dad made an appointment. At first, we all believed, and were hopeful, that this was an allergic reaction to the penicillin and an alternative could be used to cure my increasingly long list of symptoms. Afterall, it was a risk taking it, since I had never had it before, and the doctor did ask if I was allergic to it. I should add that I was experiencing shortness of breath, a fever, a runny nose, and swelling – all signs of a penicillin reaction. That being said, what I knew but failed to acknowledge was that I had been suffering these long before the penicillin, minus the swelling. The penicillin had appeared to have been some help, though, because although my leg was still in a lot of pain, the swelling of my insect bite had reduced. I was able to walk again, just with a slight limp.

The earliest appointment we could get was at about 3:20pm, so I spent most of the day lying on the sofa, doing my best to eat and drink to keep up my energy. But my ear was so painful and my throat felt so strange that I couldn't eat a lot. Grandma also came to visit and brought doughnuts for me.

For some reason, I wanted Mum with me at this doctor's appointment. Dad was currently taking care of me while Mum continued going to work. I wanted both of them there with me. Despite my optimism, it was like I was sensing something seriously wrong, but it was only a thought I had in the back of my mind. I still believed that this was just an earache and swollen throat, which would be reduced with simple medication. It's like I knew something without it ever crossing my mind. It was as if my request for both of my parents to be there was foreshadowing something very important in the history of my life.

Mum was able to leave work early and met Dad and I at the GP surgery. The car park was full, but instead of dropping me off, Dad made me walk from the next car park to the surgery, which still wasn't far, but for someone in my condition, it felt like miles. The walk to the surgery was difficult. My leg pain was excruciating, and with my walking made even more difficult by my dizziness and breathlessness, I had to hold on to my parents' shoulders for balance. The pulse in my head was getting louder and faster. My nose was running, and I was coughing everywhere. The slowest walk was making me out of breath. I was dizzy and drowsy and all the energy had been sucked out of me. My face was swollen, and I had lost all colour in my skin. But I was still standing – only just. I hadn't reached my worst just yet.

The waiting room wasn't much better either. Going to the doctors is never nice, but this time, the atmosphere was extremely unpleasant. I felt like I was in my own little world, paralysed in my body, but at the same time completely aware of my surroundings. I felt like I couldn't move, almost unconscious. Kids were screaming and punching each other in the waiting room, while I just stared into space, waiting for my name to be called, with the pulse in my brain making its presence known with increased intensity. It was all I was physically able to do – stare into space, waiting for my name to be called on the monitor, with growing anxiety as the time progressed.

I must say now that all the symptoms I was experiencing from January to March were again mostly forgotten about in this visit to the doctor. We only mentioned the major developments that had led to the appointment being made to begin with. If the events of that morning had not happened, I probably would have continued living with my health issues, continuing to take the penicillin. The penicillin had slightly cleared up the bite on my leg, and there were still beliefs that maybe my throat problems were caused by an allergic reaction. The only reason why we made the doctors' appointment was for my throat and ear, and although I have no idea why, despite the severity and increased concern of everything, I still felt no reason to address my other concerns to the doctor. They were about to find out for themselves anyway.

The GP called me in and did the normal doctor procedure,

including listening to my lungs and heart through her stethoscope. Despite how I was feeling, this was all fine. We were finally getting somewhere when I had to open my mouth and say 'Ahhhhh', although this was difficult because my sore throat made my voice croaky. Talking was very difficult, so I couldn't explain how I was feeling in the best possible detail. I tried to say everything in as few words as possible, with Mum and Dad often having to intervene.

"I can see that there is something wrong, but I can't identify what," said the GP, when she looked at my throat.

I wasn't sure if this was good or bad news – she had found something wrong, which was good and could hopefully be used to help fix me, but at the same time, what was wrong with me? Within a matter of minutes, she referred me to the Rainbow Ward at West Suffolk Hospital in Bury St. Edmunds to see the Ear, Nose, and Throat (ENT) specialist doctors, who would be much better qualified to look into cases like mine. Although I found having to go to hospital a little concerning, I wasn't too worried. The idea of my symptoms being a problem with my ear, nose, or throat made it seem like a minor issue. The only time I had been in a hospital was when I was born or when visiting a sick family member, but I wasn't too concerned about having to go myself. I was only seeing the ENT doctors; the doctor hadn't found anything seriously wrong, right? I was very optimistic and challenged my negative thoughts. The penicillin had taken care of my bite, but it was still possible that I was allergic to it. I repeated that in my head over and over. Also, the GP didn't say she was concerned, she just said that she could see something wrong but didn't know what it was. However, she was also very confident that the symptoms displayed were not an allergic reaction to the penicillin, although my parents and I remained hopeful that it was and continued to believe this. I thought this would be something that could easily be fixed, and it would be a quick stay at the hospital of one night, maximum.

Me and my family returned home for a while in order to pack the essentials for our visit. I was aware hospitals take forever to do things, so I thought I would take something to occupy myself: my iPad. Because I couldn't decide if I was hot or cold, I thought I would take a blanket to have in the car with me. Mum encouraged me to eat something as I hadn't eaten much all day due to my throat pain, so I just about managed half a doughnut, which was the last thing I would eat before my life would be changed forever. We left the house just after 5:00pm. I was in the back of Dad's boss' car – as ours had broken down a few weeks before – travelling down the A14 for a twenty-minute drive to West Suffolk Hospital, in Bury St. Edmunds, completely unaware that I would not see Stowmarket again until May.

For the first time ever, I was a patient in a hospital. I had never broken a bone before. I had never had anything wrong with me to require such advanced treatment.

The West Suffolk Hospital car park was pretty full as well – all hospital and GP car parks seem to be full these days – so I had to experience a similar walk to the one at Combs Ford Surgery. Getting out of the car was a struggle because I had no energy to move. I had to hold on to my parents for balance while I took a slow and monotonous walk to the ward, having to take regular breaks as I was so tired. The Rainbow Ward is the children's ward, treating children for all types of problems, from broken bones to long-term diseases, and it is split into two sections. Of course, knowing our luck, we accidentally went to the wrong section first. We went to the day unit first; the actual ward was upstairs. I insisted on using the lift, but Dad, still a huge believer that my lifestyle – my diet and recent inactivity – was the cause of all this, made me use the stairs.

"You need the exercise," he said.

By this point, Mum was not so sure and no longer believed the lifestyle explanation, completely agreeing with me that we should have used the lift.

Upon arrival, the receptionist at the desk made us fill in a number of forms. I had to wear two wristbands, a white one which contained my name, date of birth, and hospital number, and a red one, which listed anything I'm allergic to. I wasn't allergic to anything as of yet, but we were hopeful that the cause of my health issues was a reaction to penicillin and nothing else, so 'Penicillin?' was written on my red wristband. After that was all completed, we were directed to the waiting room, where I had to wait for the healthcare assistant to take my obs.

Observations, but almost always called obs, include taking your temperature, blood pressure, and heartrate and need to be taken regularly (every four hours) when in hospital. Depending on your condition, they may need to be taken more often. I also had to be weighed to make sure my weight remained stable – I was 57kg, which, I was to find out, would be very important information for the near future. Sometimes, obs involve having your height measured too, although on this occasion it wasn't taken.

After having my obs done, a nurse called me into the treatment room to have a blood test. First, a number of cannulas had to be inserted; four in total – one on each of my hands and arms. Numbing cream was applied to these areas before the cannulas were put inside me to reduce as much pain as possible. I find it difficult to explain what a cannula is, although to the best of my understanding, it is a needle stuck in your veins with a tube coming out of it. This can be used to extract blood for testing but also to inject a various number of medicines into the bloodstream or fluids, which go into the bloodstream to keep you hydrated. It prevents having to suffer needles over and over again in such a short space of time. If something is needed, it can just go through the cannula. That being said, cannulas are not for long-term use. The nurse supported our idea of hoping it was just an allergic reaction to the penicillin but said I would be required to stay the night in hospital just to stay on the safe side in case they did find anything else. That was fine with me.

As soon as I came out of the treatment room, I was shown to my bedspace, which I quite liked the look of to tell the truth. It was nothing luxurious; quite boring if I'm honest, despite the colourful curtains. The bedspace contained just a bed, a broken TV, a couple of chairs, and a bedside cabinet. There was no doubt that I was going to be extremely bored, but I had the company of my parents and occupied myself with games on my iPad, just to give me something to do. I'd be seeing the doctor shortly anyway, so I was hoping for some clarity on what was to come.

I became very happy when a patient next to me was ordering her dinner. Despite my pain, a cheese sandwich sounded good to me, so I was really hoping I'd be able to get something to eat. Unfortunately, the doctors made sure this didn't happen.

After I was shown to my bed, I waited two hours before the first Ear, Nose, and Throat (ENT) doctor arrived, since they'd come all the way from Addenbrooke's Hospital in Cambridge. Like the GP I had seen earlier that afternoon, the doctor couldn't see what was wrong but knew I wasn't right. This was very frustrating and quite scary too. Not even the specialists knew what was wrong. To see what was going on down my throat, the doctor stuck a small camera up my nose and down into my throat, which would provide her with a better view of everything. It was the most uncomfortable feeling ever; it didn't hurt, but still, I didn't like it! Drowning minus the water is the best way I could describe the feeling. Something was in my nose that shouldn't have been.

The ENT doctor told me she couldn't see what was wrong through the camera and would have to get her colleague, another ENT doctor, who was going to arrive later. The doctor did tell me a few things, though. One of them was that I didn't need to worry because another camera wouldn't be shoved up my nose, which was a lie. I was also informed that I may need to go to Addenbrooke's Hospital, which was about a half hour drive from Bury to Cambridge, but they were still unsure, and this was going to be determined once the results from a number of tests came through. And the third and final thing I was told was that from that moment on I was declared nil by mouth just in case any medical procedures were necessary. I was not allowed to eat or drink anything until further notice, and my only source of hydration would be from IV fluids going through my cannula. My hopes of a cheese sandwich were destroyed. All I wanted was a cheese sandwich.

An hour or so after the first ENT doctor arrived, the second arrived. I was now being examined by two doctors, both of whom were still confused over what was wrong. The second doctor put the camera down my nose and throat, which I was not happy about since I had been told that it wasn't needed again. The second doctor pretty much told me the same thing as the first. It seemed as if no one had any idea why my throat was so swollen and what the cause of my earache was. The second doctor decided it was necessary for me to have a CT scan on my throat to see what the swelling actually was.

From then it was all a blur to me as I began to rapidly deteriorate and was beginning to black out. A few moments after the doctors had visited, I was wheeled down from my bedspace to the scanning room for my CT scan. It was like my entire body had shut down, and I had to be helped by the nurses out of my bed to the scanner. Only that morning, I'd had the ability to get myself out of bed! I was now very sick, and I hated being like this. This decline happened in a matter of hours – it hadn't been long since I was walking up the stairs to the Rainbow Ward!

The scan involved me laying in a doughnut-shaped machine, which would then scan my throat and produce images for the doctors to examine. I never received the results from this because by the time they were being investigated, my blood test results came back and some new unfortunate discoveries were made ...

I was soon back to my bedspace, and my breathing was the next to deteriorate. My parents named me Darth Vader because of how bad my breathing was, which was very fitting considering I was wearing a Darth Vader T-shirt. Three nurses were surrounded by me, simultaneously holding an oxygen mask to my face which I kept refusing. Oxygen masks are uncomfortable because I always feel like I'm drowning in them, but I was young at the time and thought I had to breathe through my mouth and not my nose, probably adding to the struggle. It wasn't until around six months later that I learned how to use one properly. Despite my pain when drinking, this nil by mouth thing was getting to me as well, and although I had fluids, I felt severely dehydrated. I'd never had a drier throat. The nurse allowed me to have a few mouth swishes from a cup, but I had to spit them back out in a sick bowl. There was to be absolutely no swallowing, although I'm not too sure what the consequences would have been if I did swallow. It was tempting, I can say that.

Meanwhile, a doctor called my parents into her office. Fifteen minutes later, Mum was in tears as if her entire world had been shattered and Dad was closer to crying than I had ever seen him. I could see the redness in his eyes. I thought that Mum was just crying because she hated seeing me like that. I reassured them that I was fine and that it was just a really bad cold and an earache, and Mum reassuringly nodded. But they knew something I didn't.

***

Thursday 24th March 2016. The long day of March 23rd continued into the early hours of March 24th. I was still completely unaware of what was going on, however, by now my parents were informed of what it could be, and it wasn't looking good. All Dad could think about was what it was thought to be, and he did not accept it, thinking *not our family*. In their consultation, it was announced that the doctors wanted to transfer me from West Suffolk Hospital – where I currently was – to Addenbrooke's Hospital in Cambridge for further tests and confirmation. While I was still surrounded by nurses on my hospital bed, Mum and Dad took the opportunity to call Grandma and my uncle, informing them of the news and asking Grandma to stay the night with Kristy.

An ambulance was due to arrive at any moment in the very early hours of the morning. It was official that I was going to have to stay at Addenbrooke's and I needed an ambulance to take me. I found this quite unusual; I was already in the hospital, but an ambulance was taking me to another. I questioned all of it. It turns out that West Suffolk, a general hospital, didn't provide the treatment that I needed. Addenbrooke's was the more specialised teaching and research hospital. Treatment was already being thought about and I still had no clue what was wrong with me!

The ambulance was running late, and I believe it arrived at 1:00am on Thursday 24th March. We were told that Mum would be allowed to ride in the ambulance with me, while Dad went home to get some belongings and tell Kristy everything that was going on. Grandma was already there by the time Dad got home. It seemed as if everyone knew something before me, because at this point, I still didn't know what was wrong with me. How an earache and a swollen throat could cause so many tears, I didn't know.

The belongings that Dad needed to get included clothes for all of us, technology, and George, my teddy, who is a turtle, who I couldn't sleep without. Then we were told that Mum wouldn't be able to go in the ambulance with me because in the state that I was in. The paramedics, a nurse, and a doctor needed to ride with me, providing me with the best care possible, so Dad had to turn around halfway home on the A14 to come back to collect her. This really scared me, because I was in an ambulance heading to a hospital I had never been to before, in Cambridge, a city I had only been to on a few occasions, with people I didn't know. All I wanted was to be home and back to normal, but a new chapter of my life was not only on the horizon, but had technically already started. And I had no say in any of it.

It was about a half hour journey from Bury St. Edmunds to Cambridge, and the ride there was very bumpy. I had been in an ambulance before, taking a tour of one when I was a Badger for St. John's Ambulance back when I was very young. How I wish that this ride was for the same reason. Unfortunately, it wasn't, and I was lying on my back on the stretcher, with stickers attached to me as I was so weak that my heart needed to be monitored. Everyone was very supportive of me, and I knew that despite my situation, I was in the best hands and I was receiving brilliant care. I just couldn't believe that within a day I had been sat at home feeling ill to being so ill to the point that I was rushed between hospitals in an ambulance. It still hadn't hit me that I must have been really ill if the first hospital I went to couldn't even treat me. I was being sent to the specialists.

The only thing that was going through my mind was what Addenbrooke's looked like. I had heard about it before but thought it was a castle, so I was quite surprised when the first ENT doctor said I may have to stay there.

It was a strange feeling too. Here I was with people who I had never met prior to this day, heading to a city I can only recall going to once. In fact, I was separated from my parents and was now in a completely different county to them!

I arrived on Ward C2 in Addenbrooke's Hospital at about 1:30am on Thursday morning, which was the longest night of my life. The paramedics helped me to my bed. I thanked them and they wished me well before leaving. My condition was so bad that night that I needed to have two nurses taking care of me, Katie and Tara. I was hooked up to a machine, known as a drip stand, similar to the one at West Suffolk, where fluids continued to be pumped into my bloodstream through my cannula. My heartrate sticker was still stuck on my finger and was attached to the obs machine, and every time I moved, I set the alarm off. This got very annoying after a while and I'm sure I frustrated the nurses who had to keep coming in to switch the machine off. I was all alone in my bedspace, which I still couldn't see a lot of, with it being pitch-black in the middle of the night. The lights were off and there were patients in the spaces next to me sleeping.

Halfway through the night I met two doctors who assured me that I was going to be okay and I was in the best hands. It was reassurance that I needed. All I needed to do now was focus on getting some good sleep – or as much sleep as possible. The night was rough, and I had belly ache, but as I had eaten barely anything, I was constipated. Going to the toilet was difficult, and as I could not stand on my own two feet for long, I had to be helped to the toilet by my nurse. I was able to fall asleep until I woke up at about 7:00am to George by my side and Mum in the parent bed next to me. I was quickly reunited with Dad, who had stayed the night in the ward's parents' room.

It was Dad who gave the first indication that my illness was something serious. He promised on this day that he would not keep anything from me, and it was at this moment when he first told me that promise. Being under eighteen, my health was my parent's responsibility, but he said he would tell me everything. After my parents returned from a quick tour of the ward, he told me what was going on, but he didn't really get to the point. I had to force it out of him. I had to tell him to get to the end of it all because the fact that he wasn't explaining properly was scarier than him just not saying anything at all. He basically told me that they were hoping this was a blood infection and I would be out of hospital soon, but there was also a possibility that there was 'something wrong', which appeared to be even more serious than a blood infection. Either way, it was discovered that my ongoing health issues were all down to my blood not functioning properly. My blood had caused all of this, and whatever the problem was, I was in a critical condition.

Later on, in the morning, my family and I met a paediatric oncology consultant, who was going to explain to us exactly what was going on. I didn't want to listen because I feared that even though a blood infection is bad news in itself, it was likely to be 'something wrong'. I was worried but I was nowhere near fearing for my life like my parents were. The doctor spoke softly in a relaxed tone to Mum, both of whom were sat on the parent bed, while Dad stood behind me listening. My parents listened while I watched *Horrid Henry*, a show I had loved as a kid.

I paused the TV and forced myself to listen when I heard the words "... and this is where we find leukaemia ..."

I was shocked. My world instantly crumbled into pieces. I wanted to stop listening, but I couldn't. It was like I was listening to a horror story. From this moment on, my ears were wide open, and I was listening to everything the doctor had to say, however much I just wanted it all to stop. While I stared into space in utter shock, thoughts began firing through my head. *I have cancer? How long have I had it? Am I going to survive? Is it too late?* She continued explaining what it was and what it meant and where it was typically found in the body. I was then asked if I had any questions.

I immediately asked, knowing the answer, "Do I have it?"

"Probably, yes," she said, judging from the numerous tests taken the previous night.

Immediately after, I asked what anyone would, about my chances of survival, which was the only thing at that moment I was fearing. She said that I had good chances and if everything went well, it would all be over in six months and back to school in September. It was good to have some positivity in this dark moment, but this was if everything went to plan though, and just because my chances were good did not mean I was guaranteed an easy journey.

Ward C2 was a paediatric oncology ward; in other words, a children's cancer ward. I was completely unaware that I had stayed the night on a children's cancer ward. I had just had a consultation with a children's cancer doctor. *I had cancer.* I couldn't believe it. I was more shocked than sad. I had always seen cancer stories on the TV and on Facebook, but I always thought that happened to other people. Because of my normal life up until then, I saw myself as lucky. And yet, this was just proof that it can happen to anyone and disrupt any family. No one is exempt.

I wanted to cry but I had no tears. The fluids were keeping me going but psychologically I was dehydrated. The first thing I did, and kept doing, was apologise to my parents. I had ruined plans for Easter as we were supposed to go to Auntie Karen's and Uncle John's on Easter Sunday, which was the family tradition. I felt I had messed everything up as Kristy was sitting her GCSE exams that year and I was going to be a burden to the family when she needed all the support she could get at this time. My parents told me to stop apologising, and once I had calmed down a little and came to terms with my diagnosis, I turned to Mum and said, "I'm going to fight this!"

***

On the morning of Thursday 24th March 2016, I was diagnosed with Acute Myeloid Leukaemia (AML). To the best of my understanding, AML is where the bone marrow, which is located in the bones where blood is made – in other words, the blood factory – produces too many immature white blood cells. White blood cells are the cells that help the body to fight infections, but they need to be mature to function properly.

In the bone marrow, we have stem cells. Some stem cells form into myeloid cells. In a healthy body, myeloid cells form into white blood cells, such as neutrophils and monocytes. When someone has leukaemia, however, these cells cannot get past the myeloid stage and cannot produce into mature white blood cells. The result is a build-up of useless myeloid cells in the bone marrow, meaning that the white blood cells are not mature. Once these cells have reproduced to the point that they have taken over the bone marrow, they push out all the other healthy cells in the bone marrow. Therefore, the white blood cells rapidly increase to unhealthy amounts and start to be released into the blood, having no purpose as they do not have time to mature. The more immature white blood cells are in the bone marrow, the less room there is in the blood for the healthy white blood cells, red blood cells, and platelets. So, as the cancer increases, the healthy cells decrease, and this explained why I had felt so ill. There were few healthy cells in my blood and bone marrow; it was absolutely crammed full with useless cancerous cells. These white blood cells are called leukaemia cells, or myeloid blasts. The bone marrow was creating these blasts, and they were circulating around my body in my blood.

AML is an aggressive blood cancer and can rapidly develop within days, so it is important to start intensive chemotherapy as soon as possible to treat it. Leaving it late could potentially have caused the cells to spread to other parts of the body, including my spinal cord, which would make my battle much harder to overcome.

Symptoms of leukaemia include swollen lymph nodes in the neck and armpit, frequent infections, night sweats, weakness and fatigue, weight loss, red spots on the skin, easy bruising and bleeding, fever, pain in muscles and bones, headaches, looking pale, breathlessness, heart palpitations, and many more. I'd experienced the majority of these symptoms. I didn't realise how important blood was and how crucial it was to ensure it was healthy.

There are many different types of leukaemia, both chronic and acute. The other main type of acute leukaemia is Acute Lymphoblastic Leukaemia (ALL). ALL is more common in children, whereas AML is more common in older people. AML is a more aggressive type of cancer and needs to be treated immediately with intensive drugs, so the treatment is quicker than ALL, which is less aggressive and occurs over a couple of years. Eight people are diagnosed with AML every day, accounting for 1% of all cancers. It is more common in males than females, though the reason for this is unknown. The cause of it is unknown but factors such as smoking and increased exposure to radiation can increase the risk of getting it. AML kills around seven people a day, with 2500 deaths a year. In AML, the survival rate for people under 20 is 67%, and for older people with AML, it is approximately 24%. The treatment is very intensive and often older people cannot cope with it, hence the massive differences in age and survival rates. This is where treatments, known as palliative care, come in to give people the longest and best possible life with the disease, although this does not carry a prospect of cure.

***

For a while, I was just sat there on my bed, not really knowing what to do with myself. You're advised in hospital to take your mind off things, but in this circumstance, it was just impossible to do such a thing. Now that I had accepted my diagnosis, further worries about the consequences began circulating my brain. *What about my schoolwork? What about seeing my friends and family? When can I come home?*

The doctor who had diagnosed me quickly returned, putting her head round the bedspace curtain to give my parents further information and advice in printed material and to give me a book called 'Joe has Leukaemia'. It wasn't a 200-page academic book, rather it was a picture book with simplified and condensed information, which I found very helpful, and even today, I like to look back at it just for enjoyment. It was that book which gave me my first sign of hope – it had a happy ending, and Joe was back spending time with his family after treatment.

The book was able to explain why I had been feeling so ill over the past three months. The function of healthy white blood cells is to fight infections, but as my white cells were not mature, I wasn't able to do this, explaining the cold and cough I could never get rid of. The function of red blood cells is to carry oxygen around the body, but being low on these, it explained my breathlessness. The role of platelets is to clot the blood and repair damaged skin, but since I was lacking platelets, I wasn't able to recover from things such as the bite on my leg. It all made sense now. The consultant told me that chemotherapy needed to start as soon as possible and that day I needed to go to theatre to have a Hickman line inserted, which the play team were going to explain to me, using a teddy bear for demonstration.

***

I had never heard the term 'theatre' in terms of hospitals before. At first, I thought I was going to go see a movie or a play, which puzzled me because I had just been diagnosed with cancer. Going to theatre actually meant the operating theatre. 'The surgery room' is how I liked to refer to it.

I met the play specialists from the play team, who explained to me their role in hospital. The play specialists were there to prevent me from getting bored in hospital and would visit me every morning to ask if I wanted to borrow any board games, video games, or DVDs, as well as many other things they had to keep me occupied.

I also met Denise, who was the schoolteacher. My hospital stay was going to be long-term, judging by the doctor's estimation of six months, and I was not well enough to return to normal school. So, my education would be at the hospital for at the least the rest of the schoolyear. Denise came to say hello as the Easter holidays were approaching and it was the last day of term, but she said she would catch me a couple of weeks later to start school properly.

The play team used a teddy bear to show me how the Hickman line worked, which I was due to have inserted whenever the surgeons were ready for me. A Hickman line is pretty much a larger cannula, but instead of going in your arms, it is inserted in your chest and is for long-term use. It is removed once it is no longer needed. Sometimes called a wiggly or central line, it is a long, thick plastic tube that is inserted underneath the chest wall skin and into the large vein in the heart. A tube comes out of the chest and two lumens are attached to it in case more than one medicine is needed at a time. On the end of the lumens are bungs, which needed to be changed regularly. These are the caps on the lumens where the wires from the drip or syringes would attach – all medicines which were to go through the Hickman line (IV medication) were attached to a drip and, at a slow rate to prevent shock, would enter the bloodstream through an IV line. Coming out of the chest, the line has to be looped just in case it gets tugged so the pressure would be on the loop rather than pulling the Hickman line straight out of your chest, because that would be painful and very dangerous. If that happened, I would need immediate medical attention. Over the line site, a dressing, which was basically a giant plaster, would have to be put on, which would have to be changed every seven to ten days to avoid infections. Getting this area of my body wet was something I would have to avoid for as long as my line was in. The area of my line was also going to be checked regularly by the doctors on the ward rounds just to make sure it was looking healthy. I would receive chemotherapy, blood and platelet transfusions, and other IV medications through my Hickman line and it would also be used for daily blood tests, as blood could be syringed from the line. I was to rely on my Hickman line for almost everything regarding my care and survival, other than of course taking oral medicines and consuming food and drink.

Because it had been a dull day, the nurses found a more spacious bedspace for me. I hadn't seen the ward yet, but I was in a crowded room with three other families who had their TVs on super loud. I didn't know at the time, but I was actually in G bay, which is the bay that every family dreaded. But for now, the nurses had managed to find me a space in A, which, although it had two other families, was more spacious, had its own toilet, and even had a window. I was lucky enough to have three quarters of the window in my bedspace, so my space was a lot brighter than everyone else's. My home for the next couple of weeks was to be A1.

A1 was like all the other bedspaces and consisted of a patient bed which could recline into different positions, had a plastic-like mattress, and was covered with sheets and blankets. Next to that was a bedside cabinet with a fan on it and a parent bed, which, when not being used, could be converted into something that looked like a wardrobe. This was mostly for saving space as nothing could be put inside it; the only purpose of it was the bed. Because only one parent could stay, Mum and Dad usually took turns staying the night on the ward to start off with, until Mum had to return to work, and then it was mainly Dad. He decided he was going to undertake the bulk of the work surrounding my care, which I think upset Mum a little as she wanted to split the care. But I suppose it was important for at least one member of the family to keep working.

The parent not staying with me on the ward either went home or stayed at Acorn House, run by the charity, The Sick Children's Trust. Acorn House was located on hospital grounds, about a two-minute walk from the main hospital. Acorn House contained shared facilities, such as a kitchen, living room, and bathroom, but they had sixteen individual bedrooms for families. There were a couple of chairs in my bedspace for visitors and visiting times on the ward could be at any time, as long as they were reasonable, of course.

Sophie was my nurse on my first day in hospital, and before I went to theatre, some important forms needed to be filled out by my parents. She also needed me to change into a hospital gown for the imminent surgery, but there was much difficulty with that because I couldn't take my shirt off over my cannula. This was because I was still attached to fluids. We were all afraid that she was going to have to cut my shirt. Grandma had bought it for me for Christmas the previous year, and cutting it up was the last thing I wanted. But somehow, and I don't know how, I was able to take my shirt off and change into the gown ready for my surgery.

I can't remember when, but it was definitely late afternoon, maybe even the evening, when the surgeons were finally ready for me to go to theatre to have my Hickman line inserted. Despite having a window in my bedspace, the whole day was such a blur I had no idea of the time of day. I had been sitting in my bedspace with my parents doing nothing the whole day. Surprisingly, the upset had all blown over now – I was no longer feeling sorry for myself. I was now showing courage and strength, not allowing this disease to bring me down. Once the Hickman line was inserted, I'd be able to commence treatment the following day, so the doctors and surgeons were anxious to get me to theatre as quickly as possible. The leukaemia was rapidly progressing, and leaving it a few hours, let alone days, would be too late. Treatment needed to start *now*.

The procedure needed to be taken under general anaesthetic, meaning I would need to be put to sleep, but because my throat had swollen up so much, they were worried I would stop breathing in the surgery. So, before the anaesthetic – a thick white liquid – was inserted into my cannula, I had to take a few breaths into an oxygen mask. Dad asked me if I could count to ten – apparently no one could get as far as ten when being put to sleep. I got to around three or four until I gave a massive yawn and passed out. I was out cold, and that is all I can remember prior to surgery.

I woke up in recovery and I was in a very unusual mood. I was actually happy. It was probably the anaesthetic that made me go a bit funny. My parents were given a beeper that would notify them when I was out of surgery, giving them time to get something to eat and drink. They had gone to Costa Coffee in the hospital concourse to finally get something to eat during my surgery, waiting for me to go into recovery. Food had been the last thing on their mind, and with the current situation, Mum found eating particularly difficult.

My head was a bit dizzy because I was still recovering from the anaesthetic, but I was conscious and completely aware of my surroundings. If anything, despite the dizziness, I actually noticed nothing different than before I woke up. I didn't feel a thing. No pain, nothing. I didn't actually know what was there until Dad told me to look at my chest.

"Oh wow, what's that?" I said.

A plastic rubbery wire was coming out of a hole in my chest. The hole was bleeding, but the entire line site was covered by a transparent plaster. It was my Hickman line! Despite not feeling anything on my chest, my lower back was a bit sore.

I was informed that I also had a bone marrow aspiration, also known as a bone marrow biopsy. This is where a sample of the bone marrow is extracted from your hip via a needle, which is used to diagnose bone marrow disorders. The biopsy found that my bone marrow was crammed with 92% leukaemia cells! Over the months, I had let my condition progress rapidly. I can't imagine how long it would be until it reached 100% and what would happen if it did. I had been very close to finding out the hard way.

I also had a lumbar puncture, which is where a needle is used to extract spinal fluid to test for any disease. As a precaution, they injected chemotherapy into my spine during the procedure. If the leukaemia spread to my spine or got into my bones, then treating it would be very difficult and my chances of survival would be significantly reduced. Luckily, according to my lumbar puncture results, the cancer hadn't spread, and the chemo was injected into my spine to prevent the disease from going any further and doing more damage.

I was still not stable enough to go back to my bedspace and needed to stay in recovery for a little while longer. In the meantime, the recovery team asked me if I wanted to watch anything, and for some reason, and to this day, I still have no idea why, I asked to watch *Peppa Pig*. I'll admit, it was one of my favourites as a child. It must have been because I was feeling funny from the anaesthetic. My wish was granted, and a little while later, I had a TV at the end of my bed with a *Peppa Pig* DVD playing. The recovery team awarded me a *Peppa Pig* bravery certificate for being so brave during the surgery, which to this day I have stored, in addition to my get well soon cards, in a scrapbook dedicated to my cancer journey.

Chemotherapy was due to start the next day and I was also to receive some more information on my treatment plan in the morning. All I needed to do now was focus on getting some sleep, which in itself would be a challenge. For now, the number one rule that the hospital made me obey was that I had to sleep sitting up, enabled by my reclining hospital bed. This was because laying down flat would mean my abnormally swollen throat would crush my airways and stop my breathing.

Making my way back to the ward, we passed the doctor who had diagnosed me only that morning. She had just finished her shift and told us she was going on holiday for a couple of weeks, but she would be back. If I remember correctly, she was going to India. I had time to reflect, and I found it difficult to believe that all this had happened within a space of two days. Really, it was actually three months in the making, and I hadn't a single clue that this would be the result. Everyone gets colds sometimes and everyone gets tired, but while my body was telling me that I had leukaemia through these common symptoms, I didn't really question it. I thought everything that was going on was just a bad case of each symptom. How terribly wrong I was. Had I not started to experience the really unusual symptoms, I wouldn't have even been at the hospital yet. I honestly don't think I would have survived much longer without immediate treatment – it was that close. My body was shutting down. Now I was facing a battle, and my life was on the line.

The shock of the previous twenty-four hours is displayed in Dad's account of what happened. Writing in March 2016, he summarises my diagnosis, shows his perspective as a parent, and also provides a taster of what was to come:

This journal entry brings together a personal account of our experience of having our 13-year-old son, Jake Andrade, diagnosed with leukaemia. Understanding every situation is different, so please keep an open mind and use this as a tool to help you. Since he was born, Jake suffered from many colds, so as parents we were not prepared for the news when he was diagnosed. On Wednesday 16th March, Jake started with a cold. That same day he went on a nine-mile walk through the woods on a confidence building course with the school. That afternoon, Jake began complaining about being tired due to the combination of the walk and a cold. It was decided for the remainder of the week that Jake should rest. On Sunday 20th March, Jake was still not feeling his best and he started saying he was unable to walk because his right leg was sore. After further examination, we noticed he had a bite on his right calf muscle, and it looked inflamed and was hot to the touch. Thinking it was a spider bite, we made an appointment on Monday 21st March. We explained to the doctor all the symptoms, and at the time, the doctor recommended penicillin to help his bite heal. We did not know if he was allergic to penicillin or not, but he was given a week's dose and told to take one tablet four times a day. Excited that we had medicine to help his walking, we started the doses that afternoon. Tuesday night, Jake had not improved; in fact, he seemed to be getting worse, and he now had an additional problem; his left ear was hurting, he had a really high temperature, and his heartbeat was racing as if he was exercising. At this point, we were ready to take him to the emergency room, thinking he was having an allergic reaction to the penicillin, but after giving him medicine, his fever reduced, and we made an appointment for the following day. His appointment was at 3:20 that afternoon. When he was seen at 3:40, the doctor made the call that a trip to the ENT (ear, nose, and throat) specialist was necessary. After calling the ENT, they referred him to the children's clinic. This was how and when our story took the slowest and fastest rollercoaster ride we'd ever experienced. We managed to get to the hospital by around 5:15, and after asking questions, the doctor decided to do a scan of the neck, then they took bloods twice. The ENT specialist on call at the time put a camera down Jake's nostril. Another specialist was called from Addenbrookes Hospital thirty minutes away. Another examination with the camera followed. With all the information gathered came the devastating news that no living person wants to hear. Your son might have leukaemia, and by the way, he may have the rarest form. Immediately after, he was transferred to a specialist unit. The next day, and what I call Day 1, he was booked to receive a Hickman Line, lumbar puncture, and have an operation to retrieve bone marrow from his hip. For us, all this happened within twenty-four hours. One of the feelings we were struggling with was how to tell him he had cancer and how would he react, especially as he was old enough to understand the possibility of death. Throughout all this, Jake wanted to know his diagnosis, but we did not want to tell him until we were 100% sure. That morning, he asked us if he had cancer, and in a way, the relief that he had approached us lifted a heavy weight off our shoulders. It was heart-breaking seeing Jake processing the news and what his future may or may not be. As a parent, you feel useless and you don't know what the next day holds, let alone the next weeks, months, and years. In preparation for his operation, Day 1 consisted of conversation with doctors, anaesthetists, ENT, consultants, nurses, a housing charity, and the school representative. There were a few consent forms to fill out, all of which were thoroughly explained, but I doubt we took any of it in. The operation went very well, and Jake did not need an operation on his neck to drain fluids as it was not infected. Day 2 brought more of the same, with Jake mostly sleeping and throwing up. His chemo started and the consultant explained how the chemo works and the effects it will have both in the short and long term. The hardest thing to take was the fact that the chemo would damage his heart and there would be no chance of healing later in life. Our daughter, Kristy, was with us when we discovered this as we wanted to maintain transparency and we wanted to deal with everything together.

Chapter 3

The Battle Begins

The first round of chemotherapy and its immediate effects from March 25th to April 11th, 2016

Friday 25th March 2016. All patients had to be up early for the breakfast trolley, which started from 8:00am. The breakfast trolley had various cereals, toast, fruit, yoghurts, juice, and more. It was almost like a hotel, and in a sense that's what a hospital is – a hotel for sick people. Unsurprisingly, the food quality isn't on the same level of expectations as a hotel. Despite how hospital food is stereotypically perceived to be, by no means is it disgusting. The issue I had with it was that nothing seemed fresh when I ate from the trolley. Ward C2 did have a chef, who cooked lunch and dinner, but as it was the Easter holidays, he was on holiday, so all meals for the next couple of weeks came from the trolley.

I was up at 8:00am every morning, which was later than I used to wake up at home. That was a positive of the hospital – lie-ins. That being said, the night, and every night in hospital, is frustrating as the nurses wake you up every four hours for obs and yours and others' drip machines go off all the time. The sound of the beeping machines will never escape my head, and it gives me flashbacks when I'm reminded of such a sound. Getting a good night's sleep is not possible in a hospital. There is just way too much going on.

After breakfast – still too poorly to eat anything – my family and I met another paediatric oncology consultant at

Addenbrooke's Hospital. My parents and Kristy, who had just arrived, were all taken to an office to discuss my treatment with the doctor, while I waited anxiously in my bed, staring into space. The reason why they went off was to hear my treatment plan themselves first and sign some consent forms for my treatment as I couldn't sign them due to being under eighteen.

Apparently, the first thing that the doctor told my parents was, "We will cure this."

That meant a lot to Mum. They soon returned so the doctor could tell me what my treatment plan was and once again repeat it to my family.

I was to have four rounds of chemotherapy, with the first two rounds being known as induction chemotherapy. Induction chemotherapy aims to cure the cancer. The first cycle was to be ten days long, the second eight days of the same drugs as the first. The third was to be determined by the results of the first cycle, and the fourth was to be determined by the results of the second. If this seems a bit complex, it will become clearer as I explain each cycle in more detail. The time between the cycles depended on when my blood recovered, as the chemo was going to do some significant temporary damage to it, so it was important to focus on one round of chemo at a time.

The consultant explained to me that the first round of chemo would take ten days in total. For the first five days, I would have one dose of the drug, mitoxantrone, every day. In addition to that, throughout the entire ten days, I was to have two doses of another chemo drug, cytarabine: one in the morning and one at night. The mitoxantrone would be inserted slowly through a drip stand and would take much longer since it was a larger dose. The cytarabine was to be a much smaller dose, which could be syringed through my Hickman line by a nurse, albeit very slowly to prevent shock to the system.

Chemo aims to destroy all rapidly growing cells, so although it is successful in killing cancer cells, it is also not picky. It destroys the healthy cells too, which can lead to some negative side effects. The doctor explained to me the various nasty side effects I was to expect, which I have listed below in no particular order:

- The chemo was going to destroy all my healthy blood cells. Low red blood cells would cause anaemia, making me tired and breathless. Low platelets would put me at risk of bruising and bleeding. I would require blood and platelet transfusions to top up my blood every few days to give me an energy boost and prevent serious bleeding to help me survive. Low white blood cells, which cannot be transfused, would make me more prone to infections, and doctors would pay close attention to my neutrophils, the type of white blood cell that fights against bacterial infections.

- The treatment was going to make me neutropenic. When neutrophils reach the count of below 1.5, this is known as mild neutropenia. Moderate neutropenia is considered below 1.0, and severe neutropenia is below 0.5. The standard range of neutrophils for a healthy person is between 1.5 and 7.7. Daily blood tests would be needed to monitor this. While neutropenic, it was important for me to avoid certain foods, specifically fresh foods or foods that had been sitting out for a while, so technically I couldn't have the hospital foods on the ward trolleys (although I did as it was the only food available). This was because I would not be successful in fighting off potential infections possibly caused by bacteria on fresh foods. Fresh fruit was discouraged, although frozen fruit was fine. Having said that, the doctor said that fresh fruit that could be peeled was allowed; for example, bananas were fine, and I could eat apples as long as they were peeled. There was to be no foods such as strawberries or raspberries while I was neutropenic, unless they were frozen. Aside from food, as I would be more prone to infections, anything I owned preferably needed to be cleaned, and I had to avoid anything dirty and maintain good hygiene. The consultant told me that George was going to have to have a wash since he had nine years' worth of germs on him. The second round of chemo would be allowed to commence once I was no longer severely neutropenic, which was when my neutrophils had recovered past the count of 0.5.

- The mitoxantrone was a small but deadly bag of dark blue poisonous liquid that would enter my bloodstream. It may sound confusing, but the chemo was there to fight the leukaemia, but at the same time, my body was going to fight the chemo. My body's way of getting rid of this would be through urine, sweat, and tears. For the next few days, my urine, sweat, and tears would be blue in colour.

- Hair loss would be another side effect. Yes, hair in all places – I was asked that quite often. I was told my hair would grow back to 'normal' once treatment was over, though it would most likely be thinner and lighter in colour, having the consistency of baby hair.

- The chemotherapy would also destroy my gut lining, and I was likely to get something called mucositis, a painful inflammation of the mucus membranes. From my mouth all the way to my bottom, I was going to get ulcers, and my throat was also going to be very sore. The pain would have the same feeling as when you burn your throat after eating hot food. Eating and going to the loo would be very difficult while I had mucositis, as anything that went through the gut was going to irritate the sores. While various mouthwashes and creams could help soothe this pain, it was just a matter of waiting for the mucositis to disappear itself. Since diarrhoea was also going to be very likely as a result of the treatment, this just added to the problems and was expected to irritate the ulcers.

- Chemo makes the skin very thin, so while it was unlikely that I would be going outside any time soon, if I did it was crucial that I wore a sunhat and sun cream. This was because I would become very prone to sunburn. To protect my skin, it was important that I used odourless shower gel and shampoo, the type designed for babies.

- Nausea and loss of appetite was also going to be a very common side effect. Vomiting would be common. Because it was important that I was healthy to fight the chemo, eating was important to avoid weight loss. My weight would be monitored every two days. To manage my sickness, I would be prescribed anti-sickness medication. Also, I had to give nurses lists of what I ate and drank, and I would have to urinate in cardboard bottles and defecate in bedpans so they could make sure there was a healthy distribution of what was going in and what was coming out.

- Chemo would also destroy my taste buds, which would

make my food either really bland or make it taste weird and disgusting. Even the most flavoured food tasted bland, and pizza tasted like water. Some foods and drinks, particularly chocolate and water, would taste metallic.

- Fevers were also going to be common, and paracetamol was not allowed to be given until the doctors investigated the cause for my high temperature. This was because paracetamol could mask a potential infection, something I was to be increasingly prone to due to my weakened immune system.

- Because my blood and immune system was going to be greatly weakened by the chemo, it was important I took many medicines every day, which I could not survive without. I was required to take anti-fungal medications, potassium supplements, antibiotics, and many other oral and IV medications to help my body. My body could not fight everything on its own.

- There were also some long-term side effects, such as affecting fertility and growth, disrupting puberty, second cancers[1], and damage to the heart and spleen. Although this is rare, it was important for the doctors to inform us so we couldn't take them to court for withholding information. In the long term, my heart was going to have to be monitored and have tests done intermittently just to check for any damage.

---

[1] A second cancer is a cancer that is diagnosed after treatment and is nothing related to the previous diagnosis, rather the treatment of that diagnosis. Cancer treatment can be so damaging that it increases the risk of other cancers forming. For example, radiotherapy increases the risk of leukaemia as a result of the radiation.

Chronologically, it is difficult to place these side effects in a certain order; therefore, for the next few paragraphs, I will jump around the timeline of Round 1 of chemo. Having only been in hospital for a week and a half, I was still suffering from the leukaemia symptoms. Therefore, what I experienced while in A bay on Ward C2 was a bit of a blur between leukaemia and the chemo side effects.

First of all, the positive effects of the chemo were that I could definitely tell it was working. Don't get me wrong; to check that the chemo has successfully worked takes months of tests, but there are a few signs that indicate things are going in the right direction. After the critically ill stage, once the treatment commenced, I started to feel a lot better in myself and was able to get out of bed on my own. The swelling in my throat reduced in size rapidly, although it took a good few weeks before it went away for good. At least a month after its emergence, I was still suffering discomfort when yawning since it would strain my swollen throat. However, the swelling was going down, and as each night went by, I could gradually recline my hospital bed to a more comfortable position. I hated sleeping in a sitting position, and it had caused many sleepless nights.

Now for the not so nice effects. It is worth stating that I ended up suffering with most of the effects the doctor had explained to me.

Initially, I found the thought of blue urine terrifying. For a time, I was peeing in bottles regardless as to whether the nurses wanted to measure my intake and outtake, primarily due my fear of having blue urine.

Also, my taste buds disappeared, which wasn't pleasant at all. I went off chocolate and water as they had the taste of a 2p coin.

I also suffered from mucositis, which, along with the frequent diarrhoea, meant that the increased wiping made my bottom very painful.

I didn't experience sunburn as I didn't really go to many places while on chemo. The long-term side effects were going to be discovered much later in my journey if there were going to be any, so I didn't experience any of them in Round 1 either.

***

On Friday 25th March 2016, I started chemotherapy for the first time. To tell the truth, I remember nothing about my first day of chemotherapy other than the consultation with the doctor. I was too sick to even care about what was going on. For Round 1, I wasn't even nervous about starting treatment because, despite being aware of the side effects, nothing could have been worse than what I was already feeling. I must have been more happy than scared because finally something was going to be done about my illness.

The mitoxantrone took about an hour to pass through me because it was a larger dose, compared to the cytarabine, which was given in small syringes that the nurses could put through my line within seconds. All chemo and any other IV medications had to be flushed down with saline solution to clean the line out. This sometimes felt cold, and I could feel the cold liquid travel up my line when going into my bloodstream.

Over the next ten days, I wasn't feeling great, but that was still from the leukaemia and not from the chemo. The chemo actually helped me feel better. To me, it was clear that the chemo was working, or at least in my head it was. As the days went by, I was becoming my usual self, but still having to adapt to my new environment. There was no way the doctors were letting me out any time soon.

On the topic of my throat and why it had been swollen, by this time, we finally had the answers. A symptom of leukaemia is swollen lymph nodes, especially in the neck and armpit. I did require some checks on my throat to make sure nothing else was happening, and in my very early days of living in the hospital, I was sent to have some ultrasound scans done, but all they did was confirm the same diagnosis.

In the bay next to me (A2) was Max, who was from Norwich. Max had a brain tumour. He was eight years old and loved watching the TV show, *Miranda*, which was probably what I best knew him for. Being in a bay of three patients and their families, it could get very noisy, and hearing each other's TVs on full blast was the norm. Dad became friendly with Max's dad during our stay in A bay, and we supported each other. We had to support each other because, even though we all had visitors from the outside world, us patients and our families were the only ones together 24/7. Max was undergoing forty days of radiotherapy[2], which is a lot, and the brain tumour meant he'd have to relearn how to eat, drink, walk, talk, and carry out almost all activities all over again. I couldn't help but feel sorry for him; imagine losing all ability to carry out easy everyday tasks. In A3, there was a baby, who, like me, had just been diagnosed with AML. I think his name was Noah. While Max was watching *Miranda*, Noah was always watching *In the Night Garden*, and that theme tune, along with the beeping drip machines, is what I will always associate with my early days of hospital life. Max appeared to be getting better and was progressing in regaining his ability, though I was informed that

---

[2] Radiotherapy is a cancer treatment used either with or as an alternative to chemotherapy and is used to kill cancer cells. I did not require radiotherapy as part of my treatment plan.

both Max and Noah had sadly passed away the following year. It is sad knowing that out of the three patients in my first stay, I am the only one here today.

***

Hospital life could get boring at times, but there were always people who would try to make it more interesting. In hospital, I developed a new routine, and this was the case for most days, and even if I did not strictly follow this routine, many things I did was repetitive across the days. One nurse took care of me every day and one at night, working twelve-hour shifts. My obs were taken every four hours, either by a nurse or healthcare assistant. The nurses got to choose who their patients were, and I'm not sure if they all wanted me, but I heard that I was a popular choice because I was easy-going and just went along with everything, doing what the doctors and nurses told me. One of my nurses, Juliet, told me, "You never moan, you never complain" and that I was allowed to sometimes. I just thought I was showing simple manners and being respectful to the people who knew more about my care than I did, but it turns out I wasn't the typical patient. Some patients behaved dreadfully, which I guess was normal for a children's ward.

I would wake up at about 8:00am and have something from the breakfast trolley. I usually had marmite on toast or a yoghurt, or nothing, depending on my appetite. Eating nothing was frowned upon by literally every hospital staff member; there was a certain group of hospital staff – who we will get to later – who ensured I never went a day without eating. I always tried to get something from the trolley, even if I didn't eat it right then, because it was only out for a limited time. The chef didn't start cooking until 11:00am.

Then it would be bath time, if I was 'lucky'. Or, if I was unlucky, it was hair wash day and Dad would make me have a shower. Neither were very pleasant – the bath consisted of me sitting in a shallow pool of cold water (the hospital bath water was never warm for some reason), and the shower was warm but standing up often made me feel sick. Because of this, I always preferred the bath as it seemed the safer option. There was a seat in the shower, but I couldn't sit because I had to avoid getting my line wet. I usually covered the lumens with a Ziploc bag and had to try my best not to get my dressing wet, having to stand in awkward positions to avoid exposing my chest to the water. Because the chemo made my skin extra sensitive, I wasn't allowed the shower gel or shampoo a healthy person might have had. Instead, I had to have an odourless soap designed for babies, which worked as shower gel, shampoo, and bubble bath all in one. Also, as it was a children's ward, the towels were tiny, only slightly larger than hand towels, and I often needed more than one to get dry. It was very weird, and quite uncomfortable, being a thirteen-year-old who needed his parents to help him wash, but as it became the norm, I became more at ease with it as time went on.

Either before or after bath time, we had to wait for the daily doctor rounds that day, which sometimes consisted of consultants, but always registrars[3]. There was more than one doctor on the rounds most of the time. This involved the usual doctor procedure of getting out their stethoscope and listening to the chest and making sure everything was okay

[3] A consultant is a doctor who has completed their training, and a particular consultant is responsible for a patient's overall care. My early days in hospital involved seeing any of the oncology (cancer) consultants. After Round 2, I met the haematology team, who specialised in blood cancer. My assigned consultants were Dr. M and Dr. A, who took responsibility for my overall care.

before giving me an update on my current situation.

Every morning, depending on how I was feeling, I'd either go to the bathroom to brush my teeth or brush them in a sick bowl at bedside with a plastic cup of water. Then I'd be ready to watch TV, usually *Horrid Henry* or the *Jeremy Kyle Show*, or do other things to occupy myself until about lunchtime. At first, I was eating lunch off the trolley because the chef was on holiday, but when he came back a week later, we were told he could cook anything. That was a lie. I joked with my parents that if I asked for chicken cordon bleu, I'd be able to have it. Even the chef himself admitted that he was limited in what he could cook, and he was quite open about his feelings on how restricted he was. He did offer some good stuff, such as chicken nuggets, pizza, chips, sausages, pasta, and many other things, and he even owned a toastie machine, which he was proud of. That was enough to satisfy me. The chef was great, especially with the younger children when wearing his colourful chef uniform, and always stopped by to have a chat with my parents. Some of the things he had to say were very interesting, and it was clear that he had an interesting background and was very knowledgeable about life in general. When having my lunch, I borrowed board games from the play team, which I played with my family. Scrabble was played almost every day, as well as Monopoly, although we never finished a game because it went on forever. The chef liked to have the table clear when delivering my meals, so we had to pack away a game before every meal!

Depending on what day it was, my parents made me get out of bed for a bit so they could change the sheets. The ward liked the parents to change the bed, although sometimes it was done by the healthcare assistants. I still wasn't well enough to be venturing into the ward and seeing everything for myself, the only time I left my bedspace being to choose my breakfast or if I had to go to the showers, and I was wheelchaired to those places and back. Therefore, when I got out of bed, I just sat in one of the visitor chairs while my parents did all the hard work. I felt guilty watching them do everything, but I was feeling so unwell that any form of activity made me feel sick. Besides, even if I was well, any activity with a Hickman line is a risk.

In the afternoon, I continued watching daytime TV, starting with *Judge Rinder, Dickinson's Real Deal* (my favourite), *Tipping Point*, and then *The Chase* in the evening. I'd usually have my dinner while watching *The Chase*. In the evening, I would find ways to while away the time until *EastEnders* came on, which I would watch with whichever family member was there. Another thing that annoyed me was that the TVs shut off at 8:00pm, so sometimes to watch *EastEnders*, Mum or Dad needed to get credit from the hospital concourse to keep the TV running. After watching *EastEnders*, I just sat there until I decided it was time to get ready for bed.

This routine lasted for the next two weeks, and I was happy like that. It wouldn't be my first choice for a routine, since I did want to be active, but I accepted it. There was no resuming normal life; what else could I have done? Even if I had the power to resume normal life, doing so would shorten my life. It was important that I did anything and everything the doctors said. Hospitals are not enjoyable, and this routine helped me enjoy it the best I could. I was comfortable this way.

At first, my days were spent with both of my parents, but Mum had to go back to work nine days later, so it was decided that Dad, who luckily, had both a supportive manager and had saved up six months' worth of sick pay over twelve years of working, was going to be the one who took care of me. Here we were lucky – not every parent is going to have so much sick pay saved up, and this is where cancer can hit hard. The financial implications of cancer can be very difficult, but as we will get onto later, there are many charities who will help and support patients and their families through such a difficult time.

The only time my routine was different was if I had visitors, which I had a lot of because it was the Easter holidays, so many people had time off, and with the shock of my recent diagnosis, it was as if there was a rush for everyone to come visit me. On Saturday 26th March, I had my first visitors, my next-door neighbours, Sharon, Sean, Joe, Jas, and Esme. The chemo hadn't really kicked in yet, so I was still quite poorly, not communicating much and falling asleep a lot. It was still great to see them! They bought me some presents, including a WWE Kids Magazine to read, a ball-catching game, and a mini drone, which was kind of them. The latter two weren't the most appropriate things to be playing with on the ward, but they definitely provided me with some much-needed entertainment and amusement.

Sometimes, visitors were the best part of the hospital day. Despite feeling so ill and being in the last place I'd ever want to be, the one thing about being in hospital that I enjoyed was that I was spending quality time with my family. There was a lot more family time. But sometimes it was good to see different people and familiar faces that I had not seen for a while. There was no way I was well enough to go back to Stowmarket or see my family and friends, so in a sense, Stowmarket and my family and friends were brought to me, and I feel having visitors was probably one of the only feelings of normality I had, besides seeing my family. The best part, of course, was their company, and depending on the people, they either had a coffee with Mum in the hospital concourse, came to visit me and my family, or played board games with me. Sometimes they would ask if I wanted anything, and with my cravings while on chemo, I usually ended up with hundreds of bottles of Powerade, hundreds of cans of J20s, and hundreds of bags of popcorn and Haribo. Auntie Karen was also very good to us, as she and Uncle John would make weekly visits and would buy anything that Mum and I had on our shopping list. Some things on my list never changed; every day I was living on J20s, Haribo, and Baby Bels, but sometimes I had stranger cravings. The doctors did not frown upon this unhealthy diet.

I also received a visit from my friends, Fin and Zoe, who I hadn't spoken to properly since my diagnosis. I was very grateful to hear that they had managed to take the train and bus by themselves in order to come visit me. It was great to see my friends, even for a little while, though Zoe still managed to spill a drink everywhere and Fin kept saying rude words in front of the doctors and nurses. I remember Fin mistaking the word 'coke' for 'cock' due to the nurse's accent.

"Oh wow, you managed some coke. I thought that would be too hard on your mouth."

You can only imagine Fin's reaction!

My mouth was sore at this time, which was probably my first side effect from the chemo. Although the life I wanted wasn't best for a hospital setting, I felt comfortable and almost like I was back at home because it was like my friendship group hadn't changed. It was another thing that was still the same, just in a different setting. Fin told me that he had been covering my paper round and was using the money earned to donate to charity. He also told me he was planning a head-shaving event to raise money for CLIC Sargent and Addenbrooke's Charitable Trust (ACT), although at the time, he didn't know where or when he was going to do it. I praise Fin for everything he did in terms of fundraising and keeping my paper round going for me;

he worked so hard, all the while still having to keep up with his schoolwork, and I appreciated it very much.

I also received a visit from Mr Shades, Dad's very supportive boss, which was kind of him. He knew from experience what we were going through, as his wife had sadly died from breast cancer a few months earlier. As our car was still broken, we were using his, and he said that Dad could borrow it for as long as he liked to save on petrol. Dad was very grateful. It is kind gestures like that which can make all the difference.

Sometimes, I got visits from the Giggle Doctors. These were clowns who were dressed up as doctors, just to make you laugh or cheer you up a bit. Dr. Eye Spy visited me quite a lot; I'd say Dr. Eye Spy was the main clown, although there were many all over the ward, including the one who was convinced that she was Beyoncé. When speaking to a teacher at the hospital, he said he used to spend a lot of time in hospital with his daughter, who had diabetes, and the one thing they would always try to avoid was the clowns. They would always hope that they would be discharged as quickly as possible after each stay before the clowns arrived. The clowns freaked me out a little bit as well, but I did get quite a lot of laughs, and it was great to see them, and the kids loved them too! Nothing was more entertaining than when the clowns came and I had visitors over, because it was often the visitors being picked on!

It was important for me to be occupied in other ways as the Wi-Fi was very limited. I remember wanting to watch every WWE WrestleMania to get in the mood for WrestleMania 32, which was approaching, but I only got fifteen minutes into the first WrestleMania in 1985 because I was using all of Dad's phone data. I remember later on having to complete a survey on the ward, and although I completely forgot to add this, I strongly believe that the ward should have been installed with internet. This problem was soon fixed when a rumour went around in the parents' room of a Wi-Fi password that no one had permission for other than the hospital staff. It turns out that all of the patients were using it anyway, and after a couple of weeks or so of having very limited Wi-Fi, I was using it all the time. Nobody questioned a thing!

Every morning, I also received a visit from the play specialists, who asked if there were any board games or games in general I would like to borrow. The play specialists also had another role, and by this time, we were introduced to the Beads of Courage programme. The beads mean a lot to me because they show my story. This book would not be necessary if I could show you all of my beads and the booklet to show what they represent. I was given a long piece of string, starting with beads that spelled my name. Then, for each thing that I went through, I got a bead for it. For example, yellow beads were given for every night spent in hospital, red beads were given for every blood transfusion, and rainbow beads were for physiotherapy. There were lots of different beads for lots of different reasons, and this continued throughout every participating hospital, not just Addenbrooke's. By the end of my journey, I was able to collect 507 beads, not including the ones I'd started off with for decoration. The 507 beads, which include 109 yellow beads, still aren't complete, as towards the very end of my paediatric journey, finding a play specialist was difficult. If I ever finish the Beads of Courage programme, I'd say I'll have at least 550, and there are some beads I really need to get hold of, and one day, I hope to!

The doctors were concerned that I wasn't getting out of bed enough, and I was ordered to wear stockings, which are really long white socks that go up to your knees and are very tight. They prevent blood clots, which, due to my inactivity, I was at a higher risk from. I found them so difficult to put on, but according to Tracey, my nurse the day I got the stockings, they were easy to put on, and she told me off for not knowing how to put my socks on. She couldn't believe that I was thirteen years old and didn't know how to put my socks on. In my defence, Mum and Dad were having trouble getting those stockings over my feet, and they were forty-one and thirty-nine years old, respectively. I was very keen to get these stockings off me as soon as possible, so to get me moving around more, I had visits from the physiotherapists.

With the physiotherapists, I went on a walk around Ward C2, and it was the first time I had seen it properly. Of course, I had been to the breakfast trolley and to the kitchen door to place an order a handful of times and went to the showers every day, but I'd never really had the opportunity to explore everything that was there.

At the centre of the ward was the nurses' desk, and surrounding that were four bays (A, C, G, and H) and six independent rooms (B, D, E, F, I, and J). A was a three-bedded bay, C was a two-bedded bay, the dreaded G Bay was the four-bedded and most-crowded bay, and H was another two-bedded bay. The independent rooms were often for people who were deemed contagious, and there were signs saying 'Barrier Nursing' outside them. But some lucky people occasionally got them simply because there were no other rooms available or because the nurses felt a patient deserved a more spacious room for a change. Near the entrance, the ward also contained a school room, mostly for the primary school children, and a teenage room, strictly for teenagers only, which had lots of DVDs, an Xbox, games, gaming chairs, and a juke box. Coming out of the school room was an outdoor play area, but at the time it was being refurbished, so I didn't see much of it to begin with. At the very front of the ward was the parents' room, which was strictly for parents, and I wasn't allowed in there. I never set foot in the parents' room, so I have no idea what it looked like. At the very back of the ward were two bathrooms and a shower room, and toilets were scattered around the ward. My favourite room was the disabled toilets located near the showers as they were the most spacious, but because I was in A bay at the very start, we were very lucky that the bay had its own loo anyway, and I rarely used the other toilets.

After my ten days of chemo had finished, I was feeling much better in terms of the leukaemia symptoms, but that's not to say I didn't face any challenges. The side effects hadn't completely set in yet, although there were some. I had lost all my sense of taste, and the things I could taste tasted metallic. Because drinking – which is important anyway – is much more important when on treatment, in order to flush out the chemo, I was encouraged to drink as much as possible. As you can imagine, with water tasting like coins, it was the last thing I wanted to drink. Squash was encouraged as an alternative to give water some flavour, but the metallic taste remained, and it did put me off squash for a few years!

I was still having good and bad days in terms of nausea, but this was still due to the leukaemia rather than the chemo, and my nausea was managed by anti-sickness medications, such as ondansetron and cyclizine. I found cyclizine more effective, and sometimes it worked really well; other times, it had no effect and I was going to puke whether I had medication or not. I still had hair, and fevers were rare, as it took a while for the chemo to completely destroy the cells in my body.

One day, I was feeling well and thought it would be nice to escape the ward, which I had spent almost twelve days on, by going out to the hospital concourse. It was important to go out and enjoy things as much as I could now because this period of feeling 'well' was due to end at any moment. The worst was still yet to come.

The hospital concourse was great for someone who had just spent twelve days confined to a hospital bed, but not the most amazing thing in the world for an ordinary person. Everyone would admit it was good though. For a hospital, it was impressive, I must say. There was a Costa Coffee, a Marks & Spencer, a Body Shop, and a Stock Shop, which sold clothes and gifts. There was even a hair salon! The concourse also had an Amigos, which was a convenience store that contained daily newspapers and various magazines, snacks, and drinks. The second part of the concourse was the food court, which had a Baguette Company, a Starbucks, a place called The Spice of Life, and most excitingly, a Burger King! One time, Dad got me pancakes and a large coke from Burger King due to my changing daily cravings, which I experienced often while undergoing treatment, in addition to following the dietician's advice (which we will get to later). Unfortunately, I ate it so fast that I threw up everywhere straight after. The doctor advised that I took it easy and started with toast for breakfast and work my way up once I was feeling stronger and better in myself.

I'll tell you a funny story from the first time I visited the concourse. Easter Sunday was the week before, and it was clear, since I no longer enjoyed my Easter eggs, that I had gone off chocolate. Milk chocolate, particularly, had a metallic taste to it. As I've mentioned, most things seemed to taste metallic while on chemo. But white chocolate was different, and I enjoyed my white chocolate Easter egg that was donated to the ward, which the play team gave to me. We went to Amigos, and I asked Mum if I could have some white chocolate. The problem was that they only had small bars of white chocolate, and me being me on a good day, I wanted a large bar. I came across a white chocolate bar, which was big but sugar free. I've always advocated against sugar free products because the chemicals they put in them are worse for you and more cancer-causing than sugar. But because I was craving the chocolate, and I was already ill as it was, I wasn't bothered about whether it contained sugar or not. It was a 100g bar, and I scoffed about 75g of it when I got back to my bed on the ward. A few minutes later, I had a really bad belly ache and I had to go to the loo. Then I had to go again. And again. And again. This diarrhoea was uncontrollable! Mum, knowing what they put in sugar free products, wondered if it was the chocolate causing my sudden bowel problems. On the back of the wrapper, in clear capital letters, it read 'CONSUMING MORE THAN 25g OF THIS BAR MAY HAVE A LAXATIVE EFFECT.' It was laxative chocolate! My family never let this go and still make fun of me to this day. How was I supposed to know? Chocolate is chocolate. Who makes sugar free chocolate anyway? That defeats the purpose of chocolate!

Chapter 4

The Tube

The immediate effects of Round 1 of chemo (continued) from March 25th to April 11th, 2016

Alongside the hospital routine, visitors, and keeping myself occupied, my health issues were still ongoing. About a week into my stay, I met the dietician. At first, I was thinking: *oh no, she's going to tell me that I became ill because I was overweight and eating all the wrong foods. And therefore, she's going to say that I have to lose weight and eat a balanced diet.* Remember, that was why I thought I was feeling so unwell to begin with. I genuinely thought that. However, she told me the complete opposite, which left me puzzled. Once she explained it, it made perfect sense. My leukaemia wasn't the concern of the dieticians; they were concerned with how successfully I could cope with the chemotherapy. It was necessary to eat as much as I could to keep my weight up because this was crucial for fighting and recovering from chemo. She recommended fatty foods, such as pizza with extra cheese.

Another dietician introduced me to some supplement drinks, as, if I was feeling ill or had lost my appetite, I could drink these milkshakes, which had all the same nutrients of a substantial meal. One of these milkshakes was Scandishakes, a supplement drink containing milk powder, carbohydrate, and fat. They had the calorie intake equivalent to a full roast dinner and helped boost weight and energy and manage malnutrition. Flavours came in vanilla, strawberry, chocolate, and caramel. I was even given my own Scandishake bottle! The dieticians told me that the chef could make Scandishakes taste great by loading them up with lots of ice cream. But the chef was a critic of them, describing them as 'sickly' and 'thick, which sit in the bottom of your stomach'. He wasn't wrong. The only person who could make them 'taste great' admitted they were horrible.

There were other supplement drinks; I did like the milkshake drinks at first: the chocolate shakes tasted like the milk that is left after finishing a bowl of Coco Pops. But as time went on, the thought of them made me feel sick, and the fruit juice shakes were disgusting and made me throw up straight away. Dad tried to force these supplement drinks down me at times, and it definitely did more harm than good. Not only did they make me throw up, but it meant that I'd throw up the contents of the little food I had managed to keep down.

However bad they may have tasted, it was important I tried to drink them as often as I could because the dieticians brought on the discussion of a nasogastric tube, always referred to as an NG tube. This was where I would have to be fed through a tube up my nose with milk feeds if I was unable to eat. Therefore, it was important to keep my weight up, and if my weight went below the cut-off point of 54.77kg (I was currently 57kg), then an NG tube was necessary. Little and often was the way to approach it – eating large meals wasn't expected of me. The dieticians advised that I kept grazing throughout the day, and sweets were particularly good. Yes, the dieticians were encouraging me to eat sweets. I thought this was great at the time, but as time went on, eating just the smallest thing was going to be a challenge. Typical – when you want to eat them, dieticians will advise against eating too many fatty foods, but when you feel incapable of eating, they want you to eat as many fatty foods as possible. The dieticians also told me that it was important to keep moving around because muscle weighs more than fat, so it was worth preventing my legs from turning to jelly.

About a week or so after my final dose of the first round of chemotherapy, it was clear I was feeling much better from the leukaemia, but the side effects of treatment were beginning to kick in. By this point, I had already lost all sense of taste and had formed a number of ulcers on my tongue, which was white and fluffy. It was clear that mucositis was going to be a problem. I continued to fight, and although my weight was decreasing, it was doing so slowly, and my appetite was okay, meaning I had managed to keep it stable at around the 55kg mark. It was a loss of weight from 57kg in March, but I was slowly fighting back and keeping afloat – only just. Despite this, the dieticians started to talk to me about having an NG tube put down me, which I repeatedly refused. But the dieticians won the battle because, although my appetite was okay and my weight was above the cut-off point, they were worried that my mouth would soon be so sore I wouldn't be able to eat anything. It would also be too sore to put down an NG tube, so they'd be stuck for options. It made sense to put the tube down anyway, just as a precaution.

An NG tube is inserted through your nose, down your throat, and into your stomach. Milk-based feeds are attached to a drip machine – a different machine to the IV medications – which controls the rate of the milk-feeds going in. Going back to a couple of weeks before, when I suffered the camera at West Suffolk, I hated the thought of things going down my nose. However, the dieticians told me that I didn't have to worry about that because I wouldn't feel a thing and I would still be able to eat and drink normally with the tube in. Both of those were lies because the NG tube did nothing but disturb me and cause irritation. I do wonder if the dieticians had ever had an

NG tube put down their own noses.

Tracey, my nurse that day, kept asking me when I wanted my NG tube put in. After getting told off for not knowing how to put my socks on, I was scared of Tracey, and I'd usually do as I was told. But I was strongly against having an NG tube, and I was standing my ground! My replies were always 'later' until later became the end of the day and there was no escaping.

Tracey asked if I wanted to have my NG tube put in while I was in my bed or in the treatment room. I didn't really care because I was in a grump as I didn't want the NG tube in the first place and felt it was unnecessary as I had tried so hard to keep my weight stable. I was so angry because all that hard work I'd done to stay above my weight cut-off point meant nothing: they still put a tube down anyway. In defence of them, deep down I accept that it was for my own good.

Tracey made the decision for me and decided to get it done in the treatment room so I could have a change of scenery. I was wheelchaired (I could have walked, but I was grumpy, choosing to be difficult instead) to the treatment room, in tears. Tracey warned me that the NG tube may make me gag when being inserted and she said the best thing to do was to keep drinking through a straw. The student nurse, who was observing, passed me a cup of water with a straw while Tracey allowed me to feel the tube, which was soft and rubbery.

"See, you won't feel a thing."

She then proceeded to measure the length of the tube from my nose to my belly button, which indicated how long it needed to be. She cut the tube to size with her scissors. After that, she inserted the tube through my nose while shouting, "Drink, drink, drink, drink!", and when I stopped drinking, "Keep drinking!" It definitely made me gag, so I kept drinking like I was told. It was the most uncomfortable feeling ever; it didn't really hurt, despite feeling a bit sharp at first, but at the same time it was one of the worst things I ever had the displeasure of feeling. I was drinking and gagging at the same time, with tears in my eyes, my parents helplessly watching me. When it was done and the tube was down, Tracey pulled a sharp wire out of the tube and stuck the tube down by the side of my nose on my cheek with a dressing, which resembled masking tape. The tube continued out of the dressing and had a cap on it so I could be attached to the milk feeds. It was quite annoying having a tube hanging from my face twenty-four hours a day, but it was recommended that I put it behind my ear, which would keep it out of the way.

Like I said, I was very grumpy, and this was still the case after having the tube put down, and I did my best to show that I wasn't happy. Being wheelchaired back to my bedspace, I had my arms crossed and was in tears. Making my way back to my bed, I tripped over my wheelchair, in front of everyone, landing on the bed in the most embarrassing way possible. My attempts to be serious made me look like a fool, and I couldn't help but laugh.

As I was still eating, it made no sense for me to have milk feeds all the time. Therefore, just so my body would get used to it, I could still eat during the day and have the milk feeds at night, only at a very slow rate of 2ml an hour. The dieticians said that it would help my stomach adapt to the feeds should they need to go on at a higher rate. The tube was only there as a precaution to begin with. Therefore, I could eat as much as I could manage and have a very small, but harmless, top-up at night. After each use, the tube had to be flushed down with a special sterilised water to prevent blockages. The last thing I wanted was a blocked tube because that would mean it would have to be removed and another one would need to be put down.

An advantage of the tube was taking oral medications through it so that I could avoid the horrible taste of them. One of those medications was itraconazole, which was an anti-fungal medicine, and it tasted disgusting. It had a metallic flavour, mixed with the texture of really thick water. Itraconazole and I didn't get along, and it was usually the last medicine I took out of all the others – I had to have it twice a day, once in the morning and once at night, like most of my other medications. To take itraconazole, I had to drink it like a shot and then down a litre of orange squash. Water wasn't effective as that tasted metallic in its own right and it also still left the taste of the itraconazole. Squash wasn't perfect either as it still had a metallic, almost artificial taste to it, but it was better than having water. I would rather live on Scandishakes for the rest of my life than take another dose of itraconazole. Even worse, it had to be liquid as Addenbrooke's didn't prescribe it in tablet form. The NG tube was helpful because I could take medications without having to taste them. I could also use it to take other oral medicines, but I mostly took tablets by myself orally, as the Addenbrooke's pharmacy always seemed to be very busy. I was better off taking the tablets and saving the nurses and pharmacists hours of their time.

A further advantage of the tube was that if I was having an off-day or just wasn't feeling well, instead of having to force myself to eat something, with the fear of losing weight if I was to throw it up – which I most likely would – I could choose to have a feed instead because the rate could be adjusted depending on how much I was eating. This wasn't helpful if I was feeling sick, though, as the milk feeds would not help my nausea. If I burped, then a taste of half-digested milk that had been mixed with eggs after someone had thrown it up just before they'd died would emerge from my mouth. The tube is meant to be good at helping those who cannot eat on their own, but I found that it didn't actually do anything for the nausea, and when I was feeling sick, I usually asked the nurses to stop the feed for me because there was no way I'd be able to keep the feed down for very long. The rates of the feed were probably very small, but when feeling sick, it felt as if my stomach was overflowing with milk.

One disadvantage of the tube was that it made it very difficult to eat normally, despite what the dieticians said. Jelly was particularly easy to eat, but I can eat that without chewing anyway. The worst foods to eat with a tube in were bread products, such as sandwiches and toasties, and even pizza. These would cling to the tube at the back of my throat, dragging it down, causing pain in my nose as the tube tugged and rubbed against it. This was what brought on my worst moments in terms of behaviour, and sometimes visitors witnessed how grumpy and agitated I could get with the tube. Drinking was also an issue because I could feel the tube at the back of my throat, so if I swallowed anything, it felt like I was swallowing the tube. It wasn't a very nice feeling. Imagine having something permanently stuck in your throat and not being able to cough it up. That was what having an NG tube felt like all the time, and those days were torturous.

Another disadvantage of the NG tube was that it was really disgusting. Because the tube goes down your throat, it could be in one of two locations; the stomach – where it should be – or your lungs, if it went down the wrong way. Understandably, you don't want to be syringing water or milk into your lungs, so it was important to check the pH of the contents you were syringing out before syringing anything in. This was done by syringing out the contents of your stomach (or not) and putting it on some litmus paper; if it turned red, it was acidic, but if it was purple, it was alkaline. If it was acidic, it was in your stomach and in the right place, but if it was alkaline, then it was likely in your lungs. If you couldn't get anything out from the tube, then it was recommended to drink something dark like blackcurrant juice and suck it back up using the tube. If it came back up, then your tube was in your stomach. This procedure was carried out by the nurses on the ward, but it could be done by my parents both on and off the ward, whenever it was necessary. The reason why I found this disgusting, if you haven't already guessed why, is because I was basically putting my stomach contents on a piece of paper. Some foods were more disgusting than others – I never want to see the pH of my stomach contents tested after eating Doritos again. That being said, I couldn't help but be fascinated by how the stomach broke down hot dogs.

Unfortunately, or fortunately, however you view it – I definitely view the latter – my first NG tube didn't last long. In fact, it only lasted three days. One morning, I wasn't feeling great and hadn't yet had my anti-sickness medication. Dad made me have a shower instead of a bath, so I was having to stand up for a long period of time (though, to a healthy person, this would be considered a very short period of time to stand up for). It was hair-washing day, so there was no escaping the shower. While in the shower, I began to feel really dizzy and lightheaded and had to take a seat while ordering Dad to run and get me a sick bowl. To be fair, I did insist on taking one with me in the first place, but he ignored my advice. Luckily, it didn't come to vomiting, and I was well enough to finish my shower and head back to my bed on my own two feet. Then, Dad asked me if I would be okay for a couple of minutes so he could brush his teeth, to which I said yes as I seemed to have recovered, and if anything was going to happen, what was the chances of it being in two minutes time? As soon as he left, I felt the urge and threw up. But this time it was different. Usually when I vomited, I threw up and it was over with, but this time I felt like I had thrown up an entire cookie. What I had thrown up was massive! The NG tube was hanging out of my mouth, still attached via tape on my nose. I had thrown it up! This was something I was not prepared for – I thought if I could eat 'normally', then I could be sick normally, but the whole thing made sense now. Because I had no one with me and I had my face over the sick bowl, I couldn't reach the buzzer to get the nurses. So, for a while, I had a tube through my nose and hanging out of my mouth until a nurse spotted me, ran to me, and tore the dressing off my face as fast as she could, which hurt, and removed the tube from my nose.

It was a bit annoying that the tube was gone, considering a lady had come to visit Dad that day to train him on how to use the NG tube machine in preparation for when I was able to go home[4]. She still showed him how the machine worked but was unable to use my NG tube as an example.

I was free! It wasn't a pleasant way to get rid of something I hated – evident by the sick stuck in my nostrils as the contaminated tube was pulled out – but I was sure relieved to have it gone, and the dieticians didn't bother me with the tube again. For another four weeks.

***

By the end of the Easter holidays, I was feeling much better in myself. As I mentioned before, I was experiencing

---

[4] Once I was healthy enough to be discharged, if my tube was still in, the hospital was able to provide my family with a machine so I could continue having milk-feeds at home.

some side effects from the chemo but not all had kicked in. My mouth remained sore and was going to remain that way for a while, but it was becoming less so, and I was eating more, despite completely having no sense of taste. I still had hair – a lot of it – but was noticing the occasional hair on my collar and pillow, which was gradually becoming thicker as the days went by. It was when Auntie Karen, Uncle John, Cousin Jade, and her partner, Pete, came to visit my family in hospital that I noticed the first hair on my collar. I brushed it aside, believing it was the occasional stray hair, but it really did break me on the inside. Losing my hair upset me a lot. Many think that it's just girls that take hair loss hard, but all cancer patients do. Some nights I was in tears about my hair. Jenny, my nurse one night, told me that some people shave their hair off before it all disappears to avoid going through the painful process of watching it fall out day by day. Because the pillows were white, it made the amount of hair I was losing visible. To combat this, I found it helpful to cover a colourful blanket over my pillow so the hair wasn't as visible.

Towards the end of the Easter holidays, I met Amanda, who was going to be our Clinical Nurse Specialist (CNS nurse). We would have met her sooner, but she had been on holiday. Amanda wasn't a medical nurse, but it was her job to support me and my family and write letters on behalf of the consultant to give to schools and workplaces. She had to go through some medical forms with Dad and also provided us with contact numbers in case of emergency once I was discharged.

As I was feeling better, Amanda said it was only a matter of time until I would be discharged to Kingston House. This was the first time we had even heard of this. Kingston House, which was run by the NHS, was located on hospital grounds and about a five or ten minute walk from the main hospital. It was for patients like myself, who were not well enough to go home (I was neutropenic at this point) but well enough to be out of hospital. Therefore, Kingston House would be a 'halfway home'. School was due to start, so I would have to leave Kingston to go to school and have daily hospital check-ups at the day unit. Further information was to be given on this. Other than that, I would pretty much have freedom while at Kingston. But the number one rule was that I could not leave Cambridge.

The next day, I met Denise, the teacher, again. Because it was the end of the Easter holidays, school was due to start. Denise was mainly the English teacher, but she could teach maths to C grade. She was the main secondary school teacher, but to help with other subjects, Jason, the science specialist, would give me lessons on Tuesdays, and Richard, the maths specialist, on Thursdays. School was every day, except weekends and holidays, of course. Denise's minimum session time was ten minutes, and she recommended that we start with forty-five minutes, gradually increasing to one hour and fifteen-minute sessions, which was the maximum. School took place on the ward and could either happen at my bedside or in the school room depending on how I was feeling or whether I was at Kingston or on the ward at the time.

On the morning of Monday 11th April, the doctor who had initially diagnosed me, who had returned from holiday, was doing the ward rounds. She could tell I was feeling better in myself and gave the go-ahead for discharging me to Kingston House. The same doctor who diagnosed me would be discharging me for the first time. Despite feeling better, there were a number of issues I had going on that Dad was concerned about. One of them was that I was shaking, sometimes uncontrollably, and the other was that I was suffering from chest pains. The doctors were going to look into it, and once I was at Kingston, they would run some tests, but for the time being, they couldn't really find anything wrong so put it down to something psychological. There is definitely truth to the fact that my diagnosis caused me a lot of stress and anxiety, but me being my stubborn self, I wished they would see that it was definitely a physical problem, rather than psychological.

I was due to leave for Kingston House that evening. The move to Kingston was stressful, and I felt bad for Dad as he was on his own. Mum was back to work by this point, so she was at home with Kristy. I wasn't much use because my chest was hurting and I couldn't lift heavy objects because of my Hickman line. Because of this, he had to move out almost three weeks' worth of clutter from my bedspace and move out of Acorn House where my parents were staying[5]. I also had to wait for my medicines from the pharmacy to arrive before I could move out. Dad managed to move out of our bed space in four trips, the fourth being the final and one-way trip, which consisted of me giving as much help as I could by carrying a light backpack while clutching my chest in agony, while he was lifting fifteen super heavy carrier bags.

I was officially discharged from hospital, and I had my first breath of fresh air in eighteen days. All I needed to do now was wait for my neutrophils to reach over 0.5 and I would be ready for Round 2 of chemotherapy, and therefore the coming weeks were primarily about recovery and involved a lot of waiting, time, and patience.

---

[5] There was always one parent staying with me at hospital. The other parent usually stayed at home to take care of Kristy. However, we had access to a room at Acorn House, which was particularly helpful during the weekends, enabling the other parent and my sister to stay.

Chapter 5

Waiting

Kingston House, the later effects of Round 1, and the build-up to Round 2 from April 11th to May 15th, 2016

As mentioned before, Kingston House was to act as a halfway home. Its purpose was to keep me as close to the hospital as possible so that if I developed a fever I could be admitted back in straight away. But it simultaneously allowed me an increased amount of freedom that I would not get on the ward.

Kingston House had a number of purposes, and it wasn't just paediatric leukaemia patients and their families staying there. From what I gathered, it appeared that hospital staff used the flats as accommodation between their shifts. The patients had their own allocated block at the far end of the building, with around four flats for patient use. Each flat could have up to two families staying there, but a family was defined as one patient and one parent.

Dad wasn't too impressed with Kingston House, likely because he had experienced better at Acorn House. Though, for someone like myself, who had just spent three weeks in a hospital bed, Kingston was a luxury. It was basically a block of shared flats; a long corridor with doors on each side. Each flat had two bedrooms, one for each family, and each bedroom had two beds, a desk, a TV, and a bathroom. There was one kitchen and sitting area per flat, so we had to share some things with the other family who would be staying in the same flat.

An advantage of Kingston House as opposed to the ward was that there was Wi-Fi — well, Wi-Fi we had to pay for. I'm not like most people my age who are always on their phones, and I'm not a huge fan of social media. I'm proud to not have Instagram or Snapchat, Facebook being as far as I go. But I was finding it very hard to communicate with my friends while in hospital because the Wi-Fi was limited, and I definitely felt I had more freedom at Kingston House.

While at Kingston, I couldn't rely on the nurses to give me my medications, so it was important that Dad and I kept an eye on the clock. When we first arrived at Kingston, it was about 10:00pm, so it was bedtime straight away, especially since I was starting school the next day. I still needed to take my medication, and during this time, I was on a number of different medicines, including acyclovir (an anti-viral medication), itraconazole, potassium supplements, and ciprofloxacin (an antibiotic). These all needed to be taken since I was neutropenic and my body needed these anti-viral and antibiotic medications as a precaution, and the supplements would top up my low blood levels. These preventative medications are known as prophylaxis.

My new routine began on Tuesday 12th April. I woke up early because it was back to school day. Actually, it was my first day of hospital school. After getting ready, I went to the Paediatric Day Unit (PDU), which was attached and closely linked to Ward C2 but was for outpatients. Because it was my first day of school, Denise said she would catch me there, and because waiting times took forever, I actually had my first lesson in the waiting room. The first lesson was just about getting to know each other, and I completed questionnaires about myself, such as my favourite TV show and how many pets I had.

Denise then explained to me that the purpose of hospital school was so that I wouldn't fall too far behind my classmates back in Stowmarket, and my teachers were going to send her the work for her to complete. Denise also said she would set me homework, but not the normal homework you get at school. The biggest difference between hospital school homework and school homework is that at hospital school it is optional. I wasn't going to be under any pressure to complete it. Also, we weren't assigned essays on poems and stuff like that; instead, I had fun homework like wordsearches, puzzles, and quizzes, not so much for educational purposes but just to keep my brain busy and to take my mind off everything on the health side of things. My favourite type of homework was dingbats, which are similar to the gameshow, *Catchphrase*, where you have to guess the common phrase displayed through pictures and symbols. If I was having an off day, instead of going through the GCSE English Poetry Anthology, Denise and I would complete pages and pages of dingbats.

During the period I was in hospital, school was mostly the same in terms of content covered. For example, because I was starting my GCSEs the next academic year, we began going over the poetry anthology for English and there was a heavy emphasis on ratios for Maths, which I would soon become an expert in. We must have studied ratios for at least two months, maybe three.

Perhaps being in a different setting to the normal classroom helped me memorise content better. I was able to associate what I learned with the location I learned it in, which, I learned, during A-Level Psychology, can improve memory! I was able to memorise 'I Wanna Be Yours' by John Cooper Clarke word for word. I know that poem because it was the first thing that I ever studied in hospital school, and it was read to me in the teenage room. The teenage room was very unique because of cool furniture and items it contained.

Not all of the work I did was the same type of content. English and maths were no doubt the most important, in addition to my weekly science lessons, but sometimes, if I was having a bad day, Denise would read me some of my history textbook to prepare me for Year 10. Or, to get away from the monotony of poetry, we would do some article writing for English. 'The Wonderful World of Wrestling' was one of the articles I wrote and is one of my proudest pieces of work in hospital school. Unfortunately, I can't seem to find it either in print form or on my laptop, no matter how hard I look. My special box dedicated to my journey is missing this piece of work.

After school, I had a check-up in the Paediatric Day Unit (PDU). PDU was much different to Ward C2, and at first, I didn't like it. I soon got used to it since I was to become a regular visitor. I suppose no one really likes a hospital clinic. In PDU, there was a waiting room with a number of rooms around it, which were used by the doctors for check-ups. These rooms were also used by the nurses for things such as blood tests and line dressing changes. At the opposite end of the clinic and further down the corridor, there was a six-bedded bay for patients who just needed a bed or had just come out of surgery and were recovering. The routine in PDU involved sitting in the waiting room and waiting to be called to have my obs done, and then I would have to wait to see the doctor and the nurse for a blood test; sometimes I saw the doctor first, sometimes I saw the nurse first. The doctor would either let me go or say I needed a new medicine or blood transfusion, which would result in me and either Mum or Dad waiting for even longer until I was called to a bedspace to have my IV medication or blood and/or platelet transfusion comfortably.

On one particular day – Tuesday 12th April – after having my obs taken, I did have to have my line dressing changed. I haven't really mentioned much about a dressing change other than it needed to be done every seven to ten days, so I will explain it now. Because the dressing was a big plaster on my chest, it was quite painful to get off, and so to ease the pain, the nurses would try to unstick it either through anti-stick wipes or the 'lollypop'. The 'lollypop' was a circular sponge on a stick – hence the name 'lollypop' – and was full of an anti-stick liquid that would slowly release onto the dressing. Then, the nurse would have to carefully remove the plaster and, using the wipes or another 'lollypop', clean the line site and the lumens, then loop it back up and put a new dressing on. Addenbrooke's also put a date on the line so the next nurse would know when its due date was for a change. The bungs needed to be cleaned with a wipe, which was done after every new medication I had through my line, and were changed regularly too.

I was out of PDU fairly quick that day, but I wasn't out of hospital. The registrar who I saw was still concerned about my chest pains. Although they hadn't got worse, they hadn't got any better either. Because of this, I was sent to have a chest X-ray. This involved having to take my shirt off, and with my chest leaning on a board, X-rays were taken both with and without a deep breath. Fortunately, nothing scary came back and the doctors just put it down to stress and worry. I just said okay and agreed to it, but privately, I refused to accept that and thought there was genuinely something wrong. It was a mystery why the pains were there, and it was disrupting my breathing and I wanted to get it sorted. The pain did reduce day by day after that and soon went away for good, but it took weeks. They would return a few months later but less severely and for a smaller amount of time.

Once we were out of hospital, Dad and I were off to Tesco to go buy dinner. This would become a new daily feature. I adapted to a new routine while at Kingston. First, I would wake up and have breakfast, which was usually cereal, but if my whole family were visiting, usually at the weekends, then it would be Burger King or McDonald's. My parents were really lucky that they still had income coming in, because I am sure that eating out so often would not have been possible without it. On the weekdays, school would start at around 10:30am or 11:00am, so I would have to shower and get ready about an hour before. Because I was off the ward, it was clear that I was well enough to have the maximum amount of time Denise offered for a lesson, so school usually lasted about one hour and fifteen minutes to an hour and a half. There was no time to stop or do anything after school because it was time to go straight to PDU. Depending on how well the doctors and nurses were doing for time, I could be out in a couple of hours, but if not, I could be waiting all day. Sometimes, medicines took so long to be prepared and then infused through my line that I was still waiting past closing time and had to finish waiting in the teenage room back on Ward C2. This annoyed me. Having to wait in PDU for a check-up was the most tedious thing I've ever had to spend weeks of my life doing. If Mum was staying with me, we would then go get lunch or dinner from Marks & Spencer on the hospital concourse, but if it was Dad, we would always go to Tesco, which was a few minutes away from the hospital. If we fancied a change, we would go to Sainsbury's, although this was rare but equally exciting. We had to shop for food every day because, firstly, the time of our stay at Kingston was unpredictable, so there was no point doing a weekly shop, and secondly, because I was feeling the effects of chemo, something I might crave one day made me feel sick the next.

Therefore, we shopped on a day-by-day basis. After going to Tesco, depending on how much of the day we had left, we just stayed at Kingston House, usually playing on my iPad or watching TV.

The weekends were very different to the weekdays because I had no school, so my mornings were mostly free. PDU was also closed on weekends, so I had to spend most of my weekend sitting in the teenage room of Ward C2. This was where most outpatients my age spent their weekends on the ward. Waiting on the ward took even longer than PDU. At least I was in the teenage room, so I was able to occupy myself with various board games and card games, but there were often other patients in there too for the same reason as me and, with me being quite shy, I was limited in what I spent my time doing in the room. I preferred my own company whereas other patients liked to communicate with each other. I never really played on the Xbox, and this was definitely evident after I got beaten quite badly on a shooting game by another patient.

One advantage of Kingston was that I felt free and independent. After spending weeks on the ward, at Kingston, although I was restricted in some things, I was free to an extent. However, because I had spent so much time on the ward, I'll be honest, I did miss it. I didn't have the safety of the emergency button at Kingston, and if anything went wrong, it would be a long ten-minute walk back to the ward. After spending so much time on a hospital ward for being seriously ill, by the time you're seen as well enough, you don't want to leave because you feel protected and safe should anything go wrong. It was as if I was going out without the safety net I had had. The best way to cope with it is to just do it and take the risk, because the aim really is to get out of hospital and staying inside hospital will not help you with your ultimate goal.

By Tuesday 12th April, my hair was falling out rapidly and it was still causing me some upset, but not as much as it had. By now it was something I just accepted, and if I was going to get better, I would just have to go through the process. Because I was upset, Dad told me that when he shaved my hair, I would be allowed to shave his in return. We were going to do this together. On the evening of Tuesday 12th April, while FaceTiming Mum and Kristy back at home, Dad and I shaved each other's hair. I now looked like the stereotypical cancer patient.

I put an updated picture of myself on Facebook just to provide my family and friends an update as to how I was getting on, and I received a lot of support from my friends, classmates, and people who I had never spoken to before back in Stowmarket. I don't know how many texts I replied to that night, and there's still some I haven't replied to because I didn't discover them until much later on. In fact, I was still discovering them in the year 2020! I feel bad that I haven't replied to some; I don't like to come across as a rude person who ignores messages. I missed everyone in Stowmarket, but I could at least keep in touch as Kingston actually had Wi-Fi, unlike the ward.

Dad bought me a bandana and a hat, and he got himself a bandana too. On my first day of having very little hair, on Wednesday 13th April, I wore the bandana but decided it made me look silly so I would stick to the hat from then on. And I did stick to the hat – for a year and four months after, wherever I went, I wore a hat. It was something I grew attached to. Dad loved the bandana though and kept wearing it for at least the next week. He looked stupid but he didn't care.

My lack of hair began with me feeling upset, but it was soon something I was proud of, and it showed I was fighting back. From Round 1 of chemo, I didn't actually lose all my hair, although I lost most of it. My sides were almost completely bald, with only a few strands of hair, but on the top, I maintained most of it, except for a few patchy bits. If I rubbed the top of my head, a lot of hair would be seen on my hands, as well as dry skin flakes – it was like touching your hair straight after a haircut but with the added dandruff, which was due to my sensitive skin caused by the chemotherapy. One of my visitors did not know this, and when she rubbed my head for the satisfying feeling of touching my short, rough hair, then continued to eat her chocolates with the same dandruff-contaminated hand, you can only imagine the reaction that I was trying to hold in! I had to try so hard to hold back my laughter. I assume her chocolates still tasted nice – to this day, she still doesn't know what she did!

April 12th, 2016, was the final time my hair was how it once was. Gone were the days of thick, black, bushy hair, and the days of being bald, patchy, and light in colour were beginning. When it grew back, it never went back to how it was, and to this day, my hair is completely different in texture.

***

I lasted three days at Kingston House. Mum was looking after me on the night of Thursday 14th April, and I had just finished brushing my teeth and was in my pyjamas, ready for bed. But I was freezing cold, and I was shivering so much, chattering my teeth uncontrollably. Mum would always ask me if I was okay every thirty seconds, and I said "Yes!" a thousand times, getting grumpier each time because I just wanted to go to bed and was fed up with the constant interrogation.

We were still to purchase an ear thermometer – which

was, according to Amanda, a requirement – but for the time being, we had a smart thermometer, which could detect your temperature by holding it a few centimetres from your forehead. The thermometer was inaccurate though because within seconds my temperature changed from 38°C to Lo, whatever that meant. To Mum, it was clear that I had a fever, as my temperature clearly was not in the healthy range of 36.5° to 37.5°. But me being me, I didn't actually know the symptoms of a fever at the time (which is strange because I had suffered from so many), so I was getting grumpier and grumpier, shouting "I'm fine!"

Mum called the ward anyway, and they wanted to see me right away. So, in the freezing cold, still in my pyjamas, while suffering from a temperature, Mum and I took the ten-minute walk back to Ward C2. We arrived at around 8:00pm, just before the day nurses handed over to the nurses on the night shift. I was admitted to H bay; my new home was H2.

My nurse that night, Helen, said it may be an infection in my line, which was very common, so I needed to do a number of tests for them. The first one involved the nurse giving me a plastic bowl to pee in to produce a urine sample. I overflowed the bowl by accident and made a mess in the bathroom. She then gave me an antibiotic which went through my line, called tazocin. It made my mouth feel funny, which the nurse warned me about. She said it was strange that all patients feel that. The best possible way to describe the feeling is a mild pins and needles on your tongue, which burns but doesn't hurt and tastes metallic. Almost everything tastes metallic when you're on or recovering from chemo.

I was told that before I could go to bed, I'd have to wait for the night doctor to arrive, which could take hours. It was very boring during that time because we had left in a hurry and I had nothing to do as we had left Kingston so abruptly with no belongings. We didn't have any credit on the hospital TV either. It didn't matter what time I was watching the TV or what the volume was because, although H was a two-bedded bay, I had the room to myself as the bay next to me was vacant. I couldn't watch the TV anyway as free TV shut off at 8:00pm – typical!

Helen informed me that if I went forty-eight hours without a fever, I would be allowed to return to Kingston, but until then, I was back on the ward. The doctor eventually arrived at 11:00pm, but I can't remember what he said as I was too busy laughing at him. He had accidentally bumped his head on the TV and so Mum and I nicknamed him Dr. Bump. Yeah, things should really have been taken seriously, but sometimes, seeing something funny can make you feel a whole lot better.

Things weren't better the next morning. I woke up feeling sick, and it was clear that the chemo was beginning to show its full effect. What I was experiencing while staying in A bay was mostly the effects of the leukaemia and the immediate effects of the chemo, but the worst was yet to come from Round 1. I thought I had endured the hard bit already, but no, the chemo, which I hadn't had a dose of for over two weeks, was still yet to strike.

The doctor doing the ward rounds told me that three days at Kingston was impressive, and she had a really positive view to it, saying it was longer than expected. I was wondering what the point was. Why go through all the trouble of moving stuff out only to return three days later? She told me that despite my nausea, it was still important that I ate, and sometimes I would actually feel better if I had something in my stomach, such as a milkshake or a yoghurt. Sometimes this would enable me to feel better and eat more once something was in, settling my stomach. But that morning, I found it very difficult to eat my breakfast and the thought of any food made me feel sick. I tried to eat, but whatever I ate, I would throw straight back up. It was clear that another battle with the dieticians was imminent. A positive thing was that my mucositis had cleared, despite the fluffy tongue, which remained for quite some time. My mouth was no longer sore though.

Anti-sickness medication was prescribed to continue to help me cope with my nausea, but Dad's friend from work, who had suffered from cancer herself, gave me some hard sweets called 'queasy drops', which she had found helpful. I really appreciated the support of someone who had been through something similar. The queasy drops had some success with me. I'm not sure if they actually worked physically, but psychologically the fact that I was putting something in my mouth that was designed to stop me feeling sick actually did stop me feeling sick. This was not always the case because not even the anti-sickness medication worked all the time. In fact, most of the time it didn't. Sometimes, I was just going to be sick and nothing could be done to prevent it.

By this point, I was mostly craving Powerade and Haribo. I drank a lot of Powerade, and I was pretty much living off sweets for breakfast, lunch, and dinner. Perhaps I had too much. I scared my nurse, Stewart, and the student nurse one evening because my vomit was green!

Following this was one of the first breakdowns I had. We were now getting to the stage where the vomiting was frequent, which was too much for me to handle. I had cried in A bay because all I wanted to do was go home, and despite mostly keeping a positive attitude, I had moments of missing home, like anyone would. But for some reason, it was at this moment where I had thrown up my green vomit, where I'd had enough. I was feeling so ill. I was starting to question whether this was all worth it. Is it worth feeling so ill? What if I was fighting a losing battle? I'd be better off dead now if I was eventually going to lose.

"Am I going to die?" is what I asked Dad.

Five years later, Dad admits to me that that was the question that made him almost break down in front of me, but he knew that he had to be strong for me. It was a real low point, but it wasn't my lowest – which was still yet to come – and on the whole, I was in a positive state of mind when considering my situation.

Saturday 16th April was a sad day because for my Christmas present in 2015, I'd received tickets to go to WWE Live in Birmingham. Unsurprisingly, because I became ill and was staying in hospital, I was unable to go. Dad tried to sell the tickets but didn't make a good enough effort, and the only person interested needed wheelchair access. Typical – that was a lot of money that went down the drain! I still really wanted to go and told the nurses I was going to discharge myself from hospital, but they said I had to be over eighteen to do that, and my parents weren't going to do it for me. What was worse was that this particular day was a good one. I felt far from normal, but having been really ill, I was actually feeling quite well in comparison. I suppose it wasn't worth the risk – now being neutropenic, I had to avoid crowds, and things could quickly take a turn for the worse. There had been incidents when I was feeling great and ate a load of food, only to throw it up and feel rubbish within seconds. I joked that I was going to steal an ambulance and drive to Birmingham myself.

I suppose that Saturday wasn't all that bad though, as I did have visitors. My friends, Zoe and William, came to visit me in hospital, and it was nice to see them and create some funny jokes – I should add that some were quite disturbing. William told me he was doing a head shave for charity, which he was going to do the next day, and he did.

Speaking of head shaves, Fin and Zoe went ahead with Fin's head shave at the Stowmarket Tesco on Saturday 23rd April 2016, with 'Fin's Big Buzz' making the front page of the local newspapers. The original plan was for people to donate a small amount of money, and every donation meant a bit of Fin's hair would be cut by Zoe. For some reason Zoe was unable to do this, so someone else had to shave Fin's hair. Two managers at Tesco even had their heads shaved. Fin, Zoe, William, and a few others managed to raise an impressive £772.87 in total on that day, through the head shave and packing customers' bags at the checkouts in the supermarket, splitting it between the charities CLIC Sargent (now known as Young Lives vs. Cancer) and Addenbrooke's Charitable Trust (ACT). ACT told Fin that they would put the money raised towards leukaemia research. It saddens me how today I never speak to Fin or Zoe; I will forever be grateful for the work they put in when it came to supporting me and others in my situation.

As the days went by in H, I seemed to be feeling worse and worse. I seemed to be in a hole that I couldn't get out of, and the hole was being dug deeper. The nausea was becoming such an issue that I was having breakdowns, telling Dad that I had given up my fight and just wanted to die for it to be over with. Part of me just couldn't be bothered. Diarrhoea was also a frequent issue, with every trip to the toilet leaving behind something that looked like thrown up chicken korma in the toilet bowl. As mentioned before, my chest pains were getting better, although they were still there. They were no longer interfering, but it was still worrying as to why they were there. Because the X-rays found nothing, it was important to have more tests done, even though the doctors were adamant that it was psychological.

I was required to have a CT scan and had to lay still in a doughnut-shaped machine. Blue dye was injected into me, which would make any problems in my chest area visible. Because the scan was radioactive, Dad had the choice of waiting outside or staying in the room and wearing a funny apron. I chose to keep him in the room just so he would have to wear the funny apron. The results from the scan found nothing concerning, further proving the doctors right that it was due to stress of the current situation. I was annoyed, but what else could I have done? All the tests proved the contrary to my beliefs.

My chest pains were definitely made worse by certain medications. Up until now, I wasn't allergic to anything. The penicillin debate had been over as soon as I was diagnosed with AML. As well as having itraconazole, I also required another anti-fungal medication called ambisome. This was an IV medication, yellow in colour, which went through my Hickman line. The first time I had it, my face went red, and I was struggling for breath, clutching my chest. It was an allergic reaction. Dad went to get the nurse, who pressed the red button to notify the doctor. Apparently, it was very common to be allergic to ambisome, but the medication was important, so I had to have it regardless of whether I was allergic to it or not. This seemed dangerous to me, but I went along with it and trusted the doctors.

As soon as I had my reaction, the nurse stopped the drip that controlled the medication going through my line. She then injected a medication called piriton through my line, which helps prevent allergic reactions, then continued the medication but put it through at a slower rate. I felt a little bit better after that, but the reaction didn't go fully until the medication was done with. I required ambisome two or three times a week, and sometimes I suffered no reaction. Other times, I got it mildly, but I rarely got it as bad as my first time. I often get myself into awkward conversations about my allergies. Whenever I'm asked about what I'm allergic to, I get funny looks when I say 'ambisome', as if people – expecting me to say something like nuts – have actually heard of it. Perhaps I should say nothing when asked about my allergies.

I must have been in H bay for about a week. One morning, I had woken up to feel my bed moving. The nurses thought they would give me a change of scenery, and I was happy with the move. They moved me into D, which was a cubicle. The cubicle was vacant, so they thought they'd give it to me. I had my own room, and it had an ensuite! In the bathroom, there was also a bath, so I didn't have to travel all the way to the showers every morning. D was also much more spacious. These cubicles were designed for barrier nursing, for patients who needed to be kept separate from other patients to avoid infection. But because there were no such people on the ward at the time, I was chosen for the move. This was the closest to anything luxury on the ward.

One thing the doctors were concerned about was that I was still neutropenic. It had been at least three weeks since my last dose of chemo, maybe even more, and my blood count was increasing but only very slowly. My bone marrow was being very stubborn. It was expected to have significantly risen by then. I wasn't allowed to proceed to Round 2 until my neutrophils reached 0.5, and because the doctors were anxious to start, they made me have a bone marrow aspiration and lumbar puncture to see what exactly was going on in the bone marrow. I was due one soon anyway; I required one after every cycle of chemo to check that the treatment was working.

Unlike my first bone marrow aspiration, which was done in theatre, this was done in the treatment room of the Paediatric Day Unit. Therefore, I was wheeled in my bed from D cubicle and had my aspiration there. Under the haematologist's microscope, there was no sign of leukaemia, which was good news, but the bone marrow looked a bit empty as I was still neutropenic. The good news was that it still showed that the chemotherapy was working in terms of doing what it was supposed to, though my bone marrow wasn't doing what it was supposed to, showing only a little sign of recovery.

The lumbar puncture made me really unwell. Again, as a precaution, they injected chemo into my spine, just in case the leukaemia had spread to my spinal cord, which thankfully looked unlikely. One of the side effects from a lumbar puncture are headaches, and I can tell you that I had never experienced worse headaches – until four months later when I had one equally as painful. When the nurse asked me on a scale of one to ten, with one being the least, and ten being the most, how much pain I was in, my answer was always eleven. These headaches were a really sharp, shooting pain, like a bullet firing back and forth through my head. I spent hours burying my head in pillows, doing everything to make the pain stop. The pain was so severe that paracetamol wouldn't do, and I needed oramorph, a type of morphine, to dull the pain. Not even this worked! Oramorph also made me feel sick and very sleepy.

Eating was difficult because I felt so sick, and I even had a breakdown about it because I feared I was wasting away. That was Mum's fear too, and she was getting frustrated by my refusal to eat. Dad attempted to force the dieticians' supplement drinks down me, which was a huge mistake because I threw up everywhere straight after, which not only meant I didn't get my nutrients from the supplements, but

I also lost anything I had been able to keep down, which was not a lot anyway. I hated being forced to eat and drink because not only did it make me look like an old person in a care home incapable of thinking on their own, but also because if I could have eaten, I would have! I'm not the type of person to refuse food, and me turning it down was clearly a sign that I wasn't well. There was a reason I was turning food away: I'd throw it right back up, and I didn't like throwing up!

The chef tried to get me to eat. I had to start lightly and very slowly. I didn't eat anything special; just toast but cut in the shape of dinosaurs. Thanks to his newly discovered dinosaur-shaped cookie cutters, I was able to take my mind off the food side of things and just eat it because it was in a unique shape. I don't know how much of that made sense but, as childish as it sounds, being adventurous with the presentation of food, even if it is very simple, makes you want to eat it. That, of course, does not cure nausea, and I definitely struggled with toast, despite its simplicity. But it is a helping factor in boosting appetite. Despite feeling sick quite often, my appetite overall started to improve only slightly, and during my time in D, I never ate a proper meal.

Nausea and vomiting were becoming increasingly common, and my weight had plummeted to 51kg, which was well below my cut-off point. I remember one time feeling so sick that I had accidentally thrown up all over Dad's shoes because I couldn't find a sick bowl in time.

This led to a battle with the dieticians. Knowing how much I was determined to keep the tube out of me, my nurse asked for a second opinion from another dietician. This was because while I was losing weight and not managing any meals, I was still grazing on sweets all day, meaning I was still keeping an appetite afloat. Another dietician said that as long as I was still eating and grazing throughout the day, and I didn't lose any more weight, I wouldn't have to worry about the tube. I was thankful to be given a second chance; anything but the tube! This didn't last long though, as my weight further decreased to a worrying 49kg, and within that week, I had three NG tubes put down. I had gone from that overweight kid to the kid who had bones almost sticking out – I managed to keep my belly though.

I had three NG tubes put down because I was so sick that they didn't last long. The first NG tube I threw up after one day. The second one lasted a few hours. Because I was in so much pain from the headaches, I needed oramorph, and, as this went down my tube, it consequently made me feel sick, and I threw up everywhere. The third and final one (for the time being) actually lasted for quite a long time, as I was slowly getting better throughout the week. For someone who hated NG tubes being put down, my nurse, Amy, told me that it was the easiest NG tube she had ever put down in her nursing career so far. All I did was keep drinking like Tracey had told me the very first time.

I hadn't forgotten about school back in Stowmarket and they hadn't forgotten about me either. My head of year, Mr Carter, and assistant head of year, Miss Smith, came to visit me in hospital and brought with them Liam and Joel, who I'd sat next to in ICT and was friends with for a while in primary school. My form class, 9HL, had written me a couple of get well soon cards, and Mr Carter told me that Arran, Lorna, and Caitlin, in my class, would write me a newsletter every week so I knew what was going on back at Stowmarket High School. The newsletter allowed me to hear all the latest gossip, from relationship news to what was going on in my classes, to the smell of the toilets. This newsletter was emailed to my hospital school teacher, Denise, who then printed it off and gave it to me each week. The staff at Stowmarket High also got me an Argos and WH Smith voucher, which I was very grateful for. Mr Carter and Miss Smith had a meeting with Denise and Richard, the maths specialist, and also dropped a few schoolbooks over to make sure I wasn't missing anything. While they had their meeting, Liam, Joel, and I played a game of Monopoly, which Liam had bought for me as a gift. Unfortunately, one of my lumbar puncture headaches struck and I passed out halfway through the game, so the visit was cut short.

Around this time, I met Sue and Angela, the clinical psychologists. Because being in hospital is no doubt a stressful time, counselling was offered to me and my parents. This was usually one of the first services families received following their child's diagnosis, so Sue and Angela were confused as to why they had missed us and managed to meet us so late into my journey. It was Sue's job to look after my parents and Angela's job to look after me. Angela said that sometimes it was good to talk about my feelings, but I didn't have to talk if I didn't want to and could do activities, such as colouring, to take my mind off things for a bit instead. Being in hospital brings families closer together, but sometimes you can get a bit fed up with having your family around all the time, so counselling also offered the chance to see someone different and talk to different people, as well as give my parents a break and a chance to express their feelings and concerns. Mum really benefitted from counselling. Dad, on the other hand, preferred to bottle his emotions and didn't really show any enthusiasm for attending sessions. In fact, it was always time for him to put petrol in the car whenever Sue and Angela arrived.

As the week went by, I gradually started to feel better and the headaches began to disappear. In fact, I was so well that one Saturday, in a check-up with the doctor on the ward rounds, he said I could go into town for the day with my family. It was good to get out of the hospital, especially as I hadn't seen much of Cambridge city centre, the city I had been living in for the past month. This was also my first breath of fresh air in a couple of weeks. We all went to eat at the shopping centre, since I was really craving food, and then it all went wrong. I felt sick. Because I was feeling much better than usual, this brought on the discussion of whether I was really feeling sick or if, just because I had no sick bowl with me and had an NG tube in, my fears were bringing on the sickness. Me worrying about being sick actually made me feel sick, and I had to rush back to the ward. This was one major issue I suffered when recovering from chemotherapy. The constant nausea severely affected the chances I had when it came to continuing daily life, and anxiety of not having a sick bowl grew.

But even though I was feeling better, the big problem remained. I was still neutropenic, and the doctors could not proceed with Round 2 of chemotherapy, though they were acting as if they were in a hurry to get started. The doctors said that I may need another bone marrow aspiration to see what was going on, as either my bone marrow was just being stubborn or something was wrong. I'm more scared writing this now than I was at the time – to me, my bone marrow was going to recover when it wanted to and we were just going to have to wait. I didn't realise the implications of what would happen if it never went back to normal, and I can only imagine what might have happened. Despite my neutropenia, it was clear that I was feeling well enough to be off the ward again, and the doctors gave the go-ahead to discharge me to Kingston House for the second time.

While doctors were discharging me, and Mum and Dad were moving belongings out of my hospital cubicle, the play specialist asked if I wanted to join in making cupcakes with Jacob. Jacob was a patient on the ward, quite a few years younger than me, suffering with Acute Lymphoblastic Leukaemia (ALL). I would get to know Jacob and his family very well later on, but this was the first time I had met him. All I knew about him was that his dad used to work with my dad seven years earlier, but little did I know that only a few months in the future, our families were to become very close; housemates, to be exact.

Making the cupcakes was fun because that is the sort of thing you just wouldn't expect to do on a hospital ward. The methods of making the cupcakes were very hospitalised. Because we had to avoid fresh eggs due to it being on a hospital ward, we were required to use eggs out of cartons. Therefore, these cupcakes had a different texture to them. After making the cupcakes, we gave them to the chef to bake, and then I took them with me, and off I went to Kingston House.

***

I wasn't really sure if I wanted to go back to Kingston House because I didn't know what the point of it was. Was I going to last three days like last time? Fortunately, I was to last much longer than my previous stay.

The Kingston House routine the second time was the same as the first time. Throughout all my stays, I followed the same routine of waking up, getting ready, going to school, PDU, Tesco, sitting and watching TV, completing any homework, bed, and repeat. That being said, there were a few memorable and enjoyable times during my second stay at Kingston House.

Firstly, I was to spend a lot more time with my family. Although they had visited me in hospital before, this was the first of the soon-to-be weekly visits from Auntie Karen and Uncle John, whether I was at Kingston or on the ward. They always helped to buy Mum and I whatever was on our shopping list, especially when Dad wasn't there. Although, often, the food I craved one day would make me feel sick the next. But like I said, some things I never went off. My weekly shopping list always consisted of Baby Bels, popcorn, and J20s. When I was on the ward, I had consumed so much popcorn, the nurses were wondering why the entire ward had a cinema smell to it.

Also, when Kristy was visiting, my family and I decided to have a BBQ, But because it was Kingston House, no BBQs were allowed on site, so it was all done in the oven. It was still great to spend some much-needed quality time outdoors with the family. We had all lived as one household prior to March 23rd, 2016, and it was great to feel like we were back together again.

Denise recommended that I got a laptop for my schoolwork, and she said that Sue and Angela could help us out with getting the funding for one. This was when the Callum Pite's Smile Charity was kind enough to give me a £500 PC World voucher to choose my laptop – the same laptop I am writing this on now. I chose a red one because I liked the look of it, but it cost significantly less than £500. Instead of trying to find something else for myself, or trying to find a more expensive laptop, I decided to purchase a second laptop for Kristy. I guess I felt sorry for her, because with me being in hospital, my parents prioritised me, meaning, in the middle of her GCSEs – the most crucial year of her life so far – she was left to live on frozen chicken burgers and only really had the company of the cats. Dad did check on her from time to time, and when Mum was working, she lived at home, but for quite a lot of the time, Kristy was by herself. Family and friends did do all they could to help and invite her for dinner, and sometimes she went, but other times she turned away help. I could definitely tell that Kristy was beginning to isolate herself, and this was the beginning of her declining mental health. If I could provide some sort of gift to show how sorry I was, then I was going to do it.

Other than that, there is nothing really to add about this time at Kingston House. It was all routine. However, the end of my second stay did not result in me having to return to the ward due to a temperature. Rather, I received some very good news instead.

***

Thursday 12th May 2016. I was in PDU for a check-up as normal and not expecting anything major to have happened since my last check-up, which was the day before. However, to my and Mum's surprise, the registrar said that my neutrophils had finally recovered and had reached 0.5! I was no longer severely neutropenic, and I was ready for Round 2 of chemotherapy. This was unexpected, considering how stubborn my bone marrow had been over the past couple of weeks in growing back the healthy cells. The doctor informed me that before treatment began once again, I would have to have another bone marrow aspiration to check the effect of the chemo on the leukaemia from the first cycle. This was scheduled for 8:00am the next day. All this was a bit of a shock but fine because we had expected it to come at some point. But the doctor then told me even greater news. She said that since I wasn't severely neutropenic, I could even go home for the night, as long as I was back on PDU for 8:00am the next day. Because this procedure involved general anaesthetic, I had to be nil by mouth by 8:00pm that night.

I didn't really give Mum the choice; I said we were going home. There was the debate of whether it was really worth it, especially as this check-up in PDU was mid-afternoon and by the time we were packed and out of Kingston House, it would be the evening. She questioned if it was worth going home only to sleep, then return to hospital the next morning for my procedure and then to start Round 2 straight afterwards. Why go home only to sleep when I could go to Kingston, which was on the hospital site and was only a five- or ten-minute walk away? All of this didn't matter. No matter how far away it was, I wasn't going to turn down any chance to go home. I deserved to be home – I'd never wanted to stay in hospital in the first place. The last time I was home was March 23rd, which meant I had gone fifty days straight without sleeping in my own bed. I also missed my cats, Charlie, Perry, and Dexter, and I wanted to get home to see them. I had to quickly get my dressing and bungs changed by the nurse before we left PDU, and then after that we were free.

Because it was just Mum looking after me that day, it was difficult to just pack and go home. Although she could drive, we had accumulated so much junk that it would take at least two cars to get home in one journey, which was about an hour away. Dad, who was at work, came to meet us halfway through packing. It was then home time, and before we knew it, we were out of Cambridge and on the A14 back to Stowmarket.

I missed my home. As soon as I walked in, I found Kristy was in my chair in the living room, so I quickly kicked her out and regained it. My taste buds had also recovered, so I went to the cupboard to find my Easter eggs, which I had expected to have lots of because I hadn't been home to eat them. There were none. Kristy assumed that I had gone off chocolate for good and had eaten mine. It made me angry, but I was home for positive reasons and soon got over it.

My outlook had now changed. I didn't care that all my Easter eggs had been eaten; I just wanted to be home. And I was glad to be home! Round 1 of chemo was completed! That night, my family got a takeaway to celebrate me being home, then Fin came over for a little while just to see me. Although returning to hospital the next day was in the back of my mind, for the first time in a while, I felt a proper sense of normality. By 8:00pm, I was declared nil by mouth, and I went to sleep, ready to get up early the following day for my procedure.

***

On Friday 13th May, my family and I arrived in PDU, ready for my bone marrow aspiration. With it being Friday 13th, we were all a bit fearful of bad luck. I had no breakfast because I was nil by mouth, so I was starving and my throat was sore and dry. As permitted, I did have a drink of water at 6:00am in the morning.

Despite it not making me feel great, being nil by mouth meant I was not allowed to take my medicines. If you're wondering why that's a positive, it's because I didn't have to take itraconazole! I was more than happy to miss that morning's dose. I would have preferred being nil by mouth every morning than take a dose of that nasty stuff!

At first, it was like a normal day in PDU. We signed in as usual at the front desk and then had to wait in the waiting room for what felt like hours before I was called up by the healthcare assistant to have my obs taken. I then had a check-up with the consultant, who had to check me over to make sure I was well enough for the procedure. Then, we just had to wait. We didn't know when my procedure would be because they were not scheduled by time of arrival. The little kids went first, probably to stop them screaming in the waiting room all day.

To pass the time, the play assistant played Uno with me and my family, and although I was going to have to give that day's lesson a miss, Denise came to provide me with some dingbats and wordsearches to pass the time.

The surgeon spoke to me and my parents about the procedure, which was the same as all the other bone marrow aspirations I had – a sample of my bone marrow would be extracted from an area in my lower back and then looked at under a microscope. This time, lumbar punctures and chemo injections were no longer necessary as there was enough evidence to suggest that my leukaemia hadn't spread. From this point onward, lumbar punctures were no longer necessary as the doctors were happy that I was doing well. This procedure was just to check that my bone marrow was as close to normal functioning as possible.

We must have been sitting in the waiting room for six hours because my turn for surgery wasn't until 2:00pm. I was then put on a hospital bed, while anaesthetic was inserted through my Hickman line. Making Mum cry, I gave a massive yawn, and from there, I was out cold and cannot remember a thing. Me yawning before being put to sleep for surgery always made Mum cry, apparently due to the innocent look on my face.

I woke up in a pool of drool in the six-bedded bay area of PDU, which was also used as the recovery area. I say that I woke up, but really, I was woken up by Dad, who kept poking me with something. The procedure went well, although my lower back would be sore for a while as there was a small hole in my back, which was covered with a dressing. The haematologist could not find any signs of leukaemia under her microscope, but there were more powerful microscopes out there, so I wasn't off the hook just yet. More tests still needed to be done.

We were then told some good or bad news, depending on how you look at it. It was definitely good news for me and my family, but at the same time, it did mean there'd be a delay in receiving my next round of treatment. There were no beds on Ward C2, so I was told I was allowed to go home for the weekend, as long as I was back Monday morning for the second cycle of treatment to commence.

I wasn't allowed home just yet, however. I was required to go to Ward K3 in the hospital to have a heart echo scan done. This is because chemotherapy has long-term effects, such as damage to the heart, so it was important to monitor its health. I couldn't even go to that straight away, though, because the rules were that, before I could leave PDU, I needed to eat something and go to the toilet. I had some of Mick's dinosaur-shaped toast and went to the toilet, and then I was free to go for my scan. The scan involved sticking stickers on my chest and then using the same jelly and stick as an ultrasound; a similar ultrasound procedure was used on my heart. By the looks of the scan, my heart was healthy and the chemo hadn't had much, if any, effect on it so far.

I was then free to go home, and this time, I had an entire weekend at home, rather than just one night. The Friday night consisted of nothing special; we just had dinner and watched TV. The Saturday was more eventful, as Fin and Zoe came round to visit. They had a wrestling match, which I really wanted to join in on but was unable to due to the risk of ripping out my Hickman line. I had to be the referee instead. That evening, Fin joined my family and neighbours, who went out for a drink and some dinner. I tried to enjoy my dinner, but it was very difficult to; my NG tube was still in from a couple of weeks earlier. Going out in public with an almost bald head and a tube hanging from my nose was difficult, but after a while, I accepted that people were going to stare, and with the company I had, I continued as if I was a normal healthy person. Although I was feeling well and almost my normal self, there was no point removing the NG tube because there was no guarantee I would stay feeling well for long and it could be needed at any moment. Also, while I was in A bay, Dad had been trained on how to use an NG tube machine, and I was having small feeds at home while I slept at night, just to boost my nutrients and attempt to increase my weight ready for my next round of treatment. Besides my NG tube, which was causing me discomfort that evening, I still had a great night. The Sunday – Mum and Dad's seventeenth anniversary – was a little different. Just to get out for a while, we went to a car boot sale in the morning, and the day was followed by lots of different visitors all at different times. It was an amazing weekend home, but it went by fast. Too fast. Hospital life was going to start all over again the next day.

Chapter 6

The Dreaded G Bay

Round 2 and its severe effects from May 16th to June 20th, 2016

Monday 16th May was an early start because I was due back on PDU at 8:00am. I tried to be strong and mostly showed strength on the outside, but deep down I was nervous and fearing the coming side effects of the treatment I was about to endure. Dad was going to take me to hospital, while Mum went to work. There were some tears that morning, all from Mum, who was so happy to have me home for the weekend and was upset to have me return to hospital so quickly. Despite it going by fast, it felt like I had been home forever, but really it had only been three days. That shows just how much I missed being home and treasured the time I had there. I no longer took being home for granted.

Like many visits to PDU, it was just a normal day. As soon as I arrived, I checked in at the desk, had my obs taken, and had to see the doctor, who would give the go-ahead for the second cycle of treatment to start. The doctor always had to give the greenlight for the next round of chemotherapy to commence to make sure I was in as best possible state to fight it. Unlike Round 1, which was ten days of mitoxantrone and cytarabine, Round 2 was the same drug combination but eight days in total. The plan was for the first cycle to do most of the work and kill the bulk of the cells, and then the future cycles would be to further kill any remaining cells and prevent relapse. That meant the plan was to have less than the previous for each cycle, provided everything went well.

For Round 2, the first four days would consist of a dose of mitoxantrone once a day, and all eight days would involve one dose of cytarabine in the morning and one at night. The measurements were the same as Round 1, with mitoxantrone being a 100ml bag on a drip and the cytarabine being a small syringe. The smallest of doses could have a very powerful effect.

I spent hours in the PDU waiting room, and although I cannot remember an exact time, it was close to eight hours, with only a small number of games on my iPad to occupy myself with. I did have Dad with me, but there are only so many conversations you can have and so many games you can play. It got boring after a while. Why it took so long was for a couple of reasons. The first was that it took a while to get the chemo ready because it had to be prepared and checked. Being on the ward, you don't realise this because you have other things occupying your time. For example, there are distractions, such as the TV and board games. But in the day unit, there's nothing you can do, so you just wait hours for it. Giving chemo always required two nurses and only nurses trained and qualified to do it.

The second reason for why we were there so long was because the ward was still full. Another patient was being discharged, and this took longer than the time it took to get the chemo ready. I was waiting on PDU for a family to move out so I could go in their bedspace. And even once the patient had finally moved out, the space still needed to be cleaned and the bedding needed to be changed, which would take even longer.

At around 5:00pm, my nurse in PDU hooked the chemo up on the drip, and it was attached to my Hickman line. My first dose of Round 2 of chemo started with the mitoxantrone. Shortly after being attached to the drip, the nurse on PDU told me that the ward was ready, and she walked with me to the location of where I would be staying for at least the next week. G bay. My bed space was G1, where I had spent my first night in hospital and where I had been diagnosed on the morning of Thursday 24th March 2016.

I suppose I should just be grateful that I was 'lucky' to get a bedspace, but 'the dreaded G bay', as I called it, was an exception to that rule. It wasn't just me who hated it. Everyone hated G bay. Every family we spoke to had shared the same view as me. G bay was a four-bedded bay and by far the most crowded bay on the ward. The bedspaces were smaller than those on the other bays, and because there were so many people, no one could hear their own TV. The solution was to turn up the volume on your TV, but when everyone did this, it made things much worse. As a result, staying in G bay meant that your days would be spent listening to screaming children, snoring, and full-blast, super loud TVs, in very confined spaces with each other's property invading your own spaces. I wasn't happy about being put in G, especially since I was used to the 'luxury' of the spacious A, mostly being on my own in H, and eventually having my own ensuite room when I got to D. I hadn't stayed on G long enough to really know how it felt, but I knew from parent reviews that it was a place you never wanted to end up in. G bay was definitely my stereotype for a hospital ward.

My time in G bay was spent in much better health than previous stays in hospital, probably because I was on chemo and not yet suffering the aftermath, and my bone marrow didn't consist of 92% leukaemia cells this time either.

When I arrived on G Bay, my life as an outpatient transformed to the life of an inpatient. My nurse for the day handed me some swabs. I had to swab my armpit, nostril, and groin, which I'm guessing was to check for infections. This was the first time I'd had to do that, and I would have to do so a number of times in the future, so it surprised me that I hadn't done it until that point. Fast forward to 2021, I finally found out from my friend, Clare, who is a student nurse, as to why these swabs were necessary. Apparently, the swabs are to check for MRSA. I never received the results, so I'm guessing they came back alright.

My first night of Round 2 on Ward C2 was spent building some Lego sets, which the play specialist let me borrow. I remember building a Lego zombie and, in my time on G1, it was displayed on the bedside cabinet. Dad bought me a takeaway from Burger King on the hospital concourse, and I sat on my bed eating mozzarella sticks and watching TV for the rest of the night.

During Round 1, I was terrified by the immediate effects of the mitoxantrone, which I thought would turn me blue. My feelings towards it changed during Round 2. During Round 1, I was only required to urinate in the cardboard pee bottles temporarily, and the nurses told me that after a while I didn't have to. I chose to continue using the bottles because I didn't want to see blue urine in the toilet. It creeped me out. I guess, instead of the pee bottles, I could have just gone to the toilet as usual but just not look, but when you know your pee will be a scary blue colour, of course you're going to look. During Round 2, though, I abandoned the pee bottles. As strange as it sounds, I was actually fascinated by how the body tried to get rid of the chemo. The chemo didn't make my pee blue straight away; it took a few hours at least, or maybe even a whole day, and I remember going to the loo one time and shouting, "My pee is blue!" with excitement and fascination. After urinating three or four times after the dose of chemo, the colour returned to normal, with the blueness becoming lighter after each urination. It was never a dark blue colour like the chemo was, but rather a light blue or more of a green colour. Still, it was a weird and worrying colour for urine.

Lack of sleep is another problem I experienced on G Bay. It was no one's fault. We were all sick and all had individual problems, and I was completely understanding. However, me being my grumpy self, I did display slight frustration, but mainly to myself or my parents. A girl opposite me had a brain tumour, and one minute she was fine, but the next she would just start screaming, and it was unpredictable when it was going to happen. The screams were loud, and by loud, I mean super loud. I've never heard a louder scream, and that is not exaggerating. Words cannot describe how loud and irritating the screams were! They gave me headaches! This wasn't just every once in a while, this was constant. Sometimes it was during the night, which kept me and other patients up. These could last anywhere from one minute to hours, with short breaks in between. I'd heard these same screams when I was in my own room on the ward, and it kept me up some nights. Now, I was directly opposite them! I felt sorry for her mum, who clearly looked tired, having had to calm the girl down every time she screamed. When I came across patients like that, I knew I was ill, but I saw myself as lucky. Yeah, I was sick – really sick – but at least my illness hadn't taken over my everyday functioning.

This, combined with lack of space, did not help. G1 was clearly one of the bigger spaces on G bay, although it was still really small, and I'm guessing G2 was even smaller. The people next to me had so much stuff crammed into their tiny bedspace that their table was pushed against the G1/G2 curtain border, which ended up on our side of the bedspace. In other words, we had other people's stuff on our side, covered by the curtain.

Therefore, I lacked space on the right of me, which made my parents putting the bed down at night very difficult, and very loud screams coming from my opposite. To my frustration, my parents were too polite to say anything. At least I had an inside window on my left, but my only view of that was the toilets and the treatment room.

I hated G bay, and I spent as little time as possible on it. To be honest, I was lucky to be in G while I was feeling okay because I didn't have to rely on my bed to be my most comfortable place. I don't recall having a single school lesson on G bay, since I preferred to go to the teenage room. School was usually at bedside if I was feeling unwell, but however I felt, I was going to go to a place where I could concentrate. The play specialist also introduced me to the Ward C2 play area, which previously wasn't available because it was being refurbished. The Ward C2 play area was an outside space, man-made with artificial grass, with the hospital buildings surrounding it. I was clearly too old for it, evident by the fact that I got stuck on the slide. But, willing to do anything to get out of G, I spent a lot of time there and actually really enjoyed it. The play equipment was for the younger children, but there were still things to do for people my age and even my parents' age, such as table football. I had to avoid running because of my Hickman line, but I even went for a light jog when playing football with Dad. It was a space that I really enjoyed and appreciated, and I'd make regular trips to the play area from then on. I usually love a rainy day, but rainy days were the worst when on G bay because the play area would be closed.

I also have one other positive memory of my time on G bay. I received my 'Supershoes'! Young Lives vs Cancer, previously known as CLIC Sargent, is a charity that supports young people with cancer, and is linked to a charity who make

Supershoes for children with cancer. I was required to fill in a form about myself and my favourite things, such as my favourite games, animals, and TV shows. Someone would then receive that form, and I would end up with a pair of some very uniquely painted, personalised shoes. My Supershoes contained WWE 2k16, which was my favourite game at the time, Super Mario, because I am the best at Mario Kart and always come first, SpongeBob SquarePants, because it has always been my favourite TV show. and alligators, because I think they're cool. My Supershoes looked great! Even my friends, who didn't share the same interests as me, thought that my Supershoes were the coolest thing they had seen. I rarely wore my Supershoes because I didn't want to get them dirty, and if I did, they couldn't go in the washing machine, even though wiping them down was fine. I only wore my Supershoes once because I prefer to keep them on display, and to this day, they sit on a shelf in my room, looking as good as new.

Of course, I was going to have good and bad days and good and bad moments. These bad moments always came at the worst timing. Towards the end of my stay on G, my NG tube, which had been in since I was in D (the third attempt), was still in. Despite feeling quite well, not great but not bad, some days I did experience the slight feeling of nausea. Mum asked if everything was okay for her to go for a shower, to which I replied yes. Of course, when I had no one else around me, I started to feel sick and eventually I couldn't contain it and I threw up, only just managing to reach my sick bowl. The NG tube came out, and it was hanging out of my mouth. The buzzer to call for a nurse was down the back of my bed, and although I could have attempted to reach it, I didn't want to risk it since I was hooked to the drip stand for another medication and had a thrown-up NG tube hanging out of my mouth. It must have been at least a few minutes I was sitting with a tube out my mouth until another parent noticed me (thankfully the curtain was partially open) and notified the nurse. The nurse quickly arrived to pull it out of my nose. I learned my lesson. From this moment forward, I always made sure the buzzer for a nurse was within my reach before being left alone.

There was one advantage of being on G bay while on chemo and not recovering from chemo. As mentioned before, it meant I could spend as much time away from the bedspace as I possibly could. It gave me a reason to actually want to get out and about; anywhere but G bay! An oncology consultant was doing the ward rounds on Sunday 22nd May, which was the seventh day of chemo out of the eight. She said that she was going to send me home. I was excited, but this confused Dad and I because I was still on chemotherapy. We then found out that the doctor had read her notes wrong. The disappointment on my face was visible. Not going back on her word, she reluctantly still allowed me to go home, although on the nurse's orders that I needed to be back on the ward at "8:00pm sharp" for my nightly dose of cytarabine. The doctor said that it was important to make the most of my time at home while I wasn't neutropenic, because from my blood tests, they could see that my blood count was declining rapidly in response to the chemo. At least as I had to come back, I didn't have to go through the process of packing my bags, so I just took the things I needed, and off I went back home.

Plans changed for Mum and Kristy back at home, who were planning a quiet day. Because I was coming home, it made sense to have some visitors over. So that day, we invited Grandma, Auntie Karen, and Uncle John over for dinner. Dad and I left everyone just before 7:00pm to make the one-hour journey to Cambridge for 8:00pm sharp.

The next day, the chemo was still killing my blood cells, but my neutrophils were still – but only just – above 0.5, so I was allowed to go home again. Before going home, Dad and I stopped off at his work, where I met many of his co-workers. I was there to thank them for the two hampers they had made for me during my stays in hospital, which included different sweets and a number of games. I was very grateful for what they did because in hospital I'd live off sweets and needed games to keep myself busy, so it was perfect. When speaking to their boss, she wasn't so sure that Dad's co-workers should have got me all those sweets, and I would have thought the same had I not been ill. But in reality, it was perfect for a cancer patient and it undoubtedly satisfied the dieticians.

I also had a conversation with another man. I had no idea who he was, but he was working in the office. He gave me a new outlook on how to view my treatment. He said that it would make me feel bad, but I'd have to go through that to get better. I had never seen it like that before. I genuinely feared the chemo because I thought it would be more likely to kill me than the leukaemia itself. But now I realised it only made sense for things to be worse before they got better, and it would be completely worth it in the end. After all, why would they give me all that chemo if they knew it was going to kill me?

After leaving Dad's work, I went to go to Mum's work to see her and my cousin, Jade. Mum was keen to buy me a new wardrobe because I'd had the same wardrobe for thirteen years and my clothes were outgrowing it. So, after some very boring wardrobe shopping, I finally made it home, but only for a couple of hours before it was time to return to Ward C2. In that time, we ordered a Dominos while Mum and I caught up with WWE Monday Night Raw, which we were months behind on due to being unable to watch it in the hospital.

The morning after, on Tuesday 24th May, another day at home was uncertain. I was very close to being neutropenic the previous day, so I was likely to be now. My nurse that day, Stewart, said that it was likely to be Kingston House, so we should start packing, but there was still every bit of hope that I was allowed home for just one more day. It really would have been just one more day; I was pushing it now. I had my blood test in the morning, like I did every day, and we waited all day for the results. By 3:00pm, during my science lesson, which coincidentally was about blood and haemoglobin[6], Stewart told me that the laboratory had lost my blood and I needed to have another blood test. It would have been too late to go home anyway. The results soon came back, and I was neutropenic. So, it was off to Kingston for the third time. Although I really wanted to go home and was quite disappointed, I wasn't complaining; I was just grateful to finally be out of the dreaded G bay.

***

As I have mentioned before, Kingston House followed the same routine — school, PDU, Tesco, free time. That was the order every day. Despite the same routine, there were some changes during my third stay.

From now on, I would start seeing the haematology doctors, who specialise in blood, rather than the oncology doctors, who specialise in cancer as a whole. On the ward, I usually saw whichever oncology consultant was available.

---

[6] I rarely mention haemoglobin in the first part of this book, but it was crucial when it came to my blood tests and was discussed almost every day with the doctors and nurses. Haemoglobin is a protein found in red blood cells, which is responsible for carrying oxygen around the blood.

Now, my assigned consultants were Dr. A and Dr. M, who were haematology consultants and were mostly responsible for my care from this moment onwards. They rarely did the ward rounds, so I continued to see the oncology doctors on the ward, but while on PDU, haematology specialists were the doctors I saw the most. I met Dr. A first, who called me into PDU one day to discuss my last bone marrow aspiration, which had taken place on Friday 13th May, in more detail.

She showed us a flowchart with the risks of the leukaemia coming back post-treatment. The chart placed me in one of three categories, depending on how much leukaemia was found in the bone marrow. Standard risk meant there was the standard statistical chance of the leukaemia returning post-treatment. This didn't necessarily mean my risk was low, but it was the best category to fall into. If I was in standard risk, then Round 3 would stay with the mitoxantrone-cytarabine combination, and Round 4 would be ten days straight of cytarabine, used more as a relapse prevention course. Intermediate risk was in between standard risk and high risk, which meant that chances of the leukaemia returning were medium but could be turned around and put in standard risk if treatment for Round 3 was intensified. Unsurprisingly, high risk meant that the chemo had not worked effectively enough and there was a high risk of relapse, meaning that Round 4 of chemo would ultimately require a bone marrow transplant.

First was the good news; under Dr. A's microscope, she could see that no leukaemia was present. This suggested that the first cycle had a powerful and successful impact. But a sample of my bone marrow was also sent to Bristol, where they had more powerful microscopes, which looked for the tiny traces of leukaemia that were well-hidden and difficult to destroy. This is called minimal residual disease (MRD), which previously was only used on ALL patients until August 2015, until they discovered mysteriously high AML relapses.

To remain in standard risk, my bone marrow had to be equal to or less than 0.1% leukaemia, but unfortunately mine was 0.39%. On the positive side of things, my bone marrow was 0.39% in May, down from the 92% in March. Round 1 of chemo had worked significantly in that sense. Despite this, the progress wasn't the amount that the chart required, and I was moved to the intermediate risk category.

This worried me a little bit because I thought I was flying through things, so this was a real personal set-back for me. I asked Dr. A if this was normal, and she said that it was a good question but replied that everyone was different and for the time being it wasn't anything to worry about. Being in the intermediate risk didn't necessarily mean that I was going to relapse or I needed a transplant, it just meant that I needed intensified treatment and more of it. This meant that my treatment plan for Round 3 was going to have to be adjusted, but for right now, it was important to recover from Round 2 and see what effect that would have. Round 2 might have been enough to turn things around and put me in standard risk for Round 4, but for Round 3, I was going to remain in the intermediate category regardless of Round 2's effect.

With all this talk of the percentages of leukaemia still in my bone marrow, it brought on a major question that I had been thinking for a while. Just out of curiosity, I wondered: if chemo killed both healthy cells and unhealthy cells, why do the healthy cells grow back after recovering from treatment, but the unhealthy do not? I had wondered this for a while and finally took the opportunity to ask a registrar in one check-up on PDU. She said that the chemo tricked the body. If the body's cells – both healthy and unhealthy – were wiped out, the body would be forced to start over from scratch, relearning how to do it the old way. I found this very interesting.

I also have another funny story to tell while at Kingston, though I'm probably the only one who finds it funny. Mum most certainly wasn't amused. Chemo messes with you: one day, you can crave one thing and the next the thought of it makes you feel sick. Or one moment, you're hungry and you eat everything really fast, but then you instantly regret it the next as you feel like throwing up everywhere. One time, I was addicted to cereal, which is strange because, although I eat it from time to time, I've never been a big cereal eater. Me, the person recovering from chemotherapy, thought it was wise to eat three bowls of cereal as fast as I could, and before I knew it, I was throwing up back in the cereal bowl. My cereal bowl transformed into a sick bowl very quickly! But it kept coming, and my bowl wasn't big enough to support the amount of sick going in it, and it began overflowing and spilling out onto the table. This caused panic for Mum, who was having trouble finding a sick bowl. I learned my lesson; to this day, I stick to only one bowl of cereal!

That is all I really have to say about this time at Kingston House because, like my first stay, it did not last long. Unfortunately for Mum, she was the one who was going to have to bring me back again. It was always Dad who took me to Kingston but Mum who brought me back to the ward.

***

On the third night of my third stay at Kingston, I had finished playing a game on my iPad for forty-five minutes, and I broke my sister's high score. That was before I realised that I was playing on her account, so really, she'd broken her own score and she took the credit for it.

I'd had a good day, receiving a visit from Auntie Karen and Uncle John, and I'd eaten all my dinner, which was a sign that I was generally feeling well in myself. However, playing the game for forty-five minutes straight with no breaks made me go a bit funny, making me drowsy and giving me a headache. Mum checked my temperature multiple times before bed, which, to my disapproval, was the norm. The thermometer fluctuated from 38° to 34.5° to 38.8°. Alarmed, Mum began to panic and called the ward, who said they wanted to see me immediately. I was not happy at all, remembering the horrors of G bay only three days prior.

After a stressful walk, I was readmitted to Ward C2. Fortunately for me, I was in Room I, which meant I had my own room. It was a large, spacious, rectangular room, though it didn't have its own toilet, so I would still have to leave the room to go to the loo and have a bath or shower. It had a massive window, which gave a great view of the play area outside, but the windows on the ward did not open. My health was deteriorating in this period, not helped by the rainy weather, so all I could do was look out of the window, wishing I could be out there. At least I could hear my TV this time though.

It didn't take long for the night doctor to arrive. I had no idea what his name was, but he told Mum off for previously giving me two paracetamols when at my age I should have only been having one and a half. Mum hadn't given me paracetamol that day, so I'm not sure why the doctor wanted to know. The doctor soon got told off himself by the nurse when he kept requesting a blood test for me to be done, even though the nurses had already done it and sent it off to the lab! Mum and I nicknamed him Dr. Blood after that, a very scary but equally amusing doctor. I have no idea where Dr. Blood went, but after getting a telling off by the nurses, he was soon replaced by another night doctor, who I remember meeting previously on the ward rounds. I think he was still training, and he was now on the night shifts. His lack of experience made him sound so scared when hearing of all these symptoms – he seemed very anxious, and the symptoms I was displaying concerned and really worried him. He thought that there might be an infection going on.

In my life, I don't think I have ever felt worse. Round 2 of chemo really caused my body some damage, and after that, I'm surprised I'm still somehow alive. Sure, my bone marrow had once been made up of 92% leukaemia cells, but I was still able to go to the toilet on my own and was somehow able to complete a nine-mile walk. It was the first and only time in my cancer journey, and life so far, when the paediatric intensive care unit was actually considered an option. Mum was told that if my condition did not improve, I would be admitted to intensive care.

My temperature was reaching as high as 39°. I was shivering, but at the same time I was very sweaty. This was explained by the temperature making me very hot but my body finding ways to cool me down. This resulted in an argument with the nurses because, as I was so cold, I needed to sleep with a blanket, but they argued that it would make my fever worse, so I would have to continue shivering with nothing but a sheet. I literally had no platelets in my blood, and my body showed this by producing red spots all over my face and the rest of my body. These spots were made worse by the strain I put on my stomach and face due to constant vomiting. I was throwing up every half an hour at least, and even when I had nothing to throw up, I was still throwing up either bile or white frothy stuff. Sometimes I missed the sick bowl and threw up all over the floor. Diarrhoea was an issue, and I needed a commode to go to the toilet in because I was so weak that I couldn't walk to the toilet. Sometimes I missed the commode and there would be urine all over the floor. The conditions I was living in really were not very pleasant. I wasn't eating, and my weight plummeted, causing a battle with the dieticians over the tube. But the dieticians were aware that I was cautious of the fact that the tube would make me feel worse. I was so skinny that my bones were sticking out, which wasn't good considering I'd always been overweight. Things were not looking good, and it looked as if they were taking a turn for the worse. If my leukaemia was going to kill me, this was the moment.

I praise the nurses for their hard work, particularly Amie, Emily, and Farah. Because a fever could strike at any moment, the nurses had to work around the clock to ensure I received regular paracetamol. When the oral paracetamol was no longer having an effect in bringing down the fevers, they got the doctors to prescribe an IV version to have down my line instead. IV paracetamol worked great but left me frustrated when it wore off and I needed more but couldn't have more due to the longer intervals I had to wait. They also monitored me more closely, as the critical condition I was in meant that obs went from every four hours to at least every half an hour. The important thing was just to keep on top of everything; even if I wasn't displaying any signs of a high temperature, they would give me paracetamol anyway to keep it within the regular intervals of paracetamol doses. They spent a lot of time monitoring me and taking care of me when I'm sure they had other patients to look after too, and I'm grateful that they worked so hard to get me feeling better.

I should mention that an infection was never found, despite the symptoms and doctors' concerns. The likely case was an infection, but no test seemed to prove it. It was my body's reaction to the chemo, which proves that the treatment is scary stuff. The doctors even had to resort to a different test I had never come across before. A tube was shoved up my nose to suck up a sample of snot to see if there was anything in the snot that could be a sign of infection. At first, I was reluctant to allow them to do this because I was still fighting against the NG tube and did not want to suffer anything similar to it. I also didn't want to be seen willing to have anything inserted up my nose, which might have given the dieticians any ideas. But the nurse assured me that it wouldn't go as far as the NG tube, so I reluctantly agreed. The snot sample test had little success as there was no snot in my nose at the time, and after a number of attempts, the nurse gave up.

As time went on, with the support of the nurses and frequent doses of paracetamol and blood and platelet transfusions, my health gradually improved. I should mention, I absolutely loved blood transfusions, because after one I'd feel full of energy. I was eating more, but not much. My time in I was coming to an end after about a week, as there was a patient with more severe diarrhoea than me – if that was possible – who needed their own room for barrier nursing. The nurses moved me back to A. I was equally happy with this because I got, from what I could see, the biggest bedspace. From then on, I was in A2 – Max's old bedspace – the space next to A1 where I spent Round 1 of treatment.

The dieticians were still getting on to me about having an NG tube put down. I was feeling better day by day and eating more, although perhaps not as much as I should have been. The chef had managed to get hold of some turkey dinosaurs, which no one on the ward seemed to like, so every day I was eating turkey dinosaurs and potato waffles, something else he had just got his hands on. Who doesn't like turkey dinosaurs and potato waffles? That was my childhood. These seemed to have no effect on my weight though, and I was even grazing on Haribo every day. I was drinking a lot of milk during this time too, until I threw it up one day, which put me off having milk for a while afterwards. I was so happy one day to have managed two yoghurts for breakfast, and Mum was proud of me too, until they were dismissed by the registrar for being 'baby yoghurts'. It seemed as if nothing could be done – no matter how much I ate, no matter how hard I was trying, it didn't positively affect my weight. I could not go back on those supplement drinks, nor could I face the tube!

The play specialist let me borrow some paper and pens, and I had a genius idea to construct a chart for my weight. It had a scale of 'Original Weight (57kg)' at the top to 'Rock Bottom (49kg)' at the bottom. It even included my NG tube cut-off point of 54.77kg and some space under it labelled 'Last Chance'. I wouldn't necessarily get the NG tube if I reached my cut-off point, rather the dieticians just got on at me more until I either ate more or had no choice but to get the tube. Each day, I would weigh myself or the nurses would weigh me, and I would move the chart up and down (with a cut-out arrow stuck with Blu Tac) according to my weight for that day. I found the chart really helpful for myself because not only could I monitor my weight, but I could set myself targets, which motivated me to keep eating however bad I was feeling. To anyone in a similar situation, I strongly recommend the use of a weight chart. The dieticians knew very little of my chart, and it went mostly unnoticed by the nurses too, until Angela spotted it in a counselling session and showed everyone. One of the dieticians loved the idea and thought the chart was excellent, and the nurses soon joined in by moving the arrow for me after a weigh-in.

The problem remained. I was eating so much but I still wasn't gaining weight, which seemed a mystery. By this point, vomiting was rare, and if I was being sick, it was because I was being silly and eating too much. Things were going nowhere.

"What are we going to do?" asked the dietician, who seemed as clueless as me, but secretly knew the answer.

"The tube," I said, reluctantly.

The dietician's eyes lit up. This was the first time I ever said I needed it – the first and only time. The dietician praised my bravery for finally admitting defeat, and I could see the joy on her face. At least if I was feeling well, chances of throwing it up any time soon would be rare. So, I had an NG tube put down, which was uncomfortable, but by now I was used to it. With the help of the NG tube and continued eating, my weight became more stable, and I was feeling much better. The worst was over.

About a week into my stay on A2, while on a walk around the ward, I bumped into one of the oncology consultants, who told me some good news. First, I hadn't had a temperature in forty-eight hours, which was a sign I could be discharged. But he also told me that my neutrophils had reached 0.5, which was a shock to me. Luckily, I didn't have to go through the Kingston process again. The doctor said that as long as I drank two litres that day in order to flush my kidneys, they would be able to discharge me the next day and I could spend a week at home. I had never drunk so much water in my life!

As mentioned before, prescribing the medicine at Addenbrooke's pharmacy was a long process, so Dad and I were waiting a while to be discharged and get the appropriate medicines needed for the week. While we waited, the oncology doctor came to discuss Round 3 of treatment with us. Because I was now in the intermediate risk category, the type of treatment I was going to have changed. It was a move from the MA regimen of mitoxantrone and cytarabine, which was new at the time, to the older and known-to-work FLA-Ida combination of idarubicin, fludarabine, and cytarabine. This chemo was more intensive and was used for relapsed[7] or refractory[8] AML.

Despite being more intensive, FLA-Ida was much shorter than the previous two at only five days in total, and there was evidence to show that it was effective. Round 3 would consist of fludarabine and cytarabine each, once a day for five days, and on days three to five, I was to have idarubicin once a day, which was bright red in colour. The cytarabine dose was going to be bigger as well; I had been used to tiny syringes in Round 1 and 2, but in Round 3, it came in what looked like 250 ml doses.

This chemotherapy would have the same side effects as the others, but this certain medication allowed another side effect to come along. The doctor told me that the way this chemotherapy exited the body was through the eyes, which would cause eye irritation and could make them quite sore. So, I was going to be prescribed eye drops and eye ointment, but that was something to worry about a week later. This was just a heads up. When it was time, I was discharged from hospital, needing to return on Thursday 16th June for another bone marrow aspiration and Monday 20th June to start Round 3 of chemotherapy. Now I could look forward to a full week at home.

I didn't really do much during my time at home after Round 2. Most of the time was spent with my family and seeing my friends. I had a nice day out in Felixstowe with my parents, which was a good sign of normality. Kristy didn't spend much time with us, and I don't know where she was on this occasion,

---

[7] Relapse means when leukaemia has returned after a period of remission.
[8] Refractory AML is leukaemia that has remained after initial treatment hasn't worked.

and what we noticed from her was a growing sense of isolation, despite attempts to reach out and help her. It was a rainy day at the seaside, which made it even better. I felt a bit strange and awkward walking around in public with an NG tube stuck on my face, but I had done it numerous times before and I just had to pretend it wasn't there and that no one was looking. A few people did stare, but why wouldn't they? I know I'd stare at something unusual. It's not every day that you see someone walking down the street with a tube hanging from their nose.

I did feel like going into school for a bit because I did miss school. I never did go in in the end, and I'm unsure as to why. Perhaps it was a lack of confidence because I had the NG tube stuck on my face and I had little hair. When I returned, I wanted to look as healthy and strong as possible; I wanted to be the best version of me as possible before I came back.

We were also introduced to Debbie, the community nurse. Once every week when I was home and out of hospital, she would visit and change my dressing and bungs, as well as take my blood and send it for tests at West Suffolk Hospital. She was going to be around a lot more after I had finished treatment, but this was just a getting to know each other meeting, and some consent forms needed to be signed. At first, Debbie said something that terrified me. I still had my NG tube in at this time, and she told me that my tube would need to be changed weekly. Luckily, when we asked Jo, a nurse on PDU, if this was the case, we were told that Addenbrooke's' NG tubes were long-term, so I was okay and had at least three months before it needed changing. Not that it would last that long anyway.

On Thursday 16th June, I had my bone marrow aspiration in PDU, which was the same procedure as usual. It consisted of spending ages being nil by mouth and sitting in the waiting room until it was time for the procedure. These results were not only going to be looked at under Dr. A and Dr. M's microscope, but also sent to Bristol for another MRD test. My results would be back the next week and would determine whether I was back in standard risk, remaining in intermediate risk, or moving into high risk. This biopsy determined Round 4 – would I have a relapse prevention course of treatment, an intensified treatment, or a bone marrow transplant? For now, all I needed to worry about was having a good time at home while it lasted. I was taking things day by day.

Chapter 7

Rock Bottom

Round 3 and the major turning point in my journey from June 20th to July 5th, 2016

On the morning of June 20th, 2016, after a good week spent at home, it was now time to start the hour journey from Stowmarket to Cambridge to allow the third cycle of chemotherapy to commence. To describe my feelings, I would say I was very nervous. To me, I was only just still alive from the effects of Round 2. Round 3 was more intense, more toxic, and came in higher doses. What was going to happen to me? Was it going to make me feel worse than last time, if that was even possible? Was it going to kill me? That was circulating around my head over and over.

It was a normal day in PDU, as was always the case. Obs were taken before having a check-up with Dr. A. This was the usual procedure of listening to the heart and chest, giving the go-ahead to start treatment, and informing us of any updates with regards to my health. The doctor told Dad and I that she still hadn't received the MRD results from Bristol from my previous bone marrow aspiration, but she was due to receive them the following day and she would inform us of the results when I was on the ward. In terms of treatment, the possible outcomes would be to have a lighter treatment of ten days of cytarabine to prevent relapse if I was in standard risk, more intense treatment if I was still in the intermediate risk, or have to go to transplant in Bristol if I was in high risk. We all hoped I'd be in standard risk and that some good had come out of feeling so horrible just a few weeks prior.

A bone marrow transplant would not be a good thing since it was a very risky procedure, and it was possible that the highly intensive treatment it required could cause future complications. A transplant would only be necessary if we were out of viable options regarding my treatment and should be kept as a last resort. But I was sure that as I seemed to be doing so well, and as I had gone through all those side effects from the second cycle, it was clear that the chemo was working. I was confident – perhaps over-confident – that I would be at least remaining in intermediate risk, if not back in standard risk.

It was a whole day spent in PDU as the ward staff were still getting the bedspace ready. There were two families: me and Dad and another family whose daughter had also started a cycle of treatment again. Her dad told us that there were two spaces on the ward; one of us was getting a room to ourselves, the other was going to G, which he spoke of in a very negative tone, turning his nose up at it. But we didn't know who was getting what, and although no one said anything, I was hoping that they would get G and they were hoping I would get G.

Luckily, I got a room to myself, and unfortunately for them, they had to go to G bay. I found it funnier than I should have – I wouldn't wish G bay on my worst enemy, let alone a girl who had just started treatment. But having experienced it, I'm now aware that every patient on Ward C2 has to serve their time on G – I had done it twice already, and it wasn't going to be for the last time.

My treatment was hooked to the drip stand, and I was ready to go back to Ward C2, where I was now in E. E was a cubicle and a complete reverse of D as the two rooms were opposite each other. Like D, E had its own bathroom. I loved being in the cubicles because, despite hospital being the last place I wanted to be, it was as close to a quality stay in hospital as you could get. I was away from the screaming – although I could still hear it – and I didn't have to go to the bath area to have a bath. Instead, I had my own. And overall, it was just more comfortable.

Once on the ward, the nurse gave me my eyedrops and eye cream. Although I wasn't going to receive my idarubicin until three days' time, it was good to start with it now. Eye drops needed to be given every two hours during the day and the eye ointment at night-time before bed, which lasted longer so I wouldn't have to wake up every two hours in the night to have eye drops. I would have preferred to just have the ointment, but the drops were more effective, hence the reason I had them in the daytime. Dad was actually allowed to do the eyedrops for me, but my nurse that afternoon, Joe, did it for demonstration. She told me that mine was the most dramatic reaction to eyedrops she had ever seen. I hated the eyedrops and I made that fact very clear. They often involved battles with Dad over them. An alarm every two hours indicated when it was eyedrop time, and Dad had to change the positions of the bed so that my head was almost on the floor and my legs in the air, while I was held down with the eyedrops forced into my eyes. I don't like things going in my eyes, and they made my eyes temporarily blurry. The ointment was much easier because it only needed to be applied to the eyelids and the areas surrounding the eye, so I was able to do this myself before bed.

That was the first day of Round 3 of treatment finished. Everything seemed fine.

***

Tuesday 21st June 2016. Then June 21st hit, the date of the major turning point for my journey with Acute Myeloid

Leukaemia. This day will go down in history as the worst day of my life. No day will ever top this one – only one other day in my life can come close to this day as being the worst. My cancer journey was about to get a whole lot tougher.

Everything was fine until mid-afternoon. I had just finished having a lesson with Jason, the science teacher, while Amanda called Dad into her office to discuss my MRD results with Dr. A. Like I said, I was confident things would be fine. Why wouldn't they be? Surely the chemo was working, right?

Despite a complacent attitude, I'll admit, it wasn't until fifteen minutes in when I realised something was wrong. Dr. A was speaking to Dad in private; up until this point, I had been consulted with my family, except for the very start of my journey when the bad news first hit, so this seemed strange. Things were only kept from me if it was bad news. Nevertheless, I brushed my suspicions aside and remained confident that it would all be okay.

It was a long meeting that Dad had with the doctor, and I was sitting in my hospital bed on my own, waiting anxiously for at least half an hour, if not longer. I didn't really know what to do with myself. All I wanted were those MRD results, and I was sitting there waiting for them.

Through the door window, I soon spotted Dad coming through. When he returned, he opened the door to my room, hiding his emotions from under his hat. Close to crying, he was holding a couple of books about bone marrow transplants. My heart sank.

Knowing the answer, I tried to be strong, but my voice broke as I asked, "Good news?"

Saying nothing, he shook his head.

My world, which had already been crumbling, had finally shattered into pieces. I was shocked and upset. Absolutely devastated. I didn't cry straight away, and doing my best to keep strong, I took a few deep breaths and gave a massive sigh to process it until I ultimately lost it and burst into tears. Dad spoke to me about how it was a new chapter for me in my journey and we were going to live in Bristol for a while. Moving to Bristol and having a transplant was the only option we had – it was either that or most likely relapse and die.

This was a family emergency, so we called Mum, who was at work. We didn't want to tell her over the phone, but the fact that we weren't telling her worried her. She broke down on the phone, and Auntie Karen and Uncle John were available last-minute to give her a lift to Addenbrooke's.

From this point on, I went into a great depression and was close to giving up, if I was allowed. Being under eighteen, I had little freedom to make my own decisions. June 2016 was definitely the time when I was mentally at my lowest. I felt that all that hard work was for nothing and I had gone through all that from Round 2 for nothing. In my mind, this meant that the chemo wasn't working, and to an extent, that was true. It wasn't working, because even though it was destroying the cancer cells, it wasn't destroying enough of them. The doctors were expecting all of the leukaemia to be gone by now, and the fact that I still had some left in me after two cycles of treatment was an indication that treatment wasn't working. Strawberry laces seemed to be my comfort food, and I frequently had breakdowns, screaming, "Why me?" while shoving hundreds of strawberry laces down my mouth. Mum and I named this the 'strawberry lace meltdown'. I didn't find it funny at the time – I was just having a mental breakdown while simultaneously eating strawberry laces. Mum found it funny though, and looking back now, we do laugh about it every once in a while.

***

Everything was going so well, only for it to go so wrong, and the worst thing was that I had no control over it. I never wanted to be in this situation – I just wanted my life back or didn't want it at all. I didn't want to do anything – I stopped caring. I didn't want to die, but at the same time, I didn't want to fight anymore. What was the point? The treatment had already proven ineffective. This was yet another period of when I thought I was losing my battle.

Learning content in school lessons stopped, with Denise instead focusing on taking my mind off things, so school consisted of games of Scrabble and completing dingbats. I also had conversations with Angela, the counsellor, and Kathy, the CLIC Sargent social worker, who spoke to me about my feelings and reassured me that having the transplant was the right decision. Amanda spoke to Mum and I and told me that going to transplant was the best option for me. She said that had it been August 2015, I most likely would have been sent home with nothing wrong with me only to relapse later on. Treating it would be much harder if I relapsed as the leukaemia would come back stronger. It was scary to think that had I been in this situation just ten months earlier, I'd likely be in the standard risk category, and yet with this new technology, I was determined as high risk. The play specialist also spent some time with me, doing activities to take my mind off everything, such as drawing my name in bubble writing on a massive piece of paper and drawing whatever I wanted on there to create an amazing, personalised masterpiece. I even had visits from the people from the chapel and from the therapy dogs, who came to visit each patient from time to time. All of this support, which I had never needed before, was now coming my way.

Late June was a real low point for me, yet this only lasted a few days or so. It took me a few days, but I soon got over the devastating news and came to terms with having to go to transplant. If I didn't do it, then I'd most likely be in a worse position in the coming months or years. The doctors, nurses, counsellors, and social workers all convinced me that a transplant was absolutely necessary. Dr. A and Dr. M both said that if they didn't think it was the best option, they wouldn't put me through it.

***

Wednesday 22nd June 2016. After being given the Tuesday to let the information sink in, the following day, we, including Kristy, had a family meeting with Dr. A, who explained to us the second MRD result and briefly explained the bone marrow transplant process. First of all, the results of my MRD came back as 0.41% for Round 2, up from the 0.39% from Round 1. This did not necessarily mean that there was more leukaemia than last time, rather it was more or less the same and that sample just happened to have more of it. Thus, there was nothing to worry about in the sense that the leukaemia wasn't making a comeback. However, because treatment had progressed with no effect on my bone marrow, I was now in the high-risk category. She said that a bone marrow transplant (BMT) was the best thing for me as it was the most effective method of destroying those tiny traces of leukaemia that were likely to spark a future relapse.

So why, if it was the best thing for me, did I fear a bone marrow transplant? Why was it such bad news? The answer to this is that a bone marrow transplant is very risky, with terrifying side effects, and looking at the side effects, my mind was thinking, is it really worth it? It meant that I'd have to be away from home for quite a long period of time and I would have to take longer to recover before making a comeback. Recovery could take years.

Dr. A explained that the plan was to temporarily move to Bristol, which was four hours from home, where everything in my body would be wiped out by highly intensive chemotherapy. Unlike the previous rounds, which had weakened my immune system, this chemo would destroy it to the point where it would be completely unable to recover on its own. Then I would have a stem cell transplant, which was to be done through my Hickman line, completely conscious during the entire procedure, in which the new stem cells would begin creating a new immune system from scratch, rebuilding the bone marrow. I would be at very high risks of infections, so I would be required to isolate in a hospital room, very similar to the cubicle I was currently staying in, for at least six weeks. All contact with the outside world needed to be minimal.

The scarier stuff was to come with the side effects. There was real trouble if my body rejected the donor cells as there was no replacing the chemo damage, and the chemo had some nasty side effects in its own right. A risk was that my future depended on this – if it did not work, my old bone marrow would never come back either, which would eventually kill me. All of this was going to be explained later on in much more detail, but Dr. A was just outlining the procedure to us, so we were aware of the plan; that being to get me to transplant by August 2016. This meant that plans to return to school by September 2016 were out of the window and this would need to be set back to at least January 2017, but most likely even later, having a detrimental impact on my GCSEs.

Dr. A said that siblings had a one-in-four chance of being

a match, so Kristy was going to have to be tested straight away because the doctors needed to start looking for a match as soon as possible.

Also, she suggested that as the chemo was most likely to make me infertile, I should probably go to the IVF clinic at some point between now and my transplant to produce a sperm sample in case I chose to have children in the future. Dr. A said that this was the trade-off – it would most likely destroy my chances of creating life in order to give me the best chance of life myself. All of this was briefly touched upon because there was a lot to get through, and as time went on, things would become clearer and more certain, especially when we would meet the consultant in Bristol. There were a lot of breakdowns in that meeting; it was very emotional to say the least.

That same week, Kristy was tested for whether she was a match. From what I observed, it just seemed like a normal blood test. Mum and Dad were also tested, because if there was the slightest chance that my body would reject the donor cells, then the doctors could look at the closest match between them as my new cells. Both parents are a 50% match, which makes sense, but there are small differences that helps doctors find the best match. Using parents as donors was considered extremely risky at the time and was only to be used as a last resort on a procedure which, in itself, was already a last resort.

**

Like I said, I soon came to terms with having to go to transplant, and the rest of my time in E was spent trying to remain positive, despite a few breakdowns here and there. My physical health was okay. Feeling sick was an issue, and the anti-sickness wasn't having much effect on me, so the nurses gave me an IV anti-sickness medication, which had a greater effect on the nausea but made me feel sleepy. Therefore, I recall a considerable amount of time in E sleeping. I had lost my tube. If I remember correctly, I threw up during one of my breakdowns. My weight remained stable, but the dieticians were keeping a close eye on me, and any negative change on the scales would ensure their returning threats of the NG tube.

I have another funny story to tell, and I'm probably still the only one who thought it was funny. One morning I had a blood test, and the nurse taking my blood was still in training. Because she was left-handed, it made the process of taking blood from my Hickman line awkward. Once she attached the syringe to the lumens, she accidentally pulled the syringe too far, and my blood ended up all over me, all over her, and all over the bedsheets. It looked quite scary at first as it looked like someone had attempted to murder me and I was bleeding to death. I'm surprised it didn't stain anything – the blood was everywhere! I do wonder what happened to that nurse; I have heard that she doesn't work there anymore.

Ambisome was causing problems again. Following the weekend after treatment had finished, on Monday 27th June, the doctors decided that I was well enough to go to Kingston House. Before being discharged, however, I needed my dose of ambisome. Despite being put on at a slow rate and having piriton beforehand, a few minutes in, I began to go red, had difficulty breathing, and had a pain in my chest. It was another allergic reaction. Dad tried to press the buzzer to call a nurse, and a nurse came in to take a look, but when he cancelled the buzzer when she came in, he pressed the wrong button. He pressed the emergency alarm, so all of the nurses in mass numbers came running in! When they found out everything was okay, they gave a massive sigh of relief before returning back to the nurses' desk.

I didn't feel okay; I was clutching my chest and gasping for breath. The nurse stopped the ambisome and called a doctor to come have a look. The doctor couldn't find anything wrong, but then again, I couldn't really understand him. I don't know what country he was from, but his accent was very strong, and I found it very difficult to understand what he was saying. From what I gathered, the reaction was all put down to being psychological. That I did not believe, considering it had already been established that I was allergic to ambisome. But I guess the doctor's argument was credible in the sense that with everything I'd had to cope with the previous week, combined with my fear of the side effects of this chemo, because of what I'd suffered after the second cycle, Ward C2 was my safe place and I feared being away from it while at Kingston. Although there is definitely some truth to this, I didn't think this was causing the chest pains. I was sure it was the ambisome. After all, I had suffered an ambisome reaction before and the doctors hadn't put it down to being psychological then.

Perhaps it was indigestion, so the nurse gave me Gaviscon to see if it had any effect. It didn't work. I was asked if I wanted to go to Kingston, but I thought that after all that had happened, it would be safe to stay on the ward for one more night and look into being discharged the next day. I didn't want to stay for too long in case I was taking a bed that another patient needed, but at the same time, being off the ward made me feel unsafe when I knew a fever could spike at any time. Being off the ward was my biggest fear, especially after suffering the effects of Round 2.

On Tuesday 28th June, we were told to, once again, pack our bags and move out of the ward, because off to Kingston it was. Before leaving, however, the dietician asked for my help. She asked me to take part in some food tasting on Ward

C9 with another patient, Joe, and his mum, Theresa. Joe, like myself, had Acute Myeloid Leukaemia, and he was a few years younger than me. He was diagnosed with leukaemia in November 2014 but made a great recovery and even made it back on his football team, but unfortunately, as this was the days before the MRD test, he relapsed. Like myself, he was trying to get to transplant, but he was struggling to get to the health level required. From what I understood, they had managed to get his leukaemia close to the levels appropriate for transplant, and thought they'd make it to transplant, but the doctors decided he needed another chemo cycle before going. Unfortunately, the leukaemia came back before he'd had the chance to go to transplant and he had to start over again. Joe and Theresa had been our neighbours at Kingston House a couple of times before and we said hello when we passed each other, but it wasn't until I found out about my transplant that we started speaking regularly.

We went to Ward C9, the Teenage Cancer Trust unit, which was the teenage and young adults' (TYA) ward. I was thirteen at the time, and the reason why I wasn't looked after on C9 was because the minimum age was sixteen to be looked after there, although they accepted fourteen-year-olds when C2 was full. Therefore, I was still on the children's ward, and even once I turned fourteen, I would remain under the care of C2 as patients weren't taken on by C9 until they reached sixteen. I wasn't complaining though because I'd soon discover how lucky C2 was to have a chef – the only ward in the hospital to have a chef, as far as I was aware. C9 was a nice, modern ward and had a very spacious room, which resembled a living room. This room had a sofa, a TV, a jukebox, and an Xbox. While waiting for the food to arrive, which me and Joe would be the judges for, we played Call of Duty on the Xbox. Being one who spends hours on Minecraft or Mario Kart, Joe beat me quite badly at Call of Duty.

We also met Amy, who I would meet again in the future in a much different setting, who worked on C9 as the Teenage Cancer Trust support worker. She explained to us her role and gave us some information about Ward C9. Like I said, C2 was very lucky to have a chef. The food we were tasting was going to be offered to all patients on C9, and we were the judges to make sure it was adequate. Theresa and Dad also joined in. Like the other hospital wards, the food was all ready meals, such as macaroni cheese and chicken tikka masala. I didn't try the foods I knew I would hate, but the ones I did taste were not great, the best being the macaroni cheese, which tasted below average. Nonetheless, despite the disappointing but unsurprising taste of the food, it was great fun being a judge, as well as meeting new people and having a change of scenery. I don't know if my and Joe's opinions had any impact on whether these foods made the cut in the end[9]. I was strongly advising against feeding patients those 'meals'. Ward C2 was lucky to have a chef. If I was staying on Ward C9, I think I would have starved, quite honestly.

After the food tasting session, off I was to Kingston House for the fourth time. Nothing really major happened, and as you can guess, the same repetitive routine of school, PDU, Tesco, and free time followed. However, more time was spent on PDU than previously because I was feeling quite sick, to the point where I was unable to take my itraconazole. As a result, I spent hours on PDU having a new medication through my line, which took a while to go through. This was called micafungin, and this

---

[9] If I was to fast forward five years into the future, I think it's safe to say the foods did make the cut, so my opinions meant nothing. Perhaps it was just a ploy to get us to eat something and give us something different to do.

needed to be taken in addition to the ambisome. Knowing the effects that Round 2 had on me, I was terrified of what the more intensive and toxic Round 3 had in store for me, and during my time at Kingston, I was literally counting the days, predicting when a temperature would spike. If anything, this made me feel worse. Surprisingly, I lasted five days at Kingston, which was much longer than I'd expected.

***

Luckily, it wasn't just Mum who had to take me back to the ward. It was a Saturday, so both of my parents were there. Also, a fever spiked in the afternoon, not during the night like the previous two times, so the process of returning to the ward was easier. At Kingston, I was complaining of feeling hot and my parents could tell my face was looking red. This was a different symptom; previously, I had been shivering like I was an ice cube. Because we knew it was a fever and I'd have to stay on the ward, Dad decided to pack the bags out of Kingston in preparation while Mum took me back to the ward. *Here we go again*, I thought. *Once again, it is time to fight for my life.*

Once I was on the ward, we bumped into the oncology consultant and the registrar. They could tell I wasn't looking well and said I required a bed. When they asked the nurses which bedspaces were free, one of them replied that G3 was vacant. Great, I was back on the dreaded G bay! G3 was even smaller than G1 and, therefore, much worse. It was so uncomfortable. There was literally no space between the cabinet, the hospital bed, and the parent bed, so really G3 was one massive bed rather than a bedspace.

The consultant got the registrar to come examine me. By this point, my temperature had reached 38° so I was given some paracetamol to bring it down, while the registrar said there was a possibility of an infection. He came back later to tell me that they did find an infection but said it was okay because they had found it early and were looking to treat it with antibiotics.

With all my fear and worrying, the effects of Round 3 of chemo were nowhere near as bad as Round 2. Perhaps Round 2 was so bad that my body got used to it and knew what to expect. The night on G3 was very uncomfortable, and I spent more time sitting outside the bay rather than actually sleeping in my bedspace. That being said, it only took that one night to recover. Without any paracetamol for at least a few hours, my temperature reduced to 37.6° completely on its own. Under 37.5° was where it needed to be, but this was a major achievement. Before I could be discharged from the ward, I would have to go forty-eight more hours without having a fever. So, despite feeling almost well in myself, staying on the ward was necessary for at least a couple more days.

The next day, Dr. M, along with the haematology registrar, came to tell me the news about whether my sister was a match for my transplant. Unfortunately, she wasn't. Kristy not being a match was upsetting, but Dr. M assured me that this was not the end of the world as she only had a one-in-four chance anyway and they were looking at a couple of potential non-related matches in Germany. By this point, we were told that no news was good news. Finding a donor was a lengthy and complex process[10], so hearing nothing was actually a good thing because the only news they could give was that they were struggling to find a match. Because of the doctor's

[10] This is a process that I admittedly do not understand very well. However, to the best of my understanding, to find a bone marrow match, a blood test is taken, which looks at a potential donor's tissue type and compares it to the patient to check whether they are a match.

reassurance, I did not worry at all about Kristy not being a match despite my immediate sad reaction.

Shortly after hearing the news, the nurses informed me that they were moving me out of G3 and taking me back to the more comfortable and much more spacious A2, where I'd spent the last week or so recovering from the second cycle of treatment. I was very grateful – staying in that confined space all day was driving me crazy. I don't really remember much about this time in A2 because, unlike the first time I was there, this was a short stay. Fevers were settling and feeling sick was very rare. I had actually been gaining weight.

I do remember having a conversation with the chef, who by this point had found out that I required a transplant and was due to go to Bristol in August. He warned us that the hospital was right at the bottom of a massive hill and the accommodation, where my parents and later me, would stay was right at the top of the hill. Apparently, a lot of parents complained about this. I thought, *yeah right, it can't be that bad ...*

After only around three days on the ward, I was once again discharged. Little did I know that this would be my final stay on Ward C2. If everything went well, I was off to Kingston House until I was no longer neutropenic. Once I was no longer neutropenic, I was allowed to be off chemo for a month and a half, with at least a month of that being spent at home, building up my strength, and preparing for Bristol. I had survived a massive blow to me mentally, as well as Round 3 of chemotherapy. Despite my treatment being more intensive, the only side effect I suffered from was a couple of fevers.

Chapter 8

The Build Up

Preparing for my transplant and the future
from July 5th to August 14th, 2016

The routine remained the same for my fifth and final stay at Kingston House. By now, I was back on itraconazole, so there was no need to be spending more hours in PDU, in addition to the many hours I was already spending there.

To celebrate being discharged from hospital, Dad and I packed our bags and went straight to McDonald's. These would become frequent visits. To a normal person, this was unhealthy, but the dieticians loved it. They told me that, as I was going to transplant, it was very important that I gained as much weight as possible because one issue is that patients struggle to fight off the high doses of intensive chemotherapy. Therefore, the fatter I was, the higher my chances of success when going to transplant. Gaining weight is important when you're a cancer patient, but losing weight is treated like it's the end of the world.

Saturday 9th July was Mum's birthday, so we ordered a Dominos to celebrate, and on the following Sunday, 10th July, we all celebrated by going to the pub down the road from the hospital for a family meal with my parents, Kristy, Grandma, Auntie Karen, Uncle John, and Cousin Jade. It was the first time in a while that almost the entire family were together. And while I had to stick to the Kingston rules of not leaving Cambridge, I was happy to once again be mostly all together, albeit in a different setting.

One Saturday, my parents, Kristy, and I all had a family day out in Cambridge, and we visited Grantchester to see the river. Apparently, this is where a TV drama is set. Kristy and I were chased by a dragonfly, and it was the fastest that I had ever run with my Hickman line in. After that, we all went to an Italian restaurant for lunch; again, something the dietitians would love. Following our day out, we returned to Kingston House. I'll admit, sometimes we did break the one parent rule at Kingston, smuggling in air beds so that both my parents and sister could stay in one flat with me.

This was a long stay at Kingston, which lasted at least three or four weeks until the end of July. I should mention that I was coming to the end of hospital school at Addenbrooke's. Denise was retiring, so I was one of her last, if not the very last, students. Because it was my last lesson, instead of having a lesson on poetry or ratios, we decided to join the primary school children, who were doing fun activities to celebrate the last day. This consisted of building a tower out of dry spaghetti, joined together by marshmallows, and the aim was to balance a Kinder Egg on top of it. That was my last lesson of hospital school, and I gave Denise a thank you card, as well as some fizzy cola sweets, which she had told me many times were her favourite. On the last day, she finally realised that WWE Superstar, 'John Cena', was not pronounced 'John Senna', something she had been saying the entire four months I had got to know her. It's pronounced 'Seena'. Denise had spent our time working together trying to get to know my interests, and I had never told her the things she had said wrong! She gave me my final report for hospital school and said I should be really proud of my attendance. I had managed to attend fifty-four out of the possible fifty-five sessions, which was a very impressive attendance record for a cancer patient. It was a higher attendance than most, if not all, patients. The only lesson I missed was on the day of one of my bone marrow aspirations, giving me no choice but to miss it. It was sad towards the end of hospital school; I felt that Denise and I worked well and had built a good working relationship, and although I was undoubtedly going to be very behind on my schoolwork, I felt the knowledge I had acquired was very secure. I will always remember Denise's favourite phrase, and it is something I always try to do today: 'One minute of reading a day is better than no minutes!'

Around this time, I also met Indi, who was the trainee clinical psychologist. Instead of seeing Angela, I now saw Indi for counselling. I was very concerned about going to Bristol in the coming weeks, and I was given the opportunity to talk about how I was feeling. Throughout the period of staying at Kingston over the four weeks, I'd have counselling sessions every Thursday. Mentally, I needed as much support as I could get. It was in these sessions when I really started to open up about how I was feeling on the inside. Indi introduced a great technique, which I found really useful; it involved drawing a circle and dividing it into a number of sections for each emotion. For each section, under each emotion, I'd draw what made me feel that way. I recall drawing the blue chemotherapy on a drip stand under the sad face and explaining to Indi how the stuff scared me. In the happy box, I drew my family – they were holding me together. There was no way I could face this alone. It was very helpful to see my different types of emotions and what was causing them and be able to explain them to someone else.

On Friday 22nd July, me and my family were in PDU quite late and, near closing time, waiting for blood test results. Dr. M had told us that my blood count was increasing and I might be allowed to go home; we just had to wait for the blood test results. However, Dr. M then told us that the lab had lost my blood sample, so I would have to give it another day and return to the ward to have a blood test the next day. Losing blood samples seemed to be a common occurrence at the hospital, although I am unsure why. Sometimes if a sample was not sufficient, the labs would reject it; other times, the blood just went missing. The next day, blood tests showed that my neutrophils were 0.49. They needed to be 0.5 for me to be classed as no longer severely neutropenic. The doctors told me that 0.49 was close enough and anyway, most likely by the time I was home, they would be 0.5. Therefore, I was discharged from Addenbrooke's Hospital on Saturday 23rd July 2016. I was going to spend a lot of time at Addenbrookes in the future, but in terms of being an inpatient or an outpatient staying on hospital grounds, I was hopefully done, provided everything at Bristol went well or there was no relapse.

As I was discharged on the weekend, we had no one to return the keys to for Kingston House. So we were home while still occupying a flat at Kingston House. I needed to be back at Addenbrooke's the following Thursday, 28th July, for a check-up and a bone marrow aspiration to check how successful Round 3 was, so we returned the keys then.

Like all the other bone marrow aspirations done, my bone marrow looked fine under Dr. A's or Dr. M's microscope. The sample then needed to be sent to Bristol to see if I was still MRD positive. I would receive my MRD results at my Bristol workup plan, which was scheduled in a week and a half's time.

***

I was definitely going to transplant in August because we were informed that they had found a match from France. The exact date of my transplant by this time was still unclear. In these uncertain times, I needed to ensure I was healthy enough to go to transplant, as well as making sure I was prepared for the future. This highly toxic chemotherapy was going to affect me long-term, as well as short-term. My final few weeks at home before moving to Bristol was a balance between preparing for transplant and having much-needed time with family and friends. Although chances of death were small, I needed to treat this as my last days because no one knew when or if I would be coming back home. We were taking a risk.

After ten days at home, my first series of tests would be at my Bristol workup plan. This involved staying in Bristol for a few days to meet the doctors, to get a better understanding of the procedure, and to have tests done to make sure I was as fit and healthy as possible. We were also there to look at the social side of my stay in the city, which would technically be my second home for the foreseeable future, see the accommodation, and meet the people running the accommodation. The Bristol workup plan was going to make things more certain, and we were going to take a lot from it.

***

Bristol

Monday 1st August 2016. The Bristol workup plan lasted three days and two nights. There was a lot to get through and it could not be done all at once. Prior to the workup plan, I had little knowledge of where I would be staying or what I would be doing. All we were told was 'Bristol', not even knowing the name of the hospital. I soon discovered that the next part of my journey was going to be spent at the Bristol Royal Hospital for Children (BRHC).

It was over a four-hour drive from Stowmarket to Bristol. It was a massive move from East Anglia all the way to the West Country. Stopping halfway at the service station, Welcome Break Membury (M4), Mum received a call from Stephen, the BMT coordinator at the BRHC. He informed us about a possible trial that I could take part in. The chemo I was going to have in Bristol had nasty side effects, but they knew it worked. A trial chemo regimen, however, was known to have less harmful side effects but doctors were still unsure of success rates. If I took part in the trial, I would have a 50/50 chance of either having the harmful but effective chemotherapy or the less harmful but unknown effectiveness chemotherapy. I didn't have to make a decision right away, but we were informed so I had time to think about it.

Bristol, a city which I have since grown to love, did not give me a good first impression. Upon arrival, if I'm honest, my first impressions of Bristol were rough. Although it looked cool, there was a lot of graffiti and buildings appeared ruined because of it. Even the artwork of Banksy, which is graffiti itself, had been graffitied on. The hospital is near the city centre, so it was one of the first things I saw. It looked really nice and modern on the outside, except for the large number of people smoking by its entrance.

Smoking is something that annoys me because I didn't do anything to get ill and yet people are actively doing it to themselves. I thought a hospital would be the last place people smoked. Maybe I shouldn't be so judgemental, but seeing sick children, their distraught parents, and the direct effects of smoking should be a reminder of the danger of smoking. Wouldn't they want to avoid this at all costs? Cancer is not preventable, but there are things you can do to reduce your chances. If I'm honest, it's not just smoking by the hospital that bothers me – I'm admittedly agitated by the fact that over half of the members of my family smoke. They saw what I went through and yet they continue to put themselves at risk.

Two hospitals were located in the city centre and were both next to each other and attached. They are located on Upper Maudlin Street, one of the busy main roads, with the Bristol Royal Hospital for Children on the left and the Bristol Royal Infirmary on the right. This was quite different to what I was used to in Addenbrooke's, where the hospital was on the city outskirts and had a separate car park. Already, I would have to get used to urban life and the sound of traffic through my hospital room window.

Because the hospital was in the city centre, it didn't have its own car park, and we were given suggestions for a few public car parks. The nearest was still quite far away for someone like myself, especially as I had somehow hurt my leg. I don't know what I did, but I had a nasty shooting pain down my leg. I was in agony! To worsen things, the Ward C2 chef was right. For three days, we were staying at Sam's House, the accommodation where one of my parents and occasionally Kristy would be staying while I was isolated and where the whole family would stay when I was discharged. Sam's House was our new accommodation for the next couple of months at least, and it was located at the very top of St. Michael's Hill. Upper Maudlin Street, and therefore the hospital, was right at the bottom of that hill. With my injured leg, I was going to have to walk up and down that massive, steep hill. We were all going to have to get used to it though, especially my parents for a while and me a little later on. There was no turning back now. We were here and I couldn't get out of it.

Sam's House was accommodation run by CLIC Sargent, a charity now known as Young Lives vs. Cancer. It contained sixteen ensuite bedrooms for the families of sick children. Unlike Kingston House, which seemed to be hospital accommodation for a variety of different people, Sam's House appeared to only be for paediatric patients and their families at the hospital.

We met Sharon, who was in charge of Sam's House. She went over the rules of the house with us. It was the normal 'no smoking' and 'abuse to staff will not be tolerated' rules. She also gave us some information about the area, telling us the nearest supermarkets; there was a Co-op down the road, which was soon going to become part of our everyday life.

After signing the contract, Sharon gave us a tour of the house, which I must say was quite impressive. There were three floors in total. Each floor had a shared kitchen allocated for the residents staying in the flats of their particular floor. Neighbouring flats shared a kitchen space with their own cupboards and pots and pans, with their neighbouring flat. In other words, there were a number of kitchens within the kitchen, but an all-shared dining space between, for all staying on that particular floor. Surrounding the kitchen area were the rooms. Our flat was Room 5. In each room, there were two beds, a single and a double. If Kristy was staying, we were allowed to use a fold-up bed so the whole family could stay. The bedroom was also the living space and included a TV. Each room also had its own bathroom, which had everything in it that a bathroom should need. You could also go up on the roof if you wanted to, which Dad and Kristy would do a few times, but I never did. On each floor, there was a shared living room, where you could watch a bigger TV, play games, or just relax on the sofa. On the ground floor, there was a teenage room and a games room, although half the games did not work. Overall, although it wasn't home, despite the broken games, I don't think an accommodation could get any better, and I was really impressed by Sam's House. I would have preferred to be at home though, but anyone would. We were in the city of Bristol for all the wrong reasons.

Sharon informed us of a funded taxi service. The hospital was only five or ten minutes away, depending on how slow we walked. All we had to do was exit Royal Fort Road, the road that Sam's House was on, go down the hill, and turn left, and the hospital was there. Understandably, people who had just had a transplant were going to find it difficult getting up and down that hill, so Sam's House and a taxi company had a deal in which taxi rides from Sam's House to the hospital or vice versa would be put on the bill of Sam's House. We pretty much got a free taxi ride up and down the hill, which may seem pointless because it's a two-minute drive, but you have to experience that hill before making any judgements. Sharon said that because this was costly to CLIC Sargent, it was important to only use this taxi service if absolutely necessary and only if it was for a patient or for women walking back to the accommodation alone or with children at night.

My leg was still hurting, so we went down to the hospital for a while to try to get hold of a doctor on the ward. We made it to the main lobby at the entrance of the hospital before calling the ward. They suggested giving me paracetamol and if it didn't clear in half an hour to call them back. It helped the pain a little bit but not greatly – I think there was something else going on with my leg, although I am unsure what. Luckily, because we knew about the taxi service, we were able to get a taxi back to Sam's House and putting my leg through torture was no longer worried about.

And that was the first day. It didn't seem too bad, but this was only the first day. The scary stuff was going to begin the next day, where tests would be carried out to make sure I was fit for transplant. We would also meet my new consultant, who was going to explain everything to us.

Tuesday 2nd August 2016. After our first night at Sam's House, we woke up early to begin the first of two days of tests. The first thing we had to do was check into the hospital and provide my details. I also had my height, weight, and obs done to check that everything was still going well. This was done at the outpatients' clinic, in the basement of the hospital. I should mention that I was feeling well – my leg pain was still there but not as bad, but other than that, I was feeling almost my normal self. My hair had grown back significantly as well, although, due to the chemo, it was patchy and uneven. With it being early August, I hadn't had a single dose of chemo for over a month.

The highly toxic and intense chemotherapy I was to receive was very capable of destroying the heart, so it was important to check that my heart was healthy and not damaged by the previous rounds of chemo. The first of two tests for my heart were a heart echo scan. My heart would be made visible on a computer by rubbing my chest with jelly on a stick. This was very similar to an ultrasound. Out of this came not only images of my heart doing its job, but also a very clever graph, which I'm assuming measures the heartrate and activity. Here is another funny story to tell: because I was at a children's hospital, they had the children's show, *Bing*, on the hospital TV while I had my scan. The show involved an oversized rabbit trying to make friends with a much smaller cat, and the cat scratched the rabbit. For some reason, I found it funny and couldn't stop laughing at it. The laughing produced inaccurate results on the echo scan because it kept making the graph go really high and then back down again. The cardiologist remained calm, but I could tell he was getting frustrated.

"Try not to look at the TV just for a few seconds ... thank you."

After a few attempts, I had finally calmed down and everything looked healthy.

Following my heart echo scan, I then had an ECG scan. This was a very quick procedure, where I was required to lay on a bed and have a number of stickers stuck to my chest, arms, and legs. These stickers would produce some kind of graph, which could then be printed out, and showed the rhythm of my heart. The tests showed that I had a regular heartbeat, which was good news. Everything in terms of my heart was very well, and it was in the strongest state possible considering my circumstances, ready for the large amounts of poison it would soon have to endure.

After my heart scans, we then had to check into Day Beds. Day Beds was the PDU of Bristol – a day unit – and once I was discharged to Sam's House and eventually home, my check-ups would be on Day Beds. Because Day Beds was located on the sixth floor, this was the first time we used the hospital lifts. As unexciting as it sounds, on the first day, they were the coolest, but after a short time in Bristol, they were the most annoying lifts I've ever been in. Bristol is where *Wallace & Gromit* was animated and, therefore, there is a *Wallace & Gromit* theme throughout the hospital, with it being most present in the elevators. I will always remember approaching the orange floor and Wallace saying, "The orange floor. Sell oranges, do they?"

As soon as we arrived on Day Beds, we were sent back downstairs to get an X-ray. If you're wondering why I needed an X-ray, it was to assess my bone age. As there was a chance of the treatment disrupting my growth, it was important to be able to refer to my pre-transplant bone age in the future if there were concerns about my growth. The radiographer called me in after a short wait in the waiting room, which was full, so I spent a large amount of time standing. First, they wanted an X-ray of my wrist and my hand, which I thought was quite cool. I wanted to keep the picture, but there was a charge for that. After my hand X-ray, I also needed to have a chest X-ray. I was required to take my shirt off and stand facing a board while pictures were taken. From what the radiographers could see, everything on the X-rays appeared fine.

Next, after my X-ray, was the scary stuff that Mum and I had been dreading. On our way, Mum started crying, but Dad remained calm and said we needed to be strong for me. This was the meeting with the doctor who would go over the procedure of the transplant and the possible side effects and complications. When we arrived back on Day Beds, we met Chris. She was the specialist nurse. Chris was the Amanda equivalent in Bristol and would write letters for us, as well as support us. Chris called us into the consultation room, where we met Dr. G. Dr. G was going to be my haematology BMT consultant at Bristol.

Because we all feared it, as soon as we set foot in the consultation room, Mum burst into tears. This then made me cry. I didn't cry because I was scared, however terrified I was, rather I hated seeing Mum like that. I had caused so much stress to my family and I just wanted it all to be over with. Dr. G asked, sympathetically, if we were okay and gave us some tissues. After calming down and drying our eyes, Dr. G then proceeded to tell us about the bone marrow transplantation procedure.

The first thing he said to us was that bone marrow transplants are not a 100% cure. I shouldn't expect to be out of the woods just like that. However, it was the best option for reducing my chances of relapse and therefore it was the best thing for me. He said that no one knows what causes leukaemia or how to cure it, and if he did, he would be very rich and living in the Bahamas.

Dr. G explained to me minimal residual disease (MRD) in a little bit more detail. He began drawing circles, which represented leukaemia, on a piece of paper. After each chemo cycle, the circles were getting smaller, showing the effectiveness of the treatment. But the problem was that while the circles were getting smaller, they were not disappearing, and it was more difficult for the chemo to target the tiny traces of leukaemia blasts, which were not visible under an ordinary microscope. This is where MRD comes in.

As briefly mentioned by Amanda back at Addenbrooke's, Dr. G explained that before August 2015, MRD was only used on ALL leukaemia patients. But a larger number of AML patients were relapsing and they didn't know why. Therefore, MRD was beginning to be used, saving many lives and reducing the chances of relapse.

After the talk about MRD, I was given my own MRD results from Round 3, where I did receive some very good news. My MRD results from my bone marrow aspiration showed that my bone marrow was <0.01% leukaemia. I was pretty much in remission, but just to be safe, they couldn't say 0%. After all, this was only one sample. Despite the minor side effects, Round 3 of chemo was very successful and had put me in remission! To have a transplant, my bone marrow needed to be less than 5% leukaemia, so the fact that I was pretty much 0% was a real achievement. All I needed now was that one final stretch to victory, not to cure my leukaemia but to prevent it from coming back.

He then went over the procedure and explained how

transplant days were numbered. Treatment took place under the 'conditioning phase'. The first day of chemotherapy was labelled as Day T-10, the second was Day T-9, the third was Day T-8, and so on. The first four days of the conditioning stage would involve having two doses of the chemo drug, busulfan, every day. The busulfan took three hours to go through my Hickman line. Day T-6 would be a break day from any treatment because apparently the two drugs did not mix well. On Day T-5, from what I heard, I would have one of the most toxic chemotherapy drugs ever made, and I would start four days of cyclophosphamide once a day over one hour. The combination of these treatments would completely wipe out my immune system and bone marrow, which would not be able to recover on its own, hence the new stem cells I was to receive. My bone marrow would be completely empty after conditioning, although it is fascinating how my DNA would go untouched. Day T-1 was another break day, where I would receive no treatment.

From Day T-3, I was to be isolated in my hospital cubicle and would be unable to leave until my blood showed signs of recovery and I was no longer neutropenic. Thankfully, as I had AML and not ALL, I did not require radiotherapy. ALL patients going to transplant required total body irradiation, in addition to the highly intensive chemotherapy. If I did decide to take part in the trial, the busulfan-cyclophosphamide chemo combination would have a 50% chance of being replaced with a less harmful chemo regimen.

Transplant Day was Day 0, when I would receive my new stem cells. These cells were also referred to as T-cells. My donor was from an umbilical cord from a female in France. Because it was from an umbilical cord, the cells could have been stored for up to fifteen years, meaning my donor could have been anywhere from a couple of months to fifteen years old at the time. The procedure was very similar to a blood transfusion in the sense that no surgery was required and I would be completely conscious during the whole thing. A nurse was going to carry out the procedure, and a large syringe of stem cells would be slowly injected through my Hickman line. This would be a very slow procedure and was going to take around fifteen minutes to prevent a shock to the system. After about twenty minutes, the new stem cells would find the bone marrow in my body and start rebuilding it from scratch. I thought this was very clever and fascinating.

After Day 0, the days counted like Day 1, Day 2, Day 3, and so on. Technically, I was going to be reborn because I was going to be given a completely new immune system and bone marrow. Therefore, Transplant Day was technically going to be a second birthday for me, and because I had the same bone marrow and essentially the same blood as someone else, I was going to have a twin somewhere out there who I'm unlikely to ever meet or know.

Dr. G told me what to expect during transplant. First of all, the body's way of getting rid of the cyclophosphamide was through urine and not urinating regularly could damage my kidneys. From Day T-5 to T-1, I would be required to urinate hourly during the day and every two hours during the night. This was whether I needed to urinate or not, and I had to do it in pee bottles so the nurses could measure what was coming out. To help me go and also keep me hydrated, around this time I would start receiving fluids through my Hickman line, and they would be on constantly in addition to any other medicines I would need. This meant for four days straight I was going to be attached to a drip stand and on fluids, indirectly drinking non-stop. I would have to take the drip stand with me everywhere I went, including the shower.

In terms of side effects, I was going to expect the usual side effects from chemo, such as hair loss, loss of appetite, nausea, vomiting, diarrhoea, and fevers. They expected my throat to get very sore, and therefore, on Day 0, I would be required to have an NG tube put down. This was perfect timing because it was before my body would start feeling the full effects. There was no escaping the tube; it was an established rule for all transplant patients to have one, whether the patient felt they need one or not or whether the patient was gaining or losing weight. But because my throat was going to get so sore, if I threw it up, they promised they would not put another one down.

The cyclophosphamide was so toxic that it was also capable of causing liver failure, damage to the heart, or even death. Some can't cope with the chemo and end up in intensive care. In addition to this, there were also chances of second cancers being caused by the damage of the chemotherapy. Although this was rare, Dr. G had to inform us about this, in case it did happen and we hadn't been informed.

The chemotherapy was also likely to wipe out my fertility, so Dr. G strongly advised me to go to the IVF clinic and store a sperm sample.

Also, as the chemotherapy was undoubtedly going to weaken my immune system, I was also going to have to take an antibiotic called phenoxymethylpenicillin, or penicillin as it was commonly referred to. Despite no proof of it actually being necessary or effective, I would most likely be on penicillin for the rest of my life. As my original immune system was also going to be destroyed, all my antibodies were also going to be destroyed. Starting from scratch would mean that I had to have all my injections that I had when I was a baby all over again and also, I would be able to get chickenpox twice, having had it already when I was nine.

On top of the side effects of the chemotherapy, I also needed to expect side effects from the transplant itself. The most common side effect was called Graft vs. Host disease (GvHD). This was where my donor cells (the graft) would recognise my body's cells (the host) as 'foreign' and start attacking them. Dr. G said that it was actually good to get a little bit of mild GvHD because it was a sign that the cells were working. Symptoms of mild GvHD could include a rash or diarrhoea, however, severe GvHD consisted of vomiting, severe intestinal inflammation, and abdominal pain.

Another risk of the transplant was that my body could reject the cells altogether, in which case I would be in a world of trouble because my body would be unable to recover without them. If this was the case, the closest match from either my mum or dad would have to be used. This was risky and was only to be used as a last resort. To prevent the small chance of rejection, I would be prescribed immunosuppressants called ciclosporin and MMF, which would suppress the activity of my own immune system to allow the new cells to work.

That was it for now – to me, that consultation sounded a bit like a horror story. While it started off terrifying, we were glad that it was over, and it wasn't as bad as what we had thought it would be. It was a lot to get through, and the last few paragraphs are only a summary of the entire consultation.

Dr. G went through the biological and medical side of the transplant. About forty-five minutes later, we were going to have a meeting with Chris, who was going to go through the social side of the procedure, such as the rules of isolation, and explain more about life on the ward. Because it was a lot to take in, Chris gave us a lunch break and recommended the café across the street from the hospital, where I had one of the recommended cheese paninis before we returned to Day Beds to have our meeting.

As mentioned before, from Day T-3, I was going to be isolated in my hospital room. There were rules for this isolation, and because my body would be unable to fight an infection should I get one, it was important that they were strictly adhered to. Chris went through the rules with us, and I have listed these down below:

- The only food I was permitted to eat was either from the ward or packaged food from shops. I was to be on a 100-day clean diet, which, despite no evidence to support that it works, should be stuck to. The clean diet meant that I had to avoid foods that had been sitting out for long periods of time and most fresh foods, particularly fresh fruit and vegetables. Frozen food was preferred. The number one rule was no takeaways at all. If my parents did decide to get something to take out for them to eat, it was advised that they eat it outside my room and away from me in order to limit my cravings.

- I was even going to be limited in what water I could drink. We were given a list of the brands of bottled water I was allowed to consume. Other than that, regular tap water wasn't even allowed. All other drinking water had to come from the ward kitchen, which was boiled and then cooled down again to kill the germs. This tasted disgusting.

- To avoid bringing any germs to my cubicle, footwear from outside the ward was forbidden. My parents were going to be given a locker to put their belongings from outside the ward into. Mum and Dad were advised to buy crocs or flip flops to wear on the ward and on the ward only, in order to reduce the number of germs being brought in.

- My cubicle needed to be cleaned twice a day by the cleaners. It was the responsibility of my parents to change my bed once a day. I was also not allowed any teddies, which meant that George had to be washed and then either stay at Sam's House or live on the shelf of my cubicle in a vacuum-sealed bag.

- Regardless of how well I was feeling, the rules were that I needed to get out of bed at least once a day. Even if it was sitting in my chair for five minutes while my bed was being changed, it was better than sitting in bed all day.

- I also had to keep myself clean. Showering once a day was preferred, but if I was so unwell that I couldn't, there was a washing bowl and wipes I could have a facewash with. I was also required to brush my teeth after every meal, not just twice a day. The chemotherapy made my skin very thin, so I was not going to be allowed to use any soap, shower gel, or shampoo. Instead, I was going to have to wash myself with aqueous cream, which is used for moisturising, and I would have to do this post-transplant for quite a while too.

- Any object from outside the ward was not allowed to come into contact with me. I was not allowed to take any old books or board games to the ward with me, meaning everything I brought to Bristol with me needed to be brand new. Any magazines or newspapers brought into my ward preferably needed to be picked up from the bottom of the pile in the shop, reducing the chance of human contact. I wasn't allowed to touch any money, cards, or letters, so post for me needed to be opened by my parents. If I wanted to decorate my room and put posters up, these needed to be laminated.

- Visitors were strictly limited. I was allowed four named visitors: Mum, Dad, Kristy, and one other. No one else was allowed to visit, except ward staff. Only two of my named visitors were allowed in my room at any one time. Anyone who went in my room (doctors, nurses, and other ward staff) had to wear an apron before entering, with the only exceptions being my four named visitors.

- Because going to transplant was a lot riskier and more intense than previous rounds of chemo, I was going to have to be closely monitored. Unlike Addenbrooke's, where obs were taken every four hours, at Bristol, obs were going to be taken every two hours. Blood tests were also a lot more regular, and I would have them every day twice a day, one at 6:00am and one at 6:00pm. My blood would change rapidly from day one of conditioning past the days of my discharge.

Chris briefly mentioned that I could send my donor a thank you card. We were not allowed to know their name or where they were from, just their gender and what country they were from. I'm guessing this is because, in case the transplant didn't work, it was to avoid people sending abuse to their donors. That's just my theory; I didn't ask why in the meeting and can't seem to find anything online. After two years, if the donors give consent, you can find out who they are. I decided not to send a thank you card because all I could say was, 'Thank you for donating your cells'. I wanted to say a proper thank you and wanted to wait until I could. One day, my wish is to meet my donor, who, as of writing, I still don't know.

After the meeting, Chris gave us a tour of Ward 34. Ward 34 was the BMT and haematology ward, and this was where my transplant would occur. It was located on the seventh floor, at the very top of the hospital.

First, Mum and Dad were shown their locker. This was where they needed to put anything, as mentioned in the previous meeting, that was forbidden in my room or any footwear that had been worn outside the ward. In the locker area was also a couple of toilets, which were for the parents and staff only and were the only toilets they could use. Even my four named visitors were not allowed to use the toilet in my cubicle to reduce the chance of potential infections.

We were then showed the type of room I would be staying in. This wasn't the exact room I'd be staying in, but since it was vacant, we took the opportunity to have a look around. Amanda was right; they were very similar to the cubicles on Ward C2. Each cubicle had a bed, a table, a drip stand, a chair, and a TV. I was permitted to bring something in, like my PlayStation, to connect to the TV if I wanted to, but this needed to be approved by the IT technicians. There was also a desk on the side, with a whiteboard on the side wall. I'm guessing this was to help count down the days or to help remember what needed to be done during the isolation period – as I discovered later, all the days merged into one when isolated. Each cubicle had its own bathroom, with a toilet and a sink, and unlike Ward C2, which had a bathtub, this had a walk-in shower. I call it a walk-in shower, but it was described more as a wet room. The only way you could tell it was a shower was the fact that there was a large space of floor – the type of flooring you'd expect at a swimming pool – with a plughole and a shower head on the wall. Nothing else could show it was a shower – no curtain or anything.

Chris then showed me the playroom, which had a lot of children's toys, board games, and was full of DVDs. She didn't go into too much detail about the playroom because, as I would be isolated, it was very unlikely that I would get a chance to go in there. But it was still good to see what they had available as, like in Addenbrooke's, I'd get regular visits from the play specialists, who would bring games and DVDs to me.

After that, my parents were shown the parents' room. It had a kitchen and a few chairs and tables. This was where they could both either have a break from being stuck in the cubicle with me or make their meals, and if there were more than two of my four named visitors on the ward, the third and fourth would have to sit in there or elsewhere. Chris went over the rules of food with them, telling us to ensure that food was labelled to stop other parents eating it, as well as being clear that food past its expiration date would be thrown out by the cleaners. My parents were entitled to free breakfast by the hospital kitchen; toast and a tea or coffee. All other meals by the hospital kitchen would be for patients only.

Lastly, I was shown the hospital kitchen, which I would have no reason to go in, but we were told about the process of it. I would be given a menu in my room, and as I was going to be isolated, my parents would have to go to the kitchen and place an order for me. Like Ward C2, Ward 34 was very similar in the sense that it wasn't the stereotypical hospital food of disgusting ready meals, rather there was more choice. Chris told us that they had some really tasty food, like sandwiches and paninis, on the lunch menu.

That was it for the tour, which was more for my parents, especially since all I would really get to see of the ward was my own room.

After the tour, it was back to Day Beds for an unexpected

check-up. My leg was still hurting me and I therefore had to have an appointment with the registrar, who examined it. She couldn't tell if anything was wrong because, although I was in pain, she couldn't see anything majorly wrong. Therefore, I also had an appointment with the physiotherapist, who showed me a range of exercises I could do from my bed to help improve the mobility of my leg and ease the pain. One of these exercises included leaning against the back of the bed while stretching my toes as far as I could. The physiotherapist said that it was important for me to keep up with these exercises, but when the pain went away the next day, I stopped.

After that, it was back to Sam's House for my second night. The third day was going to consist of a visit to the dentist and a lung function test, as well as an ordinary check-up with the registrar to ensure that everything was generally still good.

***

Wednesday 3rd August 2016. The morning of August 3rd, 2016, involved a visit to the dentist. You're probably wondering why I was in Bristol for a super important work-up plan, only to visit a dentist. But the answer is simple: because of my illness, I was unable to go to the dentist back at home as I needed more specialised care, and so the last check-up I had was eight months prior. The dentist I was visiting this time was a specialist dentist, which was closely linked to the hospital and could fulfil the hospital's requirements. It was located just a few minutes away from the hospital, on Lower Maudlin Street.

When I got there, and after a short wait in the waiting room (I must say, I was fascinated by the fish tank and the massive goldfish), the dentist called me in. The first thing she did was explain why I was there. It seemed a bit strange having to go to the dentist to prepare for a bone marrow transplant. The reason why I was there was because being as clean as possible for my transplant included my mouth as well. Any holes in my teeth could have resulted in any germs or bacteria getting in there, and my body would be unable to fight it, possibly causing an infection. Therefore, it was important to make sure my teeth were as clean as possible.

I tried to keep my teeth as hygienic as possible. I did everything I could while in hospital to make sure I brushed my teeth twice a day, even if I was so sick I could only do it in a sick bowl with a plastic cup full of water. That being said, I wasn't sure what effect grazing on Haribo all day everyday had done to my teeth, and I was about to find out.

It didn't come as a surprise to discover my mouth wasn't clean. But what did surprise me was how unclean my mouth was. The dentist seemed calm but disappointed in a stereotypical dentist way; ashamed almost. She was as surprised as I was. She spotted eight holes in my teeth and needed to send me down for an X-ray to check for any more potential holes that she couldn't detect herself. She put this down to two reasons: me eating a lot of sweets probably didn't help, and Mum, Dad, the dental nurse, and I all agreed that that was probably the case. The second reason was that chemo weakens the teeth, and the acid from my constant vomiting probably helped to damage my teeth even more.

While she went to go speak to someone, we spoke to the dental nurse, who told me that instead of grazing throughout the day, which was lots of small attacks on the teeth, it was better to eat the sweets all in one go and have one massive attack instead. It just shows that doing one thing right can cause another thing to go wrong; the dieticians encouraged this to keep my weight up, but the effect on my mouth was not good. I do wonder now how many sweets I ate during my entire cancer journey. I don't know if I was proud or ashamed to need eight fillings; I was ashamed because I should have looked after them a lot better, but at the same time, I was proud because that must have been a world record!

Needing eight fillings came as a concern to the dentist, which I'm sure is no surprise since it came as a concern to all of us. I was due for a lung function test later in the day and there was no way I could have a two-hour procedure on my mouth and make it back in time for my lung function test. The dentist gave me a choice; I could either cancel my lung function test and have eight fillings all in one go, which would postpone my lung function test for when I was next at Addenbrooke's in a week's time, or I could start with a couple of fillings in Bristol, finish treatment back at the Stowmarket dentist at a later date, and make it in time for my lung function test. I chose the difficult option of having eight fillings all in one go. I just wanted it to be over with. I was then sent down to have an X-ray, and then it was off to the hospital. There would be a short break in between the check-up and my fillings as I still needed to see the registrar and a couple of medications would need to be prescribed to prepare for the procedure.

Back on Day Beds, I saw the haematology registrar. Before anything further happened, she gave me a check-up, which involved the normal procedures done when having a check-up. The heart and lungs sounded fine, and my mouth, ears, and line looked fine. After that, my parents signed some of the consent forms for my transplant. As I was under eighteen, I didn't have to sign anything, and if I did sign the papers myself, this had little meaning in terms of responsibility regarding my care. I didn't see the papers, but I'm guessing that these consent forms were along the lines of confirming that we couldn't sue them should the transplant fail or if I died as a result of it. I had known ever since arriving at Bristol for the first time that there was no going back, but it was this moment here when there was officially no going back, not that my parents would have allowed me to make that choice. The contract was officially signed – I was in for a massive risk! The doctor then prescribed me some medication to prepare myself for my fillings later on.

I hate going to the dentist when I haven't brushed my teeth beforehand. There was no time to return to Sam's House to brush my teeth, but I really needed some lunch. I ate a sausage sandwich from the hospital café on the walk to the dentist. The dentist, who was a different one from the one I'd seen in the morning, said it was okay as she had seen worse and would know what it was if she came across bits of sausage in my mouth.

The most difficult thing I had ever done was keep my mouth open for two hours. The dentist picked up on the X-ray that one of the 'holes' was actually a funny-shaped tooth. She was quite fascinated by this tooth because she had never seen that shape before. I had never seen someone be so enthusiastic about a tooth. Therefore, I actually required seven and not eight fillings, which made things a little bit better, although it was still really bad, and I wasn't proud. I was given a pair of orange glasses to put on and also had a paper towel put on me like a napkin, both of which made me look very strange.

Already, there were a couple of problems. The first arose when the dentist and dental nurse attempted to place a blue elastic cover in my mouth, which would therefore prevent any water the dentist used to clean my mouth from splashing back into my mouth. Maybe it was to prevent drowning, but I'm not sure about that. I wish they hadn't thought about putting that thing in in the first place because it took them half an hour to get it in and, once they had got it in, it fell out again! They gave up soon afterwards. It was pointless. Half an hour of the already too long procedure could have been avoided and spent doing the fillings instead. In that half an hour, I could have gone to my lung function test and back!

The second problem was my anaesthetic. The procedure was done under local anaesthetic, which was successful in numbing my mouth but had little to no effect on the pain. I kept asking the dentist for more and more anaesthetic, which still wasn't doing anything, until she was concerned that if she gave me anymore, I would pass out. I had reached the maximum limit. Passing out was almost the case when I had my bathroom break; yes, the dental procedure was so long that I needed a bathroom break. There was no effect on the pain, but I had so much anaesthetic, I began to feel dizzy and almost passed out in the bathroom. Luckily, I didn't, and I was able to return to finish the five or so fillings still remaining.

I don't know what was wrong with me, but during the procedure of my seven fillings, I began shaking. Shaking was a problem I had suffered from my first days in hospital back in A1 on Ward C2, which seemed ages ago, but this was uncontrollable and got so bad that Dad had to hold my leg down to stop it. It didn't really come as a concern to me because, as strange as this sounds, I was comfortable doing it. It felt normal, almost putting me at ease. At the time, I was wondering why Dad was so concerned about the shaking, and while now I'll admit it was odd, I still don't think it was anything that bad to worry about. I still suffer from it from time to time.

That aside, it was a long two hours, but I got there in the end. I officially had seven fillings all in one go! That surely has to be another world record. The dentist had also put a plastic coating on my teeth to avoid me getting any cavities while in hospital, once again reducing the chance of infection. As of writing, to this day, I'm not too sure where the plastic covering went; I never felt it in the first place, and I can't feel it now. I don't know if it dissolved with my food or something similar. I was also given a special toothpaste, which I needed to use instead of regular toothpaste from that moment on. I wasn't too sure on the difference if I'm honest. Colgate is Colgate to me, but I did what the dentist said and refused to use any other toothpaste from then on until the tubes ran out. And, to finish the dental procedure on a positive note, another five and a half years passed before I required another filling!

Because the surgery took two hours, it was quite late in the day and I had missed my lung function test, which was therefore rescheduled for Addenbrooke's a week later. That meant we were done in Bristol for the time being, but before leaving, we needed to go back to Day Beds to meet Stephen, who Mum spoke to briefly on the phone while we were travelling to Bristol on the first day. Stephen gave us some more information on the trial, just going over what it was again and providing us with some printed materials on bone marrow transplants for us to have a look through. He then gave us the go-ahead to go home and told us to check into Ward 34 on Monday 15th August 2016. My bone marrow transplant procedure date was finally set.

After that, we returned to Sam's House to pack our bags. Outside Sam's House, we bumped into the Krutke family: Jacob – who I had made cupcakes with back in Addenbrooke's, going way back to the aftermath of Round 1 – and his parents, Lorna and Craig. Dad knew Craig because they used to work together. Jacob had started his conditioning phase and was having chemotherapy and radiotherapy. Lorna said that he was a bit freaked out by the radiotherapy mask, which really worried him. ALL patients required total body irradiation. It made me aware that, although I was unlucky to need a transplant, others were in a much worse situation than me – at least I didn't need every bone in my body to be exposed to high levels of radiation to rid myself of cancer.

Jacob had his transplant shortly before I'd arrived for my own. Our family was to become very close to them in the coming weeks and months, and Mum and Lorna had already arranged to go on coffee breaks once I arrived in Bristol for the real thing. I was due back in Bristol on August 15th, 2016, and my conditioning phase would begin the following day. My transplant was scheduled for Friday 26th August 2016. It was official now, and there was no turning back. The contract was signed and tests and procedures were done to ensure I was in the best possible health. From now until then, I just had to finish some tests and think about and plan for my future, which was likely to be disrupted by the treatment.

***

After I finished in Bristol for my work-up plan, I began treating the next couple of weeks as if they were my 'final' days. Although I was as well as I was ever going to be, having to go for such treatment, there was always a risk, and no one was exempt from anything going wrong. I was going to have to handle crazy amounts of chemotherapy and rely on my donor cells to help me recover. These cells had to work. The cells not working was something I prayed would not happen, yet it was a possibility, and that would be the worst news any person could hear. Therefore, I spent the next couple of weeks spending quality time with both my friends and family, and since Bristol didn't cover everything, the finishing touches to make sure

I was ready for transplant and prepared for the aftermath needed to take place.

I was aware that the chemotherapy from my bone marrow transplant had a high chance of wiping out my fertility. Taking the doctors' advice, in case I wanted to have children in the future, I needed to produce a sperm sample into a plastic pot, which could then be tested in the labs and stored, and to do this, I needed to go to the IVF clinic in Cambridge. I actually went twice.

The first time I went was to meet the people and sign some papers, where I learned that sperm could actually be stored for up to fifty-five years! I was shocked by that because if I did store a sperm sample, I could have attempt to have children when I'm sixty-eight years old. Shortly after the consultation, I was shown into a spacious room, which was pretty empty and just contained a bed and a sink, as well as a vault, which I would put my produced sample in, and the lab would receive it on the other side of the wall. The aim was to produce a sperm sample in a pot. There was also a TV, but as I was under eighteen, I was strictly forbidden to turn the TV on, which put me at a disadvantage.

I must have spent a good twenty minutes in that room. I just couldn't bring myself to do it at that moment. I'll even admit that I burst into tears in Dad's arms when I came out of the room. I guess that all the stress I was under, and questioning why at thirteen years of age I was in an IVF clinic, got to me. Yes, it was all private and the door was locked, but I still felt a great sense of pressure having to do it, knowing that people knew what I was doing in that room. I exited the room, holding an empty pot, in tears, saying that I just couldn't do it. Not today.

The lady who I signed the consent forms with was really

nice about it and said that was completely normal and a lot of boys my age who come into the IVF clinic feel and react in the same way. It was a normal reaction, and I wasn't the only one, which made me feel a little bit better and less ashamed of myself.

Increasingly under pressure, with my transplant looming and knowing that my future depended on this, I knew at some point in the very imminent future that I was going to have to set foot in that building again and produce a sperm sample. I was told that it didn't have to be a large amount, just enough for the labs to be able to test it. I returned to the IVF clinic a few days later, and this time, I brought myself to do it and I did do it. I was hoping that it would be a sufficient amount to store and I could be done with the IVF clinic for the time being.

The same day, back at home, Dad received a phone call from the clinic, who said that the sample I produced was good, but chances of fertility at the time was very unlikely. All that for nothing. That meant that the previous rounds of chemotherapy had made me infertile already and so there was no point storing it. I coped with the news well, and it's something I very rarely talk about or bring up. I still don't know how I feel about it. I'm not a massive fan of kids, but what bothers me is that a future opportunity is possibly taken from me.

I did try to view it positively in the sense that there are some who have had bone marrow transplants who have been able to have kids. There is also a chance of recovery in fertility a few years after treatment. There are also alternatives out there, such as adoption. Therefore, there was some light, and my chances of having a family weren't completely diminished. I brushed this news to one side and just continued with my life; after all, I will never really know if I'm fertile until it's time to think about having children. I'm optimistic. Anyway, I had no time to be sad about my future. The future was the least of my worries – I was going to transplant the next week! The present was my priority.

After I had finished up at the IVF clinic, still in the car park, Dad received a call from Dr. G back in Bristol. I was still undecided about participating in the trial concerning the potentially less harmful but effective treatment, although I understood that if it wasn't for trials, I wouldn't be here today. At the same time, I wanted something to be done to me that was proven to work. I hate being in situations like this because I want to help others but at the same time want something that will work for me. I wish there could be a balance between the two, but unfortunately there wasn't. The worst thing was that the doctors were not allowed to advise us on this trial in case they influenced our decision, so this decision was all down to me and my family.

Dr. G said that if I did wish to take part in the trial, my parents would have to sign papers in Bristol on that day. With Bristol being four hours away, and this being at around 2:00pm, this confirmed that I was not taking part in the trial. It was not possible to sign the papers at such short notice. I was happy that it made the decision for me, but I couldn't help but feel guilty for those in the future needing a transplant, knowing I didn't take part in a trial which could well have helped them.

Back at Addenbrooke's, I had a check-up with my haematology consultant, Dr. M, in PDU. He asked if we had heard from the IVF clinic, and we told him the news. Dr. M didn't really comment too much more about it. He then went over the future with me and what to expect post-transplant. It felt really good when he was talking about the future because I was going to Bristol as if it was my final days, and he was already talking about what would happen once I was home. He said that when

I returned from Bristol, I would start by having check-ups with him or Dr. A twice a week, and this would reduce as my overall health improved. If all went well, hospital visits would reduce from twice a week, to once a week, to once a fortnight, to once a month, and so on.

Due to unfinished work in Bristol, for which my seven fillings were to blame, I also needed to go to Addenbrooke's for a lung function test. This was a funny procedure, mainly because of the man conducting it. The lung function test analysed whether my lungs were healthy and checked to see how much oxygen I was breathing in. Sitting in a transparent box with a peg on my nose, I was required to take a deep breath and breathe out into a tube until I could not physically breathe out anymore. I must have been breathing out for at least twenty seconds. The man was so enthusiastic about it, encouraging me to "BLOW! BLOW! BLOW! BLOW! BLOW! Perfect." Mum and I nicknamed him 'Blow Blow Blow Man'. The same procedure needed to be repeated a few times, including me breathing out into a tube with a peg on my nose but without sitting in the see-through box. The same needed to be done with no peg. My lung function test came back fine; my lungs were completely healthy and fit enough for what was about to hit them.

Like I said, on top of my numerous medical tests, I spent a lot of my 'last days' spending time with family and friends. A lot of my time from late July to early August was spent FaceTiming Fin and Liam and playing on the PlayStation very late at night. I did also have some quality family time, and I definitely think 2016 was the year I was the closest to my family.

With my birthday being on August 29th and my transplant scheduled for August 26th, there was no doubt that I was spending my fourteenth birthday in isolation, which I was upset by. Uncle James' birthday is August 14th, and I was scheduled back in Bristol for August 15th. So it made sense to have a joint birthday and good luck meal with my whole family on my final day in Stowmarket. I received a lot of great presents in preparation for Bristol. Dad bought me a new PlayStation. Also, I was given a number of magazines to read, and James gave me a box full of WWE Superstar John Cena gear, which included a hat that said, 'Never Give Up'. I was not going to give up. It was one final stretch and then all that hard work would pay off and I could live a happy, healthy life in the future. I was ready to get my transplant done!

Chapter 9

Reborn

The course of my Bone Marrow Transplant from August 15th to October 1st, 2016

On the morning of August 15th, 2016, my parents, Kristy, and I were all ready to go to Bristol for me to have my bone marrow transplant. Conditioning was to start the next day. All of our bags were packed. Surprisingly, everyone was in a positive mood and there were very few tears. Even Mum, who cries easily, was in good spirits. I may have showed a few, but I wiped my tears away before anyone noticed anything. I tried to be strong, but I couldn't help but shed a tear when the front door of my house closed for the final time. Privately, I was terrified, but I didn't express this too much. It was all about being positive. Negative thinking would make the situation much worse than it already was.

The plan was for Mum to stay in Bristol and look after me the entire time. Dad would spend quite a lot of time in Bristol, but as Kristy would be at home for the majority of time, he would have to go back once or twice a week to check on her, as well as do a few days at work, since his long sick pay period was coming to an end. Kristy, who at this point had done her GCSEs and was currently in the summer holidays, was going to start sixth form in September, so she mostly needed to be at home. She would stay in Bristol at the beginning and would then come to visit occasionally, mostly on the weekends.

Once we arrived in Bristol, it was a quick stop to Sam's House, where we were given our keys to our room so we could drop our bags off. My family would be staying there when there was more than two of us in Bristol. When it was just me and Mum, she would stay at the hospital with me. When Dad was there, my parents would alternate; one would stay with me, the other would stay at Sam's. Once I was discharged, I would also stay at Sam's House for a while until the doctors were satisfied enough to allow me to go home. We were in Room 5, the same room where I'd stayed on my workup plan, next to Jacob's, which was Room 6.

When I arrived on Ward 34, I was shown to my cubicle. It was very similar to the one Chris had shown me. In fact, it was the same, except I was in a corner room, so it was a different shape. Because it was a corner room, the window was smaller, but I was lucky because the room was more spacious. Lorna said we were lucky to get a corner room. My room was Cubicle 5, and Jacob, who by this point had had his transplant already, was next door in Cubicle 6, isolating. It was good to have a familiar face on a ward where I knew nobody – Jacob would sometimes wave to me from his window while I still enjoyed the freedom of walking around the ward.

The reason why I was on the ward the day before conditioning started was just as an introduction. It was so I could settle in and see my new home in more detail. I had seen a cubicle, but I'd never explored one. Also, as I lived four hours away, it would be very difficult getting to Bristol knowing that my first chemo dose was in the morning, so being early was the best way to go about it. My first nurse in Bristol, Louisa, began by doing my obs, taking my height, weight, temperature, blood pressure, and pulse. She also changed the bungs on my line and added extensions to them, so instead of two lumens, I now had four. This is because I was going to be on a lot of medications at once and it was good to be prepared beforehand.

My nurse also showed me the food menu. Although I knew there was a hospital kitchen and Chris told me that they had some delicious food, I was still worried that Bristol would have the stereotypical hospital food.

My first reaction to the menu was expressed when Mum asked what I thought.

"Not bad," I said, nodding my head approvingly.

And then I realised that it was even better than Ward C2! For breakfast, you could have toast, cereal, croissants, bacon, sausages, hashbrowns, and many other breakfast foods! For lunch, you could have paninis, sandwiches, mashed potatoes, roast beef, roast chicken, and many other lunch foods! And for dinner, you could have chicken nuggets, pizza, chips, potato wedges, potato waffles, pasta, and much more! It didn't stop there. There were desserts, such as cheesecakes, and some nice drinks, such as milkshakes and juice. The variety on offer was amazing! Of course, although the food choices were great, they were not going to be the greatest quality. They were all frozen or ready meals, but that was because they had to be. Anything of a much greater quality, such as fresh food, would have been damaging to my health and would have gone out of date easily, causing a lot of food wastage on the ward. The good thing was that there was a wide variety of food, which prevented the problem many cancer patients have: craving something one day and then feeling sick at the thought of it the next.

Because conditioning started the next day, all I was really there for was to be introduced to my hospital room. That meant, once I was introduced to my hospital room, I was free to do whatever I wanted for the day. Before that, Mum had to sign some more consent forms in addition to the forms signed on the workup plan.

We decided to go into the Bristol city centre and went to an Italian restaurant to celebrate my final day of 'freedom' for a while. For the next seven days, I would be allowed to leave the ward – that is, when I wasn't having anything through my line – but once those seven days were up, I was in isolation. I had to enjoy my final week of 'freedom'. It was a night at Sam's House and an early start the next day for conditioning to commence.

***

The Conditioning Phase

Tuesday 16th August 2016 (Day T-10). The day after my induction was the first day of conditioning, and for the next four days, I would receive the chemotherapy, busulfan, twice a day, both at 11 o'clock; one dose in the morning and one at night. The busulfan was supposed to start in the morning, but there was a slight delay and it ended up being at lunchtime instead. This meant that my next chemo dose ended up being in the middle of the night, which was unheard of on Ward C2. Including my line being flushed afterwards, the dose was so large that it took about three hours for the first dose of busulfan to go through.

This was before the two people in my cubicle at a time rule had started; although technically it already had, and no one said anything for a while. To pass the time, me, Mum, and Kristy played a number of board games. Because everything had to be brand new when brought into my cubicle, before going to transplant, my family and I had done one massive trip to Toys R Us to buy board games to keep ourselves occupied. We bought the electronic banking Monopoly, as well as the board game versions of *Tipping Point* and *Countdown*, shows I had become addicted to back in Cambridge when I was staying on Ward C2 and Kingston House.

Once my first dose of busulfan had finished, I was allowed to leave my room for the evening and have some dinner at Sam's House. I did have a breakdown there, which I tried to hide, but Kristy walked in on me when it happened. The worst part was that she was FaceTiming a friend when she found me. I was scared about the chemotherapy, and now that I'd had my first dose, I realised I truly was at risk. It wasn't like I could just turn back and say no, I don't want to do this, which, as I've stated many times, wouldn't have been possible anyway. I was so scared. I was really terrified about the future. Trying to stay strong was difficult in these situations. I just wanted to go home, and it saddened me knowing what I had left behind only the day before when we'd shut the doors to our house, ready for the four-hour drive, leaving Stowmarket behind.

Due to the slight delay in the morning, my next dose of busulfan was quite late. It was scheduled for 11:00pm, so I needed to stay the night on the ward, which was fine by me. In fact, from then on, no matter what my blood count was, I needed to stay on the ward. This was because blood tests were at 6:00am every morning and the hospital locked their doors overnight – there was no way I'd be able to enter the hospital at 6:00am unless there was an emergency. Even so, I'd hate to have to get up that early in the morning.

Wednesday 17th August to Friday 19th August 2016 (Day T-9 to T-7). Days T-9 to T-7 continued with the doses of busulfan, consisting of one dose at 11:00am and another at 11:00pm. The side effects were still yet to kick in, although I did notice that I was becoming more nauseous. This still wasn't a major problem, and I continued with life like the sickness wasn't there.

On Day T-9, I noticed that the dressing changes were much different in Bristol than Addenbrooke's. Dressing changes were a much longer procedure at Addenbrooke's. Bristol just looped the line, cleaned it a little, then stuck a giant dressing over it. The nurses at Bristol were also fascinated to see the date on my line, which indicated the date it was last changed. They thought it was a very good idea and had never thought of doing that themselves. They thought the Cambridge team were so organised!

Also, on T-9, the two-people rule came into effect, and this was learned the hard way when I had a check-up with the registrar. My heart and lungs sounded fine, but she wasn't happy that there were more than two visitors in my room at once. Dad had to vacate to the parents' room while Mum and Kristy finished our game of Countdown. I was terrified that I was going to die from this transplant, so all I wanted to do was spend time with my whole family. The two-visitor rule was not only damaging to me mentally but annoyed and frustrated me as well. My family shared my frustration too as they all wanted to be with me. I suppose it was for my safety, so we should have followed it to start off with, but the last thing you want when undergoing treatment is to have a divided family.

On T-8, I met the physiotherapist again. My leg pain had gone away completely. She was there to check that the leg pain had gone and also said when in isolation, it is important to keep in shape and it would be good to start some exercises now. The physiotherapist reiterated what the dieticians at Addenbrooke's told me: muscle weighs more than fat. For some reason, she had managed to find an exercise bike that was gathering dust and said I could have it in my room. I loved the sound of that! From then on, I had an exercise bike in my room and sometimes I would ride it even while receiving my chemotherapy. Of course, I needed to be careful and position myself in the right way to prevent stepping on my line and ripping it out of my chest while riding my exercise bike, because that would hurt and probably kill me after bleeding to death. But it was definitely a good way of preventing my legs from turning into jelly and also gaining some muscle, if very little. It was important to exercise in addition to eating a lot.

It was also during this time that I began to get the Wi-Fi set up. Although seems inconsequential, due to being isolated in a hospital room for two months, it was necessary. This was why I preferred Bristol to Addenbrooke's because they actually provided us with a Wi-Fi password when we arrived, and a permitted one too. It was a little bit annoying though, since there were different passwords for different devices and you had to provide your login details before every use. Sometimes, logging into the hospital's Wi-Fi took longer than the actual length of time I was using the internet for. Nevertheless, I was glad to be able to have some form of internet connection in my room. It is odd to think that I experienced my own mini lockdown before coronavirus was even a thing, and the pandemic really highlighted the importance of technology and internet in order to communicate with others.

Saturday 20th August 2016 (Day T-6). Days T-10 to T-7 gave my eight doses of busulfan. Day T-6 was a break day, when I would receive no chemotherapy and would be free to do what I liked. It was important that I made the most of my break day because my next break day, T-1, would be spent in isolation. Whether it was smart to be going into Broadmead, the busy Bristol city centre, when advised not to is one question, but whether it is smart to go into Broadmead when you're on chemotherapy, feeling sick, and have rapidly declining blood cells is another. My parents didn't want to go as they were worried about my health, but I said there was a chance that I was going to die anyway, so they decided to do it my way.

We went into Broadmead, and for good reason, too. Although we had bought a lot in preparation, there were still a few things I needed to get to keep myself occupied, including some wrestling DVDs. We immediately broke another rule, going into a second-hand shop to buy the DVDs, breaking the brand-new items only rule. As I write this, I have only just realised I broke that rule – we weren't thinking any different at the time. It was completely unintentional.

I was feeling quite sick and drowsy that day. Bristol had an alternative way to tackle sickness, in addition to the same anti-sickness medications offered by Addenbrooke's. Bristol's alternative was a patch; a patch very similar to what you might use to try and quit smoking. I'm not sure how it works, but you stick it behind your ear to prevent nausea. This did not work at all.

Because it was my day off from chemo, I was also allowed to spend the day at Sam's House. I needed to stay the night on the ward though, due to my early morning blood tests. We got some shopping done, going to the Co-op down the road from Sam's House to get some potatoes and other supplies. I was feeling really sick by this point but was craving a bowl of roast potatoes. I ate the roast potatoes, but due to my sickness, I threw them all up in the bathroom sink later. Being sick at least stopped me from feeling sick, and I was feeling well for the rest of the evening.

The second chemotherapy, cyclophosphamide, was going to begin the next day, so that evening, I started my four days of constant fluids. The treatment was so toxic that it could cause damage to the kidneys, and therefore, IV fluids through my line were needed to flush it out. This meant I would have to start urinating every hour during the day and every two hours at night. This needed to be done in pee bottles so the nurses could measure the amount going in and the amount coming out. Dad set an hourly alarm for when it was time to pee, and during the day, it got very annoying having to keep getting up and go to the toilet; sometimes, I just did it by my bedside with the pee bottle, praying that a nurse wouldn't walk in on me. Whether I needed to go or not, I had to force something out as it was very important to avoid kidney damage. Urinating so frequently really wasn't very healthy. For the next four days, I would be attached to the drip stand via my Hickman line, with absolutely no breaks. By constant fluids, I mean constant fluids. This involved taking the drip machine into the shower with me, doing everything I could to avoid getting the drip machine wet and getting myself electrocuted. I would finally be free on Day T-1, which would be my second break day from not just chemotherapy but everything, the day before Transplant Day.

Sunday 21st August 2016 (Day T-5). On Day T-5, I started two scary medications. The most significant of the two was the second chemotherapy of the conditioning phase, cyclophosphamide. I cannot emphasise enough how terrified of that drug I was. All I associated it with was liver failure, kidney failure, heart damage, intensive care, and death. It was quite a notorious drug. I knew that death was rare and only really happened to those who are more vulnerable, but there was still a risk. The fact that I was there in the first place was enough to prove there was a risk.

Some patients on the ward during the time I was staying there could not cope with the chemotherapy. Opposite me, there was a sign on the cubicle door that read 'PICU'. For a while, Mum and I were unsure of who PICU meant because no one was occupying the room and it was a bit of a strange name. Little did we know, PICU stood for Paediatric Intensive Care Unit and a patient had been transmitted from the ward to there. I have difficulty remembering, but I think the treatment caused a problem with his heart. This did not help my fears – a case of the treatment being too much to handle had occurred directly opposite me. Lorna told all the nurses that we'd thought that PICU was a person, which was quite embarrassing.

Although I wasn't officially isolated until T-3, I couldn't possibly leave my room from the evening of T-6 when the constant fluids started due to being attached to a drip. Therefore, Mum started going for coffee breaks with Lorna to get away from the ward for a bit. They did this every day from then on and either went to the café downstairs in the children's hospital – which was known for having good jacket potatoes – or to the Costa Coffee, which was located in the main hospital. They never sat in any of the cafes, rather they always brought their food and drink back to the parents' room and consumed them there.

The second of the scary medications was itraconazole. Yes, Bristol put me through it too. However, they were aware and concerned by the fact that I struggled with it. Therefore, after a few tries with the liquid, they prescribed it in tablet form. Addenbrooke's didn't prescribe the tablets and Bristol preferred the liquid because it was more effective. The tablets were only effective if they were taken with something fizzy like Coca-Cola. The tablets, though easier to keep down, still made me feel sick because I was taking a number of medications all at once. Sometimes, the medications that were intended to make me better were the ones bringing on the sickness, in addition to the effects of the chemotherapy.

T-5 was definitely one of the rougher days I'd had during the conditioning period. It was a day of no exercise bike and more sleeping while clutching tightly to the sick bowl as if it was a teddy bear. The sick bowl was no doubt my best friend because, despite feeling sick almost the whole day, vomiting would just happen out of nowhere. When I felt I had to puke, I had to, and it was quick.

Monday 22nd August 2016 (Day T-4). Day T-4 was a much better day than the previous. The sickness I was feeling seemed to have stopped. I got up out of bed and was straight on the exercise bike. On Dad's daily Facebook update on my health, one comment someone left was absolutely right: getting on the bike was an "F you" to the chemo and leukaemia. I was gaining strength and courage to fight through. I didn't abandon the sick bowl though, and I kept hold of it while on the bike.

The combination of chemo and heavy fluids was getting a bit much for me, and the strain on my line was painful for my chest. My dressing would have to be changed once, sometimes twice, a day because all the medications and fluids were so heavy that it undid the loop, causing a tug. It was difficult lying on a bed with this pressure; standing was even more difficult and my parents had to hold the wires to stop my chest dragging to the floor. The pressure on my line was heavy, and I constantly felt the line getting tugged out of my chest. One of my nurses gave me a Hickman line supporter, a clip that was stuck on like a dressing and held the line in place, helping to maintain the loop. Even this came undone after a couple of days.

It was important to loop the line because a tug on it would be painful, and I mean painful. A Hickman line is a wire coming out of your chest, which is inserted in your jugular vein; it is going to hurt if there is any kind of pressure on it. And it did hurt – I can tell you that from experience. I have mentioned already that the pressure was a bit much, but in fact, on one occasion, I stood on my line. I was emptying my bowels quite frequently during this time, at least three times more often than I was emptying my bladder, which was excessive itself. It wasn't diarrhoea I was producing, more something of a cowpat consistency, but I had no idea what I was eating to be having to go so often. Because my line was so heavy, I usually had to hold it while getting off the toilet, but one time I forgot to do this. All my weight – over 60kg – put pressure on my Hickman line and pulled me down with it, and I began to feel dizzy and almost passed out, having to sit back on the toilet bowl. Luckily, I didn't rip my Hickman line out of my chest, but I'm sure just a tiny bit more pressure would have done it and I would have required immediate medical attention. It was just a panic moment, and I was a bit sore for a few minutes, but I quickly got over it. The doctors looked over it and said it was fine, just telling me to be more careful next time. This is one thing about my battle with cancer which I'm still suffering from. If anything rapidly hits my chest, I automatically clutch it as if my line is still there, and I feel very uncomfortable even writing this.

Like I said, I was emptying my bowels very frequently. My cubicle was full of bedpans piled on top of each other, all containing something that resembled cowpat. It was still a bit early to be experiencing the effects of the chemotherapy, although it was definitely possible, evident by my nausea. This problem remained for at least a month, and very soon, it was to become diarrhoea. But, up until this point, no tests had been done to work out what it was. On the ward rounds one day, one of the BMT consultants told me that everyone has a weak spot in their body, and he said mine seemed to be my bottom. He wasn't wrong.

Tuesday 23rd August to Wednesday 24th August 2016 (Day T-3 to T-2). Days T-3 and T-2 were my final two days of cyclophosphamide. From Day T-3, I was officially isolated, but having been stuck on fluids for the past couple of days, I literally had no freedom and was technically isolated from the evening of Day T-6. From then on, I was not allowed to leave my hospital cubicle until my neutrophils reached 0.5 and there was evidence that my new stem cells had settled in (engrafted). I had minimal contact with the outside world, and my only view of the outside world was from a small window, which showed St. Michael's Hill. I couldn't see anything anyway as there were building works right outside. My only view was of a crane.

On Day T-3, I started a new medication called ciclosporin. Ciclosporin is an anti-rejection and immunosuppressant drug. This worked by further weakening my own immune system, which would help make my body accept the new cells because the immune system's power would be reduced, preventing rejection. However, I was allergic to the ciclosporin, which I was told was very common. Similar to the ambisome, it gave me chest pains and difficulty breathing. After the reaction, the chest pains remained, which again brought on the discussion of it being psychological. An ECG and heart scan, all of which were somehow conducted in my cubicle by bringing the technology to me rather than me going to them, showed that there was nothing worrying.

The ciclosporin was stopped and a similar drug called tacrolimus was prescribed for me instead. Fortunately, I wasn't allergic to tacrolimus, and it had the same purposes as ciclosporin. However, it was a very thick and sticky medication, which stuck to the lumens of my line, meaning that it could only go through one lumen of my Hickman line. The nurse had to put a green sticker on my red Hickman Line lumen so it was known which one the tacrolimus went through. This was helpful for blood tests, as, if a blood test was taken from the lumen the tacrolimus went through, my blood would come back with very high tacrolimus levels. Therefore, by keeping one lumen clean and using it for blood tests, the results would be accurate.

By Day T-2, my weight had also ballooned. On T-10, I was 62.6kg. However, within a space of eight days, I was up to 64.8kg. If only the dieticians at Addenbrooke's could have seen that! While this seems impressive, I wasn't actually eating all that much; definitely to be gaining all that weight. So why was I gaining? Well, I was on so many fluids that the amount of fluid going in caused me to gain weight – it was as if I was one massive water balloon. I really was having constant fluids – my body was full of water. I was very happy when I first saw my weight increase, and at first, I thought I was genuinely gaining weight by eating a lot. You can only imagine how disappointed I was when my weight plummeted a couple of days after the fluids stopped. The inevitable battle with the dieticians was unfortunately not avoided.

On August 24th, 2016 (Day T-2), a major milestone in my journey was reached when I received my final dose of cyclophosphamide, which was therefore my final dose of chemotherapy. Hopefully it was going to be my final dose of chemo for the rest of my life. I was disappointed to not be able to ring the bell after finishing treatment, which most patients are able to do. My isolation unfortunately prevented it.

Thursday 25th August 2016 (Day T-1). Day T-1 was another break day and the last day before Day 0, when I would receive my new cells. It was a rough day. Not only physically was I feeling ill, but mentally I was on the verge of breakdown. Strawberry laces even got involved, something I had managed to introduce to my breakdowns back in June.

There was good news in the sense that, by 10:00am, I was officially off all fluids, which meant that I was free from a drip stand for at least a few minutes and I didn't have the heavy pressure on my line anymore. I was only free from drip stands for a few minutes, though. Nausea began to kick in, and as I was feeling too sick to take any tablets to deal with it, I was prescribed IV alternatives.

I began to feel worse after my head started hurting. It was a really sharp, painful headache. I was asked on a scale of one to ten on how painful it was. I usually found it impossible to answer these questions because my idea of, for example, a three might be different to a nurse's. However, this time it was an easy answer for me – the pain was on the scale of ten, maybe eleven, perhaps twelve. It was up there with the excruciatingly painful lumbar puncture headaches I'd suffered back in Addenbrooke's when I was recovering from Round 1 of chemo. I'm not really one to cry when I'm physically hurting as I'm very good at working through pain, but it was awful. I've never experienced a headache worse than that. I was prescribed some tramadol, which is a stronger painkiller than paracetamol, but it had little effect. My headache fortunately went away on its own after about an hour.

As I've mentioned, I was on the verge of breakdown, and around noon, I ended up having one. I just wanted to go home. Rachael, who was my nurse that day, was really supportive and spoke to Mum and I about it. She said that she knew that I wanted to go home, but I was in hospital so I could only go home and return to normality once the doctors were happy with my health. I also expressed my concerns of having an NG tube put down, which I knew I was going to throw up. Rachael told me that an NG tube was the best thing for me as my throat was going to be so sore that I would likely be unable to eat much, and if I did throw it up, I wouldn't have to worry about having another one put down because my throat would be so sore it wouldn't be possible. She told me that 99.7% of transplant patients end up on TPN, which was a feed through the Hickman line and contained all the vital nutrients. Therefore, even if the NG tube didn't work, it wasn't the end of the world and alternatives were out there. This was news to me and made me wonder why I had to go through the NG tube at all, but I didn't say anything. I just assumed that TPN was bad news and needed to be used only as a last resort, however common Rachael made it out to be.

Once Rachael left, despite feeling a little bit better, I continued my breakdown. I thought it was sensible to eat a packet of strawberry laces and eat some mashed potato afterwards. I threw it up immediately after, and Rachael was very concerned by my pink, fluffy vomit. She was relieved when I told her I had just eaten some strawberry laces and mash – it was almost as if I had given her a heart attack.

This breakdown was early afternoon, and after everything had calmed down, I decided to go to sleep. I woke up at 7:00pm, completely confused and dazed. I asked Mum what I should have for dinner, but she told me I was too late and the kitchen had closed. I ended up having four digestive biscuits for dinner that evening, which the nurses were able to get for me from the kitchen.

It had been a strange day, and it seemed to have lost structure. I completely forgot to have a shower, so that evening I had a face wash to ensure I was somewhat clean. During that, the registrar came in to speak to Mum and I about how I was feeling for the big day tomorrow and asked if we had any worries about it. Her role that evening was there to reassure us of anything we weren't sure about, as well as answer or clarify any remaining queries. She did go over the what ifs again, but reassured me that should something happen, my mum and dad could quickly be tested as a last resort.

Having already slept for five hours, I was once again asleep that night and was ready for the big day tomorrow – Transplant Day!

***

Friday 26th August 2016 (Day 0 - Transplant Day). My emotions seemed to have swapped with Mum's overnight. Despite the previous day's breakdown, I woke up on the morning of Day 0 feeling well and in good spirits, telling everyone I craved a Domino's pizza and was ready to celebrate with one when I was out of hospital. On the other hand, Mum, who had been worried but mostly positive the previous day, was now in tears. I think it was due to a combination of feeling happy should my transplant be a success and fear of it failing – her happy-sad emotions outweighed each other, and the result was nothing but tears.

It started just like an ordinary day in Cubicle 5 on Ward 34, starting off with breakfast. By this point, my new craving was jam on toast, and it was jam on toast every day. I was eating a lot of it. Dad joined in with our daily jam on toast whenever he was staying on the ward with me. Another new craving I had was actually a drink. A father of a former patient had given away some Capri Suns to the ward because his son had gone off them. For some reason, I was the only one drinking them, and I was drinking a lot of them. Forget the fluids I was on just a couple of days before; they should have just made me drink Capri Sun after Capri Sun. After I had demolished the donated boxes, Sophie, one of the healthcare assistants on the ward, was very kind to go out of her way to buy me my own box of Capri Suns on her way home from work. We offered to pay her, but no, it was gift from her, and my family and I were very grateful.

That morning, Lorna stuck her head through the door of my cubicle to speak to Mum. She warned us of a sweetcorn smell that occurs during transplant. She had this problem with Jacob. Once the cells are infused, the patient starts to smell of sweetcorn. The patients don't smell it, but the parents do, which is a bit of a mystery. She told Mum to pay attention to the smell to see if it happened with me too.

My nurse that day, Naomi, was going to carry out the transplantation procedure. She told me they liked patients to be as clean as possible before having their new stem cells, so I was required to take a shower beforehand. This was fine with me as I preferred my showers in the mornings rather than at night. She said my new cells would be ready anywhere between 11:00am to 12:00pm so I needed to be prepared. Dad, who did not want to miss the transplant, made the four-hour journey from Stowmarket to Bristol and arrived that morning. Kristy wasn't in Bristol on Transplant Day, but because of the two-visitor rule, it was unlikely that she would have been able to be present to see it.

After having my shower, I brushed my teeth in the sink, and after finishing that, I had some reflection time. I was staring at the sink, thinking about everything. Who would have thought one headache in January would lead to me living in Bristol in August the same year? How did I get here? I'm half-

English, half-Salvadorian, a citizen of both the United Kingdom and United States, but now I'm going to have 100% French blood? I'm going to have two birthdays? Who is my twin? A tear might have escaped my eye. I said to Mum how I never would have imagined this happening this time last year when I was on holiday in Nice, France – the holiday which had helped make 2015 one of the greatest years of my life. Exactly a year later, in the worst year of my life so far, I was living in Bristol, fighting for my life. And it was funny because, exactly a year after my holiday in France, I was now to have French blood! Life can turn upside down at any moment, and while I knew that already, my reflection time gave me the chance to really think about it.

Naomi continuously asked when I wanted my NG tube passed. My reply was always either 'later' or 'never', which I think annoyed the nurse a little bit. Naomi told me that it was easier to get it over and done with sooner rather than later because there was no escaping it. I didn't have to worry about having another one put down because by the time they expected it to come out, my throat would be so sore with the mucositis that they would be unable to put one down. I finally agreed to have the NG tube put down in the morning before my transplant, and it was all over and done with. Hopefully, that was the last NG tube I'd ever have to have put down.

Shortly before my transplant, I met the music therapist. I wasn't really sure what a music therapist was, but my guess was that it was someone who would play calm music to help you relax. Every time I'd walked by on Ward C2, calm tunes were played on the guitar to half-asleep children. While this might certainly be the case on Ward C2, on Ward 34 it was the opposite. On Ward 34, it was better! The music therapist told me that being isolated in a hospital room built up stress, frustration, and energy and it was good to bang some drums to get it all out. She brought in an entire trolley of musical instruments, and with my parents joining in, me on the drums and the music therapist with the guitar, we all created a loud and awful-sounding piece of music, perhaps the worst that has ever been created. The music therapist sang while simultaneously playing the guitar, while I was banging the drums as hard as I could, with Mum and Dad playing the bongos and the tambourine. It was definitely one of the weirdest things I had ever done but that didn't take away the usefulness of the session. It wasn't about the quality of music, but it succeeded in helping me release stress, banging drums as hard as I could. Being aggressive did me good. The registrar wanted to come in to give me a pre-transplant check-up, but we didn't let her in until we had finished our piece of music. On her way out, the music therapist said that she would visit me every week for a music session, and if I downloaded an app called Yousician, she would lend me a ukulele and I could learn to play it.

The music therapy session was cut slightly short due to the registrar wanting to check me over before the transplant. This was just a normal check-up done by the doctors on the ward rounds. The heart and lungs sounded fine, my glands were not swollen, and everything seemed to be okay. Everything was well enough to go ahead with the transplant, and now that I was all prepared, the doctor gave the go-ahead. It was transplant time!

My bone marrow transplant took place at 12:00pm on Friday 26th August 2016. The procedure was carried out by Naomi, accompanied by a student nurse, who was observing. Naomi pulled out a giant syringe of my donor's stem cells, an umbilical cord from France, which looked like watery blood. The syringe was very cold; cold enough for me to see the water vapour pouring out of it. It had just come out of the freezer. The syringe was attached to the lumen of my Hickman line, and slowly, over fifteen minutes to prevent any shock to my body, the stem cells were inserted into my bloodstream. No anaesthetic was necessary; I was completely conscious throughout the whole thing, holding Mum's hand all the way. Mum had a strange belief that if she kept hold of my hand throughout the whole thing, the transplant would work. It did not hurt, rather it was just a bit cold, feeling the cells travel through the lumen and into my body.

And fifteen minutes was all it took; all the build-up it involved, with the highly toxic chemo, and it was soon to be over, just like that. This was the final major form of treatment I required, and now all I had to look forward to was recovery and hopefully getting myself out of hospital as quickly as possible.

I had just been reborn, but it didn't feel like it. I now had 100% French blood. I now had a twin; a female in France, who could have been aged anywhere between zero and fifteen at the time. It is a bit strange saying that I have a twin but they're likely to be at a different age to me. I boasted that I had two birthdays; August 29th, 2002, my official birthday, and August 26th, 2016 as my rebirth. It was still early days; just because I'd had my transplant and nothing bad had happened during the procedure didn't necessarily mean it had worked. No one would know if my transplant had worked until I showed signs that my cells had engrafted. A sign of this was no longer being neutropenic, and as you'll have worked out from previous chemo cycles, this took time. The whole thing was just a matter of time.

For a transplant, it seemed very quick. Any other transplant you hear about or see on the TV usually involves complex surgery. Naomi told me it would take twenty minutes for the stem cells to find the bone marrow and start rebuilding, which I found very clever. I asked, if it was so quick, then why go through the entire four rounds of chemo in the first place when you could just destroy it in one and have a transplant? She replied, saying that it worked like a drinks machine, getting rid of the old drink bit by bit and then replacing it with a fresher drink once empty, rather than mixing the two, i.e., getting rid of the unhealthy cells in the blood and bone marrow bit by bit until there's little or nothing left. Once your blood is rid of the unhealthy cells, you can replace them with healthy cells, giving the transplant the best possible chance of success.

Naomi told me that although the transplant was done, it could make me feel a bit dizzy and lightheaded for a little while after. There was no getting up for a couple of hours or so, meaning that if I needed to go to the toilet, I would require assistance from my parents.

After the transplant, my parents went to go get some lunch, which left me on my own for a while. The registrar came in to speak to me about how I was feeling and asked about any concerns I had for the days to come. I was still concerned about the cyclophosphamide. She told me what to expect, such as fevers, nausea, vomiting, diarrhoea, hair loss, loss of appetite, and mucositis. This sounds as horrible and it was, but it was nothing I hadn't experienced before, particularly in the first and second cycles of chemo (not so much the third). I was expecting her to say I could have liver failure, so I was slightly relieved that, when telling me what to expect, she didn't bring this up. As weird as it sounds, I felt glad hearing what the registrar had told me. The cyclophosphamide was going to have a devastating impact, but many of those severe side effects were rare, so I didn't need to worry too much; it was just something to be aware of. I was in the right place should anything happen, anyway. She also said to expect a little bit of GvHD, showing itself through something like a rash, which would actually be a good thing as it would show that the cells were engrafting.

Remember when I said that hopefully I'd had the last NG tube put down? It wasn't. I think they just said that they wouldn't put another one down so they could make me agree to it. Either that or it was pure bad luck. By this point, I did have a sore throat, but it wasn't bad enough for me not to have a NG tube inserted. With paracetamol having no effect, the nurse gave me some tramadol to help ease the pain. I wasn't using my NG tube for any feeds at the time because I was still generally eating well and maintaining a stable weight, so I might as well have used my tube for something. But the liquid tramadol blocked my NG tube. My NG tube was blocked on the same day that I'd had it put down! What were the chances of that happening? How unlucky was I? After many attempts to constantly flush the tube with water, unblocking it failed. Acting quickly because my throat was going to worsen, the nurses decided that they had no choice but to put another NG tube down the following day.

***

Saturday 27th August to Thursday 15th September 2016 (Day 1 to 20). After my transplant, I was now isolated in my hospital cubicle until I was no longer neutropenic, which would show that my new cells had successfully engrafted. Unlike my stay at Kingston House, which had a set routine, being in my cubicle involved a different structure to each day. What I did was the same – board games, watching TV, etc. – but the order I did it in was more varied. This was mostly because I had to be flexible with my time. If I needed an IV medication in the morning, I'd have to have a wash in the evening, and vice versa. Some of my days were different, both in terms of the activities I did and, of course, my health.

I will say this right now: the effects of the chemotherapy were nowhere near as bad as what I was fearing or expecting. Of course, that is not to say I didn't have trouble. It was still a very painful experience, and I felt very unwell on it. But it could be said that I found Round 2 of chemo much worse. The less-intensive chemo actually did me worse; evident by the fact that Round 2 had left me with the threat of intensive care but Round 3 had resulted in just a couple of fevers, which went away on their own. During my entire time in Bristol, I did not get one fever and nausea was not that bad, although still experienced from time to time. Most problems I experienced may have been worsened by chemo, but definitely not caused by it. That being said, the worst side effect I experienced from the treatment was by far my sore throat.

The nurses were right; my throat was going to become very sore. It started off very mild, perhaps a sore, dry throat you get in the morning as soon as you wake up. But the difference between an ordinary sore throat and a chemo sore throat is that an ordinary one usually goes after a drink, depending on how bad it is, whereas a chemo one does not. Drinking anything would burn the ulcers on my throat. It was a burning sensation, at the same time feeling like there was a large cut in my throat. It was painful, but nothing could be done; painkillers did not work. It was just something I had to live with. Eating cornflakes with a throat like that hurt like hell and brought me to tears, and even jelly gave me great difficulty in swallowing. I was actually kind of grateful to have an NG tube and only feel very moderate nausea, because my appetite did decline, although I still kept going and ate as much as I could.

I was determined to do everything I could to work around the pain and keep going, although it did, though very rarely, bring me to tears.

The milk feeds from my NG tube were not much help either; if anything, it was them and not the chemo that brought on my mild nausea. As well as topping up my nutrients and helping my non-stop diarrhoea, the dieticians thought that the milk feeds needed to be adjusted. They decided to give me a half-digested feed. This seemed to work in terms of doing its job, but the problem was if I burped, then the egg-flavoured, out-of-date milk-flavoured itraconazole taste, which was what the feeds gave, would enter my mouth, which made me want to throw up. The dieticians managed to combat this by giving me a strawberry-flavoured feed, which I was very surprised to find out existed, especially since these feeds were not for oral consumption, but nonetheless I went with it. This didn't help much either because with that, when I burped, all I got was a strawberry egg-flavoured out-of-date milk-flavoured itraconazole taste in my mouth. Also, as the feeds were half-digested, it meant that the milk was more watery and less thick, meaning it had less nutrients in it, so I required a larger quantity of it. This didn't improve matters either.

As I've previously mentioned, the half-digested feeds were also to help my constant diarrhoea., At this point I was having to relieve my bowels almost every twenty minutes, maybe even more. I had no idea what I was eating to produce so much, but my body was full of it. After more investigation, the doctors found a bug that was irritating my bowels. This bug was called clostridium difficile, also known as C. difficile, but most commonly referred to by doctors as C. diff. C. diff is what my Year 11 Biology teacher explained as a 'bacterium that gives you the craps like hell', and from experience, I can tell you that she was absolutely right. When learning about it at school, I always used to smile to myself – none of the students had any idea that I knew about C. diff from experience. The good thing was that since it was a bacterial infection, it could be treated with antibiotics, and therefore I was prescribed medication to help manage my diarrhoea, which soon improved and went away for the time being.

Another side effect of the treatment I experienced – which comes as no surprise – was hair loss. One of the nurses on the ward, Alison, said that no patient escapes Ward 34 with hair. What was different from this hair loss and the hair loss from the first two cycles[11] was that this time all of my hair went. Unlike during Round 1, instead of starting with the occasional hair on my shirt or pillow, my hair started falling out at a rapid rate, with me waking up every morning with large clumps of hair on my pillow. I wasn't upset by this because I had experienced hair loss the first time from Round 1. I had a haircut in my room shortly after my transplant, and by the time I escaped Ward 34, I was completely bald. I looked like a giant thumb or a jellybean. I was also subject to a lot of jokes from my family. Mum said I looked like a baby penguin when a few strands of my hair remained, and once it was all gone, I was given the nickname 'Slappy Sausage Head'. If I'm honest, I soon embraced the completely bald look and even took a liking to it. Some of my friends liked it too, saying it made me look more grown up.

Another issue I encountered was with my legs. I experienced a lot of pain during my isolation period. Due to my very low blood levels – caused by the chemotherapy – I required blood and platelet transfusions. I always looked

---

[11] Strangely, I did not lose my hair in Round 3. However, it did suffer significant damage in the first two cycles, so I spent the majority of the rest of 2016 after April either bald or with uneven, patchy hair.

forward to a nice blood transfusion because I'd feel amazing after one. But I also didn't have any magnesium in my blood, so I needed magnesium supplements through my Hickman line. While having my IV magnesium, as well as struggling for breath, I started to go very red and hot, but as soon as I took my blanket off, I started shivering. The healthcare assistant took my temperature, but everything was normal and there was no fever. I then started to experience something very similar to severe growing pains, and my legs began to burn. It was a reaction to the magnesium, and therefore the nurse stopped it and gave me some paracetamol. The redness and the tight chest soon cleared up, but my leg pain persisted and left me in agony. Dad was up all night massaging my legs, because I was in so much pain I couldn't sleep, the pain often so unbearable that it left me in tears just wanting the night to be over. When trying to get up to go to the toilet, my legs collapsed on me, and I almost fell before he thankfully caught me in his arms. Had he not caught me, it would have put me and my Hickman line in great danger.

The nurses called the night doctor, who couldn't find anything wrong. This annoyed me because I was in excruciating pain. But the doctor said that there was no escaping the magnesium; I needed it, so it was just put on at a slower rate instead. I can't remember what time I fell asleep that night, but it was definitely around 4:00 or 5:00am, barely getting any sleep before being woken up for my 6:00am blood test. The growing pain sensation disappeared that night, but the burning pain did remain for at least the next week, especially when I was in the shower. If water, hot or cold, touched my feet, my legs received a burning feeling. It was like I was standing in a pool of burning acid. I didn't realise how destructive magnesium could be.

August 29th, 2016, was my fourteenth birthday. I was lucky to reach fourteen after such a chaotic and traumatic year – that I had made it surprised me. Unfortunately, my birthday, as predicted, was spent in isolation in Cubicle 5 on Ward 34 at the Bristol Royal Hospital for Children. What a great birthday ... It was not the place I wanted to spend my birthday, and everyone who wished me a happy birthday that day also shared the same view. But my reply to most of them was that there were good things to come. Did I want to spend my birthday isolated in a hospital room? No. Did I want to spend my birthday recovering from the nasty side effects of chemotherapy? No. Did I want to eat hospital food on my birthday? Certainly not. Were there good things to come though? Yes. Once I was out of this place, there was even more reason to celebrate.

It did kind of suck because I wasn't even allowed a birthday cake, but because it was quite a dull birthday, the nurses did everything they could to make sure my birthday was as much like a birthday as possible. First thing in the morning, they all came into my cubicle to sing 'Happy Birthday' to me before my nurse for the day gave me a present on behalf of the play team. I received a can of deodorant, which was kind of them. Rachael made me a birthday banner the day before, which included things like Minecraft and WWE on it, which was very kind of her considering how pressured nurses are for time. I loved the banner, and it was stuck on the door of the bathroom.

Instead of my planned birthday KFC, I had the hospital's roast beef for lunch instead, which wasn't that bad. In fact, my birthday wasn't all that bad – not the best, and definitely the worst, but it wasn't the waste of a day it might seem. Everyone tried their hardest to make it my birthday, and in the circumstances that I was in, I was in surprisingly good health that day to be able to enjoy it. Besides, I'd had some pretty rubbish birthdays, such as my eighth birthday when a massive tree fell down and crushed my garden, so the disappointment of not being able to celebrate to the fullest had been experienced before. Above all, it was a birthday to remember. At least I can look back in years to come and remember exactly where I spent my fourteenth birthday. Not many people can.

In terms of keeping myself occupied while in my hospital room, I had a lot of things to do. Hospital life wasn't as boring as it seemed. I should mention, by this time, despite not feeling terrible, I wasn't feeling good enough to be able to use my exercise bike. It was just gathering dust, so the physiotherapist took it back and gave it to someone else – probably for the same reason I was given it. I'd only been given it because it was gathering dust.

The music therapist did let me borrow a ukulele, and I continued to participate in weekly music therapy sessions and was able to practice the ukulele on my own with the help of an app. I was getting good at it, and I was proud of the tunes I was creating, but there was no way I'd be able to perfect it by the time I was discharged. Not keeping up with playing the ukulele is another regret I have. I also had many of my board games I had brought with me, lots of electronic devices, some wrestling DVDs, and, most importantly, the company of my parents. I had everything I needed to survive something as boring as a hospital room, and I was surprisingly keeping sane locked inside four walls. Mentally, I had lasted a lot longer than I had anticipated.

About a week or so into my isolation, I met Kate, the assistant play specialist. Kate would visit me around once or twice a week just to play games with me, and sometimes with Mum too. I enjoyed her visits because it was good to have extra company and someone to talk to besides the four – in my case so far, three – named visitors. She introduced three really cool games to me. One of these games was called 'A-Z', which involves writing the alphabet down a piece of paper. Then, players take turns in choosing a category, such as foods, countries, or animals, and all players need to think of something for each letter, getting a point for each. But a player only gets the point if no other players have written it down either. After being introduced to this game, which only required a pen and paper, Mum and I played it a lot during our time in Bristol. I really do recommend this to any family looking for things to do in hospital because it was so simple and really fun too. I know it doesn't sound like the most exciting game, but the key to surviving hospital is keeping your brain busy with other things.

Another game we were introduced to was 'Uno Roboto', which had the same aims as Uno but involved a robot. It could be just a normal game of Uno until it would tell a player to, for example, make a nickname for another player or draw cards until they picked up a yellow card, completely messing up the game for them. It was a very cool game, and Mum bought it after leaving Bristol, and we still play it to this day when we have friends or family game nights. The robot is not popular with a lot of people.

The third and final game introduced to us was 'Caption It'. Players are given a number of funny captions and a picture, and the players have to give the best caption they can for it. The judge would then decide which caption was the funniest and best for the picture, awarding the points. Mum and I loved this game too, but following hospital rules, we were unable to get our hands on a new version of it. Mum wasn't going to risk buying second-hand from Amazon just yet. The three games mentioned above, which Kate introduced to us, are only three of the games I recommend playing in hospital. The list goes on and on when it comes to the games I played in hospital, but I can tell you at least 99% of my days involved a game of Scrabble, and Monopoly was also popular with me. The play assistant also gave me a couple of Lego sets for me to do, just to prevent myself from any further boredom, and the best thing was that she let me keep them.

Once August was over and September started, hospital life continued, but with one more addition. School started again. Now in Year 10, it was a crucial year for me with GCSEs starting. My options were History, French, and German, in addition to the core subjects of English literature, English language, maths and double science. Hospital school in Bristol was very different to Addenbrooke's. There was a school room, but it could also be done at bedside, which was where I had to start to my isolation rules. Even if I could have gone to the school room, I wouldn't have done as it was so far away. You have to remember that the biggest difference between my paediatric experiences at Addenbrooke's and Bristol was that paediatric care was distributed across several wards in Addenbrooke's and most of my tests were done in adult clinics, whereas Bristol had an entire hospital dedicated to paediatric care. The school room at Addenbrooke's was exclusive to one ward, but the school room at Bristol was for the entire children's hospital. Unlike Addenbrooke's, which had one main secondary school teacher who specialised in English and could teach Maths, in addition to a Science teacher and a Maths specialist, Bristol had a lot more teachers. There were three maths teachers, an English and history teacher, a science teacher, and a French teacher. There was even an art teacher, in a hospital, who could teach her subject at bedside! And these were only the teachers I met; I'm sure there were many more, considering there was also a headteacher. A headteacher in a hospital! I found a lot of this unbelievable. Unlike Addenbrookes, which had one full-time secondary teacher in a hospital, Bristol had an entire school in a hospital.

School started off slowly. I first met the art teacher, who – concerned by the slow start to school and anxious that the GCSE period of my school career should begin – started to teach me English by reading me poetry at bedside. School began to get more serious as the days went by, with me having weekly sessions with the French teacher, who revised the tenses with me. My favourite teacher was Dave, who was one of the maths teachers. This was because he showed very similar interests to me. Like myself, he was a WWE fan and was fascinated by the BootyOs box I had displayed in my room.

It seemed as if there was no consistency to the hospital school at Bristol. While maths and French lessons were regular, aside from that, it felt as if random teachers were showing up at my door every day. I met the science teacher but never had a lesson, most of my English lessons were taught by the art teacher, I had art lessons when I wasn't taking art, and I had one history lesson then never saw the history teacher again! However, aside from the issues I had with the Bristol hospital school, I found it good not only to recap on the educational side of things, but also just to keep busy. Some school was better than no school. I didn't mind the variety of lessons, and I was aware that the teachers were working with what they had. Despite all lessons being educational, there was still time for some fun activities, where I was able to create some drawings on iPads and play educational maths games, which really weren't helping my GCSEs considering how easy they were. Following the rules, the iPads were always covered with plastic wallets, which was a strange way to use an iPad, but having spent time in a place where everything has to be clean for your own safety, it would have been weird seeing the iPad without any covering. School was mostly every day, during which Mum and Dad would disappear to go on their lunch break or Mum would meet Lorna for their daily coffee.

Just because I couldn't have any visitors didn't mean my family couldn't have any. My time in isolation was spent, to no surprise, in isolation and away from the outside world. But my friend Ryan and his parents, Charlotte and Roy, who were coming back from their holiday in Cornwall that summer, came to meet Mum for a coffee at Costa in the main hospital concourse. Also, my next-door neighbours, Sharon, Sean, and Jas, came to visit my parents and Kristy in Bristol, and I was able to wave to them from my hospital window. Sharon had raised some money on a stall, and she kindly gave me £160 of it to spend on whatever I liked, which I was very thankful for. It really surprised me, and it was great because it gave me something to look forward to, even if it couldn't physically be opened by me.

Speaking of surprises, it wasn't just visitors I couldn't see that kept my memories of Stowmarket alive. I woke up one morning to receive some mail: a parcel from the Stowmartian, Stowmarket's town mascot. I received a mug, which when it was heated could change colour, and a few other gifts. It really made my day, and I was very grateful for the gifts and the support I was receiving from back home.

***

Friday 16th September 2016 (Day 21). Friday 16th September was a different, and rather strange, day on Ward 34. Every year, for one day, the hospital staff dress up as the chosen theme for their ward, and this year the theme for Ward 34 was *Toy Story*.

So all the nurses were dressed up as *Toy Story* characters, and I woke up to this surprise on the Friday morning. Some of the costumes were great, I must say.

There was also something else different about this day. Dr. G was doing the ward rounds, and when he entered the room, he asked if I noticed anything different about his and the registrar's appearance. The doctors weren't dressed up as *Toy Story* characters ... I eventually gave up and said I had no idea and he had to tell us.

He wasn't wearing an apron, something that was mandatory for anyone entering my room, other than my four named visitors. Dr. G told me that my neutrophils had reached 0.5! My cells had engrafted, and I was showing signs that my transplant was a success! While Dr. G spoke, the registrar examined me, and when she asked me how I felt about the good news, I said, "Let's hope it stays that way!" I was told I was now out of isolation and I could spend the day at Sam's House if I wished. I wasn't allowed to stay the night at Sam's House, because, although I was feeling much better, I still needed to be monitored and regular blood tests had to continue as usual.

I was shocked to hear this news, especially so early. As you can probably tell, it was sprung on me just like that. I had never expected it to come so soon, and I was over the moon to hear such news. By no means was this the end of my journey, but it sure was the beginning of the end, and the final stage to the main part of my journey had begun: recovery.

Despite the good news, my recent blood tests had shown very high tacrolimus levels. Tacrolimus toxicity is capable of causing nausea, headaches, and seizures. I was feeling well in myself though, so it wasn't necessarily something to worry about; perhaps my blood had just been taken from the wrong Hickman line lumen. Tacrolimus was known to be a sticky drug, hence the reason it could only be put through the lumen with the green sticker. Just to be safe, my nurse that day, Jess, told me she needed to take some blood via a finger prick. This was a way of getting some blood without having to get it out my line, which was likely to be causing some inaccurate results. No blood was coming out of my finger, so Jess took a sample from my thumb instead. And my blood started gushing out.

The results did find that the tacrolimus levels were nothing to worry about and it was likely that my blood had been taken from the wrong lumen. High tacrolimus levels were never spoken of again. I did feel the short-term effects of the countless finger and thumb pricks I received because of the failed attempts – never try building Lego so soon after having been pricked with a needle ten times!

The amazing news of no longer being neutropenic changed my plans for the day. On this day, I was supposed to have a visitor. Auntie Karen and Uncle John were coming down from Bury St. Edmunds to Bristol to visit us for the weekend, and the plan was to let Auntie Karen be the fourth of my four named visitors. Unfortunately, that meant I wouldn't see Uncle John, although my family probably would have done something and gone to visit both of them without me. However, with this unexpected, amazing news, this wasn't the case anymore, and we could spend time as a united family at Sam's House.

After my thumb prick, I was allowed to leave my cubicle. After twenty-six days of isolation, Day 21 was the day I received my first breath of fresh air. I literally ran out of the ward and into the lifts, which wasn't smart because I made myself dizzy and lightheaded afterwards. It was the first time I had run in a while, but it just showed how much energy I had accumulated in isolation.

An issue then occurred regarding how I was going to

get to Sam's House. Mum and I favoured the Sam's House taxi system, and on this day, that was what we did. However, the next day (September 17th), Dad and Kristy arrived for the weekend. There was no way someone like me, who had just had a bone marrow transplant, could get up a hill as steep as St. Michael's Hill. But Dad favoured the exercise, and he won the argument, only because he was the only one able to call for a taxi as Mum is not very good at taking her phone with her. So, I, who had just been allowed out of hospital, had to walk up the steepest hill I had ever climbed – a hill that even healthy people struggle up. I was dizzy and out of breath, and by the time I arrived at Sam's House, I had almost collapsed. Exercise wasn't appropriate just yet, and my parents realised this and ordered me a wheelchair from Amazon as soon as we got to our Sam's House room.

The weather was also boiling! It was a hot, sunny day in Bristol on the weekend of September 16th and 17th, which everyone back in Suffolk was jealous of. Back in Stowmarket, it was a cold, wet, dull day, and the entire Stowmarket High School, in my honour, completed a ten-mile walk to raise money for the Children's Cancer and Leukaemia Group (CCLG). This was a charity that I did not know much about at the time. Stowmarket High School managed to raise a very impressive £14,185.03 for the charity, and I heard many stories about events that had happened on the day. One story I heard was that a student thought it would be sensible to throw a rock at a wasps' nest, and I'm sure you can guess what happened next. The school apparently received a lot of complaints from parents about their children coming home wet and muddy, but they were quickly silenced by other parents who argued that that was nothing compared to what I was going through. They had a point – if I had a child, I would rather them face a ten-mile walk and come home with muddy clothes than watch them be ill with leukaemia, suffer four rounds of gruelling chemotherapy, relocate to a city hundreds of miles away, and then top it off with a transplant.

On the Friday, we met Auntie Karen and Uncle John at Sam's House, who were a little late because the taxi driver got them lost. The following day, when the rest joined us, Mum, Kristy, and Auntie Karen went into Broadmead to look around Primark, leaving Dad, Uncle John, and I to stay in the Sam's House room. Uncle John always has something interesting to say, so it was good to see him for a bit, though it was in a very different and slightly stranger setting than normal.

Auntie Karen and Uncle John spent time with us all weekend, staying at a nearby hotel. Because of my restrictions, I couldn't really go anywhere, so I only really saw them at Sam's. On the Saturday and Sunday I was allowed to spend the day at Sam's but had to stay the night on the ward. This would continue until the doctors were confident that I could be trusted with a night at Sam's House. We knew this would be very soon, perhaps after the weekend.

***

Monday 19th September 2016 (Day 24). I spent the night on the ward the previous night, which went well, and it was clear that I was getting better. I knew that a discharge was imminent, but were the doctors going to discharge me today? A few of the other patients, including Jacob, who were ahead in their transplant journey, had already been discharged to Sam's House, so I hoped I would be next. That day, one of the BMT speciality doctors was doing the ward rounds. She said she was going to give me a night at Sam's House, and if it went well, I would be officially discharged from Ward 34 the next morning!

I couldn't believe how quickly it had gone by – I had been told it would be four to six weeks in isolation after transplant, but I was out of isolation in three. I felt so relieved. My journey was far from over, but all the hard work had been done. It surprised me how those scary consultations with Dr. M and Dr. A were only a couple of months ago. It was a challenge and a massive risk, but nowhere near the life-ending experience I was anticipating. I was finally out on the other side, and I felt a great sense of relief.

I had gotten over the difficult period of isolation and from then on, it was all about recovery. Although I wasn't officially discharged, staying the night at Sam's House meant that it was time to start packing things up. I wasn't going to be staying on Ward 34 for much longer. Mum and I began to move out a lot of clutter that we had accumulated over the past month, including DVDs, a PlayStation, essentials, such as clothes, and boxes full of chocolate bars. We had so much stuff that we required help from the healthcare assistant, and by the time we had got the belongings out to the front of the hospital, we had missed our taxi to Sam's House and had to call for another one.

It was great to be able to spend the night at Sam's House. I felt I was finally getting my freedom back, even if it meant I had to be back on Ward 34 in the morning. That evening, Mum and I sat in the kitchen area, having dinner with Lorna and Jacob, who had at this point been discharged, and fellow bone marrow transplant patient, Reece, and his grandmother. Reece had his transplant at Bristol, coming from Slough. He didn't have leukaemia but another blood condition, requiring a bone marrow transplant. His mum, Cath, stayed with him, although she wasn't here on this occasion. We were also joined by Sam, from Somerset, whose son, Daryl, had just had his second bone marrow transplant. Although I saw him around from time to time, I never actually met Daryl because by the time I was off the ward, he had developed a really bad cough and had been isolating in his room at Sam's House. I was interested to hear that Daryl had made it in the newspapers when trying to get funding for a second transplant as the NHS only funded the first at the time. Fortunately for him, he received the funding and had his second transplant, and I believe that he is continuing to do well to this day.

***

Tuesday 20th September 2016 (Day 25). Mum and I were back in Cubicle 5 on the ward the next morning, where we finished packing everything that we were unable to take with us the previous day. The first night at Sam's was a success. There were no problems with sickness or fever, and everything had gone smoothly. Once we had finished the packing, it was a long wait for the doctor, so we passed the time playing games, including a game of the classic A-Z.

The BMT speciality doctor officially discharged me on Tuesday 20th September 2016, which marked the final time I was to be discharged as an inpatient. Providing everything went well, the life I would live, attached to the hospItal, would be done as an outpatient. She went through the strict rules of what I was required to do and not do once I was discharged.

First of all, I was to continue the clean diet for 100 days, meaning strictly no takeaways and no food that had been left sitting out for a long time, such as buffets. I was also not allowed to go to crowded places, so shopping and going to restaurants needed to be avoided. If I had a fever, unlike Addenbrooke's, where I would return to the ward straight away, in Bristol, I was required to go to A&E and go through that process instead.

Also, I was now to have outpatient check-ups on Day Beds. Unlike Addenbrooke's, there was more freedom at Bristol because I was only required to have check-ups there two or three times a week, depending on the week. I didn't understand this; I thought having a transplant required you to be monitored more closely. It was so strange how I was at risk in Cambridge but nowhere near transplant level and yet I required daily check-ups there, whereas at Bristol I had a stem cell transplant and only needed to be monitored every few days. Nevertheless, I wasn't complaining, as having to go to PDU every day in Cambridge was not only time consuming but stressful, and not having to go anywhere made me feel great.

But not going to hospital as often would be detrimental to my already suffering schoolwork. Before I left Cubicle 5 for good, Mum had a quick conversation with one of the maths teachers at the hospital school. He explained to us how school would work when I was discharged. Because I wasn't going to be at the hospital every day, school was going to be a bit hit and miss. The teachers would try to catch me on Day Beds, but while at Sam's House, I would have no schooling. This meant that for a while, I wasn't going to have any regular schooling, which, depending on how long I was staying in Bristol for, would have a severe impact on my studies. Mum said it was a shame that the teachers couldn't come to Sam's House. It was then that I realised I needed to get back to normal as soon as possible. Focusing on my future was now the priority, alongside my recovery.

***

I was now officially discharged from Ward 34, and from then on, all appointments with the doctor would be on Day Beds. I was now staying at Sam's House until the doctors told me I could go home. Therefore, I was almost free but not completely free since more recovery was needed beforehand. The good thing was that I was no longer severely neutropenic, so I spent the majority of the next few weeks feeling fairly well, with just a few issues here and there.

This was not how I felt to start off with, though. I should mention, I still had my NG tube by the time I was discharged, which, although I no longer needed, I kept for medicines and nightly feeds to help keep the dieticians away for good. On Wednesday 21st September, I was due for my first check-up on Day Beds, which was a bit earlier than I was used to, at 9:30am. That meant rushing the medicine-taking process, which I usually spread throughout the morning to prevent me from feeling sick. That morning, I took all my tablets, while Mum put the itraconazole – which, by this time, was changed back to liquid – down my tube. Following this, I rushed my breakfast and downed a glass of orange juice. None of this was a good combination for someone recovering from chemotherapy, whose gut had been torn apart by the chemo and had difficulty digesting things.

I felt relatively well going into Day Beds that morning, and I was confident it was going to be yet another good day for the progress I was making. But it wasn't, and after going to my cubicle[12], I began to feel nauseous. Suddenly, I knew I was going to be sick, and it just came out of nowhere. I asked Mum to go find a sick bowl, but she couldn't find one, and I

---

[12] BMT patients had their own cubicle in the clinic to keep them away from other patients who may be infectious.

puked all over the floor, which the healthcare assistant had the unfortunate responsibility of having to clean up. She said that it was preferable that children stop being sick before being discharged, which worried me because I was scared that I would have to return to the ward so quickly after being discharged. I soon found out that that was their explanation for not having any sick bowls in the clinic and not a health issue to worry about.

I don't think it was me being unwell as such, rather that I'd had a rushed morning and my stomach was sensitive because it had been destroyed by the chemotherapy. The NG tube was hanging from my mouth, and I asked Mum to get a nurse to pull it out, but all the nurses were busy and the healthcare assistant was reluctant to do anything she wasn't qualified to do. For at least five minutes, maybe even ten, I had a tube sticking out of my mouth. It got to the point where I couldn't take it anymore and asked Mum to take the tube out for me, and typically, it wasn't until then that a nurse finally arrived. I felt so much better afterwards and was actually relieved that the NG tube was out.

This was my only bad memory of being an outpatient in Bristol. I usually say that if it wasn't for the leukaemia and transplant side of things, I would do Bristol all over again in a heartbeat. The city I was in and the people we were with made me enjoy it so much more than expected. The next few weeks were what I saw as the golden weeks.

A lot of time was spent in the kitchen of Sam's House, and we would spend a lot of time with Lorna and Cath, and, for the first week or so, Sam. Jacob and Reece spent the majority of the time on the PlayStation in one of the living rooms. I preferred the adult company and usually spent my time in the kitchen, although sometimes I hung back in my room by myself watching daytime TV. *Jeremy Kyle's Emergency Room* was a new addition to my routine.

Soon, Daryl was discharged, and he and Sam went home, which left Jacob and Lorna and Reece and Cath. We were soon to be joined by Katie and her mum, Sue. I believe Katie had aplastic anaemia, the same condition as Reece, and was in Bristol for her work-up plan, and therefore we only saw her for a few days. It is a small world. It turns out that I went to toddler's group with Katie as she lived nearby, and although we went to different schools, she knew a lot of people from Stowmarket High School. I was even friends with some of my friends who went there. Since Dad had worked with Jacob's dad, Craig, two out of the three families we stayed with in Bristol had some form of connection to my family before our bone marrow transplants. Funny how we all got something rare for our age, we all ended up in the same place at the same time, and three of us four families had some form of connection before even ending up in Bristol.

Of course, we did not forget about Joe, who I'd participated in food tasting with on Ward C9 at Addenbrooke's and needed a transplant but was having trouble getting to that stage. Mum and Lorna checked the board of all residents at Sam's House to see if Joe's name popped up. It never did.

In terms of a routine at Bristol, there wasn't a fixed routine as such like there was during the days of Kingston House. Every day was different. The days I was due for a check-up on Day Beds were usually the same Jacob was, and so our taxi to the hospital was shared with Mum, Lorna, and Jacob – who by this point had a major cheese puff addiction due to the steroids he was having to take and was eating twelve bags of Wotsits a day. Shopping was done every day because, like I previously said, when it comes to chemotherapy, one day you fancy something and the next the thought of it makes you sick. Most shopping was done individually, but sometimes all three families (Mum and me, Lorna and Jacob, and Cath and Reece) went shopping together. I particularly remember one shopping trip to the Co-op down the road. We broke the rules because Jacob, Reece, and I, all transplant patients, were going shopping, but none of us, including the parents, really cared. There was a lot of shouting and misuse with the wheelchairs, at one point Reece running over Cath's foot. We found it amusing, although Cath did not. Jacob and Reece were both in their wheelchairs, although I wasn't because a trip to Sainsbury's with my parents a few days before had almost ended up with me being tipped out when I hit a curb. My wheelchair use lasted about a week, and after that, I walked everywhere or took the taxi to get to the hospital.

I also tried my best to maintain the illusion that I was well, doing everything I could to not become dependent on my wheelchair. The short period of time I did use it, I felt it was used unnecessarily. I only needed it for the massive hill, yet it felt like I was using it all the time.

On the topic of shopping, shops that were usually busy anyway were even more busy. Since it was September, the students were back to university[13]. Sometimes we went shopping when it was their lunchbreak, and the Co-op would be flooded with university students.

Every day, whether we had been at the hospital or not, the afternoon would be spent in the kitchen area, where all three of our families would socialise and talk about everything that was going on. We would all cook separate dinners but eat at roughly the same time. We all got through it together. We

[13] The University of Bristol is located directly behind Sam's House.

were all going through a tough time, and we were almost like a temporary family.

Kristy was doing her A-Levels back in Stowmarket, so she would rarely come visit us in Bristol. Although sometimes she would, particularly at the weekends. Dad, who was balancing taking care of my sister, working, and visiting me, would visit me at least every week, sometimes twice, meaning he made the four-hour trip to Bristol and back at least once a week. Sometimes he did the trip and back twice within the space of two days! When Dad was visiting and brought Kristy, we usually went for family days out in open spaces, following the doctors' instructions[14]. We had an afternoon out at the Clifton Suspension Bridge one day in September, and I loved it and thought the view from it was beautiful. Just before I left Year 9, in History, we'd learned about the Industrial Revolution and Isambard Kingdom Brunel, who was the architect for the bridge. We also further explored Bristol when Dad was there, although not much of it. Most of our exploring was done trying to find new supermarkets, so we could have a break from the daily Co-op and the occasional Sainsbury's. ASDA was quite popular, and Dad was the only one who was able to visit Tesco because it was on the very outskirts of the city and was quite busy.

The days in Day Beds were also different. Sometimes I would have school, other times I wouldn't – it all depended on which teacher was available. Also, sometimes I wouldn't even see the doctor. If the doctor was busy or there was no doctor available, I would see Marie, the Advanced Nurse Practitioner, who could do everything a GP could except prescribe

---

[14] You'll notice a lack of consistency. For every rule that we seemed to have followed, we ended up breaking another. Some of this was intentional, but a lot of the time it was unintentional.

medication and didn't have the title of 'doctor'. Marie's role was pretty much like the Emergency Care Practitioners that you get in GP surgeries today. Her purpose was to make sure I wasn't spending hours in Day Beds, giving me a quick check-up that would get me back out as soon as possible if a check-up was all I seemed to require. She could also provide advice and get the doctors to prescribe medications for me if need be. Day Beds was nowhere near as slow as PDU, with most visits lasting half an hour, if I was lucky, to two hours on a bad day. I was never there past closing time like I was on PDU, and I always got out before lunchtime, something I praise Bristol for.

***

So far, I have mostly mentioned the social aspects of my time in Bristol, briefly touching on the medical side of things. Below I have explained the medical aspects of my time in Bristol in more depth. A few key things happened to me that September.

First of all, because I was very prone to lung infections with my weakened immune system, I had to inhale a medication called pentamidine. Pentamidine was good for preventing lung infections, and it was necessary for me to take it, but the problem was that it was toxic. Just like chemo, I suppose. The drug was so toxic that the nurses were not allowed to enter the room while I was breathing it in and couldn't go back into the room until two hours after I had left. What I wasn't really sure about was that, if it was so toxic, how come I could breathe it in and feel fine afterwards but they couldn't go anywhere near it? For them to put me through that, it must have been very effective. I was responsible for controlling the drug and I turned the inhaler on and off, breathing it in constantly for about fifteen minutes or so until I was instructed to stop by the nurse on the other side of the door window. The entire procedure did not hurt one bit, and had I not been told, I wouldn't have realised that the pentamidine was toxic.

Surprisingly, I never got GvHD, despite the doctor's expectations. However, it was suspected that I did have it to begin with. I ended up developing a rash down below in my groin area, but the Advanced Nurse Practitioner speculated it to be thrush and gave me some cream to help deal with it. The cream did help, and the rash eventually went away. As this was thrush cream, I think it was confirmed that the rash was thrush and not GvHD.

Once I was discharged, the immunosuppressant drug, tacrolimus, was going to be cut in half, reducing the amount I was taking. This was a good thing because it showed that my body was increasingly able to cope on its own. Once I was completely off immunosuppressants, I would have to wait a full year until I could receive all my vaccinations all over again. This was because the chemo had wiped everything out from my previous immune system, including my antibodies.

I also started the antibiotic, phenoxymethylpenicillin. Despite little evidence to suggest that the penicillin is effective in reducing the risk of infection, it is thought to prevent a certain lung infection. I would be required to take the penicillin for the rest of my life. However, this was where Addenbrooke's and Bristol clashed, with different ideologies. Addenbrookes was sceptical about the effectiveness of the lifelong medication, but Bristol preferred to stick with it as a precaution. Different doctors will tell you different things, but Bristol's stance is strongly for the lifelong medication, although they are aware that it may not be that effective. I guess it is better to be safe than sorry.

Perhaps the most important of all were my blood test

results. Blood tests were no longer every day now that I was staying at Sam's, but I did have blood tests every time I was in Day Beds. My blood count continuously showed good numbers, meaning I was well and still no longer severely neutropenic. But the most important of all was the chimerism test. The origins of the name 'chimerism' are really interesting. It stems from the idea of two people living as one, and that is technically what a BMT patient is doing. In fact, one interesting fact I learned since while doing research is that if you are a male recipient with a female donor (which I was), then of course you're still a male, and if you did a swab of the cheek, the DNA collected would be XY chromosomes, meaning male. But if you looked at the DNA in the blood, it would show up with XX chromosomes, meaning female. Of course, this works the other way around if you're a female with a male donor. The chimerism test tested the percentage of donor cells in my blood, and mine showed that my bone marrow was 100% donor cells, which was amazing news! There was now no doubt that the transplant was a success! It was just a matter of my bone marrow continuing to function properly to ensure a healthy recovery and a smooth transition to normality. Surprisingly, I didn't require a bone marrow aspiration as the blood tests were enough to prove I was going in the right direction.

So, like I said, from the time I was discharged from Ward 34 to the time I was discharged from Bristol altogether, it was just about recovery and monitoring how I was doing. To keep me as healthy as possible, it was still important that I regularly took my medicines. By the time I left Bristol, despite feeling well in myself, I was still on five medications: phenoxymethylpenicillin, tacrolimus, folic acid, itraconazole, and acyclovir.

***

Friday 30th September 2016 (Day 35). It was a normal morning on Day Beds. I had just had my dressing changed, followed by a lesson on fractions with the maths teacher. We had only just received a list from Stowmarket High School on what I needed to be taught, so while hospital school was still sporadic, it was at least starting to get serious.

Chris came into my bedspace to speak to me, Mum, and Dad, who told us that she had good news. I wasn't really sure what the good news would be, and I wasn't expecting she would say what she did. My prediction was that she was going to say something about my blood tests and how I was continuing to improve day by day. I was shocked and surprised when she said I could go home!

I had done so well, and although there were still some challenges ahead, I had got through the major stuff a lot quicker than anyone else. It was expected I'd be at Sam's House for at least a month after being discharged from Ward 34, but I was actually out within two weeks of being discharged from the ward. On the ward, I had gone without a fever, and aside from my sore throat and diarrhoea, I'd only experienced the mildest of chemo side effects. A bonus was that I was one of 0.3%, as Rachael claimed, to not end up on TPN, although I don't think that's an official statistic, rather an estimation. It was a miracle to have recovered so well, and the moving on process was speedy. It sure felt great, and I counted myself lucky to have survived so well.

In such a short period of time, my family was about to leave the people we had created so many strong friendships with – the people we no doubt wouldn't have got through it all without. Chris told us that Addenbrooke's wanted to see me for a check-up the next Monday, and Bristol wanted to see me again in a month's time, but other than that, I was free to continue my recovery at home. Unfortunately, I was forbidden to have KFC on the way home at the service station, having to stick to my 100-day clean diet. The Sam's House restrictions, which I broke so many times, applied at home too – no going to busy places.

My first reaction to being told I could go home was "Let's get out of here!" But Mum remembered that that evening Kristy was having a few friends over for Dominos. Therefore, they didn't want to disturb and said I would go home the next day instead. I protested, saying I didn't trust Kristy, just because of what she had been up to recently, but I reluctantly agreed to go home the next morning instead. I kept it a secret that I was coming home, and no one knew except the people at Bristol and us. It was so difficult when texting my uncle who asked when I knew I was coming home. I had just received the news, but I had to very bluntly reply, "I don't know." So, the plan was to surprise Kristy and my family and friends when I returned home the next day.

Because I was told I could go home but decided we would have another night at Sam's House, we thought we would use the remaining afternoon and evening to explore a bit more of Bristol. Once again, we broke the rules. Looking at how many times we broke these rules, I really do wonder if we were aware that we were actually breaking them. We were definitely conscious of them because I am highlighting the importance of them here. Every family broke the rules, so it was good to know that we weren't the only ones. Judging by some families, we weren't the worst when it came to the rules either! We went to Cribbs Causeway, which is a major shopping centre and retail park in Bristol.

Reece was discharged the same day as I was, so he and Cath went home that afternoon. Katie hadn't gone to transplant yet. This left us and the Krutke family – Lorna, Craig, Jacob, and Jacob's sister, Katie, who, like Kristy, was still living at home but visited occasionally. Because we were going home, it was soon going to be just them remaining. That evening, us two families stayed up late having drinks and telling stories about the nurses and doctors we liked and disliked, both in Bristol and at Addenbrooke's, such as nurses who put their gloves on in a funny way, as well as stories about our diagnoses and the scary emergency moments in hospital. It was a great 'goodbye' evening, but these people were almost like a temporary family, and it was sad that we were already on the final evening, especially since that morning I'd had no idea I was going home. Our goodbye wasn't even planned.

***

Saturday 1st October 2016 (Day 36). I was going home, and I expressed so much joy! I couldn't wait to return to normality again, and I was so close to achieving it. I was so close to once again living the life I lived previously; a normal one. But with this joy also came some great sadness. Leaving Bristol was sadder than arriving. There were tears that morning between Mum and Lorna. We had managed to build a strong friendship with her and her family during our time in Bristol. We also felt bad for them, since they were still stuck in Bristol but had arrived before us. Jacob was getting better, but he still had a number of obstacles in his way, such as GvHD. It had been expected that I'd be the last remaining out of the social group due to my late arrival, until Katie arrived for her transplant, anyway. We encouraged them to stay strong and keep going, and we were going to see them back at Addenbrooke's very soon.

Like I said, no one knew that I was coming home. Once

we had packed our bags, we were out of Sam's House, which I didn't say goodbye to, rather a see you later, due to the fact that I was going to be returning in a month anyway. We were allowed to stay there for check-ups as well, which avoided us having to do the drive there and back in one day. It was just a four-hour drive to go, and I was straight home!

No, I wasn't. Remember when I said that Kristy had a 'few friends over' for Dominos? My suspicions were correct. As soon as the front door was open, we found sick all over the floor. Then we discovered sick all over the coffee table. Drinks were spilt all over the floor. Chewing gum was stuck on the beanbag. The bathtub was burnt, and the toilet seat was left hanging by one hinge. There was a strange substance in my room, of all places, and someone had been sleeping in my bed while I was gone. Our school photos had been destroyed because they'd been used as coasters for drinks, which had been spilt all over them. In addition to this, there was cat sick everywhere, which hadn't been cleaned up. Housework hadn't been a priority over the last month, and I understand that, but Dad had somewhat been able to keep the house in an adequate state. Now he returned after a few days to find the house completely trashed. Kristy had had a party and had trashed the house in doing so.

She was found sleeping in my parents' room with a hangover. Worried that the house was in no condition to have a BMT patient living in it, Mum drove me to Grandma's house while Dad forced Kristy out of bed, and the two cleaned up as much mess as they could. Kristy's argument was that she didn't know I was coming home, but that doesn't necessarily justify her having the party and causing so much damage, especially when she had no permission to do this in the first place, whether I was home or not. My homecoming surprise did not go to plan, and I had no time to absorb the feeling of being back home. Instead, other things were on my mind.

I had spent battling leukaemia for 192 days, and I was now home for good, but I couldn't even be at home. I was not happy. The positive side of this, though, was because there was also damage to the oven, of all things, we couldn't cook any dinner, and we had a takeaway that night. This was despite being told by the hospital the day before that I was on a 100-day clean diet. At least Kristy's party gave a good enough excuse for me to break the rule that had been bugging me for a while. All I wanted was a nice takeaway!

After the party incident was over, I finally began to settle back at home. Dad decided he wanted to do some painting in my room, but it was apparently dangerous for someone like me to be breathing in the fumes. He wanted me to sleep in the living room for a while, but I insisted that I sleep in my own bed. I think my wishes to sleep in my own bed were justified.

It was as if when I came home I turned into a grumpy old man. Because of my vulnerability, it was as if I had the power to make all the decisions. As you can imagine, as I got better in the coming months, my power did not last long, and my parents gradually became stricter with me.

The plan for the future was already underway. I was due at Addenbrooke's twice a week, and Stowmarket High School was in the process of arranging a home tutor for me so I wouldn't be too far behind my classmates once I returned. There was no date set for when I would be returning to school, because despite being well and not neutropenic, I had the immune system of a one-month-old baby. Mentally, I was ready for a comeback, but it was my physical health standing in my way.

Settling into my bedspace on the Rainbow Ward at West Suffolk
Hospital, March 23rd 2016. I have just had my cannulas inserted
and blood tests, though the results were not back yet.

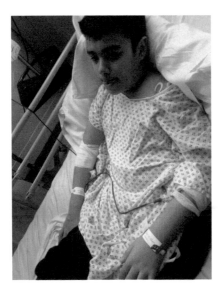

My first day on Ward C2 at Addenbrooke's Hospital, March 24th 2016.
I am preparing for my Hickman line insertion, having been officially
diagnosed with Acute Myeloid Leukaemia earlier that morning.

Kristy and I 'Keep Smiling' during
my time in A bay. I received post
from Auntie Ani in the US.

Dad and I shave each other's hair at
Kingston House, April 12th 2016.
The bandana look did not last long.

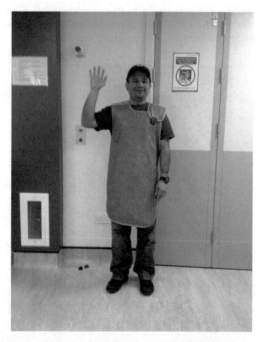

My chest pains remained a mystery and I required a CT scan.
Dad could have waited outside the scanning room but I kept
him in just so he would have to wear the funny apron.

A family BBQ during my second stay at Kingston House. I was not happy as my NG tube was causing me irritation.

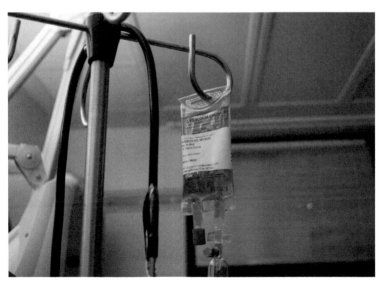

My first dose of idarabucin, June 22nd 2016. This chemotherapy drug is orange/red in colour and I was slightly scared of it.

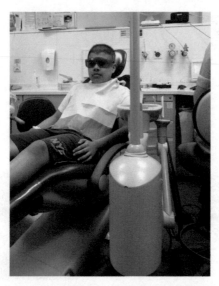

At the dentist on my Bristol work-up plan, August 3rd 2016. I originally required eight fillings but ended up only needing seven.

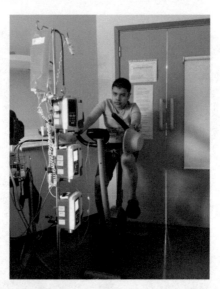

Day T-4 of conditioning, August 22nd 2016. After a rough day, I am back on the exercise bike while receiving chemotherapy. I am keeping hold of the sick bowl just in case.

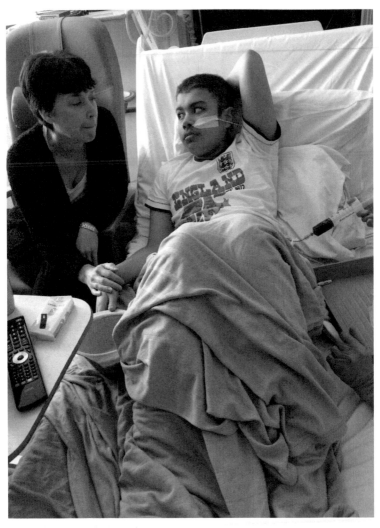

I receive my first bone marrow transplant in Cubicle 5, Ward 34, at the Bristol Royal Hospital for Children, August 26th 2016. Mum believed that if she held my hand throughout my transplant then it had a higher chance of working.

Freedom! My neutrophils reach over 0.5 and I am officially allowed out of my isolation cubicle, September 16th 2016.

'Straight Outta Chemo' – I am finally discharged from the Bristol
Royal Hospital for Children and begin my recovery at home.

Part Two
Rebuilding

Chapter 10
Getting My Life Back

The transition from cancer patient to normality
from October 1st, 2016, to January 31st, 2017

The next few months that followed was just more recovery. Despite feeling well in myself, the doctors were still not ready to let me move on to bigger and better things just yet. I remained a cancer patient after my transplant.

First, I would have to be closely monitored, but as things improved, hospital visits would reduce and become less and less regular. My aims were to be back at school as soon as possible; I didn't want to fall behind on any of my schoolwork. I was already severely behind and catching up was going to be a challenge. Because hospital school at Bristol was sporadic, and little of what I'd learned was actually relevant to the curriculum, I'd only really had a few lessons for my GCSE subjects. As soon as Bristol hospital school became more serious, I was discharged, which was great but at the same time didn't help my studies.

My health was also a priority, and my check-ups at Addenbrooke's would be twice a week and at Bristol once a month to start off the post-transplant period. I was also to have a weekly visit at home from the community nurse, who would take my blood and change my dressing and bungs on my Hickman line. Because I still needed to have regular blood tests, removing my Hickman Line was discussed, but there was no sign of it being any time soon. There was also a waiting list for the removal, so even if I was given the go-ahead, it would take a while for it to actually happen.

I now see these few months as a transition period. I was still a cancer patient who needed close and special monitoring by the doctors, and a large proportion of my life was to still be spent at the hospital. But at the same time, I was post-transplant and ready to move on. I had goals I wanted to achieve, and it was vital I used this recovery time to get back on track.

On Monday 3rd October (Day 38), I was back in PDU at Addenbrooke's, the first of my check-ups twice a week. When I bumped into one of the oncology consultants in the waiting room, he said I had done very well and none of the doctors were expecting me back so quick. They were expecting a minimum of two months, and I was back within a month and a half. Because I was a BMT patient, I wasn't allowed to be in the waiting room with the other patients, so I was isolated in the quiet side room. This was much better than the waiting room, although I felt bad when families using that room had to be kicked out and told to go elsewhere just so I could go in there. Having a transplant made me require special treatment, and needing my own room is evidence of this. My check-up was with Dr. M, who was also very surprised that I was out so early.

While, overall, I was happy with my health thus far, and if there were any problems I was already informed, I did have one concern – my skin. The waist of my trousers rubbed against my skin, which made it appear very patchy, and in some areas, including my groin, I lost pigmentation of my skin. The chemotherapy had made my skin more sensitive, and I had developed an itchy, red rash on my neck. My face was very dry and crusty, and I woke up every morning with a severe case of skin flakes, which clumped to resemble something of a white beard and moustache and also turned my eyebrows white. To combat this, I was prescribed a number of moisturising creams, such as Diprobase, and was advised to continue washing with aqueous cream rather than shower gel, or at least use non-scented shower gel designed for babies.

The creams worked for my dry skin, but the issue was that I was required to moisturise very regularly – about four times a day – and I struggled to keep up with this (not because I didn't have the time, but rather because I simply forgot to).

In terms of my rash, it could have been GvHD, but the doctor thought this was unlikely. Early attempts of treatment were as simple as changing the washing powder for my clothes. Dr. M recommended buying non-biological washing powder rather than biological, as it was likely that this could have been irritating my skin. Despite that, the doctors were not worried at all, and within my first week of being required to have two check-ups a week, Dr. M thought this was no longer necessary and reduced my appointments to once a week. I had only been home for a week, and I was really happy to see the number of appointments decrease already.

C. difficile, which I'd had while I was in isolation, had also returned by this point. This meant that I was back on another antibiotic, in addition to the penicillin I was required to take for the rest of my life. I struggled with this medicine because it was a large yellow tablet, which made it difficult to swallow. Because the doctors wanted to know how often I was going to the toilet, and also wanted a stool sample, I was required to go to the loo in bedpans. It wasn't diarrhoea, but it still had a cowpat consistency. I was producing this fifteen times a day, and the bathroom in our house was stacked with used bedpans, one on top of the other. It was quite disgusting, and the smell wasn't very pleasant, but it was what the doctors wanted, and with the amount I was producing, there was no way around it. In the meantime, in addition to taking my medication, I was told to avoid greasy foods because that would more than likely make my C. diff worse. My C. diff remained with me until December 2016, until it eventually went away and didn't return for while. I've never been the same since, though, and I seem to have very sensitive bowels, even to this day.

A month or so after my own discharge, Jacob had fortunately been discharged from Bristol. As we were both BMT patients, we both had to be isolated (sometimes together) from other patients in the Addenbrooke's waiting room. We did see them at Addenbrooke's a couple of times. On a couple of occasions, Mum and I were isolated in the same room as Lorna and Jacob, which turned into more of a social gathering once coffee and hot chocolate from Starbucks was involved. It was like a Bristol reunion already, except it was in a tiny treatment room in Cambridge rather than the communal area of Sam's House in Bristol.

And of course, once we were back at Addenbrooke's, we did not forget about Joe. We were anxious to see how he was doing because his name never appeared on the resident board at Sam's House. Dad did ask Amanda how he was doing, and she said that although she couldn't comment on private matters, she could say that he was doing very well. That was a good sign. It was a week later when Dad spotted Theresa and Joe in the day unit. Joe was doing well and had just got home from his transplant. There was no space at Bristol, and he ended up having to go all the way to Glasgow! Joe's dad had to drive from Stevenage to Glasgow and back every weekend, which made driving to Bristol and back every week look easy in comparison. We were so pleased that Joe was doing well, because we were all worried when his name didn't show up at Sam's House. Little did we know that while we were having our transplants, he was having his too! Mum requested Theresa's phone number so we could keep in touch and continue to see how Joe was getting on. Joe seemed in good spirits, and while none of us were in good health, he looked better than I had ever seen him. Things were looking very positive for him, and we were glad to see that he'd finally had his transplant, something he had been waiting ages for.

At the end of October 2016, I was back on Day Beds at the Bristol Royal Hospital for Children to have my one month after discharge check-up. I had my obs taken, which showed that my weight was 65kg, which was very overweight for me at the time. This was the highest I ever got to as a paediatric patient. I was expecting the doctors to say that I needed to limit the amount I was eating, or at least get the dieticians to tell me that I no longer had to gain, but the doctor responded by saying, "Your weight is increasing nicely".

Dr. G brought up a number of things in the consultation. First of all, my fertility was brought up because it was important to discuss the effects of the chemotherapy. Although it was likely that my fertility had been wiped out, I was told I needed to go into relationships thinking I can have children. I'm never going to know whether I'm fertile until it comes to the time that I plan to have children, and just because that one result at the IVF clinic showed I was infertile, doesn't necessarily mean that this would be the case forever. After all, I had just recovered from a cycle of chemo when I'd gone to the clinic. However, we were told that my transplant would make me infertile because in most cases that is the result, although, as I've said previously, I have heard stories of people being able to have children several years post-transplant.

He also explained the 100-day clean diet to us, providing a little bit more clarity. He said that while there was no proof that the clean diet was effective, it was there as a precaution and was just to be on the safe side. Because I was really craving a KFC, despite it not being 100 days just yet, Dr. G said I could have KFC as a treat, as long as I was sure that it was cooked fresh and not sitting out for hours. It was important I didn't eat takeaways or greasy foods too much, especially since I had C. diff.

Behind the scenes, Stowmarket High School had been working closely to arrange a home tutor for me so I didn't fall behind on my schoolwork. Although I was feeling very well in myself, despite the C. diff, my immune system was still significantly weak, and it was likely a full day at school would tire me out, and if I caught anything, then I could become very ill. This was why I wasn't allowed to return straight away, although in my early post-transplant days, I remember Dr. M telling my parents that it was important that I got ill to build my immune system and antibodies up, so I shouldn't be wrapped in bubble wrap. I wasn't so sure about the tiredness as I seemed to be full of energy and ready to make my return as soon as possible. Whatever my opinion, though, I wasn't allowed to return to school just yet, so, from October 2016, I would be taught by Jackie, my home tutor.

Jackie specialised in English and History, so this was what the majority of our lessons were devoted to, in addition to maths, which was equally important. She didn't mind when I said we were both hopeless at science and we found it very difficult to get our heads around it. After a few science lessons, we soon gave up and left it to the teachers to sort out when I returned. I was also doing GCSE French, but Jackie had no experience in French, so for the time being, this was forgotten about. Sessions were four days a week; Jackie couldn't do Thursdays as she would be teaching in a school all day. We tried to schedule hospital appointments for Thursdays to make things more convenient with regards to my schoolwork, and the hospital was very good at ensuring this and agreed my education was an equal priority. Each school session started off being half an hour long, and as my overall health and energy improved, this would soon increase to an hour and a half, which was the maximum offered. I really enjoyed home school, because although there was definitely some normal classwork, sometimes fun activities were incorporated. For example, when studying A Christmas Carol for GCSE English Literature, I was able to show my art skills by painting Marley's ghost.

Home school has its pros and cons. The best thing is that it could be done on the sofa, so I was in a comfortable setting. Also, 1:1 tuition means that you receive a lot of help from the teacher, helping you to be better than your classmates, who are in a class of thirty. But the disadvantage is that, although you may have more secure knowledge of a subject, because time is so limited, all your classmates are ahead of you by the time you return to school. Your knowledge may be more secure than everyone else's because you'd had chance to devote a lot of time to a specific topic to the point where you'd know lots about it, but everyone would know more than you in the subject as a whole. Jackie told me that the aim of home school was not to cover everything that was taught at school. It was simply not possible to do that, and falling behind was inevitable. The purpose of home school was to make sure that I didn't fall behind too much. Not falling too far behind at a steady pace was much more important than the stress of keeping up with everyone.

One day in November, I presented the cheque at school for the money raised from the ten-mile walk that the school did while I was in Bristol with the headteacher, Mr Lee-Allan, assistant headteacher Ms Ferguson, the school governor, and the three students who'd raised the most money – Kristy, my friend, Ryan, and a girl a year or two below, called Holly. Before taking the photo with the cheque, we all sat down in the headteacher's office to have cake and refreshments, which was really kind of the school to do. My friend, Liam, came into the office to see me for a bit as it had been a while; the last time I'd seen him was April.

The photo made it into the local newspaper the following day, on November 10th, 2016. I was appearing in the newspaper quite a bit, this being my third time. That being said, this was the only photo I'd had in the paper, as the other two times just mentioned my name when Fin or the school were fundraising. My face looked awful; I was practicing my smile all day in the mirror, but when it came to taking the picture, I got nervous, and instead of moving my mouth, I moved my nose, resulting in me looking like I had a scrunched-up face.

I don't really know how I reacted to all this publicity. I knew I wasn't famous, but I sure felt like it, because 2016 was the year when everyone in Stowmarket knew me as the kid that had leukaemia. If they hadn't seen my face, they at least knew my name. Months, even years later, I am still known as the boy who had leukaemia, and if I meet someone for the first time who knows about me, asking how I'm doing now is always their first question.

After presenting the cheque, Mum and I were joined by Jackie as we had a meeting with the assistant headteacher about my GCSEs. My current options were History, French, and German, as decided back in March of 2016, mere days before my diagnosis. Because of the workload, it was advised that I drop one language. I dropped German because I didn't want to throw away the French lessons I had received in Bristol. Also, I had more experience with French, having studied it since Year 5, but I had only done German since Year 9. Above all, I now had French blood!

I was given three options that were considered an easier subject, to replace German. Resistant Materials – no, I couldn't think of anything worse; I've always been more academic, loving to write essays. The scary machines often put me off, leaving me in tears in middle school, although I had grown up since then. The second option was Art, which I had considered and had actually put as a reserve choice, but I didn't really want to do it. As creative as I was, I had no passion for the subject and preferred to show my creativity in my own ways, not writing about how I'd improve on my work attempt after attempt. The third was Food Technology; I am a great chef, but due to all that washing up I'd have to do, as well as my inability to work an oven on my own back then, I decided it was not the subject for me.

Reluctantly, I agreed to do Art, despite the assistant headteacher telling me that she did not know of any deaths caused by ovens in the school's history. But luckily this didn't last long because in another meeting with the newly promoted head of year, Miss Smith, in January 2017, it was agreed that I would drop Art (I didn't have a single Art lesson in the whole time I was taking Art as a GCSE subject) and instead it was agreed for me to take only two GCSE options and devote my time to catching up with what I'd missed in free periods and through extra French lessons.

In November 2016, I went on my first holiday since my diagnosis. One of the oncology doctors on Ward C2 always said to wait before going abroad, which I did, and as a transplant patient, I wasn't allowed to fly for a year anyway. I went on a small holiday to a cottage in Hunstanton, in Norfolk, for a weekend, with my parents, Kristy, Grandma, and my uncle. It was usually the traditional family holiday, which included my auntie, uncle, and cousin. But my cousin, Jade, had got married in September 2016 – a wedding Mum and I missed because we were in Bristol – so they were saving their money. It was good to return to somewhat normality, allowing me to enjoy things that I hadn't been able to do for so long. It was good for my entire family to get a break.

Also, speaking of returning to normality, in the same month, I got my Sunday paper round back! It was a sign that I was getting stronger, even if it did just involve delivering newspapers for one hour a week. When you're a BMT patient, making small steps to recovery is the way to go. I was back earning money, which I was very happy about, although I did require some help from my parents because pulling carts put a strain on my Hickman line. Other than that, I was very happy to be finally getting some of the normal aspects of my life back, and I was very grateful for Richard at the paper shop, who had kept my round available for me during my absence.

In December 2016, I was invited to a couple of Christmas parties; the Ward C2 Christmas party and another party from a charity called Henry's Holiday Help. Henry's Holiday Help, which unfortunately as of 2020 has shut down, was a charity that granted £1000 to go towards a holiday to families of children with cancer who were registered under West Suffolk Hospital. The charity was set up by Katie, who had named the charity after her son, Henry, who was diagnosed with a brain tumour and is now doing well but still needs monitoring.

The Ward C2 Christmas party was first. Unfortunately, I was told not to attend because my C. diff was still affecting me. But that didn't stop me from showing up because not going would have messed up my plans. Grandma had raised £100 by selling homemade jam on a stall outside her house – this was to go towards board games for Ward C2. I had previously stated that the ward needed new games, considering there were always tiles missing in Scrabble. That meant a trip to Toys R Us, and we had bought lots of new games for the ward and dropped them off to the play specialists, who were running the party. Before the party began, I had to leave to avoid infecting the kids.

Fortunately, I was able to attend the Henry's Holiday Help party as my C. diff had cleared up just in time. The party was really cool because there were a number of activities designed for all ages – I made a bauble and a snowman decoration using rice and a sock. We sat with Lorna, Craig, Jacob, and his sister, Katie, at the party. The party finished with a visit from Santa, who kindly gave me a £30 Argos voucher! Henry's Holiday Help was a great local charity, who not only supported me but my entire family, who all got a present from Santa too. It was yet another charity I had benefitted from, and my family did some fundraising for them before they closed.

On December 9th, 2016 (Day 106), I was back in Bristol for another check-up. This time it was a full Bristol reunion. Jacob and Reece were due for a check-up the same day. Also, Katie had just had her transplant and was now off the ward, so she was staying at Sam's House too. Dr. G was sick on this day, so the BMT speciality doctor ran the clinic instead. Everything seemed to be going well, except my skin was still a problem, and visibly I was very dry and had a crusty face. The doctor prescribed me a new moisturiser cream to see if that would have any success.

Then, the question arose of when I would be well enough to return to school. She said that if all went well, maybe in the new year. This was now my aim; I was going to do everything I could to return to school by January 2017.

After my check-up, we stayed the night at Sam's House. That evening, my family, the Krutkes (Lorna, Craig, Katie, and Jacob), Cath and Reece, and Sue and Katie all had a takeaway Pizza Express at Sam's House, with all four of us transplant patients breaking the 100-day clean diet – again. Dad and Craig collected the pizza, but they got lost and then had to carry the pizza up the hill. Therefore, it was a cold Pizza Express we ate, but it was still delicious, and the night was amazing!

Although I was glad that I was no longer living in Bristol, I missed the people we were surrounded by, and having a one-night Bristol reunion was great. This was the first, and unfortunately final, Bristol reunion when all four families were together. We were to see the others later on, but separately. Just because we went through such a traumatic time didn't mean we didn't have any positive moments, and a positive was definitely the friends we made. The next day, my family and I went down to Cribbs Causeway to have a look around and get some lunch, and then we went home straight after.

Christmas 2016 was one to remember. Although nothing was really done differently, having Grandma, Auntie Karen, and Uncle John round, the fact that I had spent the majority of the year in hospital meant that everything seemed normal again. It was Christmas time when I realised how happy I was to be getting myself back to normal. It is hard to imagine that if I was diagnosed before August 2015 – before the introduction of the MRD technology for AML patients – there would have most likely been an empty seat at the dinner table.

***

January 2017 didn't start off too great because the family hadn't escaped cancer just yet. My cat, Dexter, was the next victim. He wasn't eating, and there was a lump in his stomach. There was nothing the vets could do, so we lost him. After planning to have a much better 2017, this wasn't the start I wanted.

Despite the bad start to the year, January 2017 was a great month because I finally felt that I was moving away from the hospital side of things – even though it was a very prominent part of my life still – and more towards greater normality. The period from January to March 2017 is what I see as the more progressive part of the transition period, where I was still closely linked to the hospital, but I was starting to drift away at a much faster pace in order to be like everyone else my age. It was a gradual process; it was impossible to do everything all at once, but I was now seeing the light at the end of the tunnel.

Returning to school was the first thing on the list. The plan was to gradually increase my days at school, and my first day back would not even be a full day, rather just one lesson (a double), in the afternoon. Home schooling would continue until I was back to school full-time.

As mentioned before, Jackie and I were terrible at science, so it was agreed that first I would go in for my science lessons. Therefore, I was gaining much-needed knowledge, doing subjects that couldn't be taught at home.

We would start with biology because that was what we'd attempted and failed at home. Chemistry and Physics had been completely forgotten about altogether, to tell the truth. I was able to reach yet another milestone when I returned to school on the afternoon of Wednesday 11th January 2017 for a biology lesson. I hate science as a subject, so I wasn't all that excited about returning to class, but returning to school was my goal, and I was happy to be back!

But, as good as returning to school was, I was worried what people would think. Surprisingly, I had never been bullied at school, despite how different and unusual I was. Like most, I had a few troubles with kids here and there, but doesn't everyone? Returning to school was what I thought would be difficult for me. When I'd left in March 2016, I'd had thick black hair. Now I was pretty much bald – my hair was slow to grow back, looking patchy and uneven, like a baby penguin with thin dark, grey hair instead. My face was paler and dry with skin flakes, despite moisturising, and I had dark circles under my eyes like I hadn't slept for weeks. My illness had transformed me. Would people even recognise me? I was the same person on the inside, but on the outside, I was completely different.

I met Kristy (Mum gave her the responsibility of looking after her little brother) and my head of year, Miss Smith, at the front of the school because I was technically a new student again. It turns out people did recognise me! Whenever I walked past people, I heard them say, "Jake's back," and teachers were saying hello and giving me a thumbs up. I didn't realise I was so well-known in the school. I did receive a lot of special treatment.

Because I was a BMT patient and needed to avoid crowds, and I had a line in, I was allowed to use the staff corridor, and on my first day back, the corridors were cleared before I could go through them. I couldn't recall ever being able to walk through the corridors at school with no one in them during break and lunchtimes. It was good to be back to school, and I didn't realise how much I missed it until I got there; everything was the same as how I'd left it – other than the twenty teachers that had left and, most notably, the broken school bell, which the school couldn't afford to replace.

Once I got settled, it was like I had never left. My actual biology lesson itself was a bit scary though because the teacher was going on about stuff that had been covered last term and told the class "You should know that!" when they got their answers wrong. GCSEs-wise, I was an entire term behind my classmates, and in terms of schoolwork, I was a year behind, which scared me a little bit. The teacher did say to me personally not to worry and just continue from where they were and catch up later, once I was back full-time. We did an experiment where we tested for proteins in foods, which was cool but scary at the same time, and I had no idea what I was doing. I relied a lot on the people I was sitting next to, hoping they would help me out, which they kindly did.

From then on, I went into school every Wednesday afternoon for biology. I was trying to avoid having to go in on Monday and Tuesday because that was physics and chemistry. However, it turned out that the class was as clueless as I about physics because the teacher had gone off sick and left weeks into the start of the year. They were getting nowhere with a useless supply teacher. All the supply teacher did was shout. I may have been physically behind the class by a term, but all I had really missed was a term of shouting, and I, as well as all my other classmates, just showed up to physics for an hour of comedy. I couldn't believe how useless the teacher was, and even worse, he was a qualified physics teacher! It also turned out that I preferred chemistry, which I actually understood, to biology which I didn't.

After a couple of weeks of just coming in on Wednesday afternoons, I then did a full Wednesday. Realising this wasn't tiring at all, I then came into school every Wednesday and Friday, both of which were full days. By March, I was back to school as often as four days a week. I only missed school if I was in a lesson with Jackie or at the hospital. By mid-March 2017, I was back to school full-time, and home schooling had stopped.

There were positives; the first being that Liam had his

friend back and, as he would say, 'the Great Depression' was over. Liam had been spending break and lunchtimes with his sister, only because he didn't want me to feel replaced when I returned. I was really grateful for that, but at the same time, I do wish he had accepted the invitations from my other friends to join them. But there were also negatives; one of them being that I would miss my lessons with Jackie. Like Denise, I felt I had built a good working relationship with Jackie, so it was sad – but at same time good – that I no longer needed her.

There was also one massive negative: I had a lot of catching up to do. I'm very good at worrying and knew that being an academic year behind and a term and a half behind in my GCSEs was going to mean that I would have to do double the work in a shorter period of time. Hospital visits meant that I had no control over my absences, which made me fall further behind. This was okay though because the teachers were going to give me a lot of support in the coming months and the important thing was for me to settle into school before trying to stress myself with a load of work. I had to take things one step at a time, and the teachers totally understood my situation, which helped greatly.

***

Tuesday 31st January 2017 (Day 158). The next milestone I had to reach was the removal of my Hickman line. Back in October, when I'd had my check-up in Bristol with Dr. G, he said that as my check-ups would get less and less frequent, they could start thinking about removing my Hickman line. The only reason for not removing it at that time was because check-ups were still very frequent and having to have a blood test twice a week with needles would be nasty and painful, but once a month wouldn't be too bad. Therefore, for the remainder of 2016, my line remained. By January, I was having check-ups at Addenbrooke's once a month, and I wasn't due back in Bristol until April. Therefore, blood tests wouldn't be constant and, not requiring any other medication other than the tablets I was already taking, I was put on the waiting list to have my Hickman line removed.

My Hickman line was removed on January 31st, 2017. Back when I was preparing for my second round of chemotherapy the previous May, an oncology consultant had described the procedure of how a Hickman line was removed. I don't remember how the topic came along, especially since I was still very early into my journey, so I was far from thinking about having it removed. She told me it was just a very hard, forceful tug on the line. This was done under local anaesthetic for adults, meaning they would be conscious through the whole thing. Having stepped on my line in Bristol, I knew how painful it was to tug it, even when it didn't fall out, so I couldn't imagine the pain of having it completely ripped out of your chest while completely conscious!

Fortunately for me, I was still classed as a child at this time, and I was to be put to sleep under general anaesthetic while the procedure took place. As much as I hated being a cancer patient at my age, sometimes I saw myself as lucky being at that age – the ward I stayed on had a chef, there was a team of play specialists to prevent me from getting bored, and I was unconscious for most of the painful things! I must say now that, although I never wanted it at all, I would have much preferred to experience cancer then rather than now or later in my life. That, of course, is not to say I will not have to face it again, later in life. My age was a major reason for why I escaped my transplant with little long-term damage, so having treatment at my age gave me not only a social advantage, but a health advantage too.

The surgery took place in a bit of a change of place. On the Tuesday morning, I had to go to Ward F3 at Addenbrooke's Hospital, which I didn't even know existed. F3 was the ward dedicated to surgery. Of course, me being nil by mouth that day, I was grumpy. But at the same time, I was very happy. As much as I knew I was going to miss my Hickman line, for reasons none other than a sense of attachment to it – something I'd relied on to save my life – my line was the most difficult thing I had ever had the displeasure of having attached to me. I was attached to it (literally) because it had been with me for my entire journey, four rounds of chemo, and I'd even had my transplant through it. But at the same time, I couldn't wait to get the thing out and have a proper bath or shower for once; a bath where I didn't have to have a plastic bag attached to tubes out of my chest or a shower where I didn't have to stand in a funny and uncomfortable position to avoid getting my chest wet. I also really wanted to go swimming, something that I couldn't do while having my line in.

When I arrived on F3, it was like any normal check-up in hospital; I had my height, weight, and obs taken. I got even grumpier when I found out that I was going to have to be nil by mouth for even longer. I had arrived at 8:00am, before most of the other patients, because that was the time I was scheduled to arrive. The plan was to be on the morning list for the surgery to take place, but I had been moved to the afternoon list.

Shortly after hearing this, we met the anaesthetist who explained why. The reason why I was moved to the afternoon list was because there were little children there who needed to be done first due to the fact that the bigger children understood why they couldn't eat and drink. Being moved to the afternoon list had some benefits; I was allowed to have another drink of water. But it was a huge disadvantage because I was going to be stuck on a hospital bed with nothing to do for hours, and also, I would have to go even longer than I already had without food. I wondered what the point was of coming in at 8:00am – my allocated timeslot – when they had known all along that other children would be there. If all along I was to be placed on the afternoon list, in my mind, I was saying, *why didn't you just make me come in later?*

Numbing cream was applied to my arms in order for me to have a cannula. If I needed some sort of medication, which was unlikely, I could no longer rely on my Hickman line, which was now being removed. No longer having my line meant that surgeries would be carried out on me like they would on an ordinary person. My line made surgical procedures easier, but I would no longer have this advantage.

We then met the surgeon who was going to be in charge of the procedure for removing my Hickman line later in the day. He described the procedure to us and required us to sign consent forms along the lines of 'we can't sue the hospital should anything go wrong'. Really, only my parents needed to sign it, but he let me sign it too. As mentioned, the procedure was simple. It was just a hard tug on the line, pulling it out of my chest, and I would be asleep the whole time. This would leave me a hole in my chest, which would need a number of stitches, leaving a permanent scar. Despite the simplicity of the procedure, I did need to be aware of the possible complications. First of all, if there was an air bubble in my line and it entered the bloodstream and reached my brain, it would likely cause a stroke. A further possibility was that while the line was being tugged, it could snap during the procedure, which would leave a piece of plastic floating around in my arteries.

Both of these were an emergency if they happened, and they would have to call the emergency medical team for help. Of course, this was rare, but it still needed to be addressed due to the low chance of it happening. The surgeon did also go over the minor consequences of the procedure, such as having a scar for the rest of my life and feeling sore in my chest for a few days, but we had been warned of this months earlier.

Someone who I had never met – but Mum had spoken to a lot in Bristol – told her that his son was allowed to keep his Hickman line in a jar as something to remember his cancer journey by. I loved the sound of this, but unfortunately the rules at Addenbrooke's were different and I wasn't allowed to do this. In fact, when we asked, the surgeon looked at us like we were stupid to even think of such a thing.

3:00pm rolled around, and it was finally my turn for surgery. I was given a *Where's Wally?* book to take my mind off of the procedure. But I didn't need the book for that reason. Surgery and being put to sleep didn't scare me one bit. It sounds weird, but I loved being put to sleep because they're the only times I sleep well. I was actually happy to be getting my line removed too – however attached to it I was – and therefore, this was not exactly a procedure I was dreading. It had been a boring day, and finding Wally was just something to do while being wheeled to theatre. Then I was put to sleep by the anaesthetist, and that's all I can remember prior to the surgery.

I woke up in the same bedspace I had been in all day. When I woke up, I saw a red mark on my chest, which was sore and had been bleeding, with stitches and four or five small plasters covering it. My chest felt strange, like I was finally relieved from something heavy. Have you ever had a hat on for so long that once you took it off, you could still feel it? I felt my line, but it wasn't there. At the same time, though, my chest felt as light as a feather.

Dad described the sewn-up hole in my chest as a bullet wound, and he said I should be proud of my scars. It showed the battle I had endured and the battle I had won. From where the numerous dressings had been over the last nine months, my skin in the former line area was significantly lighter to the rest of my body, which would take months to get back to normal. It was like when you leave a plaster on your skin for a couple of days and the skin under it is a lighter colour. Fast forward to July 2017 and I was still having conversations about how a patch of my chest was much lighter than the rest!

The surgery was a success, although I was advised to take the next day off school. I was allowed to go in the following Friday, though. Once I had eaten something and gone to the bathroom, I was free! This was the last major procedure I needed to have done at the hospital, and my remaining visits would be nothing other than check-ups.

It was dark outside. I was one of the first in the clinic and the second to last out. There was just one other family left in the bed opposite me. Before I could leave, though, like the rules on PDU, I had to eat something and go to the toilet. I enjoyed my Freddo Frog, the first thing I was able to eat all day.

I had to keep my chest dry for five days. This meant no swimming and no proper washes for five days. In other words, I just had to continue everything I had been doing for the past nine months with my line in. The stitches didn't need to be removed, since they were dissolvable. It would be sore for a while, so there was a 'no strenuous exercise' rule, not that I'd had any plans to do that anyway.

Chapter 11

Enjoying Life

Back to school full-time, my GCSEs,
hospital appointments, achievements,
and amazing opportunities from January
31st, 2017, to September 6th, 2018

At the end of January, my line was out, and I was able to have a bit more freedom in what activities I could carry out on a day-to-day basis.

Going into February, I was still at school only two days a week, but this was rapidly increasing. By mid-March 2017, I was back to school full-time. The school gave me a lot of support in trying to prepare me as best they could for my GCSEs the next year, and this difficult period of catching up with work started now. My timetable was very awkward though. As previously mentioned, I dropped art without participating in a single art lesson. This meant I had free periods. My core subjects and history lessons remained the same. The periods that were left free were dedicated to extra French lessons, a subject that had been completely forgotten about, and therefore while every French student had three French lessons a week, I had six. No one envied me for that, and people actually felt sorry for me. While six French lessons a week may have been a little excessive, I was determined to do everything I could to ensure that I didn't fall behind in the subject. The school had provided me with some French revision guides and workbooks to help me catch up on my own.

Although I could have done PE, I didn't want to just yet as I was given an opportunity for a study period in the library instead. To Dr. G's disapproval, PE wasn't my priority despite having spent a year away from full-time school! In reality, I could have done it, but since the school didn't want to pressure me into doing it, I didn't see any reason to persuade them that I could do my most hated subject. I was also given the opportunity to replace philosophy and ethics with an extra study session, but Miss Smith said that as it was only an hour a week, it would be fun to engage in an interactive lesson to move away from the academic side of things. I suppose the study period that replaced PE could have been useful, but because I wasn't supervised, I found distractions. Instead of catching up on my chemistry work, I often found myself reading the same book every week on the Presidents of the United States.

The same month was also important for my education. It was the Year 10 mock exams, or PREs, as the school called them. However irrelevant they may seem to me now, at the time this was an important indication of what I needed to work on and how much I had missed, as well as how able I was. Maybe things wouldn't be so bad. No one knew until I sat the exams. And I sat the exams like all the other students in my year, who *hadn't* missed an entire school year. They were only mocks, but I needed to show I was on the right track.

The new 9-1 grading system made the results of my mocks a bit complex to calculate because there were no mark schemes available. But, for someone who had missed a year of school, I did surprisingly well. In some cases, I outperformed some people in my class. I wasn't perfect. Far from it. In fact, I failed some subjects. Science I failed, getting three marks in my physics exam and six marks in my biology exam. You know it was bad because I'm talking about numbers in terms of marks and not grades... I literally only got three answers correct in my physics exam. I did do well in chemistry, however, which brought my grade up, although I still failed overall, only achieving a 2-, equivalent to an E.

In French, I achieved a 3, equivalent to a D, but, although this is far from great, the fact that I'd had only a handful of GCSE French lessons prior to my exam, this was a good start. The teacher marked the paper with 'Good Effort!'

Now onto the subjects I passed: I passed Maths, which surprised me because that was the hardest test I'd ever taken, achieving a 5, or a high C. In English, I achieved a 4, equivalent to a standard C.

History, which was still being calculated in the old system, was my proudest accomplishment! I achieved a B, which came as a great surprise to many, including myself. My teacher was very surprised at how well I had done after returning such a short time ago.

These mock exams were not perfect, but considering I had only just returned to school and was only two weeks into being back full-time, imagine what I could achieve in a year's time when I did my actual GCSE exams! Now I knew what I needed to work on, and I was going to work hard to improve my grades.

***

On March 12th, 2017, Grandma held an afternoon tea at her local village hall. This was to raise money for the charity, Anthony Nolan, which set up the bone marrow transplant donor register. It was these types of registers that helped find me a match for my transplant. They are very important. Many friends and family, as well as people I didn't know, attended, and Fin even helped run things. I was at the front door greeting people and selling them raffle tickets. The event was a success, raising over £750 for the charity!

In April 2017, I went back to Bristol for a check-up. We decided that instead of doing a day trip to Bristol, for which we would spend eight hours in a car for a ten-minute appointment, we were instead going to have a short holiday. It was going to be a nice three-day break.

My check-up went well and everything was okay in terms of my health. I did have a couple of troubles getting through the consultation. First of all, I had to justify why I wasn't doing PE at school to Dr. G, who believed it was very important for me to do it. I just said that I had to catch up with my other subjects, which soon became the truth after Kristy – now a sixth former, enjoying the luxury of free periods – started supervising my study sessions. The other issue I had, which made the check-up difficult to get through, was that I couldn't stay serious when Dr. G started talking about puberty and how certain parts of the body grow. I'm usually serious about stuff like this, but Dr. G's terminology wasn't what the typical doctor would use! I was quite immature, I'll admit, but Dr. G said it was okay and it was good to see me smiling. Even the accompanying doctor couldn't keep a straight face and had to stare into her computer, doing all she could to hold in a laugh. What started the conversation initially was my height, and we were quite concerned that the chemotherapy had stunted my growth. This was just discussed for now, and further action into investigating this was going to be in a year or so when the long-term damage of the chemotherapy would be tested and made apparent.

After the check-up on Day Beds, my family and I stayed the night at Sam's House. The following day, we went to the science museum in Bristol. While not overly enthusiastic about science, I have to admit that the museum was one of the coolest places I had ever been in. There was also a *Wallace & Gromit* area of the museum, which I liked because I love *Wallace & Gromit*. After visiting the museum, we went to the Bristol Aquarium, where I was fascinated by the jellyfish. This is what I wanted to see in Bristol – all I knew of previously was the hospital, Sam's House, and the Co-op!

When we finished at the aquarium, we went to Cribbs Causeway to check in to the hotel where we were staying the night. It was at this hotel where, for the first time in a year and a half, I went swimming. My line had been out for three months by this point, but I was still cautious to get my chest wet even after the five days were up because the area where my line was still didn't look right. So, I waited for the moment when it was properly healed, and now was the time. I had never felt so free! It was certainly a strange feeling, and I had to obsessively check my chest for blood, still being very used to thinking my line was in.

The next day, we actually left Bristol quite early as the next place on our list was Stonehenge, which is located in the county of Wiltshire. Back in August 2016, when I went for my work-up plan, I wanted to go to Stonehenge, which I knew was on the way to Bristol, but we never got the chance to. I was told that if you travelled a certain route to Bristol, you could actually see Stonehenge from the road. To save time, Dad never took us on this route. Now was our opportunity to go. I never realised that the actual Stonehenge was such a long walk from the entrance where the ticket stands are. It was a beautiful walk through the countryside, and the mysterious stones were fascinating!

***

Unfortunately, not everyone was returning to normality or escaping hospital life or experiencing the positives of such a traumatic experience that is cancer. I was in PDU for an appointment sometime in March (sometimes the Addenbrooke's and Bristol appointments were ridiculously close together, not so much for my needs, rather for the scheduling of appointments), and while in the waiting room, we spotted Theresa with Joe. Joe was on a hospital bed being wheeled into the six-bedded bay, and it looked as if he had just come out of surgery. I assumed he had just had a bone marrow aspiration. We just waved to them but didn't ask what was going on. If we bumped into them on PDU, Theresa would usually come speak to Mum, but strangely, this time she didn't. Once I was home, Theresa sent a text to Mum explaining why she didn't speak to us, with one of the reasons being that she didn't want to say anything that may worry me.

Unfortunately, Joe's Acute Myeloid Leukaemia relapsed in March 2017, seven months after his transplant, and his condition worsened to the point where he was admitted to intensive care. I was saddened to hear that he passed away on June 21st, 2017. I was really sad to hear that, because although I didn't speak to him as often as I should have done, or would have liked, the memories of food tasting on C9 with him and the conversations between our families in the hospital and as neighbours at Kingston House are amongst my favourite of my time at Addenbrooke's.

Joe was very important to my journey and actually an inspiration. Theresa told us he had been so well after his first battle, returning to life as it once was, and when he relapsed, he maintained a positive attitude by saying he had done it once and he could do it again. Sadly, he relapsed for a third time when things were finally looking up for him. I couldn't help but feel for his family. When it comes to leukaemia, it could have been any one of us.

My family and I attended the funeral on Monday 10th July 2017. The funeral was well-organised and did everything it could to give Joe the send-off he would have wanted. The roads to the church were surrounded by a countless number of the same breed of dogs – huskies, which were his favourite – as well as a couple of horses. We were told not to wear black, rather to wear something blue, the colour of Joe's football team. There were so many people in attendance that the church was full, and my family were amongst the many others who had to stand outside the church, trying to listen as best we could to what was being said. We couldn't really hear any of what was being said at the funeral, but we thought it was very important just to be there, not only to pay our respects to Joe, but also to support Theresa and her family. After the funeral service, Joe was taken to the crematorium in a horse-drawn carriage.

Mum and Lorna used to occasionally meet with Theresa, who seems to be doing well. I think Theresa is an inspiration too, for being so strong throughout everything her family went through, and she is still somehow smiling every time I see her.

***

I continued the rest of Year 10 in school full-time, although my attendance was still quite poor. I missed a lot of school due to hospital appointments, which were by now once a month. But those days add up, in addition to the entire first term of Year 10 I had missed. Hospital appointments were every Thursday, meaning I was missing a lot of important lessons. Appointments scheduled monthly, rather than weekly, helped things a little, but the damage to my education was still done.

I made it to the end of Year 10, and the whole school assembly was on the final day of term.

It was a non-uniform day, and I remember Mum desperately trying to get me to wear something smart. I had no idea why and refused. Afterall, why was I going to show up to school in a suit when everyone was wearing casual clothing? Little did I know, I was to be the first recipient of the school's Courage in the Face of Adversity award.

This award was set up by the parents of Jacqueline, someone in the town who had passed away from cancer. In addition to having my name on the wooden plaque, which is displayed in Stowmarket High School, Jacqueline's parents gave me a cheque of £75 to spend on whatever I liked, which was so kind of them.

The assistant headteacher, Ms Ferguson, read out my story to the whole assembly, and hearing it from someone else made me tear up a little. I'm always fine telling my story myself, but there's something about hearing it back from someone else that gets to me. After everything I endured, I had got back up in the end. When my name was finally called, I collected my award in front of everyone in assembly, and due to nerves, I tried not to make eye contact with anyone.

My entire year group and the sixth form stood up to give me a round of applause. It was a truly amazing moment, and I didn't realise how much support had built up behind me. I wish I had taken a look at the whole school clapping for me, but I was so nervous I just focused on going up to the front and sitting back down. I took a picture with Jacqueline's parents, holding the wooden plaque. It was a great end to the school year, and I was so proud to have won the award, let alone be the first recipient. I really did not expect it, and I was grateful to the teachers for nominating me in the first place. As the first recipient, I do wish in the future to have some kind of involvement in presenting the award to future recipients at future assemblies.

The summer holidays of 2017 were special. The previous year's summer holiday had not been a summer holiday at all; I had spent it being isolated in a hospital room. August 26th, 2017, would be my one-year post-transplant day, or as my family and I referred to it, 'my first birthday'. My next-door neighbour, Sharon, had the suggestion of celebrating my first birthday by opening up both of our gardens and having a BBQ, charging people for entry to raise money for a blood cancer charity of our choice. These plans were then made, and on Saturday 26th August 2017, exactly a year since my transplant, we celebrated!

We invited all our friends and family, raising money for the blood cancer charity, DKMS, which helps patients find a donor by setting up registers very similar to Anthony Nolan, the charity Grandma raised money for through her afternoon tea event. While a lot of the adults were outside socialising in the sunny weather, my friends and I stayed inside the house playing on the Wii. I do wish I'd spent more time outside with the guests, especially since it was my party, but I got a bit distracted!

My birthday cake looked great; it was a cake version of a WWE ring, which was made by someone at Mum's work. At the very end of the party, we all came outside and roasted marshmallows on the campfire. It was an amazing ending to a great evening. It was very strange receiving birthday cards with '1' on them, and some of the cards I received made me feel like a child all over again, but that was the point! That was one of the benefits of having a bone marrow transplant: two birthdays!

Many people I meet think I'm weird when I say I have two birthdays, and a lot are very dismissive when I say it, but it's all due to lack of understanding. When I explain, they soon realise that it really does make sense.

Three days later on August 29th, I celebrated my fifteenth birthday, which was an eventful day seeing my friends.

***

In September 2017, I started Year 11, which was going to be one of the most stressful school years of my life. Everyone in my year was stressed, and I understand that, but I was at a huge disadvantage because I was a year behind everyone else. Repeating Year 10 was an option and was seriously considered by the school, but I declined that offer. In my eyes, I would rather have failed trying than repeat the year. The reason why – and I know this is the completely wrong approach to take – was mostly because of friends; as they would all be ahead of me by the time I reached Year 11, I'd have no friends left in the school. While it was not the right attitude to have, with hindsight, staying with my year was probably the best decision I made!

I continued to power through, catching up with my studies. I should mention that I found learning GCSE History particularly interesting. For the Medicine Through Time unit, I could actually be an expert. I knew all about blood transfusions, ciclosporin, and the formation of the National Health Service in 1948. When I had done a little bit of reading on this on the ward with Denise, she had made me realise how important the NHS is. If I was in a place like the United States with no money, I'd be dead right now. I'm grateful to live in a country that has such an amazing healthcare system, and if it wasn't for the NHS, I wouldn't be here today. People may be surprised to hear I'm a Conservative when I say things like this, but my problem with the welfare state is when people abuse it. Any decent person would want a good healthcare system. People who live in the

UK are very lucky; our welfare state should not be taken for granted, and people should be proud to be British!

Catching up was going to be hard work, but I had to keep going and work extra hard. My goal was to achieve at least one 7 – an A grade – in any subject, but preferably History. This was going to be extremely difficult, especially for someone in my circumstances. My grades were always average at school, so I was questioning, whether I was ill or not, if I had the ability to achieve a 7? My timetable was very awkward due to the dropped course, but Miss Smith and I worked out when my study periods and extra sessions would be to fill the gaps. I would have two extra sessions of French a fortnight, and the remaining three periods would be in the computer room doing any work I needed to do, which would be provided by teachers. I now needed to learn and revise eight subjects, and it was going to be tough. While my fellow classmates were mostly revising, I was still learning!

***

In September 2017, I experienced a setback. My groin began to ache, quite badly. It was like a severe growing pain, but it wasn't going away. I had been roller-skating the previous weekend and thought I had injured myself then, but after a few days, I began to feel itchy bumps on my skin. Being in so much pain, and very itchy too, I went to the GP, and they diagnosed me with shingles.

This is worth bringing up because, as I'd had a bone marrow transplant, my immune system was completely wiped out. This meant I was now capable of getting the chickenpox virus again, which I'd had when I was younger. Shingles came from the chickenpox virus, and it can be deadly for BMT patients. Shingles only affects one side of the body, and, of course, knowing my luck, I got it in the worst place possible – my bottom and my groin.

By this point, the only medication I was taking was phenoxymethylpenicillin, which was an achievement looking back at all the medications I had been taking previously. Although it may have been too late to treat, as shingles usually goes away on its own, I was prescribed acyclovir again, and the doctor recommended calamine lotion to help soothe the itching. Scratching could make it worse, so I had to resist the temptation, which was the hardest part of it all. Having had leukaemia, I can say that shingles is up there with one of the worst diseases you can ever have. It was painful, itchy, and disrupted my sleep. I slept downstairs for three days, and my nights would be spent in the bath and rubbing calamine lotion on the spots, doing everything I could to reduce the itching. Anyone who has had the shingles will know how itchy and painful it is, and it resulted in me having to take three days off school, followed by the weekend to recover.

The Thursday of that week, I was due for a check-up in Bristol, but sitting in a car for four hours with shingles would be painful, and I'd need to be kept away from other patients. Dr. G called Dad to reschedule the appointment. That weekend, I went on the traditional family holiday as planned, as I was feeling much better, although the pain ensured that a funny walk remained for a few days after.

I returned to school the following Monday after my holiday, and I continued working hard to boost those grades. In November 2017, I was to receive a once-in-a-lifetime experience, which, to this day, remains one of the biggest highlights of my life so far.

Make a Wish

Make a Wish is a huge organisation that grants wishes to children who have had life-threatening conditions. Children can wish to have something, be someone for the day, like Prime Minister, do something, or meet someone. Prior to becoming ill, I was usually jealous of those kids I saw receiving their wish; I wanted to do what they were doing. This was because the charity went to great efforts to give children the best experience of their life. Now, I understand you have to go through a lot to truly deserve your wish.

Mum didn't want me to have a wish because she thought they were for children who were going to die. Luckily, the Addenbrooke's counsellor explained that that wasn't the case and I should have been entitled to a wish. With everything I'd been through, Mum agreed.

Behind the scenes of my ongoing hospital appointments and getting my education back on track, talks of a wish were happening. This was as far back as late 2016. We had to get references from a consultant, Dr. M or Dr. A. The references took a while, but in April 2017, we received a visit to our house from the Make a Wish representatives, Adrian and Lavinia. Their role was to get a bit more information from us, as well as get possible ideas about what I wanted my wish to be.

Adrian's role was to go through the Make a Wish process with my parents and the more technical side of it, while Lavinia was there to find out my thoughts of potential wishes. My first choice was to go to WWE Live; I had been in November 2013 and loved it and had also been due to go in April 2016 but couldn't because of my illness. Although it was likely I'd get my first choice, as WWE is very good when it comes to granting wishes, it was always good to get a second choice down. The second choice was something to do with politics because it is something I am really interested in. I wasn't sure what this would involve, but it was along the lines of meeting the Prime Minister or visiting the Houses of Parliament.

Lavinia also asked me some other questions, such as what my favourite restaurant was. She was a bit taken aback when I said KFC. I think she thought I hadn't quite grasped the concept of a wish and couldn't believe how easily pleased I was, saying I should think of something more luxurious. When they left, Adrian revealed that he liked wrestling too and told us that his favourite wrestler was The Undertaker.

Throughout the summer, I had little knowledge of my wish. It had been kept very secretive, but Mum was remaining in contact with the charity. All I knew was that my first choice was the one that was going to be granted. During the summer holidays, we received an email telling us where we could have our wish. There were WWE Live tickets for London or Glasgow. We were going to pick London, but Mum suggested that since we had been to London a number of times, it would be good to explore somewhere new. I agreed to this, especially as I had never visited Scotland before. However, I did agree with slight reluctance, because, while I was sure Glasgow would be great, I didn't know much about the city or what there was to do.

My wish was going to be a three-night stay in Glasgow, originally planned for two-nights, but my parents offered to drive so we were given an extra night funded by the charity. Because I was given three nights, Make a Wish said that we could do something else in addition to going to WWE Live. I didn't have to give anything definite, but just give them a few ideas of what I thought would be cool. I was thinking of playing the bagpipes since we were in Scotland and I love bagpipe music, but I knew this would be difficult to do and didn't expect them to manage it. It was just an idea.

As my wish was approaching, I woke up one Saturday to have received a large package from Make a Wish through the post. The mystery of what was inside made it so exciting! This package was everything I needed for my wish. First of all, I received a few gifts from the charity, including the WWE version of the board game Monopoly and a WWE bag and water bottle. I was also given a couple of shirts with the WWE logo on. We were given four Make a Wish badges, which we would be required to wear throughout our visit, and a marker pen. The marker pen clearly implied something. Going to WWE Live through Make a Wish is different to normal. This time, I was going to be meeting a WWE Superstar, so I needed to get some things to sign! Included in the package was a memory box. This contained a DVD with a 'special message' from WWE Superstar, Titus O'Neil, who confirmed I was going to WWE Live in Glasgow!

Along with this came the itinerary for my wish, which would inform us of what we were doing on each day, maps, so we knew where we were going, and a number of envelopes containing cash for petrol, spending, food, and drink. Some restaurants funded our meal, but some restaurants had to be paid for with our own expenses, and this was the money that Make a Wish sent us to help us fund it. My wish was going to take place, starting from Monday 30th October, and would finish on Thursday 2nd November 2017.

Monday 30th October 2017. I had been at school all day, desperately waiting for the final school bell. Mum and Dad, who had both left work early, were in a bit of a hurry to get going because of the long drive, so Kristy and I got picked up from school. Once we were home, we were there literally for a five-minute bathroom break and then we were on our way.

The reason why Make a Wish gave us an extra night for driving was because going to Glasgow meant an exhausting eight-hour drive, so our first stop was going to be in Harrogate, which was the halfway point between Suffolk, England, and Glasgow, and was about three or four hours away. Our journey didn't start until 3:30pm, so by the time we arrived, it was quite late, and it was very dark outside. We had time to go to an Italian restaurant, and then it was straight to the hotel, where we would be staying for one night.

The next day would be an early start. Free time was allocated to exploring Harrogate the next morning, and then we would finish our journey and hopefully make it to Glasgow by the evening.

Tuesday 31st October 2017. On Tuesday morning, after we had a delicious breakfast at the hotel, we went into Harrogate to have a look around the number of shops in the town. After that, we went to Betty's Tea Room, which I had been told was famous, but I had never heard of it prior to going there. Personally, I found it a bit overrated. It was a nice place, I'll admit, but perhaps it was just a bit too upper-class for me. At least I can say I've been in there. Once we were finished in Betty's Tea Room, we left Harrogate to complete the remaining four hours of our journey to Glasgow.

Once we crossed the Scottish border, we stopped at a service station. When we got out of the car, I noticed that the atmosphere was so much nicer in Scotland than England. It seemed fresher. The air seemed cleaner to me. I'm not sure if that's true or if that's just what I think, but Scotland does seem less polluted.

We arrived in Glasgow at around 5:00pm, just as it was beginning to get dark. Glasgow is a beautiful city. I loved seeing the bright lights as we drove past. It took a while to get to our hotel; we were only a few minutes away but couldn't work out which road to take to get to the Premier Inn. We kept going around the hotel in circles, seemingly getting nowhere. As soon as we finally made it to the hotel, checked in, and dropped our bags off in our room, we needed to go back outside and wait for our taxi. Next on the itinerary was dinner at TGI Friday's.

TGI Friday's was located in the city centre, so we got a taxi there. Dinner was completely complimentary on behalf of the restaurant, which we were very grateful for. Because it was Halloween, the restaurant was decorated with Halloween decorations and all the waiters and waitresses were dressed up in costumes. We were served by a really cool waiter, whose name I unfortunately cannot remember. He was able to predict what everyone was having from the menu, and he was mostly accurate. I didn't have to say anything; he knew I was having chicken fingers.

He was also very good at making things with balloons – he made Kristy a hat and me a water gun. When we told him that my wish was to go to WWE Live, he said he was trained in karate. Although the meal was complementary, alcoholic drinks had to be paid for. Somehow there was a mess up on the order and we had been charged for something we didn't order and the waiter paid for it himself. To thank him, we gave him a £10 tip, and once we had left, he came running down the street to thank us. I will always remember the kind waiter as someone very important to my wish. It is the little things that people do that can go a long way.

Wednesday 1st November 2017. November 1st, 2017 was the big day! It was the day of the main event of my wish. That evening, I would be attending WWE Live and meet a WWE Superstar. I did not know who I was meeting yet – it was a surprise!

The itinerary stated that the morning was allocated free time for us to go sightseeing and exploring around Glasgow. Dad wanted to go to Stirling, which is near Glasgow, to see the William Wallace monument. For someone who loves history, I knew nothing about this and didn't think to pick up a book about it until 2022. My family and I climbed the 246 steps to the top of the tower, and I purchased a goblet from the gift shop. I now get this goblet out every Christmas to drink from, adding a very unique style to my Christmas dinners.We needed to be back at the hotel by 2:45pm because the itinerary stated that 'a very special car' was coming to pick us up and take us to the Hard Rock Café in Glasgow and then straight to the WWE event, so we needed to get back to the hotel earlier to put on our WWE t-shirts and Make a Wish badges. We made it back to the hotel in just enough time to change into our wrestling shirts, and then we were back outside the hotel waiting for the 'very special car'. And that was where we saw a limo arrive in the car park! I had never been in a limo before. I was so excited, but knowing what was to come, I was very nervous too!

That was when we met Mike, our driver for the evening. He let us have some photos with the limo before we got in. He gave Mum and Dad a bottle of wine and a bottle of Coca-Cola for Kristy and me. We were all given a box of chocolates to share. When we got into the limo, it wasn't what I expected. In fact, it was better! I expected a limo to be a car with about forty seats inside, but it was just a long car with a sofa surrounding two of the four sides. It was a party in a car; that's the best way to describe it. There was a stack of CDs on the side of the limo, and we appointed Dad as DJ, who was going to work the stereo.

Our dinner reservation was for 4:00pm, but Mike said that we were a bit ahead of schedule, so instead of going to the Hard Rock Café straight away, he could drive around Glasgow for half an hour or so and do some sightseeing. I was able to see more of Glasgow this way, and I have to say, I love the city. I'm not really sure what it was about it that I loved, I just really liked the buildings and how lit-up it was when it was dark.

At 4:00pm, we arrived at the Hard Rock Café for dinner. The waiter was really jealous because he wished he was going to WWE Live too but couldn't as he was working that night. He asked if we had met WWE Superstar, The Miz, who was doing a meet and greet at GAME down the road. We didn't know The Miz had been at GAME, so it was a missed opportunity!

The Hard Rock Café meal was delicious, but due to time constraints (we needed to be back in the limo by 5:30pm), we only had time to eat half of our food. I was not very happy about having to leave my meal half-eaten, especially because I was enjoying my meal, but I couldn't miss the main event of my wish. We were then driven down to the SSE Hydro Arena, where we were going for the main part of my wish.

Outside the arena, we met Eddie, who worked for Make a Wish. He was going to escort us to the event, just so we could prove to the event staff that we were with Make a Wish. It was difficult finding Eddie at first, and Dad had to ask random men outside the arena if they were called Eddie. I wasn't the only one receiving a wish, so we had to wait for a couple of other families. One family was running late, so while Eddie stood outside looking for them, we and the other family went to go collect our tickets for the evening's event.

I was very nervous and needed to go to the toilet about

three times within the space of half an hour. I was going to meet a WWE Superstar! What was I going to say to them? When collecting the tickets, we met the two WWE representatives. When one of the representatives asked who my favourite wrestler was, I said Braun Strowman, and he told me that he was huge and you have to see him in person to realise how big he actually is. There was no sign of the third wish family, so the other representative took us backstage, where we were going to meet a WWE Superstar before the show started.

First, in a room full of thirty other people, we met the tag team, Luke Gallows and Karl Anderson. This wasn't really a meeting, rather it was an opportunity to take a picture with them. Then, everyone except the wish children and their families were told to leave the room, and the WWE representative told us to stay because we were about to meet someone 'very important'. Before the meet and greet, she gave us a goodie bag, containing the programme for that night's event and also a couple of shirts. These were what we could get signed if we wished.

After a few minutes or so of waiting with the other family, anxious to find out who we were meeting, we saw WWE Superstars, Seth Rollins and Dean Ambrose, two-thirds of The Shield, come through the door. The other Shield member was Roman Reigns, Mum's favourite, but unfortunately, Roman was sick and was pulled from the tour. Mum was very disappointed. But that was okay because, when it was photo time, I acted as the third member of The Shield! I was able to speak to both of them, but I spoke to Rollins more than the other family, and the other family spoke to Ambrose more. They were really nice, and I had a conversation with Rollins about when driving when I got older and how far from Glasgow I lived. Both signed the front of my WWE Encyclopaedia, and Rollins signed one of the t-shirts and the event programme. We also asked Rollins to sign some paper to James, my uncle, who was a big fan of him. It was an amazing experience. Never would I ever have thought that I'd have such an opportunity in my life, let alone one that cost nothing to myself or my family. Once the meeting was over, we were directed to our seats by the arena staff.

We had a great view from our seats. We were not front row, but we were not right at the back of the arena, so far away that we couldn't see anything. Our seats were in the middle section. Because the section was on a ramp, and as we were at the back of that ramp, we got a better view than the rest of the people on the section. Soon, we were reunited with Eddie, who was sat next to us, but he had to disappear again when the third family finally turned up. Because they had showed up late, they ended up having their own meeting with Ambrose and Rollins backstage while the show was going on.

The show was very enjoyable. It was a house show where the RAW roster competed. As it was a live event and not televised, I wasn't expecting any title changes or surprises[15]. I was able to see wrestlers such as Triple H – which I was very excited about and surprised by considering by this point he was a part-timer and only appeared for special events – Seth Rollins, Dean Ambrose, The Miz, Matt Hardy, Bray Wyatt, Sheamus, Cesaro, and many more.

Once the show had finished, we had to find Mike, who was going to drive us back to the hotel in the limo. I had a great evening, and it is definitely a day I will never forget. Make a Wish is a truly wonderful organisation, and I really appreciate everything they did to make my day one of if not *the* best days

---

[15] WWE Live events are known as house shows and so are not televised. The main televised shows are RAW, SmackDown, and NXT, in addition to the monthly pay-per-view events they produce.

ever. But the experience was not over yet. I didn't want it all to end, and I was fortunate that I still had one more day left.

Thursday 2ⁿᵈ November 2017. Make a Wish is amazing. As I was in Scotland, I wanted to play the bagpipes and put it down as one of the things I wanted to do. But because you have to be really experienced playing instruments like the bagpipes, I wasn't expecting Make a Wish to find anywhere that would let me play them, especially just for a one-off. But they did find somewhere!

On Thursday morning, we went to the National Piping Centre in Glasgow. My family and I were going to have a fifty-minute bagpiping lesson. The session was with Dan, a piper, who told us about all the championships he had won. Because it was not possible to learn how to play the bagpipes in fifty minutes, we had to play the bagpipes without the bags, which is how everyone starts.We were given a tube, which looked similar to a recorder, and Dan showed us how to play certain sounds by blowing into the top while covering a different combination of holes. Mum and I were really bad at playing the starter bagpipes! Dad and Kristy were okay though, and they seemed to get used to it, but their work could have done with some polishing.

For the second half of the lesson, Dan gave us a quick tour of the bagpipe museum. I found it really interesting, especially since I love history. I always thought bagpipes were just a Scottish thing, but they actually originate as far back as Ancient Egypt!

After a quick look in the gift shop, my wish experience was officially over. It was now time for Kristy's much-anticipated visit to the Glasgow city centre to go shopping. We would be back at school the next day, so we needed to make it quick for the eight-hour journey home – this time there would be no halfway stop in Harrogate.

Make a Wish is by far the greatest organisation in the world, and I had an amazing time. I will definitely do some fundraising for Make a Wish in the future so others can have as good a time as I had when I received my wish. It doesn't seem real that I have actually had a wish granted; it has always been something I've seen on TV or social media, never something I've been able to experience myself. And now I can add a wish to one of my life experiences!

***

When I returned home, I had officially been off my immunosuppressant medication for one year. I came off them in November 2016. The reason why this is important is because, once it had been a year, I was required to have all the vaccinations I'd had when I was a baby.

The chemotherapy had wiped out everything, so I was no longer vaccinated and had a risk of getting medical conditions that can be easily prevented. These vaccines include tetanus, polio, MMR, and many others. A yearly flu jab was also essential for me from now on. This was done on a schedule, so I didn't have them all at once. In fact, at the time of writing, I still haven't had all of my vaccines, and future events ended up setting me back even further for the vaccine process. For the flu jab, I'm not allowed to have live vaccines, so I need the injections each year instead of the nasal spray.

When I was back for a check-up in November at Addenbrooke's Hospital, Dr. A recommended that I go to West Suffolk Hospital in Bury St. Edmunds for some of my appointments. The only reason for this was because it was good to get to know the team for when I'd no longer need to go to Addenbrooke's. Also, West Suffolk is my closest hospital, so in the unlikely event of me needing anything, it would be good to get to know the hospital. Check-ups were still monthly by this point, but instead of going to Addenbrooke's every month, I would do alternate months of Cambridge then Bury. Of course, check-ups in Bristol continued, which were to be every six months, but soon turned yearly since I wasn't due back until October 2018.

I met my consultant at West Suffolk Hospital. Everything seemed to be fine in the consultation, although she put a heavy emphasis on the fact that, although it is rare, leukaemia likes to relapse in different places, particularly the testicular area. Therefore, she told me it was important to regularly check for any lumps or bumps.

Away from the health side of things, back at school, I was continuing to work hard, and by December, I had sat my Year 11 mocks. I would have to wait until January 2018 to find out how well I had done. Over Christmas, I was going to visit my family in the United States, but I don't think my weakened immune system was really prepared for it.

***

The USA

Make a Wish wasn't the only charity I was able to benefit from. As mentioned before, we were supported by the small local charity, Henry's Holiday Help. They kindly granted my family £1000 towards our holiday to the United States, so my family and I could visit Dad's side of the family for Christmas.

My cousin, Dalet, had been born in July 2016, and because of everything that had been going on with my health, we had not been able to visit her. My grandparents live in El Salvador, but they were going to see us in Virginia, where my Auntie Ani and cousin, Dalet, live. After visiting them for a week, Mum, Dad, Kristy, and I then planned to spend another week in New York for New Year's.

Throughout early December, I was suffering from a really bad cold, which eventually went away. But unfortunately, Dad caught something elsewhere, and – knowing my luck – with my weak one-year-old immune system, I caught it, and it was much worse than what I'd had previously. It completely ruined our holiday.

We arrived in Alexandria, Virginia, on December 21st, 2017. It was the first time I had seen Dad's side of the family after I had become ill. In fact, I hadn't seen Grandma since 2007 when we'd visited them in Maryland at Christmas and Grandad and Auntie Ani in 2009 when they'd come to visit us in Stowmarket. This was the first time I had met Dalet.

On December 23rd, Auntie Ani organised an Andrade family reunion. This was where I met many of Dad's side of the family for the first time. The theme was El Salvador because that's where they all come from, even though the majority live in the States. It was really nice to see my family – most of whom I had never heard of, let alone met!

Once the reunion was coming to an end, my family all gathered around me. While I held Grandma's hand, another family member prayed for me, praying for good health. It was very touching to say the least. I didn't understand a word of the prayer because it was all in Spanish, but I appreciated the fact that they were all praying for my health.

The lady who prayed for me had experienced cancer

herself. She told me that when she had been pregnant, she was in the difficult situation of also being diagnosed with cancer. She'd had the choice of aborting her child or dying from cancer. Choosing to keep the child, despite what doctors predicted, she had ended up surviving. At the end of the prayer, and after she had finished telling her story, she introduced her son. There they were, both healthy. She claims that this was when she found God. She even said that one day her scar from the birth had disappeared, and it was God that had made that possible.

I thought that was a very inspirational story. It was very kind of my family to pray for me, and it wasn't just my family who were praying. A lot were praying back at home during the days of Addenbrooke's and Bristol.

I am not an overly religious person. I believe that if there was a God, no child would be sick on Ward 34 or Ward C2, or any ward. If you asked me in 2016, I would describe myself as a strong atheist, but thinking now, although I don't believe in God, I do feel there is something out there that makes things happen for a reason. Whatever the answer is to whether God exists or not, I was very appreciative of all those who gave me their thoughts and prayers. Having faith and providing hope is a very effective way of getting through traumatic times, and my journey proves this. It was when I was at my best that I had the most hope and when I was at my worst that I wanted to give up.

My ill health made the holiday torturous. I tried my best to enjoy it and did to the best of my ability, making a visit to the White House, Mount Vernon, Times Square, and the Empire State Building and having a tour of New York. But, not helped by the extremely cold weather, I was full of the flu and was suffering from a terrible sick bug. I now understood why the doctor recommended not travelling abroad for quite a while after a bone marrow transplant!

I was fortunate enough to be able to return to the States in August 2019. We went over to visit my grandparents, Auntie Ani, and Dalet, as well as meet some of my family members, some of whom I had been friends with on Facebook but had never met. This time it was in the much warmer location of Tampa, Florida, and I was feeling much better than I was back in New York, making it a truly enjoyable holiday and definitely one to remember for the right reasons.

***

Once I was back from New York, I started a Monday to Saturday paper round, which I kept up with until December 2021. Kristy quit her paper round, so the round was offered to me, which I accepted. As my overall health improved, I wanted to get away from only doing Sunday rounds to doing rounds six days a week, slowly becoming more active in addition to earning more money in the process. Each day I was getting stronger, and even if it was only by a little, I wanted to increase my activity to keep getting stronger.

It was also straight back to school. I was now entering my last full term of teaching time in school. Pressure was increasing. Exams were approaching. Revision was starting.

First, I received my mock results at the end of the month. In some subjects, for me, I did quite well, but in others I was very disappointed. My greatest disappointment was History, where I achieved a 4+, down from the previous year's B. To be on track with the previous year, I should have been in the 6 range. On the positive side, I did pass everything, achieving a 4 in double Science, a 5- in Maths, a 5 in French, and a 5 in English. That was a massive improvement from what I had achieved the previous year. Now that I had passed everything, I knew what I was capable of and wanted to get better. I had one proper term of teaching time left, and then the rest would be revision and exams. The pressure was on, and my goal of one grade of at least one 7 remained.

Science was an issue though, physics being the main problem. This was an issue for the entire class, and eventually, the whole class just dropped physics as a subject entirely. Although I was at a much greater disadvantage than the rest, I was happy that we were all somewhat in the same boat regarding at least one subject and relieved from some of the pressure.

The chances of achieving my goal of at least one 7 seemed to be becoming less and less likely as the exams got closer and closer. For most of my subjects, I was being moved to the foundation tier exams. In foundation, where the questions are easier, the highest grade you can achieve is a 5, whereas in higher tiers, where the questions are harder, the highest grade you can achieve is a 9. In science, which I didn't have high hopes for anyway, I was moved to the foundation exams because of what I had missed in Year 10. In French, I was moved down to foundation because of my atrocious performance in the mock speaking exam. As soon as the teacher asked me a question in French, my response was the longest "err" in the world because I had no idea what she had asked. It's safe to say that I failed that particular exam. My maths remained good, and I stayed in the higher exams for that. For English and history, there was no such thing as higher or foundation tier; everyone took the same exam and had the same chances.

Sometimes I felt like giving up. I was hopeless at biology and chemistry, despite being okay in terms of exam results, and soon stopped revising for them, hoping I could achieve better grades in other subjects if I risked failing science.

However, with the support of all my subject teachers, through after-school, lunchtime, and even weekend and school holiday intervention sessions, I was able to get to where I wanted to be. I was at a huge disadvantage for all my subjects because I still had to teach myself content that I had missed, and sometimes I was under so much pressure, I'd only just finish learning a subject the day before the exam!

I had also applied for special consideration to the exam boards, just as a safety net if things went horribly wrong. I never heard anything from this, so I am unsure whether my special consideration application was accepted.

Despite my stress, things were looking positive. The normal exams took place in May and June 2018. French speaking exams are always early though, and my speaking exam was in April. This went much better than my mock exam. The class could plan questions for what they would ask the teacher in the exam, but I was at a disadvantage in my exam because the teacher forgot to give me an opportunity to ask my question and had to randomly give me the opportunity in a completely different topic to the one in my plan. This could have gone horribly wrong, because I only knew the possible questions I had planned. But out of nowhere, I was able to produce the words I will never forget – "Aimez vous le dessin animé?" These five words stopped my exam from being a total disaster, and I was able to pick up full marks for the question part of the exam! The teacher told me she was so proud of me, and due to my performance in the real thing – a huge improvement from the mock – I was awarded as the May 2018 Linguist of the Month.

The period from May to June 2018 was the most stressful in my life, and I often found myself revising for up to three hours a night, even on days when I had exams. I wasn't going to stop until it was all over. I was going to do everything I could to achieve one grade 7. Over two months, I sat seventeen exams, some of which contained content I had been taught entirely by myself.

And before I knew it, it was all over. Thursday 23rd August 2018 was my results day, so I was going to have to wait until then to find out my results. I don't think there was anything else I could have done to do any better. I had tried my hardest and my best. I looked forward to a thirteen-week summer holiday, which was longer than others' since I didn't have to sit the physics exam as the class had dropped it. Therefore, I finished even earlier, on June 13th, 2018. Now was time for a well-deserved break while also waiting anxiously to receive my results.

I also had other plans for the summer of 2018.

***

Find Your Sense of Tumour 2018

While at an appointment in PDU one day in April 2018, Juliet, who was one of the nurses who took care of me when I was on Ward C2, asked if I wanted to go away for a weekend on a residential. This residential was called Find Your Sense of Tumour (FYSOT), organised by the Teenage Cancer Trust. This isn't my thing; I find it very hard to meet and get on with new people. It takes me about six months of knowing someone before I really start talking to them. But I wanted to change this and thought I'd go for it. Also, in a family counselling session with Angela earlier that day[16], Mum literally ripped my non-existent social life to shreds, proving how embarrassing it had become. I decided that I was going to go for a weekend away. FYSOT was going to take place on the weekend of Friday 29th June to Sunday 1st July 2018.

FYSOT is a residential aimed at those who have suffered from cancer, where a number of teenagers from different hospitals across the UK all meet and spend a weekend together. There is one for under eighteens and one for over eighteens – I attended the under eighteen one. It is funded and organised by the Teenage Cancer Trust, so it is completely free of charge and includes a lot of fun activities, such as workshops and inspiration talks. FYSOT 2018 was going to take place at Whitemoor Lakes in Staffordshire, and I was going to be representing Addenbrooke's, the Cambridge team, along with nine other Addenbrooke's patients.

Amy, who I had met all the way back in June 2016 when I had done food tasting on Ward C9, was going to be responsible for us all, and there were two accompanying nurses: Juliet, one of the nurses who had taken care of me on C2 and who had originally invited me, and Katie, who had also been my nurse on Ward C2, including on my first night. I began as the quiet and awkward one, but as the end of the weekend drew closer and closer, I had soon boosted my confidence, proving how impactful such residentials could be.

Meeting first at the hospital, we all got to know each other as we were all going to be spending an entire weekend together. Juliet said that if I spoke to one of the other patients, we would find out that we had something in common. I found

---

[16] Kristy was having issues with her mental health. Although I remained unaffected, this often had an effect on my family, particularly Mum, and family counselling sessions were needed.

out that he had AML Leukaemia, the same as me, although, unlike me, he had been MRD negative after treatment and did not require a bone marrow transplant.

We arrived in Staffordshire as the team representing Addenbrooke's on a coach, and when we got in the building, we received our name badges and t-shirts. We were not trusted to take our own medicine, so we had to hand our medication in to the treatment room, where I would have to go every morning and evening to take my life-long penicillin. Cambridge was sharing a dorm with CanTeen Ireland, and I was sharing a room with the only two other boys from the Cambridge team.

On the Friday evening, our first dinner was provided. I loved the food there, and it did not disappoint on the first day, with fried chicken and chips being served. Food was the one thing that I was worried about because I'm a very fussy eater, but Juliet reassured me that they served beige food and was equally as happy as I was when she found out. Later that night, we all participated in a quiz, each hospital being its own team. The Cambridge team just Googled all the answers. No one noticed, but we somehow still didn't win.

Like I said, we shared a dorm with CanTeen Ireland, which was difficult to say the least. I'm sure that, individually, the kids were nice people. But together in a group, they didn't get along. The Irish kids hated each other, raiding each other's rooms, and were constantly swearing and calling people names. I even ended up in one of the Irish bedrooms, and I have no idea how I ended up there! They were also spreading rumours about, and running away from, another kid representing the Irish team, who didn't shower. They nicknamed him 'Stinkbomb'. Although I felt bad for the guy, it was his fault he was getting picked on because not only did he not shower, he was also amused by the fact that he didn't shower. The man who was responsible for the CanTeen Ireland team was more concerned with sitting in the lounge area watching the World Cup than anything else and wasn't keeping control of the kids he was supposed to be watching over.

Throughout the entire weekend, there were a number of inspirational talks. One of my favourites was from a man who had lost his legs as he had been in the army; it was really thought-provoking. If we didn't break rules, would we have rules? There were people of a similar age to us who were sharing their personal experiences of cancer. Also, someone was there to talk about being positive about our body image, as most, if not all, cancer patients have scars. Also, a man came in to have a serious talk with us about fertility and how it is affected by treatment. In addition to all of this, we also had a visit from Dr. Bob, who was going to talk to us about healthy living. I learned that potatoes should not be counted as a vegetable, although I am a strong believer that they should!

There were also a number of workshops that were going on. I attended 'Life, Doodles and Bananas', which I was very lucky to be able to attend as I was the last on the sign-up sheet. This involved doodling on a banana while thinking about life. It was all about relaxation techniques. Drawing on a banana is quite therapeutic. It involved closing our eyes and imagining feeling relaxed while doodling on a banana and then all of a sudden imagining a time when we were angry, sad, happy, or excited. I found myself softly doodling on the banana to drawing zig zags and then suddenly jamming my pen aggressively into the banana once I was made to feel angry. It was a good exercise, and it did genuinely work as a way of making me feel relaxed, but I can't say I've tried drawing on a banana ever since.

In terms of the other activities, there was abseiling and a

zip wire. I was much too scared to even involve myself in those activities, so while the nurses tried looking for me to encourage me to participate, I was hanging around in the lounge area with the Irish dude watching the World Cup, who really should have been looking after the kids he was responsible for. Juliet and Katie did find me in the end, but before they could try to make me take part in those scary activities, my foot massage was due. I did want a shoulder massage but that overran with 'Life, Doodles and Bananas', and once again I was last to sign up for a massage and feet were all that was left on the availability timeslots. I did enjoy my foot massage, though. It was so relaxing that I even fell asleep and had to be woken up!.

On the Saturday night, there was a showcase. The theme for FYSOT 2018 was circuses, and each hospital had to perform a circus-themed act, whether that was singing, dancing, acting, or something else. The Cambridge team decided to dance to 'This is Me' from *The Greatest Showman*, a very popular film at the time – which, as of writing, I am still yet to watch and will probably never watch – while throwing sweets out to the crowd. As I don't like being in crowds and was quite shy, I decided to sit back on this and support my team by watching and supporting them instead. Looking back now, I should have joined in, and if I was given the chance to do it again, I probably would have. But just attending this residential was massive progress for me.

Following the showcase, a big disco was held. I stayed away from the dancefloor, instead hanging around with a girl from the Birmingham team, who looked as if she had just finished treatment, throwing a beach ball around. When I returned, I was spotted by someone from the Cambridge team, and they got me up on the dancefloor (after a number of tries). The day before I hadn't known who any of these people were but within a day, they were the only people who could get me up on a dancefloor in my almost sixteen years of existence. I have not been on a dancefloor since.

Once the disco finished at 11:00pm, everyone from every hospital huddled around in one huge circle while the song 'We are the Champions' played. I stayed up way past midnight, playing card games with everyone representing Addenbrooke's, until one by one we all got tired and went to bed. I was one of the last to go to bed because I was now really enjoying myself. It took a while to get settled, but once I was, I ended up having a great time and I felt comfortable with this new group of people. I had an amazing night. FYSOT was great from the start, but this was where I began to really enjoy it.

Since the theme was circuses, there were some circus-themed workshops, and this was the case on the Sunday morning when we all went into the massive hall to try some circus activities. Despite looking so easy, I found plate-spinning impossible. The tight rope walk was easier than it looked, and this was where I spent the most time throughout the entire session. After that was over, we watched a play about two people with cancer, and then it was home time.

Although to begin with I was nervous and didn't know anyone who I was spending a weekend with, by the end of it all, I began to love Find Your Sense of Tumour! The Teenage Cancer Trust is another amazing charity, and most fundraising that Grandma has done by continuing to sell her jam has gone to the Teenage Cancer Trust. If there is anyone who has been invited to FYSOT but is not sure because they're nervous about meeting new people, my advice is go! Unfortunately, FYSOT 2018 was the first and only one I attended as I was slowly becoming less involved with the hospital.

Once I returned home from Find Your Sense of Tumour, it was back to Addenbrooke's the following day. Like I have previously mentioned, chemotherapy, particularly for bone marrow transplants, is capable of disrupting puberty and therefore growth. I had done a little bit of growing since my transplant; when in hospital I was 5'1", but by July 2018, I was 5'3".

Dr. A wasn't particularly concerned about my height. After all, she had seen my father, who I tower over, even though I'm still short. But just to make sure that it was unlucky genetics and not anything to do with my growth being stunted by the intensive and damaging treatment, I was due for an appointment at the endocrine clinic on Monday 2nd July 2018.

At the endocrine clinic, Mum and I needed to be measured. Preferably, they wanted Dad's height too, but he was at work, so we just told them that he was around 5'2". I was already taller than Dad and slightly taller than Mum, though not by much.

The measuring process was complicated. It wasn't just a normal tape measure that Mum and I were measured by. These were tests involved both standing and sitting to get the most accurate measurement. They even had to get a recording of my height when I was taking a deep breath and after I had breathed out. After our measurements, we were called in to see the paediatric endocrinology consultant, who would use this data to determine whether my height was due to unlucky genetics or if the chemo had stunted my growth. If the chemo had affected my growth, then I would require growth hormones. Dr. A joined us in the consultation.

The doctor asked if I had any concerns about my height, to which I said I wasn't sure. I was the giant of the family, but everyone towered over me at school. I had dreams of being 6'10".

First of all, the endocrinology doctor said that I needed to say goodbye to my dreams of being 6'10"; it was almost a certainty that it would never happen. On the positive side, he confirmed Dr. A's beliefs that my height was down to genetics and not the chemotherapy. He was able to show this by the data they had collected earlier on. A chart, formed using the many tests I had taken just a few minutes before, showed that even if I had not had any cancer treatment, 95% of the population were expected to be taller than me. That's just the disadvantage of having short parents. While I was happy that nothing major needed to be done, I couldn't help but be slightly disappointed by the fact that I required no intervention, which would have made me taller.

The endocrinology doctor also needed to examine me, as he could determine how much growing I had left by the size of my testicles. After that, he showed me something that looked like a children's toy as it was a chain of different-sized beads. He showed me the bead that matched my testicle size, and although growth was almost complete, he said it was likely I still had a little more growing to do. I had almost reached my final height, but perhaps I had some growing left.

To see if this was still the case, the endocrine clinic wanted to see me again in January 2019, and I was discharged from the endocrinology unit the same month. I was told that if I had any concerns in the future, I could always be readmitted to the clinic if I wished.

***

I was very nervous about going into school on Thursday 23rd

August 2018 to receive my GCSE results. But for someone who had missed an entire year of schooling, I had performed very well. In fact, my mouth remained open in shock for quite a while. My results were by no means amazing to an ordinary person – average at best – but they were something I was proud of, and had I not missed a year of school, I'm sure I would have been capable of much more. They were amazing for someone like me! Firstly, I passed everything. In English language, English literature, and French, I achieved a grade 5, the equivalent of a high C grade. In biology and chemistry, I also achieved a 5; I thought this had to be down to special consideration because I did not have a clue about science. In maths, I achieved a grade 6, which is equivalent to a B. I was very proud of my maths grade because I had gone from a grade 4 to a grade 6 in only one year.

But did I achieve my goal of one grade of at least a 7? I did! My proudest accomplishment was a grade 7 in History. I got an A in History! All the hard work paid off in the end, and I was so proud of my 7. It wasn't a grade 8 or 9, which I saw some of my friends get, but it didn't matter to me. The fact that I'd had almost double the workload of others in my year and still performed better than some was something I was proud of. At the following November's GCSE award ceremony, my performance in history won me the 'Outstanding Achievement in History' award, something I am very proud of, and I have the certificate on display in my bedroom.

I was very surprised and grateful to receive a congratulations card from my former home tutor, Jackie, which I didn't expect at all. I was so happy that she knew what I had achieved; Mum had texted her, hoping she hadn't changed her phone number. We emailed Amanda to let Denise know my results, but whether she followed up on this I very much doubt.

From my results, I was able to get into Stowmarket High's Sixth Form to study history, psychology, and sociology. I had decided that I was going to study history at university, hopefully to train as a history teacher or lecturer. It was clearly my best subject and one that I'm passionate about. However, becoming a history teacher would be a career I would fall back on. My main goal is to pursue a political career and hope to become an MP and have roles in government. It's unlikely, but I want to work hard to get as close to it as possible, and if I don't set these goals for myself, how will I ever achieve them?

To celebrate my GCSE results and my second birthday, my family had a day out at Newmarket races, with my auntie and cousins. My family placed a bet for me, and I was able to win £40 by betting on a horse that had a similar name to the doctor who had sent me to West Suffolk Hospital on the afternoon of Wednesday 23rd March 2016. I thought that, since I was celebrating my transplant birthday and had come so far since then, it was fitting to bet on something that related to the very beginning of my journey. And it was the right choice!

On my actual birthday on August 29th, I turned sixteen. I went to go see WWE Live at the 02 Arena in London, which was the perfect day for their one-night only tour of the UK. This was my birthday treat in addition to celebrating my GCSE results.

Chapter 12

Normality

My life from September 6th, 2018, to October 8th, 2021

On September 6th, 2018, I started sixth form, studying the subjects history, psychology, and sociology, and it was in sixth form when I started to be like everyone else. The days of special treatment and benefitting from charities were behind me. Gone were the days of hospital appointments every month. Hospital was becoming much more infrequent, but it was important that I continued attending my follow-up appointments. I was now, more or less, on the same level as everyone else, and I was to be treated as such. This was the closest to normal I had been for a while, and in a sense, things were normal, albeit with a few incorporated changes.

What hurts me, and what also makes writing this book very difficult, especially mentioning them at the start of this book, is how those friends who were so close and supportive of me at the very start of my journey are the same people I never speak to anymore. Fin, who had done all that fundraising and supported me so much when I was ill, I now no longer speak to. I was surprised, but also very glad, when he got back into contact with me in February 2021, and even though we don't speak often, it is good to hear from him from time to time. Zoe and I no longer speak, though it was nice to get back in touch in September 2022. It makes writing this difficult because my friends were a major part of my journey, with the fundraising and support. I'm very appreciative of everything they did!

On Friday 21st September 2018, Stowmarket High School did another ten-mile walk, which they had done two years previously to raise money for CCLG while I was having my transplant in Bristol. Luckily, I was able to participate in the 2018 walk! This time, they decided to raise money for the new school building, where construction was about to begin, ready for Easter 2020. Although I appreciated all the support Stowmarket High had given me, I chose to raise money for the Teenage Cancer Trust instead. This was because I had enjoyed Find Your Sense of Tumour and wanted to give back to the charity anything I could. I managed to raise £60, which wasn't much for a charity but could make somewhat of a difference. The walk was challenging but nowhere near as difficult as the nine-mile walk that I had endured in March 2016!

Back in August 2018, I had my final appointment with Dr. A in PDU. I had turned sixteen the same month, which meant that I was now ready to move to the adult haematology clinic. As a result, my appointments at West Suffolk Hospital stopped, after only having around three check-ups there. The purpose of having the West Suffolk appointments in the first place was to get to know the hospital as soon I'd have to stop going to Addenbrooke's, but after turning sixteen, West Suffolk's haematology clinic has no record of me, and I was discharged. Therefore, check-ups at Addenbrooke's remained every two months and yearly at Bristol, and Addenbrooke's was the hospital that would undertake the entirety of my care once it was no longer necessary to be reviewed in Bristol, likely for the rest of my life.

***

Friday 12th October 2018 (Day 777). On 12th October, I had my first appointment in the adult clinic at Addenbrooke's. Although

I missed PDU, the entire process of the adult clinic was much faster and better. On PDU, we would sign in at the desk and wait in the waiting room for hours until I had my obs and blood taken and then I'd see the doctor once they were ready for you. At the adult clinic, it was done by a number system and the system was fairer and quicker. All I had to do was sign in at the front and get a number from the dispenser. Once my number was called, I'd go into the blood room for a blood test, and after that it was straight to the obs room. Then, it would be a short wait until the doctor called me in.

I was previously spending hours in PDU, but the adult clinic took a maximum of an hour and a half. While I was waiting for my check-up on this particular day, Amy, the Teenage Cancer Trust support worker, came to find me in the waiting room. She told me that she understood that it was quite daunting meeting new people, and as she knew me from the food tasting on C9 and FYSOT, she offered to come into the consultation with my family and I just so I had a familiar face. That was when I met Dr. U, who was going to be, and as of writing still is, my haematology consultant at Addenbrooke's Hospital. Dr. U is the TYA lead for haematology at the hospital. He is really cool, and the consultation was really just a conversation. Amy and Dr. U seemed to know each other well because there was a very informal atmosphere to this consultation, which I liked. I was doing so well according to the blood tests that no examination was necessary. He wasn't too interested in the blood side of things, rather he wanted to see how I was doing in everyday life, and he was really surprised to hear about my 'super early paper round', with me waking up at 5:55am every morning except Sunday. We did ask Dr. U a question we had been meaning to ask Dr. A or Dr. M but had forgot about, and that was about the penicillin I was taking. It seemed to be giving me diarrhoea, and this had been happening for a while. As diarrhoea is a possible side effect of antibiotics, we just thought we would ask about it. Ever since C. diff, I hadn't been the same, which could also have been a contributing factor to my toilet troubles. Dr. U said that, while there is no evidence to suggest that the lifelong penicillin was effective, since Bristol's policy was to keep me on it, if I was coping, I should continue with it just for the moment. I was coping. Going to the loo was more of a schedule of up to seven times a day if it was bad or two or three times on a good day, rather than a sense of urgency. Because it really was up to Bristol, he recommended bringing this up with the Bristol team when I went later that month, and he would also review it next time I came for a check-up in Cambridge.

Something that had changed from this point was that, since I was no longer under paediatric care – despite not being eighteen and so unable to take complete control of my care – I was now more responsible for my health rather than my parents. From now on, I would answer calls from Jo, my new CNS nurse, rather than my parents, and if I had any concerns related to my health, it was up to me to keep the hospital informed. Mum continued to guide me through emails and phone calls for a while, but as time has gone on, a lot of the responsibility has shifted to me.

***

Thursday 25th October 2018 (Day 790). Although I had been transferred to adult care at Addenbrooke's, I was still being seen yearly by Dr. G at the children's hospital in Bristol. When I returned to Bristol, everything had changed. Ward 34 wasn't called Ward 34 anymore; it was now known as the Starlight Ward. Day Beds wasn't called Day Beds anymore; it was now referred to as the Ocean Unit.

On October 25th 2018, I had my appointment in Bristol, and I was looking so well that even Dr. G was questioning why I was there[17], He said that he hoped it wasn't a waste of drive coming to Bristol, but he liked to continue to monitor how things were going. He also told me to remain on the life-long penicillin just to be on the safe side, although there was no right or wrong answer whether I should have been on it or not.

My next check-up in Bristol was going to be in a year's time, but for the photo album and memories, I asked to take a picture with Dr. G. Like all the doctors, but especially him, he is responsible for why I am still here today. Unfortunately, I forgot to take a picture with Dr. A or Dr. M, but they are also very important for the reason I am still here today, in addition to all the nurses on Ward C2 and on Ward 34.

Because we had travelled for four hours, and it was going to be another four hours back just for a ten-minute hospital appointment, my parents and I decided to have a short day out in Bristol. It would be the first time in a year and a half I would see the outside of Sam's House, and although it seems like nothing special, we also had a look around the Co-op where I had once spent so much time. For some reason, I really wanted to go to Somerset, and I was able to. All I had to do was cross the Clifton Suspension Bridge, and I reached the 'Welcome to North Somerset' sign. Unfortunately, that was as far as I got.

***

---

[17] Some of my Bristol and Addenbrookes appointments were ridiculously close together. In the early days, this was due to timing (for example, if a two-weekly Addenbrooke's appointment overlapped with a monthly Bristol appointment). However, in this case, it was because the Bristol appointment had been booked a year in advance, whereas this Cambridge appointment was just to meet the new team.

Friday 5ᵗʰ April 2019 (Day 952). I had my second appointment at the adult haematology clinic with Dr. U at Addenbrooke's on this day. This was where I received some great news! First of all, I was told that I had the immune system of a five-year-old, which doesn't sound great for someone who was sixteen at the time, but at that point my transplant would have been only two and a half years ago, so this was some good progress.

But this wasn't the most important amazing news I received. Dr. U told me that I could now come off the phenoxymethylpenicillin, something that was supposedly a life-long medication. He said that I could come off it as I seemed to be doing well and that there is actually little evidence that it was effective anyway. This was a sign that my immune system was definitely getting stronger two and a half years post-transplant.

The only concern, which was expected, was the iron levels in my blood. When you have a lot of blood transfusions, the body receives a lot of iron, and instead of getting rid of the excess iron, it stores it. Normal blood iron levels, or ferritin levels, are 12 to 300 for males, or 12 to 150 for females. Mine were 950, giving me the nickname 'Iron Man' from Mum. Dr. U said that it was just something to monitor and this was normal and expected for someone like myself.

If the levels reached over 1000, which they were very close to, I was at a higher risk of organ failure, so if levels did increase, they would have to take blood from me every six weeks or so to balance the levels. Therefore, if my iron did reach over 1000, even how it would be dealt with wouldn't be too bad. Knowing that I was due back in Bristol in October 2019, Dr. U said that my check-ups at Addenbrooke's would now be once a year, allowing a six-month gap between Bristol and Addenbrooke's appointments, which once again was amazing progress!

***

Throughout Year 12, I also decided to become a Year 11 mentor. Knowing how difficult it was getting through my GCSEs, I thought I'd do everything I could to give support to those who needed and wanted help. My mentality was that, if I could do it, then anyone could. Every Wednesday morning, I met with my mentee, Lewis, and taught him the areas of English and maths that he found difficult. I definitely found it rewarding, especially when my mentee told me that he had learnt more in twenty minutes of mentoring than he had with his teacher for an entire year!

I still wanted to study history at university. My friends and I attended Uni Camp 2019: we stayed at the University of Suffolk in Ipswich for five days in July just to find out whether university was right for us. Meeting new people is not my thing, and I was reluctant to go, but knowing how much I had enjoyed Find Your Sense of Tumour, and since Uni Camp was completely free, I thought I'd take the opportunity. It was an amazing experience! Alongside the many fun activities and amazing restaurants that we all visited as a group, we also had taster sessions to see what a university lecture was like. My favourite lecture was the politics one, which convinced me to do a joint degree in History and Politics.

I started a weekend job in June 2019 at Glasswells, a furniture store, in Bury St. Edmunds, where Mum and my cousin Jade work. I was given the choice of the gifts department or pot-washing in the restaurant. I chose pot-washing, which, although psychologically and physically difficult, is a job I have since grown to enjoy! The good thing was that I wasn't even three years post-transplant, yet I was well enough to be able to work a difficult and fast-paced job. I kept going with my paper round too.

I was proud of my January 2020 Year 13 mock results. I achieved an A in history, an A in psychology, and an A* in sociology. At the start of Year 13, most students were going through the UCAS process, choosing our universities. I applied for the University of Suffolk in Ipswich, University of East Anglia in Norwich, and Anglia Ruskin University in Cambridge, preferring to be at a university nearby. In February 2020, I accepted University of Suffolk's unconditional offer to study politics and history, starting in September 2020.

***

Thursday 10th October 2019 (Day 1140). I was back in Bristol for a check-up in October 2019. It had seemed like ages since my last hospital appointment. Everyone there was telling me how well I was looking; it had been so long since I had been there that I was surprised they all remembered me. A few important things were discussed in the consultation with Dr. G and Chris, the specialist nurse, who I had not seen for years and was surprised to see still worked there.

Dr. G went over what the ferritin levels were all about, which has been explained above. He pretty much said the same as Dr. U. He said that it would take another six or seven years before the iron levels in my blood returned back to normal.

He also recommended that I should take Vitamin D because there is not enough sunlight in the UK. Vitamin D supplements over the counter were fine to take.

Mum was also concerned that I had been complaining of a pain in my leg. She worries a lot when I complain of pain because joint pain is a symptom of leukaemia, although I was sure it was because I was tired and had to stand up a lot at the weekends washing dishes. Dr. G agreed with my view, saying that we all get tired from time to time and as long as the pain wasn't severe, I should be okay.

Also, Dr. G was not so sure about me coming off the life-long penicillin. Bristol takes a different approach to Cambridge. He thought it was a very naughty decision made by Addenbrooke's. Bristol argues that it should be used as a precaution, but Cambridge argues that if you're doing well then there shouldn't be a reason to take it. He told me that there was no right or wrong answer to whether I should be on the life-long penicillin. A study a few years ago has shown that it can reduce the chances of getting a lung infection, which can be serious for someone with a weakened immune system. Other than that, there is no proof that it is really all that necessary to take, and therefore, Dr. G reluctantly gave his approval to allow me to continue to be off it.

In the examination, my heart, lungs, teeth, eyes, and ears were fine. Dr. G said I looked so well that I wouldn't require a blood test for this appointment. He also said that I had grown 1.5cm since my last visit to Bristol and could confirm that I had most likely reached my final height.

There was some great news to follow. You may have noticed throughout the post-transplant part of this book is that no one ever told me I was cured. I had lived an entire three years in remission – that is, I was still classed as a leukaemia patient, but I was just showing no signs or evidence that the disease was present in my body. My leukaemia will never be cured; it is almost impossible to determine. You can only go by the samples of bone marrow and blood tests. However, I was now over three years post-transplant, in remission, with no relapse, so I was Bristol's definition of a cure. My leukaemia was officially 'cured' after spending three years in remission!

But with this amazing news also came some sad news. Dr. G told me that as I was now 'cured', it was no longer necessary to be reviewed in two clinics, and as a result, on Thursday 10th October 2019, I was discharged from the Bristol Royal Hospital for Children. Therefore, I would from now on just have annual check-ups with the Cambridge team. This meant no more Bristol. I was really going to miss the Bristol team, but Dr. G said that next year I would have been referred to the Teenage and Young Adults (TYA) team in Bristol anyway, so this most likely would have been my last appointment with him.

A huge milestone in my journey had been reached! I gave Dr. G a hug and shook Chris' hand, thanking them for everything, and then I was off, out of the Bristol hospital doors for the final time, allowing me to not only continue my journey but start new ones. I am still yet to go back to visit Bristol, but I hope to one day.

***

After my final hospital appointment in Bristol in October 2019, it now became clear – if it hadn't already – that the days of constant hospital appointments were behind me. I'd still have to go to hospital, but they would soon be so infrequent that I wouldn't mind going once a year or so. I was ready to start a new chapter in my life, not as a cancer patient, but as someone who was going to fulfil their ambitions. I ended up spending the time from October 2019 to March 2020 continuing to work on my A-Levels, as well as continuing my paper round and weekend job.

Then the Covid-19 global pandemic hit, and the UK was placed in lockdown on March 23rd, 2020 – exactly four years to the day when I was admitted to hospital and diagnosed (which was confirmed on 24th March) with AML. Schools, restaurants, and non-essential shops closed. We were only allowed to leave the house once a day for exercise and were advised to stay at home, work at home, and avoid public transport. We were discouraged from leaving our area, and fines would be imposed for meeting with friends or extended family.

When evidence showed that the virus was most deadly to elderly and vulnerable people, I was advised by the government to start shielding, which would mean not leaving the house under any circumstances. It would be a lie to say that I followed shielding rules fully, with me still opting to continue doing my paper round for exercise. I also started running and weightlifting, though I did carefully follow rules with social distancing. Ensuring that I was at home as much as possible, I did not step into a supermarket from March 2020 until July 2020.

The pandemic gave me flashbacks to my time in hospital. It was a time when health took priority over work and education. Never before did I think I would have so much time to spend with my family again – the daily games of Scrabble had returned. I also used the time to attempt to get into shape. As I said, I got into running, and I was even starting to lift weights. I think it was a lockdown thing because it stopped soon after, but I was getting good, and it showed that I had very few health issues! In fact, by 2020, I think I was free from any health issues. I was a completely normal person, and I felt absolutely amazing every day!

By no means is a pandemic a good thing, but I will continue to cherish the time that I had with my family, especially at a time when we were all well, and I also felt being in lockdown with very hot weather was a well-deserved break. I had been working myself to the verge of breakdown with my A-Levels, but then everything suddenly stopped. I was concerned by how my grades would be affected, but I was happy when I found out that they would be based on teacher predictions.

I was very proud to have achieved AAA in my A-Levels. I was off to study politics and history at the University of Suffolk in Ipswich, starting in September 2020. After a long struggle with health for four years, I had finally got to where I wanted to be. Whatever the challenges that were thrown at me, I got through them, coming out stronger every time.

Before I started university – which I would be living at home for anyway – there needed to be one final trip to the hospital, and it was an important one.

***

Tuesday 29th September 2020 (Day 1496). With the ongoing pandemic, my hospital appointment scheduled with Dr. U at Addenbrooke's in April 2020 was postponed to August 14th, with that ultimately being cancelled too.

Instead, I had an appointment scheduled for Addenbrooke's on September 29th, 2020 – the same day as my first university lecture – which was a late-effects transplant clinic. This was a clinic that ran a series of tests, very similar to my work-up plan, that would test how much damage my transplant had done to me four years later. The tests I required were the following: a lung function, a heart echo scan, an ECG, and a bone density DEXA scan, in addition to a general check-up with the specialist nurse and all the blood tests and obs I needed to have done.

I was nervous about going to this appointment. It wasn't because I was scared of the tests – it was nothing I hadn't done before – rather, it was that with Covid-19 around, the hospital was going to be completely changed around with one-way systems and extra precautions, something I didn't want to mess up. For all of my tests, and for walking around the hospital in general, we had to wear face masks.

Luckily, Dad and I didn't mess up too badly, although we did at first. The first thing on my list of tests to get done was the lung function test. Automatically, we got told off for going through the wrong entrance – the entrance I had always gone through for the couple of lung functions I'd had before. Due to Covid, there were lots of one-way systems that had to be followed. But other than that, the lung function went smoothly.

I was glad to be reunited with "Blow Blow Blow man", who I remembered from four years ago before my transplant, though he looked much different. He no longer had glasses and was covered in PPE due to the pandemic. He had lost a bit of enthusiasm too, but he did have a little bit inside, so I knew it was him! He started off by recording my height and weight, and then it was the usual test of having a peg on my nose and breathing in and out as hard as I could. The only difference between this test and the others I'd had already was that this time I wouldn't be doing the test where I sat in a transparent box with a peg on my nose. I don't know why Covid restricted this procedure because it was only me who had to sit in the box, but I didn't question it. Instead, we just stuck to the breathing tube by Blow Blow Blow man's desk.

There were a few problems. First of all, Blow Blow Blow man's equipment was broken, and he had trouble fixing it. Once he had fixed it, the problem was me. The aim of the lung function test is to blow out as much oxygen as you possibly can, even if it feels like you've got no more. Because – as you can imagine – this is very difficult, I ended up taking mini breaths, subtly breathing in and out, when I was still supposed to be breathing out from the very first breath I took. It took a number of tries but I soon cracked it.

After my lung function test, it was off to the haematology clinic, where I was expecting to see the doctor. I signed in and gave my details. For some reason, every department I went to that day asked me to confirm my details, which got a bit tedious. After waiting a while in the waiting room, I was called for my blood test and went to tell the healthcare assistant that I had already had my height and weight recorded for the day. Once that was done, I ended up in the waiting room for some time, until Jo – my specialist nurse who I had met very briefly a couple of years before – called me in.

I wondered where Dr. U was, but I found out that this was a nurse-led clinic. Jo was the one doing the consultation. She had a long checklist that needed to be filled out, asking things such as how active I was, if I smoked, how much I drank, and how many times I went to the toilet. She was a bit concerned about how many times I went to the toilet, and I explained to her that I had never recovered after the C. diff, though I said it was manageable and I rarely felt a sudden urge to rush to the loo.

Jo was glad to hear that I was starting university, although she was disappointed to hear I was missing my first lecture due to having to attend the clinic. She said that she would pass it on to Dr. U as he apparently loved hearing about people going to university.

Jo did some general checks on me, saying that I had great skin for the treatment I had endured and I looked very well for what I had been through. One concern was that I had been feeling dizzy from time to time, which, as of writing, is still the case. She took my blood pressure but said that it was perfectly healthy and just said to keep an eye on it. Other than that, she was very happy to hear that my general health had been very good, and she was glad things were looking up for me. She just wanted one more thing – to get a urine sample – and once I had produced that, I was able to go to the next procedure on my list, which was an ECG scan.

The department where ECGs were done was completely unrecognisable, and Dad and I found ourselves getting lost. The ECG procedure was the same as all the others, which involved sticking stickers on my body and attaching them to wires attached to a machine. Letting the machine do the work, this ultimately shows a graph of the heart's rhythm and electrical activity. The procedure was very quick; in fact, it was much quicker than expected. All I did was have a chat with the lady about the weather and I was out of there.

The final thing to do for the day was my DEXA scan, which would measure my bone density. Using low dose X-rays, DEXA scans can show how strong the bones are. This was the one procedure that I had not had before. With it being during the Covid-19 era, this also ended up being the first appointment I ever attended on my own without my parents due to limited space for social distancing in the waiting room. I was quite nervous and anxious that I had got the wrong place, so I was glad when the lady called me into the X-ray room.

I had already messed up when I got in there because, on the appointment confirmation letter, it was recommended that I wore trousers with no metal on them. There I was with a belt on (which was easily solved) and with jeans with a metal button (not so easily solved). It worked out okay though as the lady worked around it, telling me I had to pull my trousers down and then covering me with a sheet.

She then told me about the procedure. It was really weird. It started off normal, with me just lying on a bed as a scanner scanned my pelvis area. Then, the lady got out a large, cubed cushion, which I had to put under my legs while still lying down. It is very hard to describe the position I was in, but the best way to explain it is to visualise sitting up straight on a chair and then turning the chair back 90° on the floor with the back of the chair on the floor. So, basically, I was lying down in a sitting position but with my back on the bed and me facing the ceiling. Hard to visualise, I know, but there is no easier way to explain it.

Once the DEXA scan was done, I was free to go home. I managed to make it in time for the final hour of my lecture (due to the Covid-19 era, it was online).

For some reason, I never received an appointment letter for my heart echo scan, so this wasn't done on this particular day. I did end up having it the next week, on Thursday 8th October 2020. This heart echo scan was the same as all the others, just involving the jelly on a stick, which worked like an ultrasound on the heart. This echo scan took longer than the others as it also looked at my throat and airways. Following that, everything was done in terms of tests, and I just had to wait a couple of weeks to receive my results.

I didn't really make much use of the results as it was a long letter sent through the post full of numbers. However, I can say that the fact that there were no pressing issues discussed in the review letter showed that everything was fine. Some statistics I did make use of – the iron levels in my blood were now 743, which, although nowhere near the normal level, was down from 950 the previous year and was a massive improvement from 1200 in 2017! The letter also requested that I have my annual flu jab and a cholesterol check, which could be done at my local GP surgery. I had both of these done, and as I have never received the results, I think it's safe to say that my cholesterol was fine. Overall, everything was fine, and I continued to remain well!

***

By the end of 2020, and going into 2021, despite the challenges that the entire world had and will continue to face, I ended up doing well for myself. On March 23rd and 24th 2016, everything in my life seemed to be over. If you told me that almost five years later, I would be waking up every morning for a super early paper round while attending university lectures almost every day and then going to work on the weekends, I wouldn't have believed you. If you told me on the day that I had found out I'd be going to transplant that almost five years later I'd be learning to drive and would be entering adult life, I wouldn't have believed you. If you told me that in five years, I would be thinking about my career, through my university course and also becoming a member of the Conservative Party, I wouldn't have believed you. It just shows that if you fight back and have courage, dedication, and determination, you can achieve anything and be somewhere you never expected.

This book was supposed to end here, followed by an epilogue. Being five years out from transplant, I knew that the five-year anniversary was the perfect time to get the ball rolling and start the publishing process for this book. I applied to agents but was getting nowhere, until someone at work recommended that I go to a charity, which might be able to help me out. None of the charities were willing to publish this entire book for me, but by me approaching them, they were keen to work with me and use my book as a way to get my story out to help others.

I had a Teams call with the marketing and story managers of the Teenage Cancer Trust. They talked me through potential publishing options for my book and advised that self-publishing was the best way to go. They were also really interested in what I had written about in my book, and I ended up working with them on a blog about hair loss. I sent them extracts from my book, where I talk about hair loss, and the Teenage Cancer Trust writers converted it into a blog. The blog was well-written, and I was really pleased with it, hoping it could be used as a tool for people going through something similar. It was published on the Teenage Cancer Trust website and shared on Facebook and Instagram. The blog was on there for a few months, but it has unfortunately since been taken down.

Another charity I was working with was Young Lives vs. Cancer, previously known as CLIC Sargent. They had the idea to convert my book into a graphic novel, which I thought sounded really cool. Condensed picture books had helped me greatly during the earlier days of my leukaemia journey. Of course, illustrating such a massive project takes time, and as of writing, the graphic novel is still in production, and I am unsure as to when or if this will reach completion.

I celebrated five years post-transplant on August 29th, 2021, combining it with my nineteenth birthday. I achieved five years with the all-clear on October 1st, 2021. I was beginning to share my story in an attempt to inspire others that cancer isn't all doom and gloom and you can make a comeback! The editing and publishing process for this book began in October 2021.

Exactly one week after my five-year all-clear anniversary, things started to go terribly wrong. The next page was supposed to start the epilogue. Instead, there is an entire third part of this book, where a certain happy future is replaced with one full of uncertainty.

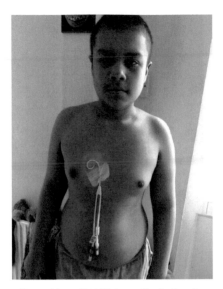

Final photo of me with my first Hickman line before its removal later that day, January 31st 2017. I had my line for 309 days.

One of my proudest moments at school when I become the first recipient of Stowmarket High School's Courage in the Face of Adversity award, July 20th 2017.

My 1st transplant anniversary birthday cake, August 26th 2017.
We invited all our friends and family to celebrate my one-year
milestone and raised money for the blood cancer charity, DKMS.

Make a Wish in Glasgow – Kristy, Mum and I in the limo, on the way to the
Hard Rock Café before attending WWE Live, November 1st 2017.

Taking a quick photo outside Sam's House just for the memories, October 25th 2018. I'd just had my routine check-up in Bristol with Dr. G.

Kristy and I on our family holiday in Gran Canaria, May 2019.

My first day of university and as a Politics &
History student, September 21st 2020.

Enjoying the weather on a day out in Bury St. Edmunds,
May 31st 2021. I am still feeling very well in myself.

Mum and I on my five-year transplant anniversary, August 26th 2021. We went out for a family breakfast to celebrate.

Celebrating five years in remission, or so I thought... October 1st 2021.

Part Three

Relapse

Chapter 13

Heartbroken

The diagnosis of my Acute Myeloid Leukaemia relapse from October 8th to December 22nd, 2021

Going into 2021, I was feeling relatively well and suffering from hardly any problems at all. I did have a problem with my throat, as I seemed to be getting sore throats quite often, but that was about it. I was doing so well that I wasn't even seen as a priority by the hospital, and due to Covid-19, my hospital appointments at Addenbrooke's kept getting cancelled and postponed. Having had my bone marrow transplant five years ago, my leukaemia was determined to be 'cured' and the late-effects clinic the previous year showed that I wasn't suffering from much damage from my treatment at all. Overall, I was very fit and healthy for someone who had been through what I had, and doctors were really satisfied with my progress.

By the summer of 2021, however, there were subtle signs that something wasn't right. There wasn't anything major to report, and I suppose what was starting to happen didn't even cross my mind as symptoms to begin with. But I was noticing that the problems I had been having with my throat were getting worse, my skin was looking very unhealthy, and any activity made me more tired, sweaty, and breathless.

I recall being unwell on my joint fifth-nineteenth birthday party, being so tired and drowsy before the party started and having to survive the day on cold and flu medicine with added caffeine. I remember a time at work when I worked so hard that my heart started pounding very fast and I became dizzy. After being discovered with my face in front of the fan, I was okay after having a five-minute sit down and downing a glass of Coca-Cola. On rare occasions, I was also falling asleep during conversations.

I guess you could count these as being symptoms, but these were very subtle. I continued functioning very well for many months, mostly free of any complaints. With the exception of my sore throats and unhealthy skin, all my other issues appeared to be sporadic and one-off incidents, and I'm not really sure if they were any contributing factor to what was going to hit me.

Perhaps I was overworking myself. Having come out of lockdown – basically months of rest – I was powering through university, learning to drive, and getting up early for my paper round, and I had taken on lots of extra shifts at work. Trying to publish a book wasn't easy either. I wasn't getting much rest, and my life was non-stop. I think my non-stop lifestyle made it clear to me that there were no pressing issues with my health. There were subtle signs and one-off incidents, but I knew what having leukaemia felt like, and I was adamant that I would not have been able to function for so long if there was anything concerning going on.

***

Friday 8th October 2021. Finally, after appointment cancellation after cancellation, I had my routine blood test and check-up with my haematology consultant, Dr. U, on October 8th, 2021. He wasn't too concerned about my health either as everything seemed the norm. That being said, by this stage in my remission, most of my consultations involved conversations about my everyday functioning and not so much the examination of any symptoms. I noticed in this appointment that Dr. U paid slightly more attention to the symptoms I was concerned about and did do an examination to check that there were no physical signs of anything concerning.

One issue I had was a lump on my hand. Due to my medical history, any lumps or bumps I discovered needed to be taken seriously. In November 2019, I had found a lump on my chest, but after being examined in the West Suffolk Hospital breast clinic, there was nothing worrying found and the lump had eventually disappeared. Dr. U wasn't concerned about the lump on my hand, and perhaps my body was just a bit asymmetrical. He told me a funny story of how he was able to get a roll of tape higher on one arm than the other and that, humans are a lot more asymmetrical than we may think.

The second issue I was suffering from was to do with my bowel movements, as in the five years since my transplant, I was still going more times than normal and my stools were not formed. Once again, the doctor wasn't overly concerned and recommended I try something like probiotic yoghurts. While it could have been chemical damage from my previous chemo, there was also a case made that I'd had so many antibiotics in my life, they had actually killed the good bugs in my body in addition to the bad bugs. Yoghurts with live bacteria would help this, although there was also speculation that I was lactose intolerant, so I was told not to make things worse if I didn't have to. Tests to check whether I was celiac were also done, as that could have potentially been causing my frequent bowel movements. Fortunately, tests came back showing I was not celiac, and it was unlikely that I was lactose intolerant.

That seemed to be it for now, and the consultation just involved going through minor ailments that I had been complaining about for some time but never thought of as something serious. On a sidenote, before the appointment ended, Dr. U did mention, and was very surprised to see, that for some reason my neutrophils had dropped below 1.0. Normal levels should be between 1.5 and 7.7.

Although he was surprised to see this, Dr. U wasn't too concerned about my moderate neutropenia and put it down to a potential viral infection, saying that neutrophils lower all the time when people suffer from infections like a cold. Evident by my sore throats, I was probably just suffering from a viral infection, which had lowered my neutrophils a bit. A good sign was that the rest of my blood count was near normal. With my clinical history, however, while not overly concerned, Dr. U wanted to be safe and booked me in for a blood test in a month's time and a telephone follow-up appointment. After a quick swab of my throat to check for any viral infections, I was sent home with few worries.

***

A week later, I received a call from my specialist nurse, Jo, who informed me that my blood test results showed a number of deficiencies in my blood. One of my deficiencies was in Vitamin D, so I was prescribed a medication called colecaciferol to top this up. These didn't appear to be normal over-the-counter Vitamin D supplements though. I was put on a very powerful first course of tablets for a week, followed by the more general tablets I was to take indefinitely after.

Another unusual thing that appeared on my blood tests, aside from my moderate neutropenia, was that I was found to have a very mild macrocytosis. This essentially meant that my red blood cells were larger than normal. It is usually very mild and causes little problems and isn't a blood condition in itself, but it can be a sign of an underlying blood condition. It was later found that I had a folate deficiency, so I was prescribed folic acid to take every day, which aims to create healthy red blood cells. I was reassured that this was nothing to worry about and in fact it was quite normal to have such deficiencies. It was good having this reassurance, but this, combined with my low neutrophil count, showed some signs that my five years of increasingly healthy blood was beginning to turn the opposite direction.

One month later, I had my check-up over the phone with the BMT clinical fellow doctor. My bloods weren't mentioned in this telephone consultation, so I assumed everything was fine. I didn't think to ask about my blood results because I thought if it was anything serious, it would have been one of the first things the doctor would tell me. It was more of a catch-up on the minor issues that I had spoken to Dr. U about regarding my bowels and sore throats back in October.

I had spent the early days of November with a suspected urine infection after experiencing a burning sensation during and after urinating for a few days. Urine infections are more common in women, so for men it could mean something more serious. I'm guessing it was down to my low neutrophils, as neutropenia increases your risk of infection. To cure my infection, I was prescribed an antibiotic, nitrofurantoin, by the GP. When looking at the label, Mum noticed that this medication had a chance of causing bone marrow damage. This was the last thing I needed, considering I was already neutropenic. I asked the doctor about this during my telephone appointment, and she said that while it wouldn't be the hospital's first choice of drug to give me, it was fine to continue taking it since I was already on it. My urine infection eventually cleared up.

What *was* a concern in the consultation, however, was that I had developed a lump on my chest, and this is what the doctor wanted to prioritise in this consultation once I had mentioned it. She started off confused, asking me if I was sure that it wasn't bone, considering I was struggling to provide exact details. I was sure something was there though. The doctor wanted me to get this checked out, so she booked me in to attend the clinic on Friday 12th November 2021.

I somehow managed to mistake a rather large spot for a lump, and the spot soon went down. I was quite embarrassed by this, but it left me wondering whether attending the clinic was really necessary now that I knew it was nothing to worry about. The day before my scheduled appointment, I phoned up Jo to cancel my appointment. The day was Thursday 11th November, Kristy's birthday, and we had plans to go see her at her university accommodation in Norwich to celebrate. But Jo had some bad news over the phone, and instead of cancelling my appointment, she wanted to see me as soon as possible.

I was still neutropenic from my last blood result, and my inflammatory markers[18] were on high. I was a bit concerned by this because the last time I was neutropenic I was recovering from chemotherapy, which was five years ago. What was causing the sudden dip in my bloods? In terms of my inflammatory markers, I had no idea what it meant at this stage in my journey, and it was a completely new concept to me, but Jo was speaking as if it was urgent.

"You're neutropenic, Jake! Instead of cancelling your appointment for tomorrow, we should really get you seen in

---

[18] High inflammatory markers include a high level of C reactive protein (CRP) in the blood. Normal CRP levels are 0-9. Anything above is a marker for inflammation, indicating anything from an infection to cancer.

the clinic today to see what your bloods are doing," said Jo.

Kristy's birthday didn't exactly go to plan. We were supposed to see her in the afternoon, but Jo strongly advised me to go to Addenbrooke's to have a last-minute blood test to see if my bloods had improved or worsened. She was able to get me booked in, and my parents and I made the unexpected trip to Addenbrooke's. We ended up being late to Kristy's birthday but managed to see her in the evening, driving straight from Cambridge to Norwich.

All the way up to December, I had gone from yearly appointments at the hospital to having weekly blood tests and telephone appointments once a fortnight. My blood tests were mostly done at the hospital, although on one occasion I went to the drive-through phlebotomy service in Cambridge. All Dad had to do was park the car in a bay, and the phlebotomist would arrive to give me a blood test from the car door!

I was still feeling very well in myself, the sore throats still on and off, and nothing really indicated low blood cells. While the appointment follow-up letters through the post started to show a decline in my red blood cells, showing a very mild anaemia, this wasn't as severe as my white blood cell drop, and the doctors never mentioned my red blood cell count when trying to get their head around my mysterious neutropenia. My platelets were still well within the standard range too. Overall, my blood count was well-preserved, except for my white blood cells, particularly my neutrophils.

On Friday 12th November 2021, I had a telephone appointment with the BMT clinical fellow, which was originally scheduled as the face-to-face appointment that I had cancelled. I'll admit that I didn't really take my appointments seriously because of how well I was feeling. If I had other plans, I'd prioritise them over my hospital appointments because everyone seemed to be panicking except me. I was well! But my neutrophils had shown no increase and had indeed dropped further. The doctor said that it was difficult to tell what the cause of my neutropenia was unless they did a bone marrow aspiration. I was reassured by this, because knowing my history, if it was leukaemia, wouldn't the doctors just tell me? From past experience, I knew that leukaemia was a result of too many immature white blood cells, and therefore I expected my white blood cell count to be abnormally high if it was leukaemia. The fact that my cells were low indicated to me that something was going on, perhaps another condition, but one that could be cured. No action was being taken yet, and the doctor told me that Dr. U just wanted to continue keeping an eye on things for now. In the meantime, I was informed that because my bloods were so low, if I developed a fever or became unwell, I would have to be admitted to hospital straight away as I would not be able to fight an infection on my own. I found this a bit scary, but I did admittedly turn a blind eye to it.

Perhaps my neutropenia was something I could control. Mum put my low immune system down to my diet, so she encouraged me to eat more fruit and vegetables. History repeats itself – these were the same explanations we had made five years prior. Having never had my five-a-day, I was actually becoming really good at eating my fruit and vegetables. One day, I even had six of my five-a-day! Mum tried to encourage me to eat a banana for breakfast every morning and always prepared different fruits and vegetables for me to try.

For a moment, there seemed to be a glimmer of hope. Maybe, just maybe, I could control my neutropenia. Things seemed to be looking positive during my Thursday 2nd December 2021 face-to-face visit to the hospital. It is worth mentioning that hospital appointments were based on blood test results from the previous week and the blood tests taken on the days of my appointments would be followed up the next week. I received good news as the clinical fellow said that while my blood test results still were not good, there appeared to be an improvement. My white blood cells had increased from 1.6 to 1.8, which was still bad considering the standard range of 3.9 to 10.2 for white blood cells, but it was an indication that the decline had stopped! The fruit and vegetables were working! The doctor said that they would still keep an eye on me, and depending on the blood test results that day, I would require a blood test in two weeks or a bone marrow biopsy. The plateau of my declining bloods was a promising sign that further action wasn't necessary, and hopefully the recovery of my bloods was underway. I had never eaten so many fruits and vegetables in my life! Mum and I went out for lunch to celebrate this news.

Friday 3rd December was a good day. I had spent the day with my best friend, Lauren, and we had finally submitted our essays for the second module of our second year of university. There was also even more reason to celebrate with yesterday's news of the ending of my white blood cell decline. Nothing was going to stop me from celebrating my good news, and I sat myself down on the living room floor to build my Lego International Space Station, something I had been waiting all day to build! Then, that evening, at 7:30pm, I received a call from the doctor, the most disheartening phone call I think I've ever had. You know it's bad news when the doctor is calling you out of clinic hours.

"Hi, is this Jake?"

"Hello, yes, it is."

"Hi Jake, how are you doing?"

"I'm alright thank you, how are you doing?"

"I'm good thank you ... So, I have reviewed your bloods

from yesterday ... and your neutrophils have dropped again."

"Oh no!"

"Yes ... and they've dropped *quite* a bit ... so I'm going to book you in for a bone marrow biopsy. What day is best for you?"

"Oh okay, erm ... either Wednesday or Thursday."

"Okay, I will try to book you in for Wednesday or Thursday. I know you're five years out from transplant, but you still need to understand the possibility of relapse ... yeah?"

"Okay ..." I said, as my heart sank. "Yeah."

"I hope that's okay. I'm sorry I don't have better news."

"No, it's fine. Thank you for letting me know."

"That's okay. Thank you, bye."

"Thank you, bye."

It was hard to let that sink in. My heart dropped and began to beat fast. The upbeat mood I was in that evening was crushed, and I packed my Lego away and just sat on the sofa and stared into space. I didn't say much that night, nor did I tell my parents everything the doctor had said. I wasn't in the mood, and I just went to bed early and cried.

The situation was becoming dire. I was losing control. I was entering a hole that was getting deeper and deeper. The life I was able to rebuild after five years was crashing down and collapsing around me.

Deep down I was worried. But knowing I was mostly feeling well in myself, aside from the minor symptoms, and not wanting to worry those closest to me, I put on a brave face. I showed no signs of fear when I told people about my situation, and I reassured everyone that the result would be good news. My family and friends were worried. I was in denial. I acted way too confident, and instead of taking a rest, I insisted that I continue with my busy life, even though, infection-wise, my neutrophils were at a dangerous level.

I was still working, meeting friends, going to university, and going for walks. When I had to sit down with my manager at work to let her know that there was a chance my leukaemia was back and I needed to take some time off for my bone marrow biopsy, I still found myself asking for overtime! My friends were very supportive when they found out my news, and Lauren took me out for Chinese food, and Liam and I went to our favourite Italian restaurant.

My life wasn't disrupted at all, and surely if it was leukaemia, I would be feeling unwell with symptoms, right? And surely, based on my history, if I had leukaemia, my white blood cells would be increasingly out of control rather than suffering a steady decline? The doctors never answered that question, but maybe that was because I wasn't asking them myself. The negative thoughts of relapse in my head were quickly replaced when I put forward these questions to myself, which I thought I was smart enough to answer.

I do think the doctors knew what was happening, but like myself, they had every bit of hope that the situation would resolve itself. I think they would have been a bit more alarmed if I was experiencing symptoms, but because I wasn't, they thought keeping an eye on me was the best approach to avoid panic, which was why investigation was a longer process compared to the first time round.

***

Thursday 9th December 2021. This was the day of my bone marrow aspiration. I had a history with this procedure, this one being the sixth in my lifetime. It was going to be a bit of a different experience compared to the previous five times, though. It was my first in over five years, and now that I was an adult, I would be awake during the procedure. When I was a child, I used to be put to sleep.

Knowing the process of the procedure and what it involved, I knew I was in for something painful. I didn't help myself the night before when I was researching YouTube videos of the procedure. Reassurance was what I was looking for – the type of inspiration where you see someone else do it so you know that you, yourself, can do it. All it accomplished was bringing back the memories of 2016.

Dad accompanied me to the Haematology Day Unit at Addenbrooke's Hospital on Thursday 9th December 2021. I had never been to this clinic before, and from what I gathered, it was a relatively new clinic. It was hidden in the corner of the courtyard, opposite the main hospital entrance. Being in the clinic instantly brought back memories. The beeping machines from all the patients receiving chemotherapy in the day unit made me slightly emotional.

I had to have a blood test, and I was taken to a room full of the typical blue chemo chairs. Next to me and opposite me were two patients receiving chemotherapy. I couldn't help but feel sad and upset, my mind telling me that *it used to be me, but it isn't me anymore*. I'll admit, I really struggled emotionally, and after my blood test – having to wait for my procedure – when I was asked if I wanted to wait in the chemo room or on the hard chairs outside, I chose outside. I didn't want to be in the chemo room. It was a reflection of who I *had been*, and it wasn't a place I was willing to be again. I had been there and done that. I could not go through it again, and I was adamant that I wouldn't.

After a short wait, a haematology registrar called me into the room where the procedure was going to take place. In the treatment room was a bed with a number of needles to the side, essential for the procedure. I had to sign some consent forms, which the doctor went through with me. She said the reason for this bone marrow aspiration was to "restage my disease". Although I had previously been aware of the possibility of relapse, here it became real that I knew what the doctors were looking for. They were not ruling leukaemia out, they were actively searching for it. Despite the brave face that I was putting on by continuing to deny any possibility of my returning leukaemia, deep inside I knew it was game over as soon as the doctor told me this.

The procedure was very painful, one of the most painful experiences of my life. I see why children are put to sleep for bone marrow aspirations, and in a sense, I wished I was a child again. I was required to lie down on the bed in a foetal position, with my shirt halfway up and my trousers halfway down. First was the local anaesthetic injection, which numbed my back to help manage some of the pain. The first needle was the most painful, what I'd imagine to be a carving knife stabbing into my spine. Once the anaesthetic was in, the doctor then stuck a needle into my hip, needing to cut into the bone to retrieve a sample of my bone marrow inside. The nerves in the body are connected, and as soon as the bone marrow was extracted into the syringe, a rush of pain shot like a bullet down my legs. I felt an awful pulling sensation. I was in agony!

Dad kept hold of my hand throughout the entire thing, allowing me to squeeze his hand when the pain became unbearable. Gas and air were offered to help me take my mind off the procedure and calm me down, but I insisted that I didn't need it, and I ended up being able to go without it. The procedure was over fairly quick – maybe after about fifteen minutes – and in the moments afterwards I lay on the bed, defenceless, and in so much pain. The doctor told me that it would take seven to ten days to receive the results of my bone marrow biopsy, although if it was really bad news or something needed to be investigated further, then I would receive a phone call within the next few days.

The next week was spent recovering, with a massive bandage covering the hole in my back. I needed to keep this dry for twenty-four hours. A scar from the procedure was expected, and when checking for it, it was interesting to see a couple of other holes in my back from my past aspirations. My platelets were still generally good, so my wound healed well. However, I was in quite a bit of pain in the few days after the procedure, and it took me a while to regain full movement in my body without agonising in pain. I made a full recovery and, still feeling well in myself, I returned to university and driving lessons the next week and planned to return to work on Sunday 19th December.

Everything seemed well after a few days when I had received no alarming phone calls. The procedure wasn't something I could put in the past, but the fact that there was no emergency to get me checked out put my mind at ease. I was previously nervous when I was told that they were looking to 'restage my disease', but evident by no phone calls, my overall wellbeing, and my relatively good blood count (aside from the white blood cells), I was confident that it couldn't have been leukaemia.

***

Friday 17th December 2021. A hospital appointment was made eight days after my bone marrow biopsy to receive the results from my bone marrow aspiration. I spent the morning in a very upbeat mood and cracking jokes. I guess I was slightly nervous, but by no means was I prepared for what was coming. The brave face that I had put on had managed to cover everything up. Once again, having had no phone calls from the hospital throughout the week had put my doubts at rest.

I arrived at the haematology and oncology outpatients clinic, ready for my appointment at 1:30pm. After having my blood test done, I was then taken to have my height, weight, and temperature recorded. The doctor was running late, and it was a very long, anxious wait in the waiting room. Because I was feeling so well, I wasn't too worried. I was expecting a bone marrow disorder that could be cured, or at least managed. Mum and Dad, however, were more concerned, but was it a parent's job to worry? While they were sat there with concerning looks on their faces, I was going on and on about how desperate I was for a Chinese takeaway.

"I'm worried about your health here and all you care about is Chinese!" Mum said.

After over an hour of waiting, Dr. U came into the waiting room to call us into the consultation room. Due to Covid-19, the rules were that I should have really attended the appointment alone, although one parent could accompany me to the appointment if necessary. The first sign that something was wrong was when Dr. U allowed both Mum and Dad into the room with me. When we were taken into the office, the next sign that something was wrong was the fact that there was an extra chair behind where my family were sitting. This was for my nurse, Jo, who had never accompanied me to my routine appointments.

However, I was relieved when Dr. U began talking to me about normal everyday life and how I was continuing to feel well. He asked about university and how I was managing my bowel problems and sore throat. If anything, it seemed like a normal follow-up appointment, and it put me at ease. Surely, if it was something really serious, this would be addressed first, right?

But very quickly after being eased in by the friendly chat, it was time to address the elephant in the room, and the doctor got straight to telling me the results of my bone marrow aspiration from the previous Thursday.

"As you know, we did a bone marrow biopsy last week, and your blood tests showed that your neutrophils have, in fact, dropped even further to 0.23 ..."

"Wow," said Dad.

"Yeah ..." the doctor continued. "And I'm sorry to say that it's something very similar to what you had before ..."

In other words, I had AML again.

"No," I immediately said.

In shock, I buried my head into my hands for one second, looked up quickly, then just stared into space for the rest of the consultation.

The room was silent.

Dr. U and Jo didn't say anything until they knew they had my full attention and knew that I was okay.

"I can't do it again," I said, almost, but not yet, breaking into tears, my head buried in my hands.

Like my first diagnosis, I had no tears to cry. It was like I was trying to cry because I wanted to, but I couldn't. Soon enough, Mum was in tears, and that set me off. Even Jo – who was sat at the back of the room –was trying to hold back her tears. We had communicated over telephone and email so many times throughout this entire journey of resolving my mysterious neutropenia, and the result was just devastating. We were all absolutely devastated.

I had always stated that my battle with leukaemia would

be a one-time thing and that I wasn't sure if I really wanted to go through the treatment process again if I relapsed. But I also always stated that if I was genuinely in that situation, I'd be so scared that I'd probably go for treatment out of fear of the cancer taking over my body.

Mum asked Dr. U what would happen if I chose not to go ahead with treatment, and he said that although drugs could be used to keep me comfortable, almost certainly I wouldn't have long to live. If we didn't act now, I wouldn't have long. How I had lived feeling so well for so long when my body was shutting down once again was beyond me. I decided immediately that I would go ahead with the intensive treatment strategy rather than the palliative route, and I signed the consent forms right there and then in the consultation room. It was the most painful contract I had ever signed, and now I know how my parents felt on March 25th 2016 when they signed the forms for my first round of treatment.

I didn't look the doctor, or anyone else, in the eye throughout the entire consultation. I stared into space, not even blinking, with tears slowly dripping down my face. It was like I was losing consciousness. The room was spinning like I was floating freely, almost like I wasn't even there, not really living the moment. It was like I was in the middle of one massive nightmare. I felt completely dead inside.

Once we had settled a bit and processed the news, the treatment plan was discussed. Dr. U said that I would need two rounds of chemotherapy and then a third, followed by a second bone marrow transplant. My treatment plan was to be the FLAG-Ida regimen, which was the Round 3 of my first battle (then known as FLA-Ida): fludarabine, cytarabine, and idarubicin, but this time, an injection called G-CSF would be added. Because I was a relapsed patient, the induction chemotherapy (the first two rounds of my first battle) for newly diagnosed patients was not considered effective, and I was to be put on the strongest chemo regimen, known to work straight away. FLAG-Ida is therefore the suitable chemo regimen for relapsed AML and refractory AML, which is the name for it when initial treatment hasn't worked.

Dr. U went over the side effects of the treatment with me, which included hair loss, nausea, vomiting, mucositis, diarrhoea, pink urine, and loss of appetite. It was nothing I hadn't experienced before. Something I also needed to be aware of was tumour lysis syndrome; such a large number of cancer cells are killed in such a short period of time that they get released into the blood. As I was older, there seemed to be more of an emphasis on the long-term side effects, and I was told the chemo would be life-shortening by about 10% to 15%. I was told that the chemo would possibly cause damage to my heart and most likely wipe out my fertility, if my first battle with leukaemia hadn't done so already. There was also a chance of death from the chemotherapy itself, with chances being as high as 5% to 10%, and there was a risk of secondary malignancy, where the chemo could potentially cause a new cancer to develop in the future. However, Dr. U assured me that, as I was fit and healthy, my chances of coping with the chemo would be a lot better, and in actual fact, they gave this chemo regimen to seventy-year-olds. He told me that if things weren't going as well as they expected regarding my treatment, they would tell me.

The entire consultation was just so sad and devastating. There were lots of tears, and my family and I had Dr. U's sympathy. The doctor said that while he understood this was difficult to take in, the fact that I had gone five years in remission had shown that my previous treatment was very nearly effective in reaching a cure and I had a reasonable chance the second time round. He said that the technology had developed in the past six years since my first transplant and improved and that anti-sickness drugs were so much better. The use of parents as bone marrow donors had massively improved over the past six years too, and there were so many new treatments that there were grounds for hope that a second bone marrow transplant would be worth it. The positivity and reassurance made me feel slightly better, but it didn't take away the fact that I'd have to go through the chemotherapy process again, something I absolutely hated. I just couldn't do it again, and I was terrified by the thought.

Something my family and I wanted to know was that if I had leukaemia, why was I feeling so well? Leukaemia is associated with too many immature white blood cells, but I was suffering from low amounts of white blood cells. Dr. U's answer to that was that they had caught the leukaemia early. In its early stages, leukaemia reduces the white blood cell count, but the rest of the blood and bone marrow remains intact. It's not until the bone marrow becomes absolutely crammed with myeloid blasts that everything starts to decline, and then immature white blood cells begin to rapidly produce. My bone marrow aspiration showed that not all of my bone marrow was leukaemia, with about 68% of it being myeloid blasts. Dr. U said that once the immature white cells crowd the bone marrow, it starts leaking into the blood and causing the symptoms I had experienced in 2016. This time, my leukaemia had been caught early, and I was able to avoid this happening.

The next question we asked was why did I relapse? That's an impossible question to answer as no one knows what causes cancer. But it is something you should always ask the doctor. Dr. U said that my last transplant was very nearly there last time, almost entirely getting rid of my leukaemia, but it just wasn't enough, and my leukaemia had most likely grown back slowly over time.

My chimerism tests in 2019 showed that my blood consisted of 100% donor cells, but by October 2021 my blood was 98%, then eventually 33% by December 2021. That was quite a depressing blood test result to receive. Still, I had done well to last over five years in remission, and Dr. U said that hopefully my second transplant wouldn't just put me in remission for five years but for life.

Dr. U's response tied into the next topic: the plan of action. While he understood that Christmas was very soon, he preferably wanted my treatment to start the next week because he was worried that I would lose my advantage if I delayed treatment any longer. They had caught my cancer early and it would be much harder to treat if left after Christmas. From past history, we knew how rapidly AML can develop. My family's plans for Christmas were therefore out of the window.

He said that I would be staying on Ward C9, the Teenage Cancer Trust unit, which treats teenagers and young adults aged sixteen to twenty-four. He said that it was preferred that I stayed on the ward, especially for Round 1 of chemo, to see how I reacted to it, but more time at home was negotiable for Round 2. Of course, for my bone marrow transplant, which would be done at Addenbrooke's, not Bristol, this time (Addenbrooke's doesn't do paediatric bone marrow transplants), I would be required to isolate in a hospital room for over a month.

Now that I was once again a cancer patient, Jo gave me an emergency helpline number, which I could call at any time if I was feeling unwell, and also an information sheet, which informed me of my treatment plan and its side effects. Jo would no longer be my specialist nurse while I was under the care of C9, and I would now be under the care of the TYA team and Rosie, the TYA specialist nurse.

Dr. U said that we would leave things for now as he understood that it was a lot to take in, and I would hopefully get a call the following Monday about getting a bed on the ward. I was allowed to go home, but Dr. U advised that now that I was very neutropenic and prone to infections, I should be very careful. I needed to avoid Covid at all costs, so that meant no going to shops or restaurants, and if I had any visitors at home, they needed to shower and change before seeing me. Now was not the time to get Covid as it would cause a delay to my treatment, and it was likely I'd be very unwell.

Leaving the doctor's office, down the corridors, out of the hospital, and into the hospital car park was probably the hardest part of the entire day. The silent walking gave us time to process the news. Mum and I literally broke down, and we often stopped for family hugs in the middle of the corridors. I hardly said anything. When not crying, I made a slow walk, staring far into the distance, like all the light had been taken from my life. That day's news was a massive, absolutely devastating, mental blow to me.

It couldn't have come at a worse time. In the short-term, it was Christmas, and due to Covid, visiting was restricted and there was a high chance that Christmas would be spent on my own. In the long-term, the implications for my future were devastating. I was in my second year of university, I had a weekend job, and I was so close to booking my driving test. And leukaemia had attempted to sweep that all away from me. Again.

Now that I was a cancer patient, I was prescribed some new medication. I still had to keep up with my colecalciferol and folic acid. In addition, I now had to take acyclovir, Posaconazole, and Co-Trimoxazole Forte tablets, which worked to prevent infections during my neutropenia and rounds of chemotherapy. This shocking news made us forget to go to the hospital pharmacy to pick up these prescriptions. The last thing we wanted to do was spend any more time in that hospital.

We had left the car park, so we had paid for our parking ticket, but we still needed to get the new medication. Mum was nominated to go to the pharmacy while Dad and I did circuits, driving around the hospital grounds. Addenbrooke's pharmacy can take a while, and we were driving around the hospital for at least forty-five minutes. Meanwhile, Mum was overwhelmed, and the stress of picking up my medication in the pharmacy was all too much, and she broke down.

My best friend, Lauren, had been waiting for me in Bury St. Edmunds pretty much all day, waiting for me to tell her when I was returning from the hospital. We had plans to go out for dinner, expecting everything to be good news and the appointment to be over quick. Of course, these plans had changed, and I decided to invite her over to my house instead to break the news in person. She waited quite a few hours, which I really appreciated, before we picked her up in Bury and went home. She already knew it was bad news, especially when I broke down in the car, but she was very supportive and did everything she could to take my mind off the situation and offer me words of encouragement.

Already at home was Kristy and her boyfriend, Bogdan. There were a few hugs when we got through the door, and the unpleasant atmosphere pretty much confirmed I had bad news. The six of us – Mum, Dad, Kristy, Bogdan, Lauren, and I – sat in the living room, mostly in silence, when I broke the news to everyone that my leukaemia had returned. I found breaking the news easier than I had thought it would be, but that's not to say I didn't get through it tear-free! I announced that the plan was for me to have a long-term stay in hospital to have two rounds of chemotherapy and a third followed by a second bone marrow transplant. The room was silent, with Lauren trying to break the awkward silences, and there were lots of tears and hugs.

I made the decision that I would carry on with university because Lauren told me I had to. I had my doubts, but she insisted that I continue because our goal was to graduate together. I hoped that the university would support me with flexible assignment deadlines and recorded lectures. However, I had to give up my paper round and quit my driving lessons as I could not possibly do these things. Work remained uncertain, with me choosing not to hand in my resignation notice but take time off in the hope that I would recover well enough to do such a physical job in the future. Because I was aware of the side-effects of treatment, I wasn't even sure if I'd ever be well enough to return to work, or perhaps even be alive to return to work.

Despite being so shocked by the news, I was so hungry as I hadn't eaten anything since my marmite on toast that morning. I insisted that we had Chinese that night, which we did, and it was very enjoyable! I think I was the only one who wanted it and people didn't eat much, but the day had been awful, and I wanted something to make me happy.

We all kind of separated to give each other space. My parents and Kristy decided to sit in the conservatory, while Bogdan, who we could all tell felt quite uncomfortable being stuck in the family emergency, spent the evening upstairs. Lauren and I stayed in the living room. The mood that day was depressing, but the Chinese food made it a somewhat good ending to a terrible day. The enjoyment didn't last long when realising that there was still a major obstacle ahead for me and my family.

None of us really slept that night, and I slept in my parents' bed, mainly because Mum didn't want to be away from me.

***

The weekend was a difficult one. I insisted that we did our best to continue as normal, and since I was still feeling well, every day consisted of a thirty- or forty-five-minute walk. Trying to keep life as normal as possible was difficult, because whatever we did, there was still a large thundercloud looming over our heads.

On one of my walks, I had, what I saw, my first sign of good luck. When bad news strikes, you look for these signs. A cat with three legs came limping towards my parents and I. Clearly, the cat had been through its own challenges, but it was still standing. It was friendly to my parents, but it particularly took a liking to me and sat on my feet. To me, this was a sign as if it was guarding me, protecting me, and showing signs that everything would be okay. I met the same cat a couple of days later, and it did exactly the same. I don't know if my diagnosis had just made me crazy or if this was a genuine sign that I was being protected.

The day after my shock diagnosis was difficult because the psychological effects were beginning to show. I did my paper round in the morning, which I expected to be for the final time, before breaking down in tears after I had delivered to the final house. I was still feeling well, but because I knew I had leukaemia and had felt so unwell the last time I'd had it, it was almost as if I was expecting these symptoms to start straight after diagnosis. I began to feel my throat swelling up, but this was probably the strain on my throat from the constant crying.

My chest pains were back, and I was noticing changes to my body, such as my skin not healing and hard, painful lumps on my face. It was a severe outbreak of spots, probably as a result of the stress. It was likely that these symptoms had nothing to do with the leukaemia since it was still yet to make its presence in my bloodstream, but knowing I had cancer made me think that I *had* to be feeling ill. It was a horrible feeling!

Although I felt like going for walks to clear my head, most of the day was spent staring into space, completely empty, with tears in my eyes, or sleeping. That night, I had a massive breakdown to the point where I almost stopped breathing and we came very close to ringing the emergency helpline number that Jo had given me the previous day. I guess it was something close to a panic attack. Crying on Mum's shoulders, amongst my blubbering, which was understandable, I apologised to everyone in my family, particularly Kristy, for being such a burden to them and told them that all I'd ever wanted was a normal life. I never wanted a life plagued by cancer, and yet by nineteen years old, I had got it for a second time.

The Sunday was even harder because, for all we knew, I could be in hospital the next day. We were still unsure of when I would be admitted to hospital, and not knowing when my final day at home would be left painful thoughts. *Would I ever come home again?* I expected to be in hospital the next day. I was so scared, and it was the fact that I'd be staying on my own that scared me the most. We still didn't know the rules of the ward, and due to Covid, we knew that visiting would be severely restricted. Packing my bag was upsetting, and I wished to have no part in it, leaving it to my parents. I didn't want to see the suitcase. That day, all I did was cry, sleep, and stare into space. Mum's eyes were also heavy from all the crying.

Lauren came to visit me Sunday evening, and I soon

began to feel better and my normal self. It was quality time that brought a little spark of the 'old me' back, although the spark did not last long once she had left. She had made a box of things for me to keep busy with in hospital, including a couple of puzzles, a book about the moon, and a notebook with my birthstone on it for me to start writing Part III of my book. I really appreciated this, and it meant a lot to me.

I received a lot of support. My friends, family, neighbours, co-workers, and friends of my family were all behind me. My friendship group had been going through some trouble, but Ryan, Skye, Alfie, Clare, and Will all decided that the best way to support me was to unite, and they all put together a lovely Christmas present for me and continued to keep in contact with me throughout the difficult waiting period. I kept in contact with my co-workers, particularly my friend, Bobbie, who was very supportive of me during the time I was waiting for a hospital bed.

I told Liam about my relapse last. I feared this conversation with Liam the most because, although times had changed and we were both adults now, I knew how much my past diagnosis had affected his schooldays. In fact, I had known I had leukaemia for two days before I built up the courage to tell him. In the end, it was easier than I had expected, and his response, 'Love you brother', meant a lot.

I was very surprised to have received a message from Fin, who I hadn't spoken to for ages. He wished me well and said he wanted to see me before I went into hospital for treatment. Unfortunately, plans to meet never happened, but the fact that I hadn't spoken to him for so long but he was still affected by my news meant a lot to me.

Dad set up a Facebook group called 'Jake's Leukaemia Fight'. It still exists today. We post updates about my health, and others can post to encourage me, wish me well, or keep me entertained while staying in hospital. We got quite a few members when the group was set up on Sunday 19th December! I couldn't believe all the support that had built up around me. Dad started with the posts, but I gradually took over and began to treat the group more like a blog, and I found tracking my journey was very useful!

Pressure on the NHS due to Covid-19, and also the fact that Ward C9 was smaller than others, meant that there was difficulty arranging a bedspace for me. Dr. U did not want to leave my treatment for another week out of fear that I would lose my advantage, and therefore he wanted me in hospital that week. But before I could be admitted, I had to take the necessary precautions, as well as wait for a discharge on the ward.

Monday 20th December 2021 ended up being the final day of my paper round, not the previous Saturday like I had planned. I was still feeling well enough to walk, so I thought I would show Kristy how to do her former round as she would be covering for me until the company found someone new. It wasn't as difficult saying goodbye to my round the second time as it was the first. I found myself not caring so much, and I just went up to any customer who opened the door and told them that it was my last day and the leukaemia was back, as if I assumed they knew my medical history.

The same day, I was back in the haematology outpatients clinic because I had to have a Covid swab to check that I was negative before I could be admitted to the ward. There was still no news on a bed, so I asked the healthcare assistant doing the swab if there was any news. She said that the bed manager would give me a call to arrange a bed for me, but in the meantime, I was free to go home. The healthcare assistant also gave me some reassurance when she said that the people on Ward C9 were really nice and I'd be absolutely fine. This put me at ease because I was worried about returning to hospital on a different ward. I was used to C2, the children's ward. My Covid swab was negative, but unfortunately, still no bed was available for me.

While in the waiting room that day, I received my second sign of hope: I had achieved 73% on my history essay for university. This was the only 1st I had achieved in a history essay, and I was so proud of myself! While I had decided already that I would go through the difficulty of continuing university during treatment, this was my sign of encouragement, telling me that I could do it.

As I said, psychologically, I was making myself unwell, and the fact that I was worrying so much made me fear that somehow overnight I'd lose my advantage and the cancer would spread around my body. I had been dying for weeks, not knowing I was. But as soon as I knew, I thought things would drastically change. I was desperate for a bed because I just wanted treatment to start. Waiting was a frustrating process, and while there was no doubt that the hospital staff were doing their best, in my mind, I was feeling forgotten about. I was in a constant state of panic.

On the Tuesday, it was expected that there would be a bed for me by the evening. Unfortunately, there were still no beds available as the ward had an emergency case. The ward had enough female beds but did not have enough male beds, so I had to wait until the next day to see if a bed was available. I was really starting to panic, psychologically feeling that my advantage was slipping away.

On Wednesday 22nd December, I received a call from the bed manager, who informed me that a couple of people had been discharged and there was now a bed available for me! She said Ward C9 were expecting me and I could arrive in my own time during the day.

I was so unlucky to have relapsed over five years after my transplant, and I was even more unlucky to be one of the sixteen to twenty people in England every year who need a second bone marrow transplant. Indeed, my case must be very rare. I didn't want to do this; I had never wanted to do this. But I understood that if I didn't go ahead with treatment, then I'd have weeks to live, and going through treatment was worth the sacrifice if I could remain here on Earth. And even if I didn't survive my battle with leukaemia, at least treatment would buy me some more time with my family and friends. Of course I was terrified, but I adopted this positive mindset. I was ready to get treatment done!

Here, the toughest rollercoaster ride of my life was to start all over again.

Chapter 14

Infection

Settling back into hospital life, Round 1 of chemotherapy, and its immediate effects, from December 22nd, 2021, to January 8th, 2022

After my call with the bed manager, although I was told that I could come to the ward in my own time, I desperately wanted to get there early. This was because I didn't want to face the sitting at home anxiously waiting. Unfortunately, this didn't go to plan, and Dad made us late.

Now that Christmas was pretty much non-existent, opening my presents had been spread sporadically throughout the week. My parents had bought me a new laptop, which I received that weekend, and I decided to open my final few gifts, Christmas cards and get well soon cards, shortly before leaving for the hospital.

Because I didn't know when I was coming home, I felt the need to say goodbye to every room in the house. Saying goodbye to my room was most difficult, and In one of the weirdest moments ever, Mum joined me, and we were both stood in my room for a good five minutes, staring, trying to hold back the tears before finally closing the door behind me. We left just after 1:30pm before stopping off to get lunch – my final Greggs sausage roll for a while. We ate in the car in Stowmarket ASDA car park and then continued our journey, arriving at Addenbrooke's Hospital just after 3:00pm.

Leaving the car and walking from the car park to the ward

was difficult. Mum, Dad, and Kristy, and I all carried my bags, suitcases, and boxes to the ward, all ready for me to move in. Going down the stairs was particularly difficult as I was so full of anxiety that I was shaking uncontrollably with every step I took, looking like my legs were going to collapse and I'd fall. I surprisingly didn't cry, continuing to put on a brave face, but I was desperately trying to hold back the tears, shaking due to nerves. This was the most difficult moment of my life, and I felt uneasy when we entered the lifts to the ninth floor of the hospital and approached the doors of Ward C9 – my new home.

Because of Covid rules, I was only allowed to have one visitor with me, and this visitor had to be the only visitor during my entire admission. Before entry to the ward, the named visitor was required to show a negative lateral flow Covid test. Mum was chosen to be the one visiting me, but when I was on the bay, I was not allowed anyone to stay the night with me, so she would have to go home and come back the next day. That meant being in a bay would be quite lonely in the evenings and mornings. If I was lucky to have my own room – a side room, as they were called on the ward – arrangements could be made to have Mum stay with me. The one visitor rule meant that Mum was the only one who could help me settle in on the ward and unpack my bags, so Dad and Kristy had to wait on the benches outside the ward

Approaching the door of Ward C9 was a horrible feeling. When I was first diagnosed back in 2016, it wasn't as bad because being admitted to hospital had happened unexpectedly and it was a rapid change. I was too sick to even care. But this time round, I found it so difficult because I had celebrated five years of remission. It was the best five years of my life. I had taken part in so many charity experiences, survived my GCSEs, achieved three As in my A-Levels, got a job, started my politics and history degree, spent so much time with my family and had some great holidays, made amazing friends, and was so close to booking my driving test. I also thought about the time and money I had put into this book, which I was getting so close to publishing. It was approaching its final editing stage, yet I had to put things on hold to write this unexpected Part III. Because I had such great experiences over the past five years, it was almost as if I was signing my life away, and as soon as I set foot on the ward, there was no going back.

We waited outside the ward for a while to be let in, and once we were let in, we were welcomed by the ward clerk, who showed me my bedspace: I had the choice of Bed 6 or 7. I chose 7 because there was a window next to it. It was just me and one other patient in there, and he wasn't exactly the friendliest of people. In fact, as soon as I arrived, he shut his curtains. Unfortunately, I was to be in the bay to start off with, but the patient opposite me was soon to be discharged anyway, and I'd most likely have the entire room and toilet to myself. After I had put my bags down, the ward clerk gave Mum and I a tour of the ward.

I had visited Ward C9 back in 2016 when Dad and I had participated in the food tasting with Joe and Theresa, which felt like ages ago. The ward consisted of one three-bedded bay and five side rooms. It also contained a day unit for outpatients, the PDU of C9. There were also a couple of quiet rooms and, probably the most spectacular room on the ward, the social zone. The social zone was where I had tasted the food with Joe, and it hadn't changed one bit! It had the same purple sofas and the massive TV. Its technology had been updated, though. There were also other things to do in the social zone, such as a game of darts or pool, and it even had some arts and craft supplies!

The ward clerk also went through how the ward worked and showed Mum the relatives room. In terms of food, there wasn't a chef like on Ward C2, but instead a housekeeper, who would provide the patients with fresh water and meals throughout the day. There was a set menu for the ward, which we could ask for at any time. Food was available twenty-four hours a day. All we had to do was press the buzzer, and the nurses or healthcare assistants could even cook for us if necessary. It was the typical hospital food, consisting of microwave meals, so food was very easy to prepare, and I was told it would be no trouble for the nurses.

After the tour of the ward, the ward clerk said that, as nothing would be started until the next day, I was free to go to the concourse for a bit. There I was reunited with Dad and Kristy, who were waiting outside to take Mum home after she had helped me unpack. They were surprised to see me back! We went to get a drink before Mum and I headed back to the ward. Dad and Kristy went up to the doors of the ward with me, where I gave my final goodbyes and hugs before I closed the ward doors behind me.

Mum helped me unpack some more and put my clothes in the wardrobe and sat with me until 6:00pm. In that time, we met the ward doctor, who went through the treatment plan and confirmed all the medications I was taking.

I could tell that my neighbour was a difficult patient to deal with. During the consultation with the doctor, it was amusing seeing the startled look on her face every time he said, quite possibly, the worst swear word you could use, which seemed to be his catchphrase. Then he forgot that he was attached to his drip stand, so he shouted his favourite catchphrase again, this time in agony! He then decided that he'd had enough and just got up and left, unofficially discharging himself.

"Did we say he could go?" asked one of the nurses, confused.

"He just got up and left," replied another nurse.

"We didn't sign the discharge papers."

"Well, he's gone."

Mum and I nicknamed him Mr. Grumpy.

Mum left at around 6:00pm, and I was sat on my own in my hospital bed for the remainder of the evening. Because my neighbour opposite me had decided that he wasn't going to wait to be discharged and would just leave himself, the nurses let me move into his bedspace as it was more spacious and a bit more private. I had gone from Bed 7 to Bed 8 in only a few hours. During that time, I was able to quickly FaceTime Lauren and reply to all my messages and also write down all my reasons to live:

- Go to Edinburgh with Lauren on my twentieth birthday.

- Be alive to look after my family and continue to be there for Mum.

- Complete my Politics and History degree and graduate with Lauren.

- Visit Stockport with Liam and see the air raid shelters.

- See my friendship group reunite.

- Tour of Bury with Bobbie.

- See my family be happy.

- Future trips and holidays with Lauren – Israel, the US, etc.

- Return to work as soon as I'm well enough.

- Complete a Master's degree and PhD in History and become an academic.

- Eat Chinese food.

- Publish my book!

- See my graphic novel with Young Lives vs Cancer get published.

- Do more work with the Teenage Cancer Trust – blog, share my story, etc.

- Destroy cancer!

- See my family in the US and El Salvador. See my grandparents, Auntie Ani, cousin Dalet, and my new baby cousin on the way. Visit my extended family and the family I've never met.

- Eat Italian food and finally celebrate the end of 2021 as planned.

- Start a blog to help people going through something very similar.

- Write a book on British Prime Ministers, US Presidents, and British general elections.

- Go for long walks in the fields and in the rain.

- Delayed Christmas celebrations for when I'm out of hospital.

- Finally pass my driving test.

- Build more Lego.

- Continue my goal of watching every WWE PPV ever produced.

- Visit the US with my family and watch a Royal Rumble live.

Lauren had told me to write down all my reasons to live. I promised her that when the going got tough, I'd look at all my reasons to live. However big or small, however long- or short-term these goals were, my list of reasons to live were to be an inspiration for me to get through yet another battle with leukaemia. It was a reminder for me to realise what exactly I was facing treatment for. She gave me a notebook with my birthstone on it, just to make it more personalised, and this is what my reasons to live are contained in, as well as the rough notes needed to formulate the third part of this book. Our goal was to go to Edinburgh for my twentieth birthday, which would also be my inspiration to get through this massive challenge and give me something to look forward to when there were brighter days ahead.

***

That evening, treatment had technically started. When I'd had this specific type of chemo combination before back in 2016, it was called FLA-Ida – fludarabine, ara-C (cytarabine), and idarubicin. This was the intensified treatment that I had needed when the first two rounds were not effective. For relapsed patients, it is introduced immediately. Now, it was called FLAG-Ida. The 'G' stood for granulocyte-colony stimulating factor (G-CSF), which was an injection used to boost the production of white blood cells, making the effects of chemotherapy-induced neutropenia shorter and less severe. This was a daily injection over six days, starting on the first day of treatment. On the second day, I would start fludarabine in the afternoon and cytarabine in the evening, one dose of each over the next five days. These infusions would be delivered via a drip machine. On days three to five, I would have my dose of idarubicin, which would be administered by a nurse via a large syringe into my line. The G-CSF injection went either in my tummy or the fatty bit of my arm.

I didn't like the daily injections, and even worse, I required one more than before. Gone were the childhood days of wearing the stockings to prevent blood clots. I now had to have a blood thinner injection called dalteparin. I absolutely hated the dalteparin, though it wasn't the needle that was the most painful part of the injection; it was the liquid inside it, and it would cause my arm to sting for a few minutes afterwards. The dalteparin injection was always the worst part of my day!

Depending on anti-sickness medications and fevers, throughout the next couple of weeks, on some occasions, I was having at least four or five injections per day!

Because I had arrived on the ward in the afternoon and the process of getting settled in was slow, I had missed the hours of the kitchen. The nurses were able to make me some toast, but there was a mess up on the order and I ended up with double the amount! So, for dinner that night I had four slices of toast with butter. I agreed with the healthcare assistant when she told me that NHS toast might be the best toast ever! There's something about the type of bread used and the butter that makes it taste delicious, but, as with everything when you're on chemo, enjoying food too much soon makes you want to throw it up – as I learned with toast.

After dinner, it was time for bed – the big day was tomorrow!

Thursday 23rd December 2021. I woke up bright and early on Thursday morning. It was going to be a busy day. For breakfast, I had another two slices of toast. It seemed as if all I was eating was toast!

I was given the go ahead by the nurses to have a quick shower, which, little did I know, would be my final shower line-free for a while. Because it was Christmas time and almost all of the patients were at home, I was on a bay on my own, which meant I had the bathroom to myself. As soon as I came out of the bathroom, there was a porter standing by my bed, waiting to wheel me down to the surgery room to have a peripherally inserted central catheter (PICC line) inserted.

No Hickman lines were available to order at this moment in time. A PICC line is very similar to a Hickman line. It is a plastic tube going into one of the main arteries in the heart, with a couple of lumens coming out to allow blood tests, chemotherapy, and other IV medications. The difference between a PICC and a Hickman is that a Hickman comes out of your chest, whereas a PICC is inserted in the centre of your arm.

I was taken down to the hospital's vascular access department on my bed by the porter, who parked me in a bay. I waited for the specialist nurse doing the procedure.

When the specialist nurse asked if I knew the reason why I was having a line inserted, I told her that my leukaemia had come back after five years of remission.

"We'll fight it again!" she said.

She then spotted George, my teddy turtle, at the end of the bed.

"Who's this?" she asked, squeezing his head.

"That's George; he brings good luck. He was with me

through my first journey, and he'll be with me again."

George got a lot of attention wherever he went. Everyone on Ward C9 loved George!

The nurse went through the risks of the PICC line with me, the main one being a risk of it getting infected. As was the case with most procedures, now that I was an adult, there would be no general anaesthetic. I was going to be completely awake for this procedure. I was slightly nervous, because I was going to be awake while having a tube inserted in my arteries and up near my heart!

But however uncomfortable it was, the procedure was fascinating. I was covered in a blue sheet so I could not see the procedure taking place, but I could feel it. The nurse first injected my arm with local anaesthetic so I would not feel pain in the affected area. Then, she made the incision in my left arm, located the main artery in my arm by using an ultrasound, and followed the tube up the artery and into the heart, guided by the ultrasound images. If the ultrasound couldn't detect anything, then I would have been required a chest X-ray to check my line was in the right place, but fortunately this was not needed. The procedure was a little bit sore, but on the whole, it didn't hurt as much as I thought it would. All I could really feel was the nurse pushing the tube up my arm.

Immediately after the procedure, there was a lot of bleeding, so it took a while for the nurse to stop it. Once it had stopped, she dressed the PICC line and put a white bandage sleeve over it to keep the lumens tucked in and protected. She also gave me a blue plastic sleeve, which I would be required to wear in the shower to avoid getting my PICC line wet. When Mum came to visit me later that afternoon, she was surprised that so much had happened already!

After the insertion of my PICC line, I was wheeled back to a bay to recover while I waited for a porter, who picked me up and took me back to my bedspace on C9.

"Did George bring you good luck?" asked the specialist nurse as she held the doors open to help the porter.

"Yes, he did," I said, as I was being wheeled out of the department.

My arm was quite sore for a while, and I found adjusting to a PICC line difficult at first. I found it better than the Hickman line because showering was going to be so much easier, but because I move my arms more than my chest, I feared that I'd accidentally pull it out, especially in the earlier days. It took a bit of getting used to.

Shortly after my PICC line insertion, I met Rosie, who would be my TYA specialist nurse. Because it was Christmas, she was getting ready to have some time off, but she popped into my bedspace just to say hello and introduce herself. She provided me with some printed materials and booklets on relapsed AML, the Young Person's Guide to Cancer, which is produced by the Teenage Cancer Trust, and books on bone marrow transplants. Rosie also gave me a gift on behalf of the Teenage Cancer Trust, which was pretty much a hospital survival kit. This included clothes, a blanket, shower gel, and much more! I really appreciated the effort that everyone had gone through to make Christmas time at hospital as much like a normal Christmas as possible!

The majority of the day was spent either reading or complaining of toothache. The ward doctor came to see me just to check that everything was still going well. When I complained of my toothache, she said that the hospital dentist was closed for Christmas, and while I could go to the A&E dentist, she didn't really want to send me there. For someone with low white blood cells, it would have been dangerous for me to be around people who hadn't been tested for Covid. I didn't get my teeth fixed until February, which meant, for a couple of months, eating caused immense pain!

At 4:00pm, Dr. U came to see me on the consultant ward rounds. Consultant ward rounds were Mondays and Thursdays, usually late afternoon. The ward doctor would do ward rounds every day, Monday to Friday, almost always in the morning or early afternoon. At the weekends, the doctors doing the ward rounds were the haematology registrars, who were also responsible for doing the ward rounds on Ward C10, the adult haematology ward.

It was the first time I had seen Dr. U while I was an inpatient, and it was so weird seeing him on the ward when I was used to seeing him in the outpatients clinic. This was the final check-up with the doctor before chemotherapy was to commence. Dr. U said that obviously it was psychologically extremely difficult, having relapsed so late post-transplant, but they had found it early and hopefully we were going to nail my leukaemia treatment, not just for five years but for life! It was good to hear some words of encouragement, full of energy and optimism, as we prepared to blast my leukaemia back into remission! Unfortunately, that did mean I would have to face treatment all over again, but we were hoping that the benefits would outweigh the costs.

Almost immediately after the ward rounds with the doctor, my chemotherapy was ready. It was time for my first dose of fludarabine. This was my first dose of chemotherapy and the first time I had been hooked up to a drip machine in five and a half years! I put it on the 'Jake's Leukaemia Fight' Facebook page, and there was so much support for me. Dad encouraged people on the group to post anything about my interests to entertain myself with in hospital, although I questioned how much Dad knew me when he told everyone I liked politics from every country and made me out to be a massive EastEnders fan when I am only a casual viewer! He also said that I liked music, which I do, but I know absolutely nothing about it and most of the time just listen to whatever is on the radio. And he even said that I was a fan of *Peppa Pig*, which was true, but I didn't want everyone to know that! I took *Peppa Pig* as a joke though, considering it was important to me at the start of my first battle, and some funny videos related to it were posted on the group.

Lorna, whose family we had made friends with in Bristol, even set up a GoFundMe to help my family with food and travel costs and also to get some treats for me. This raised an impressive £2575! I was very appreciative of all this support coming my way. Lorna also got in touch with the charity, the Liam Fairhurst Foundation, who were very kind to send me a gift of £500. I was very grateful! I spent some of the money on a Lego space rocket.

I was really fascinated by how the FLAG-Ida chemotherapy combination worked, and I took advantage of my relapse to really become immersed in the topic of haematology. When doing research on my treatment, I was able to find out that the fludarabine changes the DNA in leukaemia cells to prevent their growth and reproduction. Fludarabine is also able to boost the activity of the cytarabine by making leukaemia cells more sensitive, therefore killing more cancer cells at a faster rate. Idarubicin works in a similar way to cytarabine, by destroying the DNA of cancer cells and then killing them. Throughout my course of treatment, the G-CSF injection would be given to boost my white blood cells and make my period of neutropenia following treatment last a shorter amount of time. I found it so interesting how all of the drugs were different yet so similar and worked so well in combination with each other to achieve a remission.

No chemotherapy drug is ever pleasant, and I could feel the metallic taste in my mouth already. But other than that, I actually got on well with fludarabine, and it didn't make me feel too ill. Mum sat with me until the fludarabine had gone through me and ate dinner with me while we played a game of Scrabble. She went home shortly before my dose of cytarabine as the rules were that parents who weren't allowed to stay had to leave the ward by 9:00pm. Having been feeling moderately well on the fludarabine, the same could not be said for the cytarabine later on that night. I began to feel really hot and sweaty almost as soon as the 250 ml infusion of cytarabine began. Known for causing high temperatures, I became very ill with a fever, and I was all alone.

"I don't feel well! Please come early tomorrow morning!" I pleaded to Mum on the family group chat, with lots of crying emojis.

The night was rough, and I just wanted my mum with me. I found it a lonely night, stuck in a three-bedded bay, alone in absolute darkness, with most patients off the ward to celebrate Christmas. Cancer is difficult at the best of times, but having to face it alone at Christmas, in the middle of a pandemic, was really challenging.

Also, I was suffering from the side effects of the G-CSF injection, which causes a stabbing back pain. Luckily, this was controlled quite well with paracetamol. The night doctor came to visit quite late to check that everything was okay. The cause of the fevers was still unknown, as it could have been the cytarabine, which was the original thought. That said, because I was admitted to hospital when I was severely neutropenic, before any treatment, it could have been an infection.

***

Christmas Eve was the next morning, and I woke up feeling awful. I was sweating uncontrollably, and I felt very lightheaded and dizzy. When the nurse took my temperature, it was well above 39°. I tried to get up but the nurse told me not to because it wasn't safe, and she made me lie back down. She grabbed a cold, wet towel and placed it on my forehead to help cool me down. There I was, lying on my back in bed, with my trousers rolled up to my knees and a wet towel on my forehead. I looked quite silly. The nurse gave me some paracetamol and made me drink some water to keep hydrated.

The search for an infection was underway, and the first of a series of tests took place on Christmas Eve. I had a heart echo scan, which collected pictures of my heart through an ultrasound. The porter who took me to my scan was really nice to me. He seemed to know every hospital staff member, and as he passed them in the corridors, everyone told him their plans for Christmas. I think he felt a bit bad for me, and he apologised to me for having to hear about everyone's exciting plans, and he understood that it was probably a sensitive topic for me, considering I was in the last place I'd ever want to be for Christmas. While I'll admit that it did put me in a depressed mood, I told him I didn't mind. Just because my Christmas was going to be rubbish didn't mean I wished everyone else's to be. He said that while hospital wasn't the ideal place to be celebrating Christmas, he said that they would try their best to make it as Christmassy as possible and patients do at least get offered a Christmas dinner.

Fevers continued on and off throughout the day, and once Mum left on Christmas Eve, it turned into another depressing evening. I ended up having a good night though.

Lauren didn't want me to be alone on Christmas, and on the night of Christmas Eve, she FaceTimed me. I was too sick to talk much as I was suffering from high fevers, terrible back pain, and newly developed diarrhoea, but she just talked at me while I listened. I'm not sure how much I took in, but I was responsive. She stayed up and fell asleep on the call, just so I would have someone to wake up to on Christmas Day. I really appreciated it, and it meant a lot to me, especially considering my constantly beeping drip machines probably kept her up. The Wi-Fi cut out at about 4:00am but I was still happy that I wasn't completely alone during the first few hours of Christmas Day.

Christmas Day was undoubtedly the worst Christmas I have ever had and probably ever will have. The only good thing to come out of it was that because my diarrhoea was so uncontrollable, I needed to have my own room, so that took me off the bay, even though I was in a bay on my own for the time being anyway. The ward was pretty much empty as most of the patients had managed to escape for Christmas.

I was now in Room 3. I was very sick and spent the majority of the day sleeping. On Christmas Day, I started the chemotherapy drug, idarubicin, which I was to have for three days. This was usually timed before my fludarabine and cytarabine doses, so I had it around lunchtime. The chemo was given by a nurse via a syringe over a slow rate of ten or fifteen minutes, so no drip stands or infusions were necessary. This differed from when I was having FLA-Ida back in 2016, when I'd had it as an infusion. Because I was very sick at this point, and I'd only had the drug for three days, I knew very little about my idarubicin doses, and most of the time I was asleep while they were being administered. No photos exist of my doses.

It upset me knowing that people were out there having Christmas dinner – the thing I enjoy the most about Christmas

– so, despite not being hungry at all, I took up the hospital's offer of a Christmas dinner. Of course, it wasn't going to be the best quality, and it was a microwave meal, but for a hospital, it did its job. You have to give the hospital credit for trying to make a Christmas stay in hospital as Christmassy as possible. Christmas dinner was also offered to Mum too, but because I was feeling sick, she felt bad to take up the offer when I'd be seen struggling with my food. I eventually ended up ordering one, but one bite of pig in blanket resulted in me throwing up my empty stomach contents. Having felt sick for the entire day, I actually felt better once I had thrown up.

The night of Christmas Day and the early hours of Boxing Day was probably the worst night I'd had in a long time. Although I had moved into a side room, it was unexpected news, so Mum hadn't brought belongings with her to stay the night. This meant that I was on my own again. My temperatures were very high, and my diarrhoea was uncontrollable, with me having to go at least every half an hour, sometimes more often. Because my stools were so loose and watery, absolutely no pressure needed to be put on to relieve my bowels. It just all came gushing down like a waterfall as soon as I sat down and, soon enough, when I made any movement in bed.

As I had a fever, I was very dizzy and lightheaded, and I ended up getting stuck in the bathroom after feeling like I was going to pass out. I had to press the emergency alarm, which was embarrassing because the nurse and the healthcare assistant had to walk in on me on the toilet, with my trousers halfway down, diarrhoea still gushing down the toilet.

My embarrassment only increased when the nurse asked, "Do you need to change your underpants?"

My underpants? I was questioning it until I looked at my pants and pyjama trousers and saw a massive brown stain. It turned out I had managed to defecate the bed without even realising it, and the nurses had to change the sheets of my bed while I was stuck in the bathroom. I was so embarrassed, and I tried to avoid seeing those particular nurses for a few weeks, hoping they'd forget what had happened in time.

Once I was out of the bathroom and in the comfort of my bed again, my fever reached so high that I was lying on my back again, with cold wet towels on my forehead, while another nurse washed my arms and legs with more wet towels. The fan was left blowing full blast in my room.

Fevers continued throughout Boxing Day and on Monday 27th December. I was really struggling to cope with the chemotherapy, and its toxicity was a real shock to my system. One chemotherapy drug is bad enough, but when you have afternoon idarubicin, evening fludarabine, and night-time cytarabine, you become overloaded!

That Monday consisted of my final doses of Round 1 of chemotherapy, but there had been chance it wouldn't end so soon as my temperature was so high that receiving a dose of chemo would be considered unsafe. I had a very high fever, the highest it had ever been, at 40.2°. To this day, that is my highest temperature record. My oxygen levels were also beginning to drop, and for a couple of days I had to wear an oxygen tube in my nose to raise my levels. Even when I went to the toilet or took a shower, I was required to take an oxygen tank with me as it was not safe to have the tube out of my nose for even a short period of time. I was very unwell.

Still trying to find the source of these fevers, the nurse tried to carry out an ECG. I'd had many ECGs before, where wires were attached to stickers on my body to detect the heart rhythm. But I was so hot and sweaty, the stickers just peeled straight off. When the doctor came in to check me over, he looked at the inconclusive ECG results. It was quite funny watching him examine the inaccurate results in so much depth, with a confused look on his face, only for him to say, "I can't read this!"

The doctor told me that if my fever didn't go down then it wouldn't be safe to have my dose of cytarabine that evening. Worst case scenario would be that it would get delayed until the next morning, so I guess it wasn't all that bad. I was going to have my chemo regardless of the timing. I just had to keep powering through.

"You will get better in days, not hours!" the doctor said to me.

Because I didn't want my chemo delayed, especially the very last dose, I did everything I could to get my temperature down on its own. My room had the windows wide open, the fan on, and the air conditioning blowing full blast. It did the trick, and combined with paracetamol, my temperature went down to a safe level to have my final dose of the first cycle of chemo.

I should mention that by this point, it was determined that the fevers were not caused by the cytarabine, as previously thought. The source of the infection was still unknown, so doctors prescribed a combination of IV antibiotics to reach all parts of the body. Despite my infection being unknown, there was speculation of it being a problem with my heart. On the heart echo scan done a few days prior, it showed either a uniquely shaped valve or a bacterial growth in the heart. Luckily, on further inspection by the cardiology consultant, it appeared to be a uniquely shaped heart valve, although this did mean that we were still unsure of where the infection was coming from. We will never know where the infection was located.

Once I had finished the first round of chemotherapy, I

began to feel better. I was put on the very strong IV antibiotics, meropenem and vancomycin, which appeared to be working. My CRP levels, or infection markers, seemed to be coming down as well. Everything appeared to be going in the right direction, and while fevers remained for the time being, they were nowhere near as high or as frequent. Recovery from the first round was underway, and on Tuesday 28th December, I had my first blood transfusion in over five and a half years.

Around this time, I also met the dietician, a meeting I was absolutely dreading. To be honest, one of the things that scared me most about my relapse was not knowing what the dieticians were going to do to me. This time, though, I was happy with what she had to tell me.

One of my biggest fears about returning to hospital life was the dreaded NG tube. The dietician told me that in paediatrics, the dieticians use a *random* weight cut-off point to determine whether an NG tube is necessary. I couldn't believe it! The many months I had been battling those dieticians, who acted as if losing 3 kg was the end of the world, only to find out that, after all, the cut-off point was just a random estimate and not a pressing concern? I would have resisted the NG tube much more as a paediatric had I known that fact, especially since the tubes were mostly useless anyway. The dietician also told me that now that I was an adult, even if they believed that an NG tube would genuinely be the best option for me, I could just say no anyway. She said that I should at least try some of the supplement drinks though.

"Have you tried Scandishakes before?" asked the dietician.

I hated Scandishakes! I had actually managed to keep my weight relatively stable throughout the tough infection I was experiencing, although my weight had shown a very slight dip.

The dietician made me promise to try the supplement drinks. I never did try them. Like the paediatric dieticians, she made Scandishakes seem like the tastiest milkshakes in the world and made them out to be so much better than I knew they were.

Overall, I was satisfied with what the dietician had to tell me. I was glad to have much more autonomy over my diet and weight than I'd had under paediatric care. And in fact, for the rest of Round 1 and the entirety of Round 2, a dietician never came to see me! When I had stayed on Ward C2, they visited every other day! I have nothing against dieticians, and I actually really liked the adult dieticians, but when you're a cancer patient, they can be extremely annoying, especially the paediatric ones.

Going into the new year, the chemo had done its job as my blood counts were flat. My white blood cell and neutrophil count were 0.0, my platelets below 10, and my red blood cells also very low. I required blood and platelet transfusions to top up my blood every other day. But as my infection markers had come down and fevers were beginning to stabilise, there was talk of me being discharged home.

The nurses wanted me discharged as they weren't actually having to do much for me once I was better, and it seemed unnecessary to keep me in. But the doctors, aware that my counts were flat, wanted to delay my discharge for as long as possible to give me the best chance of avoiding another infection. If I did catch an infection, unfortunately, unlike when I used to just turn up on Ward C2 straight from Kingston House, I now had to go through the A&E process from home. This would take up to six hours in order to get readmitted to the ward. The consultant said that if they were to discharge me, I'd have to be very careful at home.

The nurses won the argument over my discharge, and the

process of getting me home was underway. After seventeen days of absolute hell, I had somehow made a miraculous recovery, and the change from infection to no infection was very quick.

I was discharged from the hospital on Saturday 8th January 2022. I had done very well as it was expected that I would spend twenty-one to twenty-eight days in hospital for my first stay, but I was out by seventeen. As I was severely neutropenic, a close eye had to be kept on me and appointments were made to attend the Ward C9 day unit on Mondays, Wednesdays, and Fridays for blood tests, dressing changes, and any IV medications or transfusions necessary.

I would see my appointments, letters, and test results come up on MyChart. MyChart was an app or website that I hadn't yet set up. In 2016, we didn't have apps like this to track our progress, so times had really changed! It took a bit of getting used to as I'm very old fashioned and prefer pen and paper, but it soon turned out to be very useful. For most of my time as a paediatric, I had no clue about my blood test results, other than when the doctors told me my neutrophils had reached over 0.5. Now, I had full access to every blood test result, every appointment made, and every update regarding my care, which was very helpful! I always used to wait excitedly when my blood tests results would be updated at 6:00pm every evening, and I could track the increase or decrease in my blood counts!

Chapter 15

The Ferocious Groin

The later effects of Round 1 of chemotherapy from January 8th to February 8th, 2022

My first visit to the day unit was on Monday 10th January. It looked very similar to those chemo rooms you see in photos, with a number of comfy chairs with drip machines beside them scattered across the sides of the room. It was a lengthy process, arriving at 11:30am for my appointment, then having blood tests and having to wait for the results. Waiting for the results took at least a couple of hours, and then once the results were released, the doctor had to review them. If everything was okay, I could go home, but if my bloods were low (which mine were), then they had to order a unit of blood to be transfused. Getting the blood ready took even longer! And even worse, my bloods were so low, I needed blood and platelets! So, I waited about four and a half hours, had a platelet transfusion, which took over half an hour, then had to wait another hour for my blood to be prepared, which then took an hour and a half to be transfused! I wasn't able to escape the ward until 6:30pm.

Rules were that only patients under seventeen were allowed to be accompanied by a family member in the clinic, and since I was nineteen, Mum had to wait outside the relatives room. She was enjoying her free time, spending seven hours reading her book and doing puzzles. Me, on the other hand, got bored of reading and didn't think to bring a charger for my Nintendo Switch or my phone, which I liked to preserve the battery power for. It was the slowest seven hours of my life, and I was potentially going to have to do this three days a week!

Tuesday 11th January was a planned day off from the hospital. I should mention that probably the biggest advantage of being an adult with cancer and not a child was that I had more freedom. Paediatrics were required to be reviewed in a clinic daily, whereas an appointment for me was now only necessary three days per week. These appointments were for blood tests, transfusions, and various other treatments, done completely by the nurses. There was no requirement to see a doctor for these appointments unless you asked to see one or they needed to see you for something. When in PDU, I had to see a doctor every day! And there wasn't much change in terms of my health – I was still severely neutropenic and anaemic as an adult, just as I was as a child.

Unfortunately, Tuesday's scheduled day off from the hospital was not to be. I had been complaining of pain in my testicles for over a week, and with certain developments in that area seeming to get worse, I phoned the hospital. The ward doctor was concerned about a potential infection, and I needed to go into hospital to get checked out. However, the ward day unit was busy, so I had to be seen in the Cancer Assessment Unit (CAU), which was the day ward for the oncology and haematology outpatients clinic. This was the adult equivalent of PDU's six-bedded bay.

It was a different experience because, rather than being with teenagers and young adults, like I was used to, I was now in a proper adult ward. Some of these patients were elderly. There were eight bed spaces on this unit, and it was all open, so I passed the time by people-watching. I found it funnier than I should have when a constipated lady kept walking back and forth to the toilet, holding her stomach, and was telling the nurses that her laxatives weren't working. I'm not so sure why I found it so funny, considering my own situation of inconsistent bowel movements. But I think it was the fact that she was so open about her constipation, in front of everyone, that it made me put a label on her as the constipated lady.

I wasn't a fan of the CAU. While the staff were very nice and Mum and I were offered drinks and biscuits by the very kind and helpful healthcare assistant, it was an unpleasant atmosphere. Being with the old people who needed fluid from their stomach drained or couldn't take their tablets because they were not a manageable size was difficult to have to watch. It is quite a difference seeing young adults with cancer and older adults with cancer. I understood that we were all sick, but the older patients looked a lot sicker, and some of the things I saw was quite sad.

Luckily, I was out of the unit within a few hours, with my blood results still flat but above the transfusion cut-off point. After an examination, the doctor also found no concerns regarding a potential infection and told me that, while everything looked fine, I should let them know if my symptoms worsened.

Because I came to hospital unexpectedly on the Tuesday, I was allowed to have both Wednesday and Thursday off, hospital-free, provided there were no issues. As I was severely neutropenic, I did hardly anything during my time at home. If I was a child, I would have been staying at Kingston by this point, so being at home would have been something more special back then, with lots of celebration once my neutrophils hit the 0.5 target. But all throughout this week, my neutrophils were 0.0, and the chemo had made me so anaemic that I had no energy anyway, so most of my days consisted of sitting on the sofa and watching TV. Like my first round of chemotherapy in 2016, it always seemed as if the bone marrow took longer to recover after the first round than it did for subsequent rounds.

On Thursday, I had my haircut. Despite not losing that much hair, I noticed a few hairs on my pillow every morning and felt that it was only a matter of time before it started falling out rapidly. It didn't upset me like it did the first time, although my initial reaction to having a bald head was a shock. I told myself that I had been there before, and that was enough to get me through it. I'd had hair for so long, and to see it go again was a bit of a blow. My beard remained intact, and I began my new look with the bald head and the beard, and it was something I came to embrace.

***

Sunday 16th January 2022. I managed to last eight days at home, which was impressive for someone as severely neutropenic as I was. I also noticed that, in my blood test results, my white blood cells were slowly creeping from 0.0 to 0.04, which is hardly impressive, but a sign that my bone marrow was trying to rebuild.

I began feeling unwell on the Friday of the week that I was at home. I spent the morning in the Ward C9 day unit, and while my bloods were super low, I was on the borderline of needing a transfusion. It looked as if I could get away without a transfusion that day, but that was pushing it, and there was no doubt that I'd need one by Monday. Therefore, my visit to the hospital that afternoon was quick and just involved having a blood test, waiting an hour and a half for those results, and then a dressing change. After that, I was free to go home, but having extremely low red blood cells in my body made me very tired and breathless. This continued into Saturday, and along with these symptoms, I started feeling hot flushes. My temperature remained good though, and it was just something to keep an eye on.

On Sunday, I woke up feeling a little bit better than the previous day. But as the day progressed into the afternoon, I began to feel worse. After a video call with my extended family, I noticed that I was very tired, breathless, and in a lot of pain. My groin was giving me issues, feeling like my skin was broken in the area between my groin and right leg. It felt almost as if I had carpet burn on my groin, and the irritation was worsening my mobility. Also in pain was my neck, which was very sore, feeling like I had been rubbing it with sandpaper.

Things suddenly got worse when my thermometer read a temperature of 38° but then kept fluctuating from really high to really low. Mum called the haematology helpline, and the haematology nurse told her that I needed to go to A&E as soon as possible. Because I had spiked a fever of 38°, it was a potential infection and therefore deemed an emergency, meaning I needed IV antibiotics within one hour.

It is generally advised that you go to your local A&E, which in my case was West Suffolk Hospital. But because I did not know the haematology team there, in case I was admitted again, Dad drove us to the Addenbrooke's A&E. The helpline nurse said that this was absolutely fine as long as we arrived as soon as possible. She informed the on-call haematology registrar that I was arriving in A&E.

If it was true that I needed IV antibiotics within one hour, I'd be dead already. A&E was a horrible experience and not one I wished to live again. Firstly, the drive to the hospital took over an hour. Even though that was our choice, surely it wasn't that much of a pressing emergency if the nurse had allowed such a long travel time. But then once we arrived at the front door, we had to wait in line and go over any Covid symptoms before I was triaged. If I was to die of an infection at any minute, why wasn't the priority getting me seen rather than running through a checklist of symptoms that I didn't need the hospital for? I was then directed to the emergency department, where I was left waiting for twenty minutes while the nurses at the front desk had a chat. The doctors on the ward always told me that if I caught an infection while neutropenic that it was an emergency and I needed to be seen straight away.

After I had waited twenty minutes, the healthcare assistant arrived and took my obs. It showed that I had been right to come into A&E as my temperature was 38°, confirming the true temperature from the previous fluctuating results on my thermometer. The healthcare assistant asked me to take my coat and jacket off as, while I was going to be a bit shivery, it would help my temperature naturally go down.

Soon after, a nurse checked me in and had to go through all my details again. Here, I will further emphasise my point. I understand that you have to do the relevant checks to make sure you have the right patient – maybe your date of birth and hospital number – but is it really necessary to go through who you live with, your occupation, and your ethnic background when you're supposedly dying of an infection?

Mum was then told that she would be unable to stay with me due to Covid restrictions, so she returned to the car while I was taken into an ambulance bay. I felt a bit uneasy being stuck in the A&E department on my own, especially overnight.

In the ambulance bay, a nurse took a blood sample from me and also took blood cultures. Blood cultures are interesting – they involve putting a sample of blood into a couple of bottles with solutions inside it. These are then taken to the lab to see if it grows any bacteria, looking for a potential infection. It was annoying because, despite having a PICC line, blood cultures had to be taken peripherally, requiring a needle in my arm. A cannula was also put in, and I cannot emphasise enough how much I hate cannulas. You can feel the needle poking your vein from the inside!

Once that was completed, I needed the toilet, so the nurse showed me where it was. Then came the embarrassing part of my time spent in A&E, with me getting lost and walking around the department, aimlessly trying to relocate where I was supposed to be staying. There were so many doors, I couldn't remember which door I had come through! A&E was a maze. A healthcare assistant soon helped me out when I passed by asking for help and admitting I was lost, and she managed to direct me to where I needed to go by getting my notes up on the system.

Once I was back in my room, the healthcare assistant took a few swabs from me, one of them being a Covid swab. This was important because the number one rule of A&E at this time was that it needed to come back negative to be readmitted to your usual ward. Waiting for the result was also time-consuming, hence the reason it took even longer than the usual A&E process. The healthcare assistant then took me to the bed area of A&E, and I was taken into my own room. Ironically, my cubicle was called C9.

As I had been feeling unwell and had a temperature of 38°, I almost certainly had an infection. To keep me alive before seeing the doctor, I had a couple of antibiotic medications and fluids running simultaneously. I suppose I was lucky to have had my cannula put in earlier as both lumens of my PICC line were in use, in addition to my cannula, with me having three medications at once running through my bloodstream.

Although I'd had blood cultures taken when I'd first arrived in the ambulance bay, for some unknown reason, more were needed. Because my line and cannula were in use, the nurse needed to put a new cannula in, and with both arms in use, the best place to put it was in the back of my hand. The nurse struggled to find a vein, and after poking the veins at the back of my hand with a needle several times, she accidentally slipped and hit what seemed like the bone in my hand! The effect was a very sharp, shooting pain in my hand, and my vein began to swell three times the size and bleed. I had a very large, hard lump emerge on the back of my hand. The pain was excruciating! The nurse was very apologetic and gave up on trying to insert any more tubes in my veins. I didn't mind – I understood that mistakes happened. She gave me some tissues to help stop the bleeding.

A&E itself was very uncomfortable. The beds were very different to the hospital beds on the ward, and it felt as if I was lying on an ambulance stretcher. It was a very cold, hard mattress – the type of bed you'd expect in a prison. There were no sheets or pillows, which I'm guessing was because A&E isn't for a long-term stay. Nevertheless, it was still uncomfortable, especially as I was suffering from a high temperature and was feeling very shivery. I wasn't allowed any paracetamol until the source of the infection was investigated, so even though the antibiotics had already gone into my bloodstream to do its job, I couldn't take anything that would potentially mask anything serious. Therefore, I just had to let my temperature skyrocket and hope it would reduce on its own.

Because I had the IV fluids going through at such a fast rate, I was desperate for the loo. But when the nurse came in to take my obs, which showed no improvement in my temperature, he said that he didn't want me going to the toilet because there were two positive Covid patients beyond my room. Therefore, I had to urinate in bottles in my room. Being stuck in that cubicle was one of the most uncomfortable experiences of my life, and I spent six hours in there!

I soon met the haematology registrar, who had been informed of my arrival. She did a thorough examination to check for any infection. As I was feeling pain in my neck, she had a feel of it to check for any swollen glands. Luckily, there was no sign of this. She was a bit suspicious of the groin pain though and pressed down on the areas where I was feeling pain. She couldn't see or feel any signs of swelling. However, the fever was enough evidence to show that an infection was going on, so after a quick chat about university and being careful to avoid infection at home, she told me that I would need to be readmitted to the ward, with the plan being to try to get me onto Ward C9. Getting onto Ward C9 unplanned was difficult though because there were only eight beds. Before I could be admitted to the ward, my Covid test from a couple of hours prior needed to come back as negative. If it was positive, I'd have to go to a special Covid ward. That was what the delay in A&E was about: waiting for the negative test.

Once all my IV antibiotics had finished, the nurse came to detach the wires from me. My IV fluids kept running. She told me that my Covid test had thankfully come back negative, and they were just waiting for the porter to arrive to take me to the ward. There was still uncertainty over which ward I was going on. When I asked the nurse, she didn't know, although she knew it was a haematology ward. This put in my head that I was either going to D6, the haematology and neurology ward, or C10, the adult haematology ward. I was surprised when another nurse arrived with the porter about half an hour later to tell me I was going to Ward C8. *Ward C8? What ward even was that?* I thought. As I was starting to feel really shivery, before we took off, the nurse finally let me have some paracetamol, and my fever began to go down.

Quickly before going to the ward, I needed to have a chest X-ray in the A&E department. The investigation for finding the source of the infection was underway already. The radiographers were very kind and supportive of me and didn't even make me stand up. They positioned the bed and the X-ray machine to where I could quickly have it done while in my bed. Following this, the porter and nurse took me to Ward C8.

Ward C8 was the orthopaedics ward, which treats spinal injuries and conditions. I thought it was a bit odd, but knowing the pressure on C9 sometimes, I didn't question it. The odd non-cancer patient used to show up on Ward C2 from time to time. The A&E nurse arrived at the nurses' desk to check me in, but they told her that all their beds were full and they weren't expecting me. It must have been close to thirty minutes that I was lying there on my bed, in the middle of the ward corridor, while the A&E nurse made phone call after phone call, trying to find the correct ward for me to be on. I didn't mind; I knew these things could happen from time to time when nurses got their notes wrong. The porter was getting annoyed though, having to stand there and wait, huffing and puffing louder and louder.

It was soon made apparent that instead of C8, the nurses meant C9, and finally, after spending half an hour on a spinal injury ward, I arrived on C9 at just gone 2:00am on the morning of Monday 17th January.

I arrived on the ward, wheeled on my bed, looking pretty much dead. The nurse on shift was surprised to see me.

"What happened?" she asked. "An infection?"

After transferring everything from my A&E bed to my new bedspace in the bay (Bed 6), I thanked the porter and the A&E nurse before they left. The porter was grumpy for having to spend half an hour on a spinal injury ward with me and walked off, but the nurse wished me the best. I was now back on Ward C9, so I was required to go through the admission process all over again. I was given a new inpatient wristband and was required to take the MRSA swabs. I then had my height and weight measurements taken. After that, I didn't get to bed until about 3:00am, but once again, in the space of three weeks, it was time to play the game of finding the source of infection.

***

When I woke up in the morning of Monday 17th January, the groin pain had not improved. In fact, it had worsened. My walking had significantly gotten worse, and I could not stand up straight. I avoided getting up unless I had to go to the toilet, and when I walked, I was severely hunched. Sometimes I needed to hold on to a nurse, Mum, who I was reunited with later that afternoon, or my drip machine to avoid my legs collapsing. Coughing or going to the toilet put intense strain on my groin. It was a sharp, shooting pain, but also very sore, as if there was a deep cut. I was in absolute agony!

The doctors still could not see or feel any swelling in my groin, and neither could I. It was a mystery as to where the infection could be coming from. An ultrasound scan of my groin was booked, but in the meantime, the protocol measures of trying to find the infection were still underway. My chest X-ray from the previous night was clear, so it wasn't a chest infection. I did have an ECG in my bedspace to see if it was a problem with my heart, but this also looked fine.

I was informed that the ultrasound scan that was booked was for the groin and testes. I was fine with the groin because that was where the pain was coming from, but I wasn't the most comfortable with the testes being examined because it is an uncomfortable area at the best of times, let alone having to have a stick pressed hard against them. In hindsight, I'm glad that the procedure was done, because it found the source of infection.

The ultrasound involved the typical jelly on a stick, which was then applied to my groin and testes to detect images from inside the body using soundwaves. The stick hitting my groin was painful at first, but then I realised that the cold jelly really helped soothe my pain, and I enjoyed my groin ultrasound in comfort! From the images, the radiographer could detect nothing wrong with my groin, but noticed the blood flow in the tube of my right testicle was larger than the left. The groin pain was on my right side. Most likely, this was an infection called epididymitis, and this was the cause of the pain and probably the fevers. I was prescribed a course of antibiotics, and I was expected to recover well from it.

It appeared to be a mystery as to how I had managed to contract epididymitis. I was asked if I had partner, which I didn't. When I saw the haematology consultant on the ward rounds, he said that epididymitis is usually associated with chlamydia, a sexually transmitted disease. For obvious reasons, this was very rare amongst their haematology patients. He said that it was just likely that, as my blood counts were so low, bacteria had got in the area to cause the infection and this had brought on the pain. He said everyone seemed to have a weak spot. Going back to what the consultant in Bristol had told me five years ago, my weak spot used to be my bottom, but since then it had definitely changed!

After being constipated for a few days and unable to even try going to the toilet due to the strain being so painful on my groin, I soon developed diarrhoea. This resulted in me being moved into my own room. I spent a few days on the bay, and once again I happened to be the only one in there.

The pain started to worsen, and I was really struggling now – it was unbearable. The haematology doctors were in consultation with the urology doctors, who were much better qualified for this kind of infection and were able to prescribe the best combination of antibiotics. I also met the urology consultant as doctors thought it would be a good idea for him to have a look at it.

The consultation with the urologist started off in quite an amusing way because when the consultant entered my room, he found me sitting on my chair on the other side of the room, opposite my bed. It was funny because I was stuck and was trying to get to my bed. I was sat on my chair as my bed had just been changed by the healthcare assistant. He needed to get me on the bed to examine me, but I was in so much pain that I was stuck there, and I had to make a painful, hunched, walk to my bed, like an old man in a care home.

The consultant said that while it could be a bacterial infection, which the prescribing antibiotics would help with anyway, it was usually common for epididymitis to be caused by a viral infection, and therefore it was just a case of letting it clear up on its own. From what he could see, there was nothing too severe when examining the testes and my groin, with no sign of fluid build-up. He was able to explain the reason for my pain though, and that was because in that particular area, the muscles are connected, and the pain from the groin was pulling on everything. That was why it hurt so much when I coughed or strained to go to the toilet.

"Do you want to sit back down on your chair?" asked the doctor, after he had finished with the examination.

"No, it's fine. I had actually been stuck there because I

couldn't walk. Here is where I wanted to be!"

He started laughing.

The urologist recommended ibuprofen as that appeared to be most effective for managing pain caused by epididymitis. However, the haematology doctors didn't want me on that as my reduced platelet count meant that taking ibuprofen increased my chances of bleeding. Wanting to save paracetamol for my fevers, I was prescribed codeine for the pain. But this made me constipated, and due to my refusal to take laxatives, the doctors didn't want me on that either. I refused to take laxatives because, as I was in so much pain, I wanted to avoid going to the toilet as much as I could. I feared that if I had diarrhoea, that would mean having to get out of bed more often. As a result, I was prescribed oramorph, liquid morphine, to help dull the pain.

None of my painkillers really worked, and I was always in agony when I moved. Sitting or lying down was fine but moving was unbearable! Cold compression helped a bit, and I spent most nights sleeping with a massive bag of ice stuffed down my pants. It was actually good if I spiked a fever during a period of immense pain because paracetamol and oramorph worked great in combination with each other, and these were the only times when my pain relief showed some signs of working, although the effects still weren't great.

Going into the weekend of Saturday 22nd and Sunday 23rd January, I saw the weekend haematology registrar on the ward rounds. On Saturday, symptoms were about the same, and before leaving the room, the registrar said that when he was doing his training, one of his lecturers told him that 'your dangly bits' take longer to heal than most parts of the body. Therefore, it was just a case of waiting for things to clear up either on their own or with the help of the antibiotics. By Sunday, however, the swelling had got much worse, and it was now visible. What doctors couldn't even feel just a week earlier they could now see, and my groin was massive. On examination, the doctor thought it felt more like a hernia than an infection. He got the surgeons to have a look.

The surgeons took me by surprise. They came barging into my room, and the one doing the consultation was not gentle! He asked me where the pain was and yet he still pressed down as hard as he could!

"Hmm, yeah, feels like a hernia," said the surgeon, agreeing with the registrar on the ward. "If it is one, it will need surgery."

The surgeon told me that I would be booked for a CT scan to confirm and diagnose the hernia. In case I needed any surgery, I was declared nil by mouth and only allowed to consume clear fluids for the time being.

The CT scan was not nice at all. The worst bit is before the scan, where you have to have a cannula put in because they cannot connect the blue dye tubes to the lumens of a line. I hate cannulas! Then there was the difficulty of deciding which scanning machine to put me in. I'd had so much radiation in my time as a cancer patient that the radiographers were concerned that it would be too much for me, especially if I was going to continue having scans throughout the remainder of my treatment. Therefore, I had to wait a short amount of time for the machine that produced less radiation. I also hated the blue dye that gets injected into your bloodstream during the scan as it caused hot flushes and left me feeling like I had wet myself. On this occasion, however, the burning sensation I received on my groin actually seemed to soothe the pain, almost as if something was burning the pain away.

A couple hours later, I received the results from the CT

scan. The results came quick. I could eat and drink again, as luckily there was no hernia! I was amazed that a doctor and surgeon were both in agreement that it was a hernia, yet it wasn't! What it appeared to be was a swollen gland in my groin, and the haematology consultant said that almost certainly the cause of this was an infection. The source of the infection, however, was unclear. Was it the epididymitis or an unrelated second infection in the same area?

Doctors wanted another ultrasound to see if the epididymitis had cleared up, and the radiographer was able to confirm that it had. The blood flow in both testes was normal. This was good news as it appeared that the recommended antibiotics by the urologists and microbiology team and the general IV antibiotics for neutropenic fevers that I was taking had worked effectively in combination with each other.

The problem with my groin remained, though.

***

On the same day of my second ultrasound, which was Wednesday 26th January, I had a bone marrow biopsy. If the pain I had been suffering already wasn't bad enough, I now had to face the massive needle in my hip again. The reason for this biopsy was to check for any lingering disease now that my counts were beginning to recover. After being stuck on 0.0 to 0.04 to 0.0 again, my white blood cells were on the up! My platelets were also showing signs of recovery. I still needed blood transfusions though, as red blood cells are always the last to recover. I was particularly impressed by my neutrophils, which had reached 1.25 by this point. Having been below 1 in October 2021 and 0.23 by December, this was a small sign that I had responded well to treatment thus far!

The biopsy, carried out in the Ward C9 treatment room by one of the registrars on the ward, was nowhere near as bad as the one in December, with the only severely painful bit being the anaesthetic needle. Other than that, it was a mostly painless procedure, probably because I was in so much pain already that it wasn't possible to feel anymore. The aspiration did cause an expected sore back for a little while afterwards.

It would take a week to receive the results of my biopsy.

***

Despite the severity of the pain in my groin, doctors had determined that I was well enough to not need my own room and they had to prioritise other patients. I reluctantly gave up my room to be demoted back to the bay, and I was not happy! I didn't like the bay because my neighbours were noisy. It seemed that they were friends, and I was in between the two. I didn't speak to them much, but we did all communicate on one occasion, shouting over the curtains. We were saying how it was okay to be grumpy and told each other how long we had been in hospital for, almost as if it was a competition.

I was on FaceTime to Lauren, telling her how grumpy I had been.

"It's okay to be grumpy!" shouted the patient opposite me. "I've been here since 2020!"

"I've been here since December!" shouted the patient next to me.

"I've been here before and was able to escape this place for almost six years and now I'm back and have been here since December!" I aggressively shouted back over the curtain, shutting them and the conversation down.

"Ohhh woahhhh, hahaha," said the patient opposite me.

It was clear that I had won the competition.

The pain and the swelling of my groin only seemed to worsen, and when the ward doctor, who hadn't seen it in a week, re-examined it, she was surprised by how red, swollen, and inflamed it was. By this point, it was a very solid, hard lump, which encompassed the entire right side of my groin. It looked like it was going to erupt at any moment. When the haematology consultant arrived to take another look later in the day on the ward rounds, he said that it would need an ultrasound and a biopsy, which would involve sticking a needle in it to see what they could suck out and test in the lab. He seemed very confused by what this groin problem was.

The biopsy took place on Friday 28th January in the ultrasound department. By this point, I was becoming a regular in the ultrasound department. The radiology consultant went through the procedure with me. First, he would inject local anaesthetic into my groin to help numb the pain. Then, using the ultrasound, he would detect the lymph nodes in my swollen gland and try to suck one of them up into a syringe, using another needle. Because the nodes move around after being touched, the procedure would be like trying to pick up a marble with a chopstick, and the consultant warned that he may have to move the needle around quite a bit in my groin to catch it and quickly suck it up.

"This procedure is quite tricky, so sorry if I start leaning on your man bits there," said the consultant as he made his preparations for the biopsy.

The sample would then be sent to the lab for inspection to answer the question of whether my swollen gland had been caused by an infection or, very possibly, by the AML. That was a concern, as back in 2016, one of my symptoms for AML was a swollen gland on my neck. The groin being affected by my leukaemia was a possibility.

As soon as I lowered my trousers for the biopsy, the consultant took a look and was a bit taken aback, shocked by my ferocious groin.

"The anaesthetic isn't going to work on something that red and inflamed!" he said, eyes wide with shock.

I loved this consultant because he was unintentionally funny. I found it difficult to take him seriously because he had his facemask taped to his nose and mouth. His biopsy felt like a biology lesson at school, and he was very enthusiastic about his subject.

"Explain to me in your own words what I'm about to do to you."

"Erm ... so, you're going to get a needle, erm ... and then ..."

"It could just be a few words, like stick a needle in your groin and take out a sample of your lymph node."

"You're going to stick a needle in my groin and take out a sample of my lymph node."

"Perfect!"

He injected my groin with anaesthetic anyway just on the off chance that it would work. Then he began to find the affected area using the ultrasound equipment. The nodes looked normal. My gland was completely normal. He even told me the exact measurement, which was well within the perfect range for a lymph node. It was not swollen at all, showing the complete opposite result to what the CT scan had detected earlier that week.

Because of this, the consultant changed tactics. Rather than trying to suck up a gland he knew would be normal anyway, he stuck a needle in multiple areas of my groin to see if he could suck anything up, which would then be sent to the labs to see if it would grow anything, and another sample would be kept to look at under a microscope. The consultant did exactly what he said he would and held the sample up to show his assistant.

"It's pus!" he said, shocked and fascinated at the same time, holding the test tube in the air, staring at it in awe.

He showed me his test tube, which showed something inside resembling pus from a popped spot. It seemed like finding the pus in my groin was the most exciting thing the consultant had done all day. He told me that this was definitely an infection, and rather than a swollen gland, the swelling was as a result of hard, infected tissue. The ultrasound showed that there was no fluid to drain from my groin, and out of the pus that the consultant was able to get out, there wasn't much of it. He was able to conclude that this would go down either in its own time or with my continued course of antibiotics.

After my biopsy, I was wheeled back on my bed to the ward. I was in so much pain, and I could still feel the sharp needle firing back and forth through my groin, even though it was long gone. Mentally and physically, I was exhausted. I felt like I had been thrown off a skyscraper, splatted on the floor, scooped back up, and forced to live.

Now we knew that it was an infection in itself, and not a swollen gland caused by an infection, treating, and explaining my groin problem became easier. My infection had probably started off with the epididymitis causing disturbance to the area. As my blood cells, particularly the neutrophils, had begun to recover from chemo (white blood cells are also made in the glands, located in the groin), there was so much activity in that area when these neutrophils had attempted to munch up my epididymitis, it had ultimately overwhelmed my groin and resulted in the eruption that it was.

Back on the ward, the haematology consultant prescribed

the antibiotic, meropenem, which is known to be quite strong. Doctors were hopeful that this would cure my infection, and the consultant assured me that, he believed, now we knew what it was, it would soon settle down.

If everything that I had going on wasn't enough, during this time I developed a cough. This was very painful due to the strain it put on my groin. The good thing about having a cough was that I was deemed contagious, and I was able to move out of my bedspace in the noisy bay and return to my own room. I got Room 3, my favourite room!

"You were very sick in this room. Why is it your favourite?" asked the nurse.

"It's *my* room. We have a lot of history."

I began to feel a lot better once I was in my own room. I started off with difficulty walking but as the week progressed, I found myself just hopping out of bed with no pain. It was still sore to touch, and shower time was extremely uncomfortable. The swelling was still a massive, hard lump, but most of the pain had disappeared, which was a good sign. It appeared as if the meropenem was working.

I was due for yet another ultrasound on my groin to check the progress of the infection. Isolated pockets of fluid were discovered in my groin, and what the radiologist was worried about was that this could accumulate into one big pocket of fluid that would need to be drained with a needle. Whether this happened, though, was just a matter of waiting and seeing, and if my groin remained with just tiny pockets of fluid, it would just be absorbed into my body in its own time. The good sign was that my mobility was improving, and the doctor advised me that, as it was very easy to become weak in hospital, I should start walking around again. The viral tests conducted as a result of my cough all came back as negative, and I was not contagious, so I was allowed to go to the hospital concourse. I was able to see Dad for the first time since I had last been home, as he met Mum and I for Burger King. This was on Wednesday 2nd February.

***

On Thursday 3rd February, Dr. U was doing the ward rounds. He had some good news to tell me. My blood count was generally good, my white blood cells and platelets at a normal level, and the results from my bone marrow aspiration done the previous week showed all healthy and normal functioning cells. Although the MRD test would take a little longer to come back, under the doctor's microscope, it looked like something close to a complete remission. I was very happy with this news! Also, with this great news came even more – the plan was to get me discharged that day!

However, Dr. U also said that he was anxious to get my next round of chemo started before we gave the leukaemia any chance to grow back. The next round would be less intensive, removing the idarubicin from the FLAG-Ida regimen to just become FLAG. He also said that he wanted my infection to fully settle before I started the next round. Because I was getting better, the haematology team agreed with the microbiology team that it was safe to move me off IV antibiotics to oral antibiotics, which I could have at home. The day was Thursday, and he said that the plan was to get me home that evening and come back the following Tuesday, 8th February, for an ultrasound on the groin. Just in case there was a bed available, I was told to bring some overnight gear with me to start the next round.

Four days at home wasn't a lot of time, but we accepted it,

knowing that the leukaemia could grow back at any moment. It was a bit different to my previous time at home because I was no longer neutropenic and was actually allowed to go places. My family and I tried to make the most of our time at home, and I was able to come say hello to my friends at work and go out for a Chinese with my family.We wanted all four of us to go out for Chinese food, so Kristy had to come down from Norwich. Despite being unwell, Kristy tested negative for Covid on a lateral flow test. She began to worsen as the weekend went by, and then after taking another test, it turned out that she was positive. And I had been exposed to it ...

Chapter 16

Banned

Covid-19 as a cancer patient and the delaying and course of Round 2 of chemotherapy from February 8th to March 5th, 2022

While I had already been exposed to Covid unknowingly for a few days, in the off chance that I hadn't caught it, Kristy left the house and went back to her accommodation in Norwich to get away from the household. For the remainder of my scheduled time at home, I had continued testing negative on lateral flows, although I was beginning to feel mild symptoms. My main symptom was a sore throat, but I could feel a cough beginning to develop.

I arrived at the haematology and oncology outpatients department on Tuesday 8th February for my clinic appointment as planned, but I failed the 'Do you have any symptoms of Covid-19?' question at the front desk. I had attended the hospital because I had tested negative that morning. Just to be safe, Mum and I were separated from the rest of the patients until the receptionist took us to a room to get my temperature taken, as fevers are a symptom of Covid. I was 37.1°, which was a good sign. Then I was taken to another room to take a PCR Covid test, which give more accurate results than the lateral flows due to increased sensitivity. Rather than seeing the doctor then starting treatment as planned, I was then sent home to wait for the results, and my consultation with the doctor was moved to a telephone appointment.

I was feeling a bit low, knowing that Covid was a potential setback to my treatment. I felt even worse when at 2:00pm, I received the result. I tested positive. This put me in an even lower mood. After being hit with infection after infection, I now had another one thrown at me! This was my first Covid infection since the pandemic had begun, and I had done very well to avoid it until then. Now was not the time! Not only did I have to worry about Covid itself and becoming severely ill with it because of my vulnerability, I also had to worry about the delaying of my treatment. Everything was so uncertain, and this could not have come at a worse time.

At 5:00pm, I had a consultation with one of the haematology consultants I hadn't met before. I was supposed to meet him in the clinic earlier that day, but Covid had changed that plan, and it ended up being a video call on the hospital's Attend Anywhere software. He was surprised when I told him that my test came back as positive, and therefore, he said that my treatment would most likely have to be pushed back a bit longer. Of course, my family and I had a few concerns, but the doctor was able to put us at ease.

Firstly, when I had been neutropenic, I had to return to hospital if I developed a fever. I was no longer neutropenic, but we wondered what would happen if I developed a fever due to the virus. The doctor responded by saying that while my symptoms would hopefully remain mild, since it was Covid, fevers were to be expected. He said that he would like us to let the hospital know if I did develop a fever as there was a small possibility that it could be something serious not related to Covid.

The second concern was the delaying of my treatment. Because I had Covid, doctors did not want me to have treatment that could worsen my own condition, nor did they want me near other neutropenic patients when I was infectious. The day I was discharged, Dr. U seemed keen to get me back in for the second cycle before the leukaemia had any chance to grow back. The consultant said that delaying my treatment by another seven to ten days wouldn't be an issue, but he would be a bit concerned if it was delayed by another five or six weeks.

The appointment as a whole was very helpful, and the haematologist even went through the transplant procedure with my family and I again. I left the consultation reassured that catching Covid wasn't the end of the world and I just needed to focus on recovering from it before chemotherapy could commence.

***

The following day, I had seemingly got much worse. Mentally, I was okay, having had my reassurance from the doctor the previous evening, but physically my symptoms were worsening.

My TYA specialist nurse, Rosie, called Mum that evening to see how I was doing and also provided us with a plan for the second cycle of chemo. The current government guidelines for isolation at home were ten days, but if lateral flow tests taken on Day 5 and 6 showed as negative, then I could leave isolation early. Government guidelines applied to me everywhere except the hospital, which I had to stay away from for fourteen days. However, because my bloods needed to be taken and my line dressing needed to be changed, I was allowed in the hospital's isolation clinic on Day 5 to have these done. To return to Ward C9, I needed two negative PCR tests on Days 11 and 14. If these came back negative, I would be admitted to the ward for my chemotherapy to commence on Wednesday 23rd February.

As soon as Rosie called, it seemed to be the perfect timing to be calling a nurse, as I began to feel awful! I had spiked a fever of 38.4°, which increased to 38.6° a little while later. Although fevers were to be expected with the virus, because of my clinical history, it was vital that I phoned the emergency haematology helpline. Rather than sending me to A&E straight away, since I was no longer neutropenic, the protocol was to wait one hour to see if the temperature went down on its own. I was allowed no paracetamol. If my temperature did not improve, I would have to go to A&E and possibly be admitted to a Covid ward, or I would have to go in for blood cultures and then be sent home. Even though fevers were expected in my situation, being a chemotherapy patient meant that fevers were treated like any other infection.

I'd had a horrible experience in A&E the previous month, and the thought of having to go back there reduced me to tears. I didn't want to go and told my parents that I'd rather stay at home and die than ever go back there, which sounds extreme, but it was the truth! Desperate to avoid A&E, I began to panic, but my parents feared it would make me feel hotter and definitely put me in A&E if I didn't calm down.

The helpline nurse told Mum to call back in an hour to notify her of any changes in my temperature. An hour later, despite fluctuating temperature readings, we managed to settle on 37.6°. My temperature had indeed gone down on its own, and this was my only fever with the virus. I had just had a nap, and according to the helpline nurse, it was common to get a bit hot and flustered when having Covid. I avoided A&E!

Thankfully, the rest of my symptoms were mild, aside from the nasty cough, which remained on and off for a couple of weeks after. I was pretty much back to normal within a couple of days. On Monday 14th February, I was able to go into hospital for an overdue dressing change and blood test. It was a unique hospital experience to say the least. I wasn't allowed in the main hospital in case I caused an outbreak and infected the neutropenic patients, so I had to meet Rosie in the car park at the back of the radiotherapy department. She then let me through the door, and I was taken into Room H, the dreaded isolation room. I waited a short while until she came back in full PPE, and I had my bloods taken and dressing changed.

By Friday 18th February, all of my symptoms had disappeared, except for the on and off cough. My lateral flow test came back negative, and I was allowed back into hospital for an ultrasound, which had been postponed. This ultrasound was to, once again, check my groin. My groin had pretty much healed by this point. When in hospital, it was massive, red, and inflamed, which then reduced to a hard lumpy wall along the side of my groin, but now there was just a bony knobbly bit on the corner of the right side of my groin, below the waistband of my trousers. I saw the same consultant who had done the biopsy on my groin, and he could tell just by looking at it how much it had improved. The ultrasound didn't pick up anything concerning, and most of what he concluded came from just having a feel of the area with his hands. He said that the knobbly bit was just scar tissue left over from the infection. He told me that it would either take ages for it to go down or it may never go down at all. The good news was that the infection was gone, and after a month my groin was infection-free!

In the space of two months, I had suffered from three life-threatening infections and Covid-19. The infection blizzard from December 2021 to February 2022 was finally over! Things were finally looking good, and I looked forward to four more days at home until chemo started on the planned date of

Wednesday 23rd February. All I needed was two negative PCR tests and I could get back on Ward C9!

Or so I thought ...

***

What I hoped would be a small setback for my treatment plan ended up being what I saw as a never-ending battle with Covid, a virus I didn't even *have* anymore. The hospital policy stated that I needed to show two negative PCR tests on Days 11 and 14 before I could return to Ward C9. Since I had recovered from the virus within a couple of days, I thought this would reflect on my tests. Unfortunately, it didn't, and a positive PCR result was to remain with me for quite a while.

My planned PCR test for Day 11 – the same day as my final groin ultrasound on Friday 19th February – did not go to plan due to an unusual reason: the weather. There was a storm going on at the time, and as most test centres were in an outside setting, it was deemed unsafe to have them open. Therefore, I missed my scheduled PCR test that day. This was slightly annoying, and worrying too, as I was anxious to get treatment started, and with the hospital not getting back to me in time about doing a test there instead, my parents and I decided that we would just have to get one booked early the following day.

Thankfully, the weather improved overnight, and I was able to have my test in Bury St. Edmunds as planned. I expected my result to come back negative. After all, my severe symptoms had only lasted two or three days, and even though there were on and off long-term symptoms, I would have thought that seven days in isolation and a further three before my test would give me a negative result. But it didn't, and when I woke up the next morning on Sunday 20th February,

I was disheartened to see the email informing me that I was still positive. The delaying of treatment was already a concern, and as a plan was in place to get started, I was worried about how Round 2 would be affected.

I emailed Rosie and my leukaemia specialist nurse, who I had never actually met in person, about what the potential options would be regarding the plan to get treatment started. Having been worried about delaying it for a long time, I decided that I'd take any plan that allowed me to commence treatment as soon as possible.

Treatment ended up being delayed for almost another week. I was assured that I had not been forgotten about, and all of my doctors and nurses were working hard to formulate a plan that would be the least-traumatic experience and in my best interests. By Tuesday 22nd February, I received a call from my leukaemia nurse, but unfortunately the options we went through regarding the next stage of treatment were not very pleasant.

The first option would be to have my chemotherapy as an outpatient. Under this option, a hostel on hospital grounds, very similar to Kingston House many years back, would be booked for Mum and I to stay in. We would then be able to make a short walk to Room H, the isolation room, at the back of the hospital for me to have daily treatment there, enabling me not only to start treatment but also to be close to my family. However, there were a couple of disadvantages to this option. Firstly, I was known from Round 1 of my second battle to not get on well with cytarabine, and my family, the doctors and nurses, and I would have all preferred me to have a bed on the ward just in case something bad should happen. Any reaction would have resulted in a trip to A&E. Even worse, if I was able to survive my five days of cytarabine unharmed, the effects of it would not be pleasant. Being a chemotherapy patient, an infection was pretty much a near certainty, and it would be very likely that I'd end up on a ward at some point. Since I was still testing positive for Covid, I would have to stay on a red ward, not C9.

The second option would be to have my treatment as an inpatient, but for the same reasons, I would not be able to have it on Ward C9. If I went for this option, I would receive my chemotherapy on a red ward, meaning strictly no visitors for infection control reasons. This meant that, while I'd be well looked after, if I was feeling unwell, I would not be able to have the emotional support from Mum. It would also mean that while the haematology nurses would come to see me on the ward to give treatment, the round-the-clock care that I would require throughout the day would not be given by the doctors and nurses that I knew. Overall, being on a red ward was to be an isolated, lonely, and unpleasant experience.

That left the third option – waiting and seeing. As soon as I could show a negative test, my nurses were keen to get me admitted to Ward C9. Of course, it was important not to delay treatment any longer than it already had been, and if a negative test could not be achieved within the next five days, the doctors and nurses would debate over which of the first two options would be in my best interest. In the meantime, I was advised to keep testing over and over to get a negative result, and it was getting to the point where the staff at the test centre recognised me! Unfortunately, I had no luck, and every test came back positive.

This was a frustrating experience, and the more I read and learned about Covid tests, the more frustrating my dilemma seemed to get. First of all, I learned that PCR tests could show as positive up to ninety days after the initial positive test! The

PCRs were considered more trustworthy than the lateral flows because they were more sensitive. But the issue was that they held me back because they could detect disease that was no longer contagious! I had done my ten days in isolation, my lateral flow tests were negative, and I was no longer showing any symptoms.

I completely understood that it was important to keep away from other patients on the ward, especially neutropenic and transplant patients, but I was not contagious anymore, and the likelihood of me spreading the virus to them was very low! Also, if I was so contagious, then why could the nurses from the ward come to see me in the isolation room, potentially putting themselves at risk of catching Covid and passing it on to the neutropenic patients on the ward? Nothing about the hospital's two negative PCR tests policy made sense, and if anything, my family, friends, and I thought it was wrong to be denied the treatment I desperately needed. As I said, I was all for protecting other patients on the ward, and having been neutropenic myself, I know how important it is to be protected from infections. But doing my time in isolation was enough, according to government guidelines. So why wasn't two weeks enough for the hospital?

The problem with the hospital's policy was that there was too much focus on what *could* happen and not on what was happening. Restricting Covid in a hospital is highly important, especially for the vulnerable. But I was a vulnerable patient, and I got mild symptoms. Not every vulnerable person was going to become seriously ill with the virus. My life and my future were literally being played with because I was denied the treatment that I needed over something that had very little chance of happening. I was not a threat to anyone.

This isn't just the view of myself, my family, or my friends.

I heard from the staff at the test centres that this problem was happening quite frequently. Even my nurses, who were doing everything they could to fight my case to get me back on the ward, agreed that this was a stupid rule. They said that if they could let me on C9, they would, and I was even advised to complain to the higher-ups as they seemed to be turning a blind eye. We never did complain, and I was very grateful to have a fantastic team of doctors and nurses around me during my endless battle with Covid. I was certain that they were doing everything they could, and not allowing my treatment was a factor beyond their control.

***

I was given five days to achieve a negative test, starting on Wednesday 23rd February. If I was not negative by Monday 28th February, which seemed the likely case, then doctors decided that the best option would be to have my treatment as an outpatient.

In the meantime, I was still showing up to the test centres for Covid tests, and I was attending Room H for blood tests and line care. We were hopeful for a negative test by the Monday to ensure a smooth admission to C9, but it was important that I was prepared for all options.

On Friday 25th February, in my weekly Room H appointment, Rosie took my bloods and changed the bungs and dressing on my line. She also gave me a quick Covid swab, both of us praying that it would come back negative. It was important to prepare for the worst-case scenario, and she showed me the plan she had devised for the commencement of Round 2.

Round 2 was going to consist of the FLAG regimen

(fludarabine, cytarabine, and G-CSF), removing idarubicin from the combination since doctors were happy with January's bone marrow biopsy results. The dosage of the cytarabine would also be reduced, from 250 ml per dose for Round 1 to 100 ml per dose for Round 2. The fludarabine would stay the same as it was for Round 1, with 100 ml per dose. Chemotherapy was to last five days in total, with my fludarabine infusion in the morning and cytarabine later in the afternoon.

The plan was to move into a hostel, called Elsworth House, on Sunday 27th February. Elsworth House was massive block of flats, and it wasn't clear who exactly was staying there. I'm sure everyone used it for different purposes, as sometimes I'd see hospital staff and fellow C9 patients and patients from other wards staying there. The hostel also had a palliative care office, so I think people worked in the building too.

Elsworth House was very close to Kingston and was slightly closer to the main hospital. That evening, my first G-CSF injection was due. Because of the timings of the G-CSF injection, it would be me having to administer the injection myself rather than a nurse, and I'd be expected to inject myself for the next six days too. Knowing that I'd never had any experience in administering injections before, Rosie gave me some quick training on what to do, and I ended up injecting G-CSF into an orange. I learned not to inject straight into the orange, rather to do it at an angle to prevent it from hurting more. The needle had a spring, and it just sprung back up as soon as I was done injecting. I was quite proud of myself, completing what I saw as the first stage of my nursing training! An orange was my first patient, but I couldn't help but feel nervous knowing that the next person to be injected would be myself!

Every morning, from Monday 28th February to Friday

4th March, I was expected to show up at the back of the radiotherapy department for my chemotherapy. I'd have to call a phone number to be let in, and a nurse from C9, in full PPE, would then come to collect me to get me hooked up to my fludarabine drip. Another chemo-trained nurse from the outpatient department would also be present to supervise the nurse from C9, helping to check and administer the chemo before going back to what they were doing. Even though, by this point, Mum would be allowed to sit in the isolation room with me, it was still deemed unsafe to be left by myself, and the C9 nurse would have to sit with us while my fludarabine went through.

Each fludarabine infusion was to last half an hour. Once the fludarabine had gone through, and after a quick flush, the nurses would then hook me up to a pump, which would contain the cytarabine inside. Known as a CADD pump, this machine was programmed to start the cytarabine infusion four hours after the start of my fludarabine. I was going to be attached to this machine for five days straight, with no breaks, and the drug was going to be infused when I was in the hostel. I'd have to go for walks with it, shower with it, go to the toilet with it, and sleep with it. Everywhere I went, my CADD pump went with me. Each cytarabine infusion lasted four hours, and the pump would be changed daily during every Room H appointment.

My treatment plan for Round 2 was scheduled to come to an end on Saturday 5th March 2022, with that day consisting of one final G-CSF injection in the evening.

***

Sunday 27th February 2022. Treatment as an outpatient was not ideal, but I had no choice if I wanted to get started. As much as they wanted me to, the nurses just couldn't let me on Ward C9. There was no alternative other than facing the hardship and taking the risk of something going wrong outside of the hospital ward.

After a few eventful weeks at home, my family and I set off for the next stage in my journey. I was sad having to leave after so long but also excited to be getting the show on the road. Having to go through it just meant that the end was closer in sight.

We were required to collect our keys from the Addenbrooke's Treatment Centre (ATC) to get into the hostel. This was eventful because as it was a Sunday, the ATC was closed and no one was operating the front desk. We desperately needed our keys! The security guard directed us to the main hospital reception desk, but the receptionist just directed us back and told us to phone a number. After a number of tries getting the phone to work, Mum ended up being put on hold for ages until a woman arrived from behind, taking us by surprise, to give us our keys. Our booking for Elsworth House was to last until the end of March, so we had it just in case we needed to be nearby the hospital for any reason after my second cycle was completed.

It was a quick stop at Elsworth House to drop our many belongings off. We were going to explore it a little bit later on, but we needed to go to Tesco first to stock up on food. The excitement of the morning had previously outweighed the sadness of my situation but going back into the very same Tesco for the first time in years brought back the memories of 2016. I remember visiting the very same Tesco every day when I was staying at Kingston House, and these flashback memories made me feel slightly emotional. I was really uneasy about going in there and felt a desperation to leave. As I've said with regards to my December 2021 bone marrow biopsy, I'd never realised how much the past had affected me until I came face-to-face with it.

Once we had finished going shopping, it was a quick stop by the ward. I was banned from the ward, but Mum wasn't, and she was required to pick up my G-CSF injections for me to administer myself. I was allowed to wait outside the doors of the ward, but I just couldn't go in. Apparently, the nurses thought it was a good thing that they hadn't seen me and didn't realise I was having to have my treatment as an outpatient due to Covid! With the chaos that was going to occur in the next week, I'm sure it soon became a well-known fact why I hadn't been seen on the ward for over a month!

After the quick stop to C9, we returned to Elsworth House to settle down a bit and unpack. In normal times, this would have been a shared flat, but because of Covid restrictions, we had the flat to ourselves. One room wasn't in use and remained locked, while Mum and I had access to two bedrooms, so Dad could stay if he wished. Shared was the kitchen, bathroom, toilet, and lounge, but once again, due to Covid, we had the flat to ourselves, and it was pretty much our own for the next month.

That evening, I administered my first G-CSF injection. I'd had my training on how to give myself the injection, but no one had told me I had to make the solution. I had to work with a syringe that was pre-filled with water, and then with a larger needle, suck the contents into a powder solution, mix it, then suck it up again. Then I had to replace the larger needle with the smaller needle ready for injection. It took a couple of attempts. The first was an absolute failure when I accidentally pushed all the water out of the syringe. But the worst thing was checking for air bubbles. Trying to eliminate the air bubbles caused me to create more, and I eventually gave up and just injected it. I'm not sure if that was smart, but I didn't suffer any problems doing it. The injection wasn't going into my bloodstream, which would have caused a stroke if there were any bubbles, rather it went through the first layer of fat on my tummy. I didn't find injecting myself too traumatising. I did my best, injecting at an angle, just like I was trained. While it hurt, there was only a tiny bit of bleeding, which I was able to patch up. For the next six days, I always dreaded G-CSF time. Making the injection was the worst bit, and when Dad came to visit, I asked him to make it for me. I even trained Mum up on it, but for the most part, I did it myself.

Aware that my freedom was expiring rapidly, Dad decided that he would take Mum and I out for dinner. I was still feeling really well, although I could tell that bone pain was going to become an issue after the G-CSF. Thankfully, it was just that one dose that gave me trouble, and I was absolutely fine in subsequent days! After dinner that night, it was time to say goodbye to feeling well. Tomorrow, I knew my body was in for a real shock.

***

On Monday 28th February, I woke up early to attend my 9:30am appointment in Room H. Waiting outside Room H was the most tedious activity you could ever spend your time doing. It was a great start when I had to call a phone number to be let in but received no response. Thankfully, I was able to call Rosie, and she managed to contact C9, and the nurse from there let me in.

The nurse administering the chemo was late, but it wasn't her fault. Firstly, the place where the chemotherapy was made didn't open till 9:00am, and mine wouldn't be ready until 10:00am. This then had to be collected and checked, and a nurse had to come down from the ninth floor to the outpatients' department to see me. It was all very complicated, and no one knew where they had to be or at what time.

I was the problem. Ward C9 had managed to avoid the dreaded Room H so far, and I was the first and only patient on the ward at the time who was having this problem. At least I can say I've made history on Ward C9! I heard that receiving treatment in isolation happened quite a lot to the older patients, but when my situation arose, it put the nurses in a state of panic, and they had no idea what they were supposed to do.

For a 9:30am appointment, I finally entered Room H at 11:30am, passing the time by waiting outside on the cold hard ground with Mum and shopping for lunch. Round 2 of chemotherapy had officially started by 12:00pm, with the first of five fludarabine infusions! This took half an hour to go through. I was known to feel well on fludarabine, and nothing major happened while it was going through. All that I was really noticing was a metallic taste in my mouth. Having chemo feels like you drank petrol the week before but the taste hasn't gone yet and you've been left with a very subtle taste in your mouth and throat.

Once the fludarabine was done, I was hooked up straight away to the cytarabine. This was what we feared, and the nurses on the ward had been having conversations about me earlier that morning, knowing how much I really did not get on with that drug. They weren't so sure how safe it was allowing me to have this unsupervised.

Extensions were put on my PICC line lumens just to give me some more space, and a cassette with 100 ml of cytarabine was attached to a CADD machine. The machine's screen looked like the top of a card machine, but rather than a keypad at the bottom, there was just a cassette with chemotherapy labels. I found the word 'cassette' interesting. It had nothing to do with tape players, but I'm guessing it was called a cassette because the chemo was contained in something of a similar shape. Now I was going to be attached to the CADD machine for five days straight with no breaks, and this was going to be challenging! I hoped I wouldn't forget that I was attached to it, because from experience of forgetting that I'm attached to drip stands, I knew it would hurt!

Usually, patients receiving chemo as an outpatient with a CADD pump would be able to take their treatment with them in a backpack, but despite one being ordered for me, it hadn't arrived in time. So, for the remainder of the day, I was walking around with what looked like an oversized calculator and a smaller bag of saline solution for a flush. I got a lot of stares in the pharmacy that day when Mum and I were sent down to collect my medicines.

I had to be hooked up to the cytarabine then, but it wasn't programmed to start until four hours after the start of my fludarabine dose. Therefore, the cytarabine was going to start at 4:00pm, once we were back in the hostel. Mum and I were nervous. We began the countdown, and soon enough, 4:00pm rolled around and the machine started to make a noise, indicating that it was functioning properly. I was used to 250 ml doses of cytarabine at a faster rate, but here I was only having a 100 ml dose every day, over a slower rate of 25 ml an hour. This hopefully would cause less shock to the system, and it appeared that way to begin with. Two hours in, the cytarabine seemed not to be having much effect. *I can do this*, I thought. Then it all went wrong.

About two and a half hours into my first cytarabine dose

on Monday, I began to feel sick. Nausea was expected while on chemotherapy, so there wasn't much of a concern. But then I started to feel *really* sick, and I felt the sudden urge and just threw up everywhere. Often after throwing up, I would feel better having got it out, but more and more kept coming. I almost overflowed the bowl twice! Vomiting was uncontrollable, and I could hardly breathe as I felt the sick clogging my airways. More and more just kept erupting from my mouth, and as soon as I was done throwing up everything I had eaten and drank that day, my empty stomach paid the price as I gagged uncontrollably, throwing up nothing but bile and then saliva. The strain on my tummy and upper body caused excruciating pain, and my face, also severely strained, reacted with a huge outbreak of spots. The severe vomiting fit left me with chest pain for a couple of days after.

This was unfortunately the disadvantage of having chemotherapy as an outpatient. No one had informed Mum and I when I needed to start my anti-sickness medication. Usually on the ward, I would have had my admission and the nurses would prepare the appropriate medicine. But because we were left on our own, we didn't know what medicine I could and couldn't take as medication protocols change within cycles and we hadn't received the protocol. We didn't even know that I had medicine to pick up at the pharmacy until we asked the nurse in Room H. It turns out that I should have had my anti-sickness before my first dose of chemotherapy, and I needed to take it regularly throughout the day. And there I was, having a dose of chemo with absolutely no protection from sickness.

My vomiting was getting so severe that night that Mum called the haematology helpline. I was still testing positive, and I wanted to avoid A&E at all costs, especially when the nurse on the phone said that I may require an overnight stay if they did not get on top of my sickness. The concern was me becoming dehydrated. If I was throwing up so much, it was unlikely that I was able to replace the fluids I was losing, and this could have become very serious. The nurse advised that I take an anti-sickness tablet and see if I kept it down. If I couldn't, Mum was told to call back. I wasn't able to keep it down, and my vomiting was so loud that the nurse actually asked if it was me that she could hear on the phone! She said that A&E were expecting me, and it may just be that they would give me an anti-sickness injection and send me back to the hostel, but an overnight stay was a real possibility.

Perhaps due to the fear of A&E, my sickness settled after the phone call with the nurse. I woke up still feeling rubbish the next morning, so Mum phoned Rosie, asking for advice. Rosie supported Mum, who was clearly upset and worried about me, and assured her that it was very normal for me to feel that way. The FLAG chemo regimen is tough, hence why they prefer to give it as an inpatient. She was able to construct a chart for us, with the key being to keep on top of the sickness before it starts. I was required to take regular anti-sickness drugs: ondansetron, domperidone, and a steroid called dexamethasone. I had been prescribed cyclizine, but since this had the same mechanism as one of the other drugs, I was advised to hold off for the time being.

The nurses absolutely loved dexamethasone, describing it as a wonder drug, and said that they themselves were even tempted to take it! It makes you eat and drink and keeps you awake, so it was advised that I didn't take it at night. I couldn't believe I had never taken it before – the drug was amazing! Over the next few days, I couldn't stop eating, and my weight increased! I was eating double, perhaps triple, what I was eating before – much more than I was even when I was healthy. My face did puff up a little, but that was expected when taking steroids, and overall, my face wasn't as swollen as some of the other patients I had seen on steroids. The highs of the drug – eating, drinking, and keeping me awake – sadly were not enough to keep away the lows. While the medication left me feeling very awake, it ended up causing sleepless nights, even when I hadn't taken any at night-time. The dexamethasone also made me feel quite depressed and paranoid at night, and I'd stay up worrying over the littlest things.

The first day of chemotherapy was the worst one, and from then on, things were a bit smoother. We finally had a plan to get regular anti-sickness drugs into me, and nausea soon became a problem of the past. In terms of coping with being attached to a machine 24/7, I soon got used to it. By Tuesday of Round 2, a bag had finally arrived, and I wore my chemotherapy like a backpack and carried that with me everywhere I went. I think Rosie, who was doing my chemo that day, felt a bit bad. When she opened the door to let me in, I had been stood out in the pouring rain, with nothing to protect my electronics that I had to carry with me, completely exhausted after a night of vomiting. She soon chased up a bag for me.

Showering was very difficult because it was just not possible. I had to avoid getting my line wet, but at the same time I had to avoid getting the electronic machine wet! I couldn't wear my blue shower sleeve, nor could I cover the bag effectively because the wires were not long enough. Going five days straight without a shower was not only unhygienic but would also be strongly frowned upon by the nurses due to my increased infection risk. I ended up having to take a shower without actually getting in it, only getting half of my body directly in the water when it was hair wash day.

Despite the practical issues of receiving the

chemotherapy itself, as I've said, the rest of the time my chemotherapy was administered went smoothly. My history with cytarabine resulted in fevers, but I did not get a single fever while on the drug. However, a blood test from Tuesday – the second day into my second cycle – found something a bit concerning. My CRP levels (infection levels or inflammatory markers) had for some reason skyrocketed to 142. Normal levels should be between 0 and 9. I hadn't yet spiked a fever, and my white blood cells were super high (due to the G-CSF, my white blood cells were 32.0, the normal range being around 3.9 to 10.2). I would be required to have another blood test the next day to monitor what my infection levels were doing. As I was still Covid positive, being admitted to the ward was something we really didn't want, and in the meantime, doctors wanted to hold off on antibiotics. It was going to take a few days for my blood count to go down, and perhaps the G-CSF was doing its job fighting the infection artificially before I naturally began to suffer. A closer eye needed to be kept on me, and if I had any symptoms of infection, such as fevers, shortness of breath, or increased heartrate, I needed to call the haematology helpline without hesitation.

Thankfully, by Wednesday, my CRP levels dropped to 100. This, somehow, coincided with a negative Covid test. I managed to dodge a massive bullet! Thursday was a complete disaster of a day when the nurse wasn't informed that I needed to have my dose of chemotherapy, and the outpatients receptionist refused to let me through the door. Mum and I were stood outside the back of the radiotherapy department for almost an hour, in the cold and wet, waiting to be let into the isolation clinic. The nurse was not happy when she discovered that no one had let me in and put a complaint in to the oncology outpatients department. Another nurse was kind enough to provide Mum and I some free snacks and drinks as an apology. We were not angry, because we understood that nurses are busy and it's completely normal for plans to go wrong. The receptionist should have just let us in rather than making a sick chemotherapy patient wait in the cold and rain!

What happened that Thursday just increased the motivation of the nurses to get me admitted back to Ward C9. Having chemotherapy as an outpatient just wasn't practical. I had finally tested negative on a PCR, and with recently policy changes, just one, not two, negative tests was necessary, so I was allowed to come back. My infection levels were also something the nurses wanted to monitor me on, and even though this showed a drop to 50 by Thursday, keeping a close eye was important.

After my appointment in Room H on the morning of Thursday 3rd March, I was back on the ward by the evening. I didn't have my own room and I was back on the bay, but I was receiving my chemotherapy where it was safest – the ward. I had been gone for over a month. The last time I was there, my groin had been the most famous thing on the ward. The healthcare assistant said I was like a little celebrity, having been back after disappearing for so long. Also, famous for my ferocious groin, which I'm sure put a label on me for the rest of my time on C9, she couldn't believe I could walk so fast! Apparently, I was like a space rocket. All the nurses and healthcare assistants were surprised to see me walking – it was like they had never seen me so well on the ward before! That was also because I wasn't in for any emergency. They just wanted me on the ward for monitoring, and being discharged to the hostel, or maybe even home as soon as treatment finished, was a very real possibility. In fact, my CRP levels dropped again to 25 by Friday, and going into the next week, they were normal, at <4.

I was glad to finally be on the ward. While I preferred the food we were cooking at the hostel, I felt safer, and I'd have the relevant checks to make sure I was functioning well. So far into my second chemotherapy cycle, I was feeling okay, except for a bit of brain fog, feeling but not being sick, and weakness in my heart. Nausea was well-controlled, and my confusion was getting better, but I was feeling a lot of pain in my chest area, and at times it felt like my heart was dropping. Having regular obs and check-ups with the doctor put me more at ease than it did being independent and calling out-of-hours helplines. A further advantage of being on the ward was that finally someone I trusted was administering my injections again, so I was certain that it was being done the right way.

Freedom day was Friday 4th March, when I was finally disconnected from my CADD pump at 8:00pm. This marked the end of my final dose of Round 2! I was relieved to finally be detached from the CADD pump, and I was able to have a proper shower for the first time in over a week! Evident by my dropping infection markers, both the doctors and nurses agreed that it was no longer necessary to be taking up a bed on the ward, and I was discharged on Saturday 5th March from what was the shortest hospital stay in my life thus far.

While the doctor said we were allowed to go home, since we had the hostel and I was due to attend the ward day unit on Mondays, Wednesdays, and Fridays for blood tests and potential transfusions, Mum and I decided it was best to stay in the hostel. Also, if something such as a fever happened, which was a strong possibility, then it would be easier to reach A&E from the hostel than from home an hour away. It was all about taking the most sensible option, and since we were entitled to keep the hostel booking, we thought, why not keep it? I managed a few hours at home on Sunday, just to visit, but I was used to hostel life by this point and more comfortable there. It worked well when we had stayed in Kingston House, so it made sense to play it safe while we had access to Elsworth.

On the day I was discharged, I also received something very nice through the post! I received my second pair of Supershoes! If you remember much earlier in this book, you'll know that Supershoes is an amazing charity that assigns an artist to hand-paint a unique pair of shoes for children, teenagers, and young adults with cancer. Kathy, my Young Lives vs. Cancer social worker, remembered me from six years ago and referred me for a second pair. It was interesting to see how little I had changed when comparing my second pair with my first, with WWE, SpongeBob SquarePants, and Super Mario all being top features. I also requested that the planets of the solar system be added to my shoes, a turtle, and also a star with a crown on top, which is the logo that represents my nickname, 'the Brightest Star'. I love both pairs of my Supershoes, and both are proudly displayed on the shelf in my room!

Chapter 17

Dodging Bullets

Recovering from Round 2 of chemotherapy
from March 5th to March 24th, 2022

My number one goal, since the terrible experience I'd had in January, was to avoid A&E at all costs. It was so bad last time that there was no way I could go back, so I did everything I could to avoid spiking a fever or infection. But knowing my terrible record at fighting infections, I anticipated a fever to come sooner rather than later. A lot of my time in Elsworth was spent waiting for a fever to spike at any moment, and I often said to the nurses on the ward that, if I was to get a fever, I hoped it would be while I was on the ward, just do I could avoid A&E!

Mum and I both agreed that as spiking a fever was a very high possibility, it would be best to remain in the hostel for the majority of my time recovering, in case I'd have to return to A&E. I also thought that being on the hospital grounds was safer in terms of controlling infections, as my CRP levels always seemed to increase when at home. We had our room at Elsworth House booked until the end of March, so in the chance that something did happen to me, Mum would be able to stay nearby if I was admitted to a bay on C9. Also, my appointment times for the Ward C9 day unit varied; some were as early as 9:30am. It would be a rush to drive there and back, considering we lived an hour away. The hostel turned out to be very handy indeed.

I managed a few hours at home on Sunday 6th March as doctors were happy for me to go home, some unaware that we were even staying in the hostel. I still wasn't neutropenic, as the G-CSF had done a great job at sustaining my white blood cell count. But it was drastically going down, from 32.0 the previous Tuesday to 9.0 three days later on the Friday. That was still a good white blood cell count, with the standard range being 3.9 to 10.2, but as you can tell by a drop that quickly, the chemo was doing its job. My white blood cells began to drop rapidly after my G-CSF injections finished, and by the end of the next week, my count was flat at 0.0.

The chemo was very slow at killing my red blood cells. Doctors like to transfuse if the haemoglobin, a protein in the red blood cell that carries oxygen around the body, falls below 80. But for the first couple of weeks after my treatment had finished, my haemoglobin fell from 113 to 96. The standard range for haemoglobin is between 135 and 172, and anything below that means you are anaemic. I had been anaemic for a while, mildly since October 2021, and my red blood cells never fully recovered or reached the standard range after Round 1 of chemo. This is because they are always the last blood cells to recover after treatment. When my bone marrow was showing signs of recovery a couple of weeks after Round 2, evident by my improving but still severely low white blood cell count, my red blood cells were still dying.

Probably the scariest thing during my recovery from Round 2 was my platelet count. The standard range for platelets is 150 to 370. Doctors like to transfuse when they reach below 10. Low platelets cause easy bruising or bleeding, and something like a cat scratch to an ordinary person could make a person with low platelets bleed for a very long time. Bigger cuts could make someone with low platelets bleed to death. And if they reached below 10, what is known as severe thrombocytopenia, there is a high risk of internal bleeding without any apparent reason. On

Monday 14th March, my platelet count was 3. I knew my platelets were low as my gums wouldn't stop bleeding, but I didn't realise that they were *that* low. The nurses couldn't believe it! I had a platelet transfusion, which kept my platelets at a low but safer level until Friday. Blood and platelet transfusions did not top my blood up to the standard range, rather they gave my bloods a boost to a safer level.

The scariest thing was surviving the weekends. I felt safer in the hostel, but we went home at the weekends, mainly because Mum wanted to. I guess you have to have some time at home! But if my platelets were low on a Friday (they were 15 on Friday 18th March), because I was above the transfuse level, I would be sent home without a transfusion and told to come back on Monday. I therefore needed to be very careful when at home because I was living with dangerously low platelet levels. At home, the cats were always in their playful mood, so I spent most of my time trying to avoid them because I knew they'd do anything to unintentionally kill me. Because I cut and bled easily, I was also more prone to getting infections through these cuts as a result of my white blood cell counts. Low platelets and no white blood cells are not a good combination, and it was the perfect recipe for an infection!

Round 2 also gave me the strangest case of hair loss. From Round 1, I lost the hair on my head but managed to maintain my beard. Because there was such a long interval between Round 1 and Round 2, my hair had the opportunity to grow back. It was patchy, uneven, and gave me a rattail, but in terms of colour and consistency, it grew back more or less the same as it was before it fell out in January. Round 2 was strange because my hair loss was a complete reverse of my hair loss from Round 1. I had lots of hair on my head, but my beard fell out! I woke up most mornings with beard hairs all over my pillow, and if I had a white shirt on, hair would be visible all down it. It fell out with ease – all I had to do was touch my beard and there would be hair all over my hands. Sometimes beard hairs would be on my plate after I had finished eating! Because I had low platelets, I couldn't risk cutting myself, so I didn't shave. This left me with a very patchy beard, with patches looking shaven while parts of my beard were still well-preserved.

***

My first day in the Ward C9 day unit post-Round 2 was on Monday 7th March. This was the same procedure as my previous visits in the day unit. My bloods would be taken, after which would be a couple of hours of waiting until my blood test results were back. Then action would be taken depending on what needed to be done, whether that was a blood or platelet transfusion, or both.

I had done really well on the first week, requiring no blood or platelet transfusions on Monday, Wednesday, or Friday. My red blood cells were slow to decrease, and my platelets, while really low, were still above the transfuse level. However, I did have a funny turn in the day unit on Friday 11th March.

I had just finished eating my lunch, and all of a sudden, I had an awful pain in what felt like my chest but was actually in the upper gastrointestinal tract. I had also been complaining of pain in my rib cage all week, which could have been down to my anaemia or thrombocytopenia. With these pains, I began to feel very hot and sweaty. In fact, I had so much sweat on my hands that I couldn't even open my water bottle, and patients were just staring at me, watching me trying to get my bottle open. It made me look really weak, so I was embarrassed!

Oh no, I panicked, *I have a fever. It's going to be an*

infection! At least it's on the ward so I won't have to go to A&E to be admitted!

The nurse did a full set of obs, which showed that my blood pressure and pulse was normal and my temperature was 36.6°, so we had no idea what was going on there. But she wanted me to see the ward registrar just in case, which meant I'd have to wait in the day unit for even longer.

The doctor did the necessary checks and a full examination. She looked into my mouth and could tell I was suffering from a bit of mucositis. Mucositis was the only other thing aside from low blood counts that I was suffering from Round 2 of chemo. My gums, not helped by my low platelets, were really sore and bled often. I was brushing my teeth with a baby toothbrush and using a mouthwash, which, although it burned my mouth, worked really well on my gums. The rest of my mouth was fine though, although the doctor could see a bit of bruising.

She had a feel of my rib cage and there was nothing concerning, but she said the pain I was pointing to on my chest was quite a vague area, so it was difficult to know what it was. What I was probably suffering from was a case of acid reflux and heartburn. Because the chemotherapy destroys the gut lining, the acid from my stomach irritated the gastrointestinal tract, causing very painful heartburn and indigestion. I was prescribed a medication called omeprazole, which I had to take before breakfast every morning, which works to prevent the stomach from producing too much acid.

I managed to spend the Saturday and Sunday at home, which was uneventful, considering my blood levels. My neutropenia, anaemia, and thrombocytopenia, all caused by the chemotherapy, ensured that I'd have no protection from bleeding or infection and no energy, even when doing easy everyday tasks. Because of this, I took it easy when at home, especially when I knew I was in desperate of a platelet transfusion.

Mum and I spent the weekend at home with Dad, who would then drive us back to Elsworth House on the Sunday night. I was back on the Ward C9 day unit on Monday 14th March, and I seemed to have dodged another bullet. My CRP levels, which test the level of inflammation in my body, indicating a potential infection, had risen from <4, which they had been for a few days, to 53. This was an indication that an infection and quite possibly a fever was imminent.

The registrar was quite alarmed by this and asked me if I was having any problems. A few days prior, I had been having toilet troubles. During the day I was normal, but in the night, I was having to urinate every two hours, sometimes even hourly. I attributed this to the dexamethasone, which I had been weaned off since finishing my course of treatment, as it is a drug known to keep you very awake. The doctor was a bit concerned about me having to urinate so often during the night, so just to be on the safe side and to check for any infection before it could escalate, I was asked to produce a urine sample. Everything from my urine sample appeared fine, except for the traces of blood that were found in my urine. The doctor was not too concerned about this, considering my platelets were 3 on this day, and having severely low platelets is known to cause blood in urine. I had just had a platelet transfusion to correct this, so, provided that the set of obs that the nurses were to do were fine, I could be sent back to the hostel. My obs were fine and I was free to go, but if I had any signs of a fever or feeling unwell, I was told to not hesitate to call the emergency haematology helpline.

By Wednesday 16th March, I seemed to be doing well again.

My platelet transfusion from the previous Monday had done a good job of keeping my platelets above the transfuse level. Even better news was that my CRP levels had decreased to 44. This was still high, but an improvement from 53.

Then, on Friday 18th March, I dodged another massive bullet. The previous day, I received a call from the matron at the hospital. She informed me that I had been in close contact with someone with Covid-19 when I was in the day unit on Wednesday a couple of days ago. The matron told me that I had to do lateral flow tests for the next ten days, even though she said that the risk of the positive patient transmitting the virus to me was very unlikely but she was unaware that I was still in my ninety-day period of no testing. I was still ninety days out from my own Covid infection. In this period, reinfection was unlikely (but not impossible), and hospital policy was to not swab anyone who were within their ninety-day period before a hospital admission. I was confused about whether this applied to lateral flows or PCRs, so I took a test anyway to be on the safe side in case the ward asked me to provide evidence upon entry. I took the lateral flow, and from what appeared as a very faint second line, I had tested positive for Covid. Again! Because I remembered the horrors and awkwardness of Room H, I thought I'd dispute that result and take another test to test the reliability. Once again, I received a faint second line, indicating a positive result. I couldn't exactly show up to the ward and lie about being negative, so I contacted Rosie, asking what I should do.

First of all, Rosie said that it was highly unlikely that I had caught Covid in the day unit that Wednesday, so if I was positive then it was likely that I had contracted the virus from somewhere else. Also, because I was still in my ninety-day period of no testing, it was likely that I was showing a false positive. Nevertheless, a positive result had to be taken seriously by the hospital, and because of this result, due to the most complicated rule ever, I wasn't a red patient, nor was I a green patient: I was now an amber patient.

Being an amber patient meant that I was still allowed on Ward C9, I just had to be isolated from everyone else. Instead of being on the day unit that day, I had to have my blood test and PICC line dressing change in the small treatment room of the ward, isolated from the other patients. I wouldn't be able to stay on the ward. As soon as my tests were done, I had to return to the hostel, and they would call me to tell me my results if I needed any transfusions. Also, the hospital couldn't trust my lateral flow result and had to do their own. They also did another PCR to see what that result would come up as. The hospital's lateral flow was negative, so I was wondering what my two faint lines from earlier that morning meant. However, my PCR was unfortunately positive.

Rosie spoke to infection control and virology, who agreed that as I was still in the ninety-day period of no testing, and because my lateral flow at the hospital was negative, it was most likely that my PCR and lateral flows that morning were just showing a false positive. Most likely, I was just shedding Covid and I wasn't contagious to anyone. As a result, I was considered a green patient again, and Rosie put up a note on the hospital's system to explain that I was a green, in case I had to be admitted to the hospital but was showing a positive test. I dodged a massive bullet and was happy to return to the Ward C9 day unit the following Monday! Had the matron been aware that I was on a testing ban, and had I been smart enough not to test, then the chaos of that Friday could have been avoided.

Despite the good news of still being green, I didn't receive the best blood test results that Friday. My white blood cells were still flat but showing signs of recovery at 0.2. My neutrophils were 0.02, and my platelets 15. My haemoglobin was 96, which showed that my red blood cells were still declining. Still, both my platelets and haemoglobin were above the transfuse level, so I didn't have to return to the hospital that day. Most worrying of all the results were my CRP levels. They had gone from 44 on Wednesday to 110 that Friday. Doctors were a bit concerned and would have liked the nurses to have done a set of obs on me had they known sooner. They couldn't because the Covid dilemma had forced me to receive my blood test results via a phone call, so I was in the hostel and not in the day unit.

I spent the weekend at home living in fear that a trip to A&E was imminent due to my raised CRP. Also, I was aware of my platelet levels and did everything I could to prevent bleeding to death, including having to bury myself in cushions to avoid the cats scratching me. I'm sure cats can detect thrombocytopenia because they did everything they could to attempt to kill me when I was at home. Luckily, it came to nothing over the weekend, and I was happy to have a reduced CRP level of 88 on my next visit to the day unit on Monday 21st March. These CRP levels, which I had never heard of as a paediatric, constantly kept me on edge during my second leukaemia battle. I think talk of CRP should be banned in hospitals just because of the psychological distress they cause!

After having flat blood counts for two weeks, I was happy to hear my blood test results on my Monday appointment. Over one weekend, my white blood cells had managed to increase from 0.2 to 1.3. I wasn't taking G-CSF anymore, which was a bonus! In particular, my neutrophils had gone from 0.02 on Friday to 0.46 by Monday. I was still severely neutropenic, but finally there was evidence to show that the neutropenia was on its way out. I thought my platelets were still going down, but in two days, they had managed to go from 15 to 43. Although still low, I now had *some* platelets to protect me from bleeding! These results would only continue to increase as I recovered from Round 2 of chemotherapy.

As expected, my red blood cells were on the decrease. As one of the haematology registrars had said on the ward, they are always the last to recover. My haemoglobin had decreased from 96 to 93, which was a small decrease and still above the transfuse level of 80, but still a sign that my anaemia wasn't disappearing just yet. During Round 1, I needed a blood transfusion the day after finishing my cycle, yet during Round 2 I had gone over two weeks after finishing my cycle without needing one!

With my bloods on the increase, and the ward continuing to keep an eye on me three days a week, I began to feel safer being away from the hospital in the case of infection. With our booking at Elsworth coming to an end by the end of March anyway, Mum and I decided it was safe to move out of the hostel on Thursday 24th March. I was keen to go home, but because I had spent the past month at Elsworth House, like Kingston, I was going to miss it as I had a sense of attachment to it.

In this section, I've only really talked about the health side of things during my Round 2 recovery. In the next section, I talk about how I coped with life in the hostel.

***

Hostel life wasn't as bad as it may seem, and Mum and I did everything we could to make the most of it. We were very restricted in what we could do, and the majority of time was spent sitting on our beds, reading, doing university work, watching TV, scrolling our phones, or playing on the Nintendo Switch.

On a hospital day, the time I woke up depended on the time I was scheduled for my appointment in the day unit. Mum was always up early for breakfast. Appointment times could vary from 9:30am to 1:30pm. My appointments were mostly scheduled for 9:30am, which, despite the earlier mornings, I actually preferred. Not only did it mean I could have my blood test earlier, which would allow my results to come through sooner, allowing me to get out sooner, it was when the day unit was at its quietest. The later appointments left me struggling to get a seat in the day unit, and I usually had to move drip stands and rearrange chairs just to sit down.

Also, I'm known to be quite grumpy, and I like to sit away from people. I was particularly annoyed by a family in the day unit, who would always enter, dump their belongings on two chairs to claim their seats, and disappear for the rest of the day until they got their blood test results, all the while I was tripping over drip stands to find a chair! Sitting and waiting in the day unit was usually a good opportunity for me to do my university work, and however boring it was waiting there for hours for blood test results, it did provide valuable time that I used wisely. Unlike PDU, which was a slow process, to be fair to C9, they were quicker, and sometimes I was out within a few hours. When having to wait for blood and platelet transfusions, the process could be slow, but that was more of a problem with the people preparing the blood and not so much the ward itself.

The times I woke up depended on my appointment times. Every day, I woke up and took my tablets before breakfast. What I had for breakfast usually depended on my appetite or what Dad had bought for us when he came to visit. Because I was on the prophylactic antibiotic, ciprofloxacin, I couldn't take this medicine with milk products as they made the medication difficult to absorb. Therefore, I had to stop having yoghurts, porridge, and cereal in the mornings and evenings when I became neutropenic and required the medication. My breakfast varied from croissants, toast, bacon sandwiches, sausage sandwiches, and much more. Hostel life was much better than ward life!

Then, after a quick shower, on Mondays, Wednesdays, and Fridays, I'd go to my appointment on Ward C9. Mum usually walked me to the door of C9, then she went shopping at the Marks & Spencer in the hospital concourse for lunch. If you remember from my time at Kingston five years prior, you'll know that shopping is a daily feature of hostel life because you don't know when you'll be admitted to the ward. However annoying it may have been, we had no choice but to shop on a day-by-day basis.

Depending on what time my hospital appointment finished, Mum would meet me either outside the ward or outside the hospital, and we would walk back to the hostel together. Most often, I ate my lunch in the day unit. Sometimes I was out early enough to have lunch with Mum in the hostel, but most often I would bring my own lunch to the ward. Occasionally, I would order something from the ward kitchen, but I tried to avoid this as much as possible because I really wasn't a fan of the food, and knowing transplant was the next stage in my treatment, I knew I'd pretty much be living off it in the future!

After lunch, all we really did was sit on our beds relaxing and catching up on daytime TV. *Tipping Point* and *The Chase* were a must-watch. By this point, the pressure of taking care of me and balancing a job was a bit too much for Mum, so she was able to get a sick certificate from the doctor and claim sick pay, ensuring an income. This also left her with lots of spare time, and we had the time to watch daytime TV, play on the Nintendo Switch, and read books.

Almost every day, Dad would join Mum and I for dinner in the hostel. Because where he worked was closer to Cambridge than where we lived, he would drive straight from work to see us. He rarely stayed the night, as he had to return home every evening to feed the cats. It was good to have the three of us together, even if it was just for a couple of hours a day.

When not at hospital or at home, it left us two days of the week (Tuesday and Thursday) with no plans. If I was feeling a lack of energy, the majority of the day would consist of sitting on my bed, watching daytime TV, doing university work, or writing this book! I think this frustrated Mum a little bit as she wanted to get out of the four walls of our room, and sometimes she took advantage of my hospital appointment days to go for a long walk around the hospital grounds.

On a day off when I was feeling well, however, our days would be a lot more eventful. Sometimes I joined Mum in the daily shopping routine, but only when the hospital was quiet due to the fact that I was doing everything I could to avoid infections and A&E. We also used to get a Costa Coffee from the concourse and sit outside with my hot chocolate and her coffee and have a good chat about my diagnosis, while wondering how the patients we had met six years ago were getting on.

On most of my days off, Mum was able to get me out for a walk. Despite being anaemic, I could walk, and I often managed a half an hour walk around the entire hospital grounds. Sometimes we took the route that led to the road outside the hospital, round the back of Kingston House. Seeing Kingston

House and the alleyway next to it brought back the memories of 2016. Towards the end of March gave us some lovely weather, and Mum and I began to escape the four walls of our hostel room a little bit more and spend some time outside.

Once I had recovered fully from Round 2 of chemo, we knew that preparation for my transplant was imminent. In the meantime, I'd be continuing my appointments on the Ward C9 day unit three days a week, but already the next steps were being thought about.

Chapter 18

Preparing for Battle

Preparing for my second bone marrow
transplant from March 24th to April 14th, 2022

Thursday 24th March 2022. I had been attending the Ward C9
day unit on Mondays, Wednesdays, and Fridays for a few weeks
by now, but I was due for a clinic appointment on Thursday 24th
March. On the sixth anniversary of my diagnosis with Acute
Myeloid Leukaemia, I attended the bone marrow transplant
clinic with Mum.

We signed in at the reception desk of the haematology
and oncology outpatients department at Addenbrooke's
Hospital. Because of my appointments every three days, my
blood tests from the previous day were good enough not to
need a blood test on this day, although I still needed to have my
weight and temperature taken. After a very short wait in the
waiting room, the receptionist said that the clinic upstairs was
ready for me, and we were directed to Clinic 1A of the hospital.
Our consultation was going to be with Dr. U, who was going to
explain the transplantation procedure to Mum and I.

Dr. U and I first had a general conversation, catching up
on how I was doing. He was surprised that I still had hair on
my head and asked how I had found Round 2. I said that it was
nowhere near as bad as the first round. He said that that was
good, and also expected, as the removal of the idarubicin from
the regimen would have slightly reduced the chemo's toxicity.
Dr. U also asked how my groin was. Due to my lengthy bout with
Covid, I hadn't seen him in a while. I was pleased to tell him that

my infamous groin infection had fully resolved.

Dr. U reviewed my blood counts from the previous day, and he was happy with the results. My neutrophils had reached above 1.0, and my platelets, while still low, were on the increase at 87. My red blood cells were still low, but that was expected since they took a little bit longer to recover.

After the quick chat, Dr. U got to explaining the transplant procedure with me. My first transplant was much simpler. I'd had ten days of highly intensive and high-dose chemotherapy to wipe out my bone marrow to the point where it would be unable to recover on its own. I had then received my new stem cells from an umbilical cord donor from a female in France. After a month in isolation to avoid infections, I had then successfully engrafted, and I had been discharged. Dr. U said that my second transplant was going to be a little bit different to that, and a little bit more complicated, yet there was going to be a lot of similarity.

Because of my relapse, it was unlikely that chemotherapy alone was going to secure a long-term remission. With this transplant, there would be a higher focus on building up an immune system rather than relying solely on the chemo to kill the remaining leukaemia cells not visible under the microscope.

My transplant was going to be a haploidentical allogeneic stem cell transplant, and the doctor told me that my donor was most likely going to be Dad, who was actually in the hospital himself on this day, undergoing a number of tests to ensure he was fit and healthy enough to donate his cells. Mum would also have been perfectly fine to donate her cells to me, but Dr. U said that they had looked at small differences between each of their blood tests and Dad seemed to be the most suitable.

Each parent is only a 5/10 match each, which makes sense as you are half your mother and half your father. When I'd had my first transplant five and a half years before, a procedure like this was considered very risky and only as a last resort due to the high chance of rejection. But since then, modern medicine and technology had improved massively, and using parents as donors is becoming more common. This was a relatively new procedure, having only been trialled since around 2002, used more commonly in recent years.

The plan was to get me admitted to Ward C9 to start the conditioning phase of transplant on the week commencing April 10th, 2022. I'd then receive the chemotherapy drugs, fludarabine and cyclophosphamide, throughout the conditioning phase, which would wipe out my bone marrow. It was going to be a lot of chemotherapy, but I was actually on the 'reduced intensity' conditioning programme. The reason behind having less-intensive chemotherapy was because I had already had intensive treatment for Round 1 and 2, which had put me in remission. In addition to the chemo, I would also require low dose radiotherapy to wipe out any remaining cancer cells and further suppress my immune system. Radiotherapy would be a completely new experience for me.

After the conditioning phase, I would receive Dad's stem cells on Transplant Day, or Day 0. My transplant would involve a procedure exactly the same as my last, as an infusion through my line. With Dad being a 5/10 match, there was a likelihood that these cells would be a bit of a shock to my body. In what is known as cytokine release syndrome, for a few days after Transplant Day, it was expected that I'd be very sick with high fevers. Dr. U said that if they left me like that then I'd most likely become very sick and could potentially develop severe Graft vs. Host Disease (GvHD). As Dad was only a half match, it would be likely that his cells (the graft) would perceive my cells (the host) as foreign and would begin to attack my cells. This could show as a rash or diarrhoea.

To prevent this, on Day 3, I would receive more of the chemotherapy, cyclophosphamide. This aimed to do two things. The chemo would end the fevers caused by the cytokine release syndrome, but it would also work as a great prevention for future GvHD. This then brought the question of whether this additional chemotherapy would just kill my donor cells. The answer was no. It was expected that Dad's cells would be more hyperactive, whereas my cells would be weaker. Dad's cells were likely to be slightly more resistant to the chemo, whereas the chemo was likely to kill mine. I would also be on a couple of immunosuppressant medications, which would suppress my own immune system to give Dad's cells a higher chance of engrafting. Therefore, if this went to plan, Dad's cells would begin to attack the remaining leukaemia cells in the body, which is known as the Graft vs. Leukaemia (GvL) effect, in addition to building up a completely new bone marrow. So, while the chemotherapy and radiotherapy conditioning would do its best to wipe out my remaining leukaemia, the focus of this transplant was to build up an immune system to attack the cancer cells. Because my previous transplant was a cord donor, these were technically baby cells that had not yet matured. Using Dad's stem cells would mean that I'd have a more mature immune system, and in turn, his would be more likely to know what a cancer cell was and detect and destroy it.

If all went to plan, like my first transplant, I would be isolated in my hospital room for at least a month until I showed signs that I had successfully engrafted. The first sign of engraftment would be my neutrophils reaching over 0.5. I would be seen at least once or twice a week in the Ward C9 day unit and the outpatients clinic after being discharged home, and once doctors were happy with my progress then they would begin to wean me off my immunosuppressants. This could take anywhere from a month to a year. Once I was off immunosuppressants fully for a year, then I could think about having all my vaccinations again.

Dr. U then went over the side effects of the procedure. The side effects of the chemotherapy were nothing I hadn't suffered before. The chemo was likely to cause nausea, vomiting, total hair loss, mucositis, and diarrhoea. It undoubtedly would cause my blood counts to be severely low. Low red blood cells would cause anaemia, which would cause tiredness. Low platelets would put me at high risk of bleeding, bruising, and internal bleeding, and low white blood cells, particularly low neutrophils, put me at risk of life-threatening infections and high fevers. There was also a chance that the chemo would cause toxicity to the brain, heart, eyes, liver, kidneys, and pretty much every organ it could reach. Of course, there were also long-term side effects that I needed to be made aware of. These included second cancers, and the treatment would not be good for my fertility either.

The radiotherapy was going to be at such a low dose that it was unlikely to harm me too much. There was a possibility that it could make me feel a little bit sick afterwards, but this was expected to clear soon after my dose. In terms of long-term side effects, my dose would be so low that there wouldn't be many, although I was going to have an increased risk of cataracts in the future.

In terms of the transplant itself, side effects included acute GvHD. Mild acute GvHD showed up as a rash or diarrhoea, although there was a chance that I could have GvHD for a very long time in the future, which would be known as chronic GvHD. Dr. U said that if I was going to get chronic GvHD, it didn't necessarily mean I'd have it for ever, it just meant I'd have to stay on my immunosuppressant medication for longer. Most people who get GvHD get it mildly.

The topic of GvHD is a complex one. It is known that there is an association between GvHD and the GvL effect. It is hoped that a haploidentical transplant causes the GvL effect, but it is also important to reduce the toxicity of the GvHD as much as possible. Therefore, it is all about finding a balance between the two by limiting the amount of GvHD but producing as much GvL as possible. This is very difficult to do, although Dr. U did tell me that GvHD was not completely essential to get a bit of GvL.

Another possible side effect of the transplant was that the donor cells could have trouble engrafting. If my red blood cells were having trouble increasing, then they would top me up with blood transfusions until they started to recover. This was the same with my platelets – if they were falling behind then they would top me up with platelet transfusions until I showed signs of engraftment. White blood cells, however, were going to be more of an issue. Transfusing white blood cells is very rare due to the high risk of side effects. If my white blood cells failed to engraft then doctors would have to give me more of Dad's stem cells in the hope that it would give them a boost to start engrafting. Of course, there was also the risk that my body could reject the donor cells altogether, which would not have very good implications for me or my future and would most likely have fatal consequences.

The most difficult thing to take in from my consultation with Dr. U was that even if my second transplant was successful, my chances of the leukaemia coming back in the months and years afterwards would be 50%. If the leukaemia decided to make a comeback, as the doctors would be closely monitoring my blood levels, they would hope that there would be enough warning to give me more of Dad's cells to fight the leukaemia cells in a last-ditch effort to prevent a relapse. This was an advantage of having a half-match transplant, as you can continue to destroy the cancer cells with more and more of the stem cells, in what is known as donor lymphocyte infusion. This therapy was known to be very successful in some cases, and Dr. U told us about how it had been successful in one of his patients, which the hospital had written a story about.

That's not to say that a relapse would be smooth for me though, and although the doctor didn't tell me this, I knew that if my leukaemia came back like it did in December 2021, it would most likely be game over for me. I was about to have my second transplant, the maximum funded by the NHS and also the maximum a body could endure. One bone marrow transplant is damaging enough!

Dr. U told me that he and all the haematology consultants believed that this was the best option because I had proven that chemotherapy alone was not enough to secure a long-term remission. I needed to rely on these new stem cells to attack the leukaemia hiding in my bone marrow.

Mum and I had a number of questions about my transplant. We were concerned that I had caught leukaemia from a gene of either Mum's or Dad's, and despite no family history of it, we feared that, if Dad was to be my donor, it could have come from his side of the family. Dr. U said that while his answer would have been different if there was family history, because there wasn't, it was safe to say my leukaemia had not come from my parents. My relapse was not a new cancer that had developed after my last transplant either; I was just very unlucky to get my old blood back, which had begun to rapidly produce leukaemia cells again. The leukaemia was down to my own DNA creating mutant cells.

Also, what about my blood group? My blood type was O+, whereas Dad's was B+. As a result of my transplant, eventually my blood type would become the same as Dad's once I had successfully engrafted. I found this interesting!

Once Dr. U had gone through the procedure with me, he asked whether I wanted to wait and digest the information or sign the consent forms there and then. Knowing that this was the only option that provided the best chance of securing a long-term remission and a happy and healthy future, I decided to sign the papers during the consultation. The plans for my transplant were finally being put in place! Like my first transplant, I needed to have a number of tests done to ensure that I was healthy enough to endure the crazy amounts of treatment, but these were to be done at a later date.

Meanwhile, Dad was having his own tests and consultations with his own doctor and specialist nurse. He, too, was now under the care of the haematology team at Addenbrooke's, but as a transplant donor. He writes his account of the day, March 24th, 2022:

I received a call from a nurse, who asked if I could go in for a blood test and speak with a doctor. The nurse, Jenny, also explained that I might have to go and have an ECG. I asked if my wife, Heidi, would be receiving a call too, and she avoided the question, saying their computers were not working. I figured that they would not be able to tell me because of privacy, but I thought it was worth a try.

On the day of my appointment, I arrived early. I went straight to get my blood taken, but it was time for my appointment, so I went to the clinic to see the doctor, per Jenny's instructions. When I arrived at the clinic, they told me to go back and get blood drawn because the doctor had not arrived. I hurried back, hoping that I had not lost my place in line. I managed to get in, but the phlebotomist did not know what blood test I needed. While the phlebotomist was trying to figure out my tests, I received a call from Jenny, telling me that the doctor had arrived and I needed to return to the clinic.

Consultant Dr. B greeted me. He was a very nice man, who explained why I was there. It was apparent, but this was the first time I had been told they were looking at me to be Jake's donor. As he started to explain, I realised that this was not an explanatory session, but an actual plan for me to be a donor. I asked when they were looking at transplanting and if they had already looked somewhere else. Dr. Brian said that they wanted to start by the middle of April at the latest and that it was unlikely that a match would be found. This was the point in the conversation where it got very real, and the seriousness of Jake's treatment plan finally hit me. We would know whether the transplant had worked in approximately a month or two.

I knew Jake was also seeing a consultant simultaneously, and I wondered how his conversation was going. I wanted nothing more than to be there with him and Heidi. The consultant continued to explain that they did not know too much about Jake's plan as they were only allowed to support me as the donor. Jenny made it very clear that she would lose her license if she spoke to Heidi or Jake. I asked if I was allowed to talk to Jake and Heidi about my procedure, and they said that was my choice. Having worked in a hospital setting, I understood why they have these procedures.

Dr. B asked questions about my health, previous operations, Covid vaccine, and if I was sure that I wanted to be Jake's donor.

Without hesitation, I said yes. What parent would say no if they had a chance to save their child's life? Anyway, I knew this involved a higher risk for Jake, but I also trusted the consultants that they had Jake's health in mind. Dr. B explained that I would need to take blood tests to check for HIV, syphilis, hepatitis, and a rare disease called human T-lymphotropic virus (HTLV), similar to HIV. These results would take up to two weeks to return and must be repeated after thirty days and sometimes before transplant. I would also be tested for Covid, have a chest X-ray, ECG, vein examination, urine test, and MRSA swabs. All these tests would happen right after seeing Dr. B.

When Jake started conditioning, I would have to isolate two weeks before harvesting my cells for transplant. A few days before the transplant, I would go to a clinic where they would insert needles into my veins, and a machine would circulate up to twelve litres of blood. The device would separate my blood, plasma, and cells and return my filtrated blood to me. Separation of the blood would be done in six hours, over one or two days, depending on how quickly my veins could pump blood. Also, before this procedure, I'd have to inject G-CSF four days prior. G-CSF would help my cells become more active in the bloodstream. G-CSF could be administered in the clinic or by myself. Jake had to do the same during his first and second round of chemotherapy, so I was familiar with the injection and the side effects. Dr. B explained some side effects, including bone pain, enlarged liver, headaches, and tiredness, but there were no long-term side effects. If my veins could not pump enough blood out, I would be going into theatre to remove stem cells by hooking a Hickman line to one of my jugular veins or going into my bone marrow on each side of my hip.

Once the process was explained, Dr. B checked me from head to toe. Nurse Jenny then took me to a separate room, where one of the healthcare assistants swabbed me for Covid and MRSA and took my blood pressure, height, and weight. Jenny then took me to get blood tests and explained where I had to be and when.

After explaining that the phlebotomist had had trouble looking for me in the system, Jenny said that she would go with me to sort it out. Jenny showed the phlebotomist what bloods I needed, and that was all sorted. Eleven vials of blood later, my vein decided to stop giving, so they had to use another vein, which was not helpful. The phlebotomist had to resort to squeezing the last drops of blood from the line into the tube. This was not a good start, and I hoped I could do better during the harvesting phase.

I headed to get my veins checked, where I met a lovely nurse who had trouble getting his apron on. I think he finally managed to get it on, on the third attempt. He was excited to see me and show me the machine I would be hooked up to for six hours. He told me to have a delicious breakfast in the day because I would need the energy. However, he also said I could not leave the bedside, and if I needed the toilet, I would need to use the commode. I wasn't sure how I felt about this. It was a choice between breakfast or using the commode. I figured it would be better to have a good breakfast!

My next stop was a chest X-ray, which took no more than five minutes. I stood in front of a metal object, taking a deep breath, and got zapped.

My final stop was an ECG, which was equally as quick. Again, the technician was very excited about stem cells. He said that if you look at heart cells created from stem cells or normal heart *cells under a microscope, they beat individually.*

Regarding the Covid vaccine, Dr. B asked that I don't take the Moderna booster fourteen days before giving stem cells; it was twenty-eight days for Pfizer.

After my consultation with Dr. U, Mum and I were reunited with Dad, who had just finished his appointments and was waiting for us in the clinic downstairs.

Because of my recovered blood counts, Mum and I believed it was safe to move out of the hostel and return home full-time, rather than just visit at the weekends. I had done so well to avoid a fever and infection from Round 2, considering the fluctuating CRP levels. After the consultation, we returned to Elsworth House to move all our belongings out. Leaving was sadder than arriving as Elsworth had been our home for the past month! But I didn't miss it enough to want to go back.

Once we had moved out and posted our keys in the return box, we went for a family meal at the pub down the road, then I was back home. I was happy to be home! The next few weeks leading up to transplant was going to leave me bombarded with hospital appointments to check I was healthy going into transplant.

***

Friday 25ᵗʰ March 2022. I thought it was a normal appointment in the Ward C9 day unit. By this point, we had moved out of the hostel and handed over the keys, so from now on, we were travelling back and forth from home to appointments.

I had my blood test as usual. I had also somehow been bitten by an insect on my tummy while I was still neutropenic.

This caused the bite to become infected, and it became very sore, red, and inflamed. The registrar prescribed flucloxacillin, a type of antibiotic, which seemed to be working as the pain was improving. Just to be on the safe side, the nurse swabbed it and took a picture of it for the microbiology team to investigate. Other than a dressing change for my PICC line, I was expecting that to be it.

The nurse began to prepare for my dressing change, but then she noticed that on my notes, Dr. U had written that I could have my PICC line removed. When going to transplant, as I was going to be on a lot more IV medications than before, I needed something that would bleed back easier, could be accessed easier, and could have more lumens attached, and overall, something that would be more convenient for both me and the nurses. For transplant, having a PICC line wasn't ideal, and it was time to bring back the trusty Hickman line! The insertion of my Hickman line was booked for Tuesday 5th April. As my blood counts were up, Dr. U didn't think there was any reason to need a line from now until then and therefore authorised the removal of my line to give me a little bit more freedom during my time at home.

"Do you want your line removed now?" asked the nurse.

I was a bit taken aback. I thought when Dr. U had mentioned the removal of my line in the previous day's consultation that I'd have to go back to the place where I'd first had it inserted to get it removed. Yet the nurse was able to remove it in the day unit, exactly where I was sat.

The procedure involved pulling my PICC line out of my arm. I was worried that it would hurt, but I was reassured by the nurse and another patient opposite me that it was painless, and it actually tickled rather than hurt. Anaesthetic was unnecessary.

I took a picture of my PICC line in my arm for the final time, just for the memories. Then the nurse told me to take a deep breath, applied pressure to the line site, and within a second, tugged the line out of my arm. She was right – it did not hurt at all. The feeling was a sliding sensation, and I felt the tickling feeling once it was out rather than when it was being pulled out. Once it was out, the nurse let me take a picture of what the line looked like. It was quite long, and I was surprised that a tube that long had been living in my arm for four months. Also, the fact that my line was that easy to pull out made me feel uneasy. How did I not accidentally rip it out?

***

Like my first transplant, there was always the fear of something going wrong, and I wanted to see everyone before I left. My limited time at home meant there was a rush to see all my friends because no one knew when or if I would be coming home.

I spent the weekend of March 26th and 27th with Lauren, who was the only person outside my family and hospital staff who I had actually continued to see regularly since December. With transplant causing so many uncertainties, Lauren and I wanted to spend as much time together as possible before I went back to hospital, and she usually came to visit me whenever she was free, mostly on evenings during the week and at the weekends.

Lauren managed to get some of our classmates and lecturers from university to contribute and buy me an amazing present. Of course, I couldn't be doing a politics and history degree and not receive a political gift from my university friends! They all wrote me a lovely card and bought me a Lego

White House, which was so cool! I really appreciated my gift, and while the intention was probably to give me something to do in hospital, I ended up building it as soon as I received it.

I was aware that I hadn't seen Liam since a couple of weeks before my diagnosis, and I arranged to meet him on Friday 1st April. It was great to see him and his family, who kindly had me over for dinner. Liam and I brought back the classic, and slightly disturbing, jokes that we had created years before! We're the type of friends who can go ages without talking but just pick up where we left off.

I also arranged to see my group of friends, who I had hung around with in sixth form, and we all continued to meet from time to time. Some of them I hadn't seen since even before December, going back to September or October! They all came over for Chinese, and it was great to see them. I felt exactly like my normal self again. They all kindly contributed and made me an awesome Easter chocolate box. I was so lucky to have such supportive friends, and they all mean so much to me.

Unfortunately, while I focused on seeing my friends, family time was not to be. Covid struck the household again, and this time the victim was Mum. Mum got it quite badly, and while Kristy and I had only felt rough for a few days when we'd had it in February, Mum seemed to have a bad cough and runny nose for days! There were a few worries with Mum catching Covid. The nurses wanted Dad to be very careful, as he was going to be my donor and needed to isolate for two weeks to avoid catching the virus before he donated his cells. With my transplant being less than two weeks away, we were very worried about this! Also, while I wasn't too worried about catching it in terms of getting ill, I was concerned that catching the virus would mean that my transplant would be delayed and I'd get sent back down to Room H! That was one place I refused to go back to.

I was hoping that as I was in my ninety-day no-testing period, I'd be immune to the virus, but I was aware that my white blood cells had been reduced to 0.0 by the chemo since my last infection and my immunity would be slightly weaker, if not wiped out. I was taking lateral flow tests anyway, as the new policy on the ward was that patients, in addition to parents, had to show a negative test before entering.

I felt a bit bad for Mum. I think we should have been a bit more caring regarding her health, and in normal circumstances, we would have been. But having a future transplant patient and donor in the household with a Covid-positive family member, she ended up being banished to her bedroom, unable to leave unless she needed the toilet! I didn't see much of Mum during my days at home.

Monday 28ᵗʰ March was just a routine blood test on the Ward C9 day unit. My bloods were continuing to increase, showing that my bone marrow was doing its job correctly.

Tuesday 29ᵗʰ March was my only break day from the hospital that week, and I think that fact was getting to me. I was in a very depressed state that morning, and rather than making the most of my day off, I just spent the morning lying in bed thinking about all the what ifs of transplant. My hospital appointments, which included my three blood tests per week, as well as the tests to ensure I was fit and healthy for transplant, took up four days of my week. Therefore, my home time wasn't really spent at home. I was travelling to hospital frequently, which I found quite difficult to cope with. Added to the fact that Mum had Covid, I wasn't spending any time with my family. The thought that this could well have been my last time at home in a state of relatively good health, I felt it was time wasted.

I was lucky to get a bit of family time with Dad and Kristy. While Mum was upstairs in her bedroom, we went to Ipswich on

Thursday 31ˢᵗ March to listen to a talk by Professor Brian Cox. It was a great experience and very interesting too! It was the first time I had been somewhere so busy for a while, and knowing that Covid rules had been relaxed, I felt a bit uneasy about getting out and about. I think it was a questionable decision to go, but I think I deserved something to look forward to before everything happened. The way I viewed it though was: (1) the virus was already in the household so I had a higher danger of catching it there; (2) if this was my final couple of weeks, I might as well live my life and do the things I wanted to enjoy; and (3) what was the difference between sitting in a theatre with lots of people and walking past lots of sick people in the hospital? I knew I had to be aware of Covid, and I did not want a repeat of what had happened before Round 2, but I thought the pros outweighed the cons. It would have been more depressing to just stay at home, knowing I was about to undergo intensive treatment, and seeing Brian Cox would be a once in a lifetime experience. Not many people can say they have done that!

By this point, I just felt that everything was getting on top of me. Despite all my challenges, I felt as if I had been successful in swatting away everything negative that had been thrown at me. With transplant-related mortality being as high as 20%, I needed to have a number of tests done to ensure I was healthy enough to endure such treatment, including a lung function test, a heart echo, and a kidney test. I also needed to have my Hickman line insertion and a bone marrow biopsy to see the effects of Round 2. It seemed as if I had hospital appointment after hospital appointment.

I was starting to drown in university work. The university had been really supportive of me and allowed me to defer my assignments. Most assignments I was able to submit on time, and, in fact, I was actually seeing an improvement in my grades, most likely because I had so much time that I could really focus on my assessments. Some, however, I had to defer, and these deferrals, while helpful at the time, all accumulated to a single assignment deadline, and this happened to fall on my transplant preparation week. If all my hospital appointments and procedures weren't enough, I had a political negotiation assessment, globalisation report, and a presentation and essay on the Cuban Missile Crisis due!

I was lucky to be supported by my personal tutor, Scott, who I had been having weekly check-ins with since January to track my progress with university, every Thursday on Microsoft Teams. Scott was really supportive and did everything he could to make my university experience as easy as possible during my difficult time. I really appreciated all the work and genuine care he put in to ensure I could progress with university through treatment.

The problem with my assignments was soon resolved with another deferral, and I was able to work on what I could until the summer. The main priority at this stage was focusing on my health and ensuring I made it to transplant, not only as healthy as possible but on time!

***

Wednesday 30th March 2022. Like my Bristol work-up plan in 2016, my tests to ensure I was fit and healthy enough for transplant took place over a couple of days. These tests were done at Addenbrooke's as I was going to be lucky enough to have my transplant on Ward C9. I was happy that I didn't need to travel as far this time like I had to for my first transplant!

My first appointment was actually at home – a telephone appointment with the radiotherapy consultant. I had never had radiotherapy before, although the amount of time I had spent at the back door of the radiotherapy department waiting to be let in Room H, I should have been able to find my way around the department with ease. Because radiotherapy was a new concept to me, the consultant explained the procedure over the phone.

Firstly, about a week before radiotherapy started, I would need to go down to the department and have a chest X-ray. Custom-made lead plates would be made for my lungs, using these X-rays to shield my lungs from the harmful radiation. To accurately mark where these chest plates needed to be positioned during treatment, I would require two small permanent tattoos on my chest and back. The tattoos needed to be permanent as they were used as references for each treatment, even though I only required one dose. After the preparation, the treatment would then be allowed to commence.

My radiotherapy was going to be low dose total body irradiation (TBI). Given as an inpatient, I was going to be taken to the radiotherapy department, and radiographers would blast my entire body with high-power X-rays to kill any remaining cancer cells and to suppress my immune system before receiving my new cells. I would only need one dose of this, and it was scheduled to start once the chemotherapy part of my conditioning phase had been completed.

Even though Dr. U had said in the consultation the previous week that the radiotherapy would be such as low dose that it was unlikely to cause long-term problems, the consultant still went over the side effects, which still very much applied to me. Because I was having radiotherapy in combination with high dose chemotherapy, it was likely it was going to make me feel pretty rough. I was advised to attend the clinic in my pyjamas or boxer shorts, and as the radiation could make me feel quite sick, I would be required to take anti-sickness tablets before attending the department. In the long-term, I was going to be put at a higher risk of developing cataracts in the future, which is a condition that causes a blurring of the lens in the eye. Cataracts are more common in people aged sixty and over, but for people who have had radiotherapy, doctors generally predict them to develop ten years earlier, so I have a chance of developing them in my fifties. I was told to never ever smoke and stay away from cigarettes for the rest of my life as I was going to have an increased chance of secondary cancers due to the radiation.

After my quick telephone appointment, it was then straight to Addenbrooke's Hospital. The first of my many tests was going to take place in the Ward C9 treatment room. It was time for my bone marrow biopsy, something so painful I had been dreading it all week! This was done by two haematology registrars. They were surprised that I had never used gas and air before, which is generally used to calm patients down before the procedure. With this being my eighth bone marrow aspiration in total, and the third one I'd had while awake, each aspiration became less and less painful. The biopsy from December 2021 caused excruciating pain, even for a few days after the procedure. The January 2022 one took place at the same time as when my groin was the most famous thing on the ward, and all the pain was so focused in that area of the body that it seemed to absorb the needle pain in my back. The March 2022 one, while it was undoubtedly painful, and the sharp, shooting pain down my leg was very difficult to endure, wasn't actually as bad as I was expecting. Maybe it was because I was distracted by having a conversation with the doctors about university, bone marrow transplants, and the book that I had written while they were syringing fluid out of my bones.

The registrar placed a massive bandage on my back, and after a quick chat with the registrar about Chinese food, I returned to the Ward C9 day unit for a routine blood test before I headed off to my next appointment. The effects of my bone marrow biopsy didn't last long, although the pulling, shooting pain down my leg that I had always experienced during the procedure lasted longer than usual. Usually, I only felt this pain during the procedure, and once it was done my legs felt fine. But on this occasion, I felt the sharp pain for a day or two afterwards. The best way to describe it is a toothache sensation, but in your legs. I did walk a bit funny after my biopsy, but things returned to normal within a couple of days.

After a quick break in the hospital concourse, it was straight down to the lung function clinic for my lung function test. I almost very nearly didn't make it in. I failed the "Have you or anyone else in your household had coronavirus symptoms in the past ten days?" question. Mum was positive. Honestly, I was going to lie because I really couldn't be bothered with this Covid rubbish anymore. But Dad said I had to tell the truth, so I ended up having to wait a few minutes while the receptionists ran back and forth in a panic, trying to find answers as to whether they could let me in. I had a lateral flow test from the morning in my pocket as proof that I was negative. After a worrying few minutes, the receptionist came back to tell me that as long as I was negative, I was fine. I was able to breathe again!

It was a short wait in the waiting room, and then a woman called me to have my test. First, I had my height and weight taken, which was the norm before a lung function. Then, I had to sit in a transparent box with a peg on my nose, breathe in and out normally into a tube until the tube shut, and I had to sit and pant, then as soon as it opened again, I had to take a deep breath in and then breathe out as much as I could. Every last little bit of breath that I could get out was worth it, and I was even advised to hum into the tube to get as much breath out as possible. Another test I had to do involved coming out of the transparent box, but still with the peg on my nose, breathe into a tube and then take a very deep breath of oxygen, hold my breath for five minutes, and then get as much breath out as I could. The third and final test involved taking a very deep breath and blowing out as fast as I could until all the oxygen had been squeezed out of my lungs.

This was the first lung function test I'd had without Blow Blow Blow man, and I'm starting to think that Blow Blow Blow man wasn't as enthusiastic as I thought he was. I think it's just part of the job, because the woman was equally enthusiastic: "Breathe in IN IN IN INNNNN ... and ... BLOW!"

My lung function test was scheduled for 2:15pm, and my heart echo scan was at 2:30pm. Because of the Covid dilemma at the lung function reception desk, and the fact that I was waiting a while in the waiting room, I wasn't able to make my heart echo in time. While I had my lung function test, Dad phoned the cardiology clinic for me to inform them that I'd be late. I lost my 2:30 slot, but I was told to attend my appointment anyway. I had the choice of either waiting in the waiting room until I could be seen or reschedule for another day. There was uncertainty over what time I would be seen, as since I had lost my slot; the cardiographers were getting through the remaining patients first. Therefore, there was a chance that I wouldn't be seen until 4:00 or 5:00pm.

It was closer to 5:00pm when I was seen. Probably the most interesting thing about having such a large gap between my relapses was seeing how many people I knew from before in my first battle that still worked at the hospital. I had seen my former CNS nurse, Amanda, a couple of times, but she did not recognise me or Dad. It often made me quite sad when seeing my former specialist nurse just walk past like she'd never seen me before. I did look very different to how I did in 2016, though! I recognised the cardiographer straight away! He was my favourite when I was staying on Ward C2! Understandably, he didn't recognise me, but he said it was very possible that it was him I used to see many years ago.

"Yes, there's only one Bruno in this department. It probably was me!"

The heart scan itself was the same as all the others, using ultrasound equipment to look at images and make measurements of my heart. I always found it fascinating to hear my heart beating on the computer. The cardiographer said that everything looked fine from what he could see but he needed to review the results in more detail and make more measurements.

Thursday 31st March 2022. Thursday was also a long day, but I only had to attend one clinic: the Nuclear Medicine Department. Having to go to the Nuclear Medicine Department sounded a bit scary, and I wondered what it would be for. As I knew I'd be having radiotherapy, I associated the words 'nuclear' with 'radioactive' and thought maybe this would have some form of connection. But no, I had to attend the department for a kidney test. The Nuclear Medicine Department was not as scary as it sounded. They should really change their name!

I was scheduled to be in the department all day, so it was an early start. Once I arrived, it was a very short wait in the waiting room before I was called downstairs to go to the nuclear scanning rooms. The woman conducting the test then told me what the procedure involved.

I was going to be injected with a radioactive substance. Following the first injection, I would then have three blood tests, spread hourly throughout the rest of the day. Depending on the amount of substance left in my blood, they would be able to test how well my kidneys had filtered it. The injection was at such a low dose that I did not need to worry about any side effects or long-term harm.

Before being injected, the nurse had to do a vein check to work out which arm would be most suitable. The vein on my left arm was chosen for the injection, and my blood tests would be taken from the right. I was injected with the small amount of substance in the morning. The liquid was transparent and just looked like a thick, watery substance. Once the injection was in, which didn't take long, the nurse then got out an interesting machine. I had to spread both arms out, and the nurse held the machine a few centimetres away from each of my arms. This machine could detect the radioactive substance in my body. If the numbers showed the same value, which mine did, then it was evidence that the injection had gone in properly and was equally distributed around my body. The substance did not affect how I felt at all; I felt completely normal.

My appointment for the Nuclear Medicine Department that morning was for 10:30am, but by the time I had signed in and waited in the waiting room, it was about 11:30am. I didn't have to return to the department for my blood test until 1:00pm. I didn't have to stay in the department while I waited, and I was allowed to wander off elsewhere if I wished. Dad and I decided to go to McDonald's in Cambridge before returning for my first blood test.

I didn't like the blood tests because I absolutely hate cannulas! To make things easier, and to avoid having to be pricked constantly with a needle, it was just easier to put a cannula in. By now, I was regretting saying goodbye to my PICC so soon, because I was getting poked with a needle for blood tests about four times a week! I think I'd prefer this over a cannula though. Cannulas are so uncomfortable, and as soon as you move your arm, you can feel the needle poking your vein inside your body!

After my 1:00pm blood test, bloods had to be taken hourly. The next would be at 2:00pm and the last at 3:00pm. Dad and I waited in the hospital concourse for the second and third intervals. I was relieved when the 3:00pm blood test was over and I could have my cannula removed. I had been expecting to return home with the ability to power our microwave, but the Nuclear Medicine Department was nowhere near as terrifying as I had thought!

Tuesday 5th April 2022. The weekend before Tuesday 5th April left me feeling very depressed. Despite the removal of my PICC line causing needles three or four times a week, I was enjoying the freedom of having full movement in both arms and the ability to take a proper shower. I felt freer and was managing longer walks. I was able to go out alone, which I hadn't done since the day before my diagnosis. So the thought of having a Hickman line put in again was quite deflating.

I arrived at the Vascular Access Unit at Addenbrooke's at 9:30am. It was an early start as my appointment letter said I needed to expect to be there for hours.

Dad had to leave once I checked in at the reception. Once again, Covid meant that visiting and accompanying a patient was restricted. Patients were required to show a negative lateral flow test before they could have their procedure. The woman waiting next to me was asked to show her negative test, or what she thought was negative.

"Have you got a lateral flow on you?"

"Yes, I did it in the car on the way. Ta-da!" she said, as she proudly showed her lateral flow test.

"That's two lines ..."

"What? There wasn't this morning! I did it quickly in the car and it was just one line!"

"Let me get my colleague."

The lady turned to me and said, "I was negative this morning!"

We laughed. I felt sorry for this woman, having had similar trouble myself. A short while later, the nursing assistant came back with the nurse practitioner to speak to the woman.

"Please, it was negative this morning! Can I do another one now and show you? I promise I'm negative!"

"Hmm, yeah, two lines. I'm sorry, we can't accept that. We will reschedule."

The woman's mood changed from jokey to annoyed. She got up and left.

I have a whole chapter written on my struggles with the delay of receiving treatment due to Covid, especially when you don't even have it. Although I do acknowledge that the woman could well have been positive. I understand that it is important to keep both patients and hospital staff safe from the virus, but I cannot stress this enough: cancer is much more important than a virus! Cancer means certain death if untreated, whereas Covid is a risk. Some get it severe; some get it mild. The hospital really should have prioritised what *was* happening over what *could have* happened! This woman was clearly in the unit for a reason. She was having a line inserted so she could start treatment. How could you deny someone treatment over a virus they might not even have?

Luckily, I had tested negative that morning, and I was 100% sure that my lateral flow showed one line. Provided I hadn't caught Covid from the woman who was sat next to me, I was good to go. The practitioners and nurses were a bit suspicious over my records, as even though I had managed to get that one negative PCR test to be admitted back to the ward the previous month, I went back to testing positive straight away. That's why they recommend not to swab after ninety days. However, I had brought my lateral flow in to show that I was negative, and they let me in.

It was a short wait in the waiting room before I was called into the bay area of the unit. This was where I was going to wait and prepare for my procedure and recover afterwards. There were a lot of Hickman lines that needed to be inserted on this day, so the practitioners were getting through a long waiting list of people. Not being able to have anyone sit with me while I waited made things a little bit boring, and I didn't anticipate how long I'd be waiting. I just sat playing Mario Kart, a recurring addiction of mine, until it was my time for surgery.

After some time, a student nurse practitioner came to see me, accompanied by an experienced nurse. She was going to explain to me the procedure of having a Hickman line inserted. As you'll remember, when I had my first Hickman line, I was under paediatric care, and they put me to sleep for the procedure. Now I was an adult, I'd have to endure the painful procedure while I was awake.

The training nurse showed me a real Hickman line, which they used to show patients as a model. She showed the long tube and the lumens, which would be the visible part of my line as it was going to be hanging out of my chest. Then, she showed me the cuff on the line. Where the tube would come out of my chest, the cuff was designed to allow my skin to grow around it and secure the line in place. Stitches would be needed for a few weeks before the skin around my line healed fully to the cuff. The nurse then explained that, using X-rays to work out where the line was going, they'd continue to insert the line up my chest and through the jugular vein, entering near my heart.

The area where my line was going to be inserted was going to be injected with local anaesthetic to dull the pain as much as possible. As I wasn't going to have any general anaesthetic to put me to sleep, the practitioners recommended that I be sedated during the procedure. I needed to have a cannula put in, and a drug would be injected into me that would make me feel like I'd had a few drinks. It wasn't to further help with the pain, rather it would just calm me during the procedure. I was advised to not sign any legal documents or drive for a couple of days after having sedation.

The nurse then explained to me the potential risks of having a line. A Hickman line insertion is generally very safe, and there were not too many risks from the procedure itself. A rare risk of the procedure was that the line could puncture my lung, and in that case, a small drainage tube would be necessary to allow the air in my lung to escape. The nurse said that she just had to inform me of this, and in her career thus far, she had never seen it happen.

After the procedure, it wasn't uncommon to have a bit of bleeding. If my line did bleed, I was advised to apply pressure below my collarbone for five or ten minutes. If the bleeding didn't stop, then I was told to call the haematology helpline emergency number that I had been given. I also needed to call the same number for a dressing change if the bleeding of my line was larger than a 5p coin.

A common side effect after the procedure was also pain,

not only in the area where the line would be inserted, but also down my arm. The feeling the nurse described was that it would feel like being kicked by a horse. Having just had a procedure, it was possible I would feel like this for a few days, but once again, I had to phone the haematology helpline if my pain appeared to be worsening.

It was also possible that I'd get an infection in my line, and symptoms varied from feeling generally unwell to high fevers. If the infection was caught in time, then there were things doctors could do to treat it, but in some cases, there was a possibility that the line would have to be removed.

Also, I was at an increased risk of blood clots as having a tube in my vein meant that the blood would have to work harder to get through my arteries.

Next was the topic of line care. Judging by the look of remembrance on my face, the trainee nurse knew very well that I had previous experience with Hickman lines. Of course, dressing changes were the same as before, and the line had to be looped to prevent a tug on my chest. My dressing would need to be changed every seven days, or sooner if I got it wet or it became unlooped. Showering was going to be difficult as I could not get the dressing wet, and if I did, I needed to call the helpline number to get booked in for a redressing.

I was given a couple of tips by the nurses. Firstly, I had to stand with my back to the shower, trying to avoid getting all my upper body wet. Also, it was useful to buy Ziploc sandwich bags, which I could put my lumens and bungs in, and then lift the bag up and tape it over my dressing to prevent as much water getting on it as possible. I also needed to avoid having any sharp and pointy objects near my line. If my line broke, then it was possible that an air bubble could get into my bloodstream and cause a stroke. So I wasn't allowed to cut my lumens with scissors or stab my line with needles, not that I had any intention to do that anyway.

All that was left after the consultation was to sign some consent forms. Following this, the nurse handed me a hospital gown. I had to remove all clothing and jewellery from the top half of my body, and I was given some anti-bacterial wipes to give myself a good wipe and clean before the procedure commenced. Then, I changed into my hospital gown, which was more difficult to put on than I had thought. I was given two gowns. One had to be put on like a straitjacket, which was the main gown that was essential for the procedure. The second one was to be worn like an ordinary coat, which would just protect my dignity. After a few minutes of waiting, the practitioner called me into the surgery room.

Once I was in the room, the practitioner asked me a few questions to show that I knew about what I was having done to me. I then had to lie on the bed while the practitioner brushed a yellow antiseptic liquid over my chest and neck. The practitioner did a vein check to see which side of my body the line would go in best, and he was able to see that I'd had a Hickman line before by the scar on my chest. He decided to go on the left side (my previous line was on my right), so once my second Hickman line was removed, I would have matching scars! While the practitioner was doing his preparations, his two assistants were standing at each side of me. One attached a blood pressure cuff on my left arm to monitor how I was doing during the procedure, and the other put a cannula in my right arm to inject the sedation. I don't think the sedation worked because I didn't even notice it!

Once I was sedated, the practitioner then injected local anaesthetic into multiple sites on my chest to ensure the pain was dulled as much as possible. He then began to make the incision into my chest, which allowed the line to enter under my skin, and then made a second incision under my collarbone, which provided the line entry into my jugular vein. Using several X-rays to track his progress, he continued to push the line through my vein and into the area around my heart. This was a little bit painful, but more uncomfortable than anything else. I could feel the plastic tube being forced up my arteries, and it wasn't pleasant. Once the line was in, the practitioner made a couple of stitches, one of which would dissolve, and the other would have to be removed in two to three weeks. The procedure was completed after the holes in my chest were stitched up, and a dressing was quickly stuck on me to keep the line looped and in place.

I spent about half an hour in recovery before the nurse who had inserted my PICC line back in December 2021 said that I could think about getting ready to go home. I was in quite a bit of pain, and the nurse was right when she said it would feel like getting kicked really hard by a horse! I have never been kicked by a horse, but a Hickman line pain is definitely what I'd imagine it to be like! I was advised to take whatever I had been prescribed in the past to manage the pain and to phone the number if the pain was becoming unbearable. When I texted Dad to tell him I was leaving the clinic, he was already outside, and he was wondering why I looked so ill. The anaesthetic and sedation gave me a headache, and overall, I was just hurting.

The headaches took a couple of days to clear, and the pain settled after almost a week. It was really difficult to adapt back to a Hickman line. I thought having had the experience six years ago would be enough for me to slip back into old routines, but really, having a Hickman line is just a pain to have attached to you, and I wished I had my PICC back. The PICC line restricted me a lot, was always blocked, and was generally just annoying.

Hickman lines don't often get blocked, and one of the main reasons for me having one was because it would bleed back easier. However, if you thought a PICC line was a pain, times its annoyance level by a thousand and you get a Hickman! At least with the PICC, I was able to shower properly by covering my arm with a blue sleeve, but with a Hickman I had to tape myself with sandwich bags, and even then, I had to avoid getting wet! I had to wash and dry my hair simultaneously to avoid a drop of water dripping onto my dressing. My body was literally folded at a ninety-degree angle to prevent getting any of my upper body wet, and the shower head faced the wall to stop any water hitting me. Hickman lines left me afraid to shower.

***

I finished the week following my Hickman line insertion by attending my appointments on the C9 day unit. While I wasn't very happy to have a Hickman line, the nurses loved it! PICC lines always seemed to get blocked, whereas the Hickman was much more convenient for them.

Every time a nurse went to get a needle prepared to take my blood peripherally, I'd tell them I had a Hickman line. Every nurse had the same reaction, anywhere along the lines of, "Ooh you have a Hickman line", "I love a nice Hickman line", or "Oh you have a Hickman line! That's bangin'!" Unfortunately, I didn't share their joy.

Once the week finished, the appointment notifications for the C9 day unit mysteriously stopped coming through on my MyChart account. I knew that the plan was to be admitted back to hospital for the week commencing 10th April, but we were still yet to receive any news on this. When I asked the nurse on my last unit appointment before the 10th, she said that looking at my letters, my beliefs of admission were true, but my name was nowhere to be found on the admission list for that week. The nurse told me to go home and wait for a phone call from my specialist nurse.

I looked forward to at least a few more days at home!

***

Tuesday 12th April 2022. Three whole days away from the hospital was impressive! I couldn't wait for a fourth.

I asked Rosie about news regarding my admission, and she told me that the plan was to get me admitted to Ward C9 either Wednesday night or Thursday morning, but she needed to confirm this. Reassured by the fact that I was going to hospital soon anyway, and that no appointment notifications came through, I thought I could enjoy the remainder of my time at home.

On Tuesday morning, I received a call from Jo, who had been my specialist nurse when I was under outpatient care and was also the transplant coordinator. I was hoping she would confirm when I'd be admitted. Instead, she told me that there were a number of tests outstanding that I needed to get done that, for some reason, hadn't been done the previous week. I needed a chest X-ray, an ECG, and a blood test, and I'd also get booked in to the C9 day unit for a dressing change. Preferably, she wanted all of this done on Tuesday afternoon.

No! I thought, *I hate being called in on my day off!*

Knowing that my transplant was looming and the situation was serious, I had no choice but to say yes. Here was another day of my life spent at the hospital, this one unplanned.

First, I attended my ECG in the cardiology department. I'd had many ECGs before, all of which tested my heartbeat and rhythm. And like most of the ECGs in the cardiology department, I was in and out of the department in a heartbeat! But when I was on the ward and I needed an ECG, since it was one of the protocol tests to carry out when an infection and fever spiked, I was almost always hot and sweaty, which made the stickers fall off my skin. Applying ECG stickers all over my body was the most tedious procedure and was painful to watch! As soon as you think all of them have stuck, one falls off. As soon as you fix that one, another sticker falls off. It was always a nightmare!

Following my ECG, I was told to go straight down to the X-ray department to have my chest X-ray before going to the Ward C9 day unit. I arrived and attempted to check-in at the front desk, only to be turned away. Despite needing a chest X-ray, the receptionist could not find anything booked under my name. I was advised to go to the ward and let them know so I could be booked on the system for my X-ray to take place later in the day.

I went to the C9 day unit for a blood test and a dressing change. Nothing was really significant about this visit to the ward since it was just a normal blood test through a Hickman line, but it was the day of my first dressing change for my new Hickman line. It really wasn't a pleasant experience. It wasn't that it was painful, it's just that it was slightly uncomfortable, and I don't like the thought of wires coming out of my chest. I definitely missed my PICC line! I am left with painful memories of my first Hickman line, but I was able to cope quite well. I have to admit, my second Hickman line did make me feel quite squeamish, although I did enjoy torturing my friends from time to time, showing them the monstrosity that was coming out of my chest and wedged into my heart!

Thankfully, Jo said I didn't have to wait for the results of my blood test, so I escaped the ward very quickly. The X-ray was booked, and it was back to the outpatients X-ray department.

The chest X-ray was very quick. I didn't have to wait in the waiting room long, and that was the longest part of the whole visit. The procedure was slightly different to my previous chest X-rays though. Usually, I had to put my chest up against the board while holding the handlebars behind the board. Then I'd have to take a deep breath. This time, there were no handlebars, and I put my chest as close to the board as possible, taking a deep breath, while the backs of my hands were on my side. I wondered what the difference in procedure was all about, but I'm guessing all chest X-rays aim to achieve the same thing.

After my X-ray, I was all done for the day and I was able to enjoy the evening and the following day at home, hospital-free. All that was left on the list of visits for my work-up plan was Thursday's appointment at the radiotherapy department for my radiotherapy preparation. Then transplant preparation would be complete!

When I'd be admitted remained in question, however. Rosie told me that the aim was to get me admitted Wednesday night or Thursday morning, but this now seemed unlikely. The ward appeared to be full, and only one transplant room was available. Two patients were scheduled for a transplant at the same time. This meant that I was in competition with another patient over the bed, and there was uncertainty over who would get there first. I just had to wait for the phone call to tell me when I'd be admitted.

***

Thursday 14th April 2022. My radiotherapy appointment was scheduled for 9:36am. I don't know what the precise time was all about, but it nevertheless meant an early start for the family as we lived an hour away from the hospital.

Dad also had a hospital appointment on this day. His haematology consultant had given him a phone call the day before to tell him that he had been approved for donating his cells and had passed all relevant tests. This was excellent news! Dad was in for a routine blood test, a Covid swab, and also had to pick up his G-CSF, which he had to inject himself with to make his cells more hyperactive. While Dad was getting his appointments done, Mum accompanied me to the radiotherapy department.

When we arrived at the department, the receptionist allocated us to a specific waiting room. There were a number of waiting rooms in the department, and you were assigned one according to your needs. There we met an old man, who looked about seventy years old, who broke the ice and made conversation with us. He seemed to know everyone in the waiting room. They were all old men with prostate cancer, and their timeslot in the department made the waiting room seem like a social gathering. The man told us that about five of his radiotherapy friends had actually flown to Cambridge from Jersey just to receive their treatment. The man looked well, considering he had cancer. He told Mum and I that if you don't laugh, you cry, and he did his best to make light of every situation. He joked that once I was done with leukaemia, I'd have prostate cancer to deal with next! I hope not, but then with what life has thrown at me over the past few years, I wouldn't rule it out. The man asked if I'd had radiotherapy before. I said I hadn't, and he showed me a photo on his phone of the machine. He told me it took a couple of minutes and you couldn't feel a thing. It was nice of him to introduce himself and make Mum and I feel more at ease about the radiotherapy procedure. *It can't be worse than chemotherapy,* I thought.

After the conversation with the man, a radiographer called me into the room. Already I was quite fascinated. I was taken into a dark room with a computer, which didn't surprise me, but the journey didn't end there. I was directed through a long maze-like corridor, which was dark but lit up with purple lights. It felt as if I was at the bowling alley or was about to play a game of laser tag, or maybe visiting a modern cinema.

We were joined by another radiographer, who went through the general questions with me, such as what my name and date of birth was and where I lived. Once we got through the check-in, the radiographers explained the procedure to me. When I would have my dose of radiotherapy, which was booked for Wednesday 20th April, it was important that the lung plates I required were positioned correctly to ensure that my lungs were protected from the radiation. Therefore, in my radiotherapy preparation, the radiographers had to make a few measurements to make sure they lined my chest up to the lasers in precisely the right place.

I decided to wear jeans on this day, which wasn't helpful as I wasn't allowed to wear metal when the measurements were taking place. Therefore, I had to stand in the dark room in nothing but my underwear and had to hover over a bicycle seat in the corner of the room. The radiographers then aligned green lasers to my chest and made measurements on my chest, marking where the plates needed to go. It was important that the measurements were 100% accurate, so I had to be slightly adjusted into position by the radiographers, and the process was repeated on my chest and back many times. Once they had made the markings on my chest and back, the radiographers then left the room, and I was required to stand as still as possible while a number of X-rays were carried out to check the markings were in the correct place. The radiographer then tattooed my chest and back with tiny dots, which would be helpful for my dose of radiotherapy the next week. The tattoos were so tiny that they were barely noticeable, and if anything, they just looked like another mole on my skin. I was then allowed to get dressed and return to the waiting room while they reviewed the X-ray images. As soon as they were happy, I was allowed to leave.

There was still no news on when I'd be admitted, but I was running out of my anti-fungal medication, Posaconazole. The previous day, I asked for more medication to be prescribed for me so I wouldn't run out at home. As Mum and I were still waiting for Dad, we went to the pharmacy to pick up the Posaconazole. I was then told by the pharmacist that the doctors had discontinued my medication and they advised me to phone the clinic that I was under to ask if I still required it.

I tried to phone Rosie, but after receiving no answer, Mum phoned the ward. That was when we received the shocking news that they were expecting me on the ward! I had got the bed! No one had thought to tell us that though, and had we not been baffled by the pharmacy incident, I would have been sitting at home completely unaware that medication needed to start straight away to prepare me for treatment. Being admitted came as a shock because, despite knowing that Wednesday or Thursday was the aim, we'd thought there was a delay due to a full ward. Therefore, I hadn't said my proper goodbyes, and while the packing had been done, we hadn't brought my suitcase to the hospital.

Before I could be admitted, I needed to do a PCR test. That involved a trip to the haematology and oncology outpatients department. I was a bit nervous by this, considering I hadn't had the best of luck with PCRs lately and I was still in my ninety-day no-swabbing period. If the result came back positive, I was worried that it would jeopardise my treatment. I was reassured by the ward that even if my PCR was positive, as long as I could show a negative lateral flow upon arrival, then all would be fine. I thought that rule was stupid and questioned the whole purpose of having to take the PCR test in the first place.

My family and I were allowed to go home for me to collect our suitcase, as well as finish some of our packing. It also gave me the opportunity to say goodbye to the home and my cats, who I would not see for a while. Once we were finished at home, we had to go straight back to the hospital to get the next – and hopefully final – stage of treatment completed. It was time to wipe out my AML for good!

Chapter 19

The Big KO

The course of my second bone marrow transplant from April 14th to May 7th, 2022

When I wrote my list of reasons to live back in December, there were a mix of long- and short-term goals. Indeed, some were very long-term goals, like seeing this book get published. They were undoubtedly my reasons to live and every reason why I was going through the treatment process again. But when going to transplant, I thought it would be good motivation to think of starting goals to start the process of regaining normality. This was when I decided I'd also set myself some post-transplant goals:

- Resume driving lessons as soon as possible.

- Finish my second year of university with a 1st.

- Return to work by September, or December at the absolute latest.

In some way, these goals were written in my reasons to live, but I was a lot more specific this time and added my ideal timeframes. With my longer-term goals in mind, I saw these three goals as the most achievable first. These goals were my motivation to just get through the next stage of treatment and gave my courage to get through it! They would serve as the launchpad for what I would see as bigger and better things ahead!

***

Thankfully, both my PCR and lateral flow tests were negative, and I was readmitted to the ward on the afternoon of Thursday 14th April 2022, ready to start the conditioning phase of my second bone marrow transplant. Upon arrival, the nurse directed us to where I would be isolating for at least the next month. I was in Side Room 1. For the first week, I'd be allowed out of my room, but after that, I was to be in isolation until I showed signs of engraftment.

It wasn't until I arrived at hospital that I understood the full plan of what would happen to me. Dr. U went through the procedure with me during my March 24th consultation with him, but he didn't go through the specific details of when transplant would be or how many days I would need of conditioning. This transplant definitely seemed less intensive than my first. I would receive six days of conditioning altogether. Days T-6 and T-5 each involved a dose of fludarabine (100 ml over thirty minutes) and cyclophosphamide (1000 ml over two hours). Days T-4, T-3, and T-2 would each consist of a 100 ml dose of fludarabine. Day T-1 would be my total body irradiation (TBI). Transplant Day (Day 0) would be on Thursday 21st April 2022. Days 1 and 2 would be the period when I was expected to become very sick with high fevers, which would then hopefully be brought under control by two further 1000 ml doses of cyclophosphamide on Days 3 and 4, respectively.

You may also remember from my first transplant that during the work-up plan, we had a meeting with the specialist nurse about what I could and couldn't do during my time in isolation. Addenbrooke's was a lot less strict than Bristol. Addenbrooke's provided details advising what to do and what not to do during my isolation period through a few printed materials and booklets. There was no mention of the 100-day clean diet, rather the booklet advised that I carry on with a neutropenic diet until I was off immunosuppressants. The advice provided no information on how regularly my bed needed to be changed or how often I needed to shower, or what I needed to shower myself with. In fact, when I told a nurse on C9 that Bristol had made me shower every day, she was shocked, telling me that they didn't expect transplant patients to shower as much just because of how rough they are likely to feel. There were no rules on what I could bring with me, meaning that books and games didn't necessarily have to be brand new. I could open my own post, didn't have to laminate any papers before they came into contact with me, and if I wanted to, I could bring my own bedding into my room. Mum didn't have to buy separate footwear or put any footwear from the outside world in a separate locker before entering my room. I thought it was normal transplant protocol, but no, Bristol was just very strict!

At Bristol, I was allowed four named visitors, and two of those visitors were allowed in my room at any one time. However, Covid ensured that this time round I was only allowed one visitor, and this probably contributed to my thoughts that this just seemed to be an admission with mostly ordinary rules, just slightly stricter and prolonged. Really, the number one rule of this transplant was that I could not leave my room once my isolation period had started.

At first, I found it really difficult to settle in my new room. I was concerned about having to live off hospital food. The variety on Ward C9 was nowhere near as amazing as Ward 34. I was lucky enough to be re-diagnosed following a review of the neutropenic diet, and when I was neutropenic, I was allowed to order food in or get something from Burger King on the concourse, provided we were certain it was cooked fresh. Because of my transplant, I lost this luxury, and while I could have individually wrapped snacks from outside shops, my meals would be solely based on the Ward C9 menu. This was difficult because, being a fussy eater, the only things I ate on the menu were pizza, roast chicken, chicken nuggets, jacket potatoes, chips, half of an all-day breakfast, cheese sandwiches, toast, cereal, and sponge pudding. At least half of these foods I'd had some sort of bad experience with, either throwing up after eating them or the taste in my mouth leaving a bad memory that would worsen my nausea with just a simple reminder of the food. That reduced me to only ordering pizza, jacket potatoes, and toast from the ward, as they were all I could stomach! But it was important that I ordered these sparingly, because just feeling sick while eating these foods was enough to put me off them forever! It really worried me knowing that I had to last at least one month on a very limited menu, and I feared that the dieticians, who I had managed to keep away for so long, were going to make a comeback.

My second fear was adapting back into hospital life. It was definitely going to affect me mentally. I had the experience of staying in hospital for ages following my relapse, especially during my first admission, and again when my groin was the most famous topic on the ward (doctors were still asking me whether the swelling in my groin had completely healed by this point!), but after being banned from the ward due to Covid and surviving Round 2 with very little side effects and only requiring a two-night stay, I wasn't sure how well I'd handle at least an entire month in hospital, possibly even longer. It upset me knowing that my family and friends were out there living their lives, while I was stuck in a hospital room just to increase my chances of one day being able to live mine. Something I had managed to refrain from doing for so long finally got to me, and I did become angry at the world for my problems. I just thought, *why me?*

The evening of Thursday 14th April was spent settling back in. It was Easter weekend, so it was likely that the hospital was going to have a very lonely feeling to it. That being said, the nurse told Mum and I that all of my chemo had already been made in preparation for the weekend, which meant I'd be able to get it out of the way a lot sooner and hopefully have the weekend to myself, potentially being able to leave my room.

***

The Conditioning Phase

Friday 15th April 2022 (Day T-6). Day T-6 started early when I was woken up by the nurse who was coming to the end of their nightshift. Part of my transplant protocol was to start ambisome, the anti-fungal medication, which I'd had as a paediatric and was one of my known allergies. It was essential that I had this medication, but the nurses needed to ensure that I wouldn't suffer a terrible reaction. The nurse therefore gave me a small dose of ambisome, mixed with saline, via my line. Any reaction to the medication would show up through the test dose. Thankfully, I did not react to the test dose, and doctors and nurses began to think about taking the drug off my list of allergies.

I required ambisome on Mondays, Wednesdays, and Fridays. My earliest doses in 2016 had included piriton, an antihistamine. Because I passed the allergy test, the nurses now just put the drip on at a slow rate to avoid the ambisome causing a shock to the system. I didn't have a reaction to ambisome this time round, so I was surprised when they started giving me piriton beforehand in later doses. My ambisome doses were very inconsistent. Some days a nurse would give me piriton, other days they wouldn't. I guess it couldn't hurt, but I do wonder if I'm still allergic to it.

Once the nightshift nurses handed over to the dayshift nurses, I was told that they wanted to get my IV medications done as early as possible so I could have the rest of the day to myself. I had my first dose of the chemotherapy, fludarabine, that morning, meaning my conditioning phase was officially underway. It was a 100 ml dose over half an hour, which was what I had been used to for Rounds 1 and 2.

I was shocked when the nurses arrived almost straight after my fludarabine finished with a 1000 ml bag of cyclophosphamide! Cyclophosphamide was the chemo drug that had terrified me as a paediatric, but now I saw it as just another ordinary chemo drug. I was concerned by the litre bag of chemo, but from my previous transplant, I understood the intention of the drugs was to wipe everything out in my body to the point where my cells would be unable to recover on their own. I knew that the doctors wouldn't put me through it if they thought it was going to kill me.

The first day of chemo didn't bring too many problems. I was feeling a bit sick and had a metallic taste in my mouth, as was the case with most of my first days of chemo. Once all of my IV medications for the day had been completed, I was free to do what I liked. My nurse told me to make the most of my time because, preferably by Day T-1, they wanted me to isolate. Mum and I decided to go outside and sit on the benches in the grass area, where we used to sit and have a Costa when we were staying at Elsworth.

Saturday 16th April 2022 (Day T-5). I wasn't able to get out and about like I had been the previous day due to a slight delay in receiving my chemotherapy. Day T-5 brought the same as the previous, one dose of fludarabine followed straight after by a dose of cyclophosphamide.

I was doing my best to pass the time, which I found more difficult than I thought. I knew I had gone off a lot of foods as a result of the chemotherapy, but the constant games of Mario Kart while receiving chemotherapy had left me with an unfortunate association with the two. I played Mario Kart to death, and now the thought of playing it sometimes makes me feel very sick!

Regarding my health, it was important to protect my bladder. Cyclophosphamide can possibly cause the bladder to bleed, so frequent drinking and urinating was required to manage this. I also took a medication called Mesna to protect my bladder. It was very important that I drank enough, also to avoid being constantly hooked up to IV fluids. As always, the nurses and healthcare assistants asked what I'd had to eat and drink, and I had to urinate in bottles so they could measure my intake and outtake.

What I didn't realise is that my levels of hydration could be detected in my blood pressure, and I was experiencing moderately low blood pressure. Every time this happened, the nurses told me I needed to drink more to avoid IV fluids. I was managing roughly a litre on my own, with two litres being the required amount. It was just so difficult to drink, especially when feeling nauseous!

Sunday 17th to Tuesday 19th April 2022 (Days T-4 to T-2). Each of the three days involved a single dose of fludarabine, once again 100 ml over half an hour.

Nothing really happened during these few days, although I noticed that nausea was starting to become an issue. My weight had been kept stable during my first few days, despite the cyclophosphamide making my mouth and throat taste like metal. Now my weight was showing a very slow decline.

I was happy that the chemotherapy part of my conditioning regimen finished on Day T-2, though I was slightly disheartened by the fact that I would require more cyclophosphamide on Days 3 and 4. My conditioning regimen was going to finish on Day T-1, with my TBI.

Wednesday 20th April (Day T-1). The radiotherapy department had strangely precise appointment times. I was scheduled to attend the department at 8:18am. A porter was going to take me down from my room in a wheelchair.

I don't know what happened to my 8:18am appointment but the forms for my radiotherapy had not been signed, and I could not go down to the department until they were completed. There was a bit of uncertainty that morning, with me not knowing when I'd be going down. The nurses and the haematology registrar rushed around trying to get my forms and a plan in place.

It must have been at least 10:00am before a porter came into my room to take me down to radiotherapy. I took a sick bowl with me just in case, as by this point, I was feeling slightly nauseous, and I was told that the radiotherapy would make me feel rough anyway. I checked into the department, and the receptionist directed me to the waiting room. The waiting room was busy – so much for keeping me isolated!

The wait was short, and it wasn't long before the radiographer wheelchaired me into the room where I'd receive my radiotherapy. In the room were two radiographers, one student radiographer, and a physicist. A lot of preparation was necessary. I had to take my shirt off. Usually, I would have been required to stand in my boxer shorts, but the radiographers decided that my pyjama bottoms were thin enough. While the student observed, the two radiographers made measurements on my body and stuck stickers on me – one on my head, two on my side, two down the waist of my trousers, and one on both ankles. A few crosses were marked on my chest and back, which I was told would eventually wash off. Then, using the permanent tattoos that I'd had put on a week prior, the radiographers aligned me to a green laser, and once they were happy, they put a plastic board in front of me, which contained my custom lung plates. The role of the physicist was to watch the radiographers measure and align me and provide advice to double check everything was in the correct place.

Once all the preparation was done, I was required to stand over the bicycle seat again, and facing forward in my aligned position, the radiographers placed a heavy rubber material around my neck just to further protect the areas of my body that were sensitive to the radiation. They then shut the lights off, pressed the radioactive alarm, and left the room, while I stood watching the machine circle around and blast me with radiation. I didn't see the lasers, nor did I feel anything. It was completely painless, and if anything, it was like a prolonged X-ray. It took about a minute, and I was also required to turn around and have my back exposed to the radiation, repeating the process again.

I was wheeled back into the waiting room and reunited with Mum, who came down to the department with the porter and I. While I didn't feel a thing during the radiotherapy itself, I felt the effects very quickly! As soon as I returned to the waiting room, I fell asleep in my wheelchair. It made me very sleepy!

When I returned to my room on the ward, I jumped into my freshly made bed, which the healthcare assistant had changed for me while I was gone. All I wanted to do was sleep! The tiredness was unbelievable. There were quite a few interruptions, with it being time for obs and having to have my breakfast, so I didn't get the sleep I really wanted. I was awake most of the morning, but I finally managed to have a nap in the afternoon.

Halfway through my nap, Rosie popped her head through the door just to see how I was doing. There was some confusion over whether my radiotherapy dose that morning was my only dose. I was told that I only needed one dose, and on my protocol, it clearly stated 'TBI – once'. However, I had an appointment come through on MyChart for another radiotherapy appointment at 5:36pm. Rosie seemed just as confused as we were, as my conditioning regimen stated 'once' but also stated that the amount of radiation was 2Gy. I didn't know what that meant, but apparently 2Gy was a lot of radiation for one dose. Rosie said that usually radiotherapy doses were split into two, one in the morning and one in the evening. She phoned up the BMT nurse just to double check, and she was right. My radiotherapy wasn't done. Even worse, what I'd had that morning was the lighter dose, and I'd receive a heavier dose of radiation in the evening as night-time was when I was most likely to sleep.

I have no idea what the point of the super precise appointment times were because they were never stuck to. Scheduled for 5:36pm, I didn't get wheeled down to the radiotherapy department until 6:30pm. A porter arrived, only for the radiographers to arrive at the same time, both with the intention of taking me down to radiotherapy. The radiographers thought they'd save the porter a job, so they were the ones who took me down. They were the same radiographers who had done my preparation the week before. They were very nice, having a chat with Mum and I, and they told me that they had done their training at the university I currently went to. We also had a chat about our favourite game shows, and we both agreed that *Tipping Point* was the best!

The second dose of radiotherapy was torturous and uncomfortable. Luckily, the measurements had been done that morning, so the preparation process went a lot quicker. Unfortunately, it was a heavier dose, and because my chest tattoos had to be accurately aligned to the green lasers, I had to stand in quite uncomfortable positions.

The radiographers did ask if I was in a comfortable position and tried to make sure I was as comfortable as possible. I thought I could survive in the same place for a minute or so, so I wasn't too bothered. I just didn't realise how long I'd have to stand uncomfortably for! It had to be done, and it was vital that I did not move because moving out of place would have caused damage to my lungs.

The heavier dose forced me to stand uncomfortably for at least three minutes at a time. I had a dose on the front of my body for three minutes, then a short break, then on my front again for another three minutes. This process was repeated on the back of my body, making the second part of my radiotherapy twelve minutes in total. My morning radiotherapy consisted of one dose on each side for a shorter period of time, whereas my evening dose consisted of two doses on each side, at longer intervals. I was the last patient in the radiotherapy department that day, and once the radiographers returned me to the ward, their shift was up.

I was back in my bed by just after 7:00pm and missed the housekeeper when I returned, so the healthcare assistant made me some marmite on toast, which at this point I couldn't stop craving. I slept very well that night!

I was relieved when it was all done. I had completed my radiotherapy, and the conditioning phase for transplant was completed!

Thursday 21st April 2022 (The Forgotten Day 0). Dad had been injecting himself with G-CSF for four days to boost his cell production, in preparation for harvesting his stem cells. This was the day when he was going to donate his stem cells. While Mum and I were downstairs on Ward C9, Dad was above us on Ward E10, attached to a machine for six hours straight, which collected his stem cells. The plan was for his cells to be collected, processed, and then brought straight to me for transplantation, scheduled for 4:30pm.

Dad wasn't allowed to move due to being attached to the machine and therefore couldn't really communicate with us very well. He was able to send a few selfies, and I was fascinated by the bag of stem cells he had collected in a bag above him. It was strange to think that very soon, they'd be infused into me.

I saw lots of different people in the morning and early afternoon before my scheduled transplant. First was a visit from the chaplain. He was there to have a chat with Mum and I, and he wished me well before my transplant. He asked me a few questions about my plan for the future, and I said my priority was to resume my life before December 2021 as much as possible, although I did really want and need a holiday too. Edinburgh in August 2022 was on my mind. The chaplain said that he was going to pray for me shortly before my transplant, which was very kind of him.

Next was a visit from the ward doctor, who saw me every day during the week. She asked if an NG tube had been mentioned in my Thursday 24th March consultation with Dr. U. She said that as the chemotherapy was likely to make my mouth and throat very sore, there was a possibility that I wouldn't be able to even swallow. Of course, it was important that I was eating and drinking regularly throughout the day to fight the chemotherapy. Therefore, they preferred to insert an NG tube in transplant patients as a precaution, and this was something they were thinking about doing to me within the next couple of days.

I stood my ground. I was over eighteen now. There was no chance, absolutely no chance, of me having an NG tube!

The doctor said that she would get the dietician to see me as she was the one with the expertise in the field of NG tubes. I had managed to keep the dieticians away for five months, and only when I was a transplant patient did I end up back on their radar. Luckily, the adult dieticians were so much nicer than the paediatric dietitians. In paediatrics, they would shove tube after tube down me, whether I liked it or not. As an adult, while an NG tube was advised, the dietician assured me that she would not make me do something I was uncomfortable with. She understood my hatred of NG tubes, stemming from the torture I had endured six years earlier, although she told me that adult NG tubes were different. While paediatric tubes sat in the stomach and could be inserted by a nurse at bedside, adults were taken down to the endoscopy department to have it inserted, where it would sit above the bowel. This made it less likely to throw up.

The dietician also said that in her fourteen years of experience, she had seen lots of transplants and knew that my conditioning regimen didn't cause mucositis too severely.

Therefore, there was a chance that I would get away with mucositis altogether and a tube wouldn't be necessary, although they still advised that I had it inserted as a precaution.

"Have you tried the supplement drinks before – the milk and the fruit juice ones?" asked the dietician."Yes, six years ago, and I hated them."

"What about Scandishakes?"

"I also tried them six years ago. I didn't get on with them."

"I'm really not winning with you!"

If I was adamant that I didn't want the tube but became unable to eat, there were alternative options, such as TPN, which would be a feed through my line. The dietician told me that this was her last resort. As I was prone to infections, if there was an infection in my bloodstream, TPN would actually feed the infection, making it harder to treat. She emphasised that it was important to keep the gut in use because eating something to settle the stomach would help with nausea and the gut was more protective against infections than the bloodstream.

Later that afternoon, Dad's nurse from E10 came down to C9 to update Mum and I on Dad's progress. He said that Dad had produced more cells than was needed, which was excellent news! He said that Dad was an A* donor and they were getting ready to process the cells. The nurse said that it was a shame that Dad wouldn't be able to see my transplant but told us to definitely make sure he was on FaceTime to us while the cells were going through my line.

Later that afternoon, the times for my scheduled transplant started changing, getting later and later. First it was 4:30pm, then 5:00pm, then 6:00pm.

The haematology consultant doing the ward rounds that day came to see me. He said there was a slight delay in processing the cells, and while he hoped I'd be able to have my transplant that day, they didn't want it to be too late. Because the timing of the cyclophosphamide on Days 3 and 4 were so important, having my transplant as early as possible the next day, rather than that evening, was considered an option. This would shift my entire treatment plan by one day.

The consultant asked if I had any concerns about my transplant. I was worried about the fevers that Dr. U said I might experience in the three days after Transplant Day. The doctor told me not to worry as, while I may experience fevers, they would solve them when they came. He said that almost as soon as the cyclophosphamide was infused on Days 3 and 4, the fevers would settle.

After waiting all afternoon and into the early morning, the nurse informed me that they were having trouble processing the cells. Unfortunately, Transplant Day was going to be the next day, not this day. The plan was to have my transplant as early as possible the next day, at 8:00am.

***

Friday 22nd April 2022 (Day 0 – Transplant Day). Transplant at 8:00am never happened, as there was yet another delay! The delay gave me extra time to process and reflect on what was about to happen. I had doubts about the successfulness of my transplant, with Dad being a 5/10 match. I was terrified of the expected fevers. Half of me was excited and couldn't wait for my transplant, but the other half wanted the delay to last as long as possible, to prolong the wait of my imminent suffering.

Dad's stem cells finally arrived on Ward C9 just before 11:00am. Before I could have my transplant, I needed IV fluids over half an hour, and in the slight chance that the stem cell infusion would make me feel sick, I was given an anti-sickness medication called metoclopramide. Because Dad's blood type was different to mine (I was O+, he was B+), while it was unlikely, there was a possibility that the collected stem cells would have the odd red blood cell floating around, which could have caused me to have an allergic reaction. Therefore, I was given an antihistamine called chlorphenamine.

Two nurses gave me my new stem cells. One checked that all the information was correct, while the other controlled the infusion and would take care of my transplantation procedure. When asked how I was feeling about my transplant, I said I was worried about what was to come and had fears over my dad being a half match. The nurse told me that the chemotherapy was the worst bit, which reassured me that they were expecting everything to go to plan.

At roughly 11:10am, Dad's stem cells began to enter my bloodstream. In Bristol, a nurse had infused my donor cells through my line with a syringe over roughly fifteen minutes; this time it was like a blood transfusion. A bag of stem cells was hung up on the drip stand, although a machine was not used. Instead, the cells slowly dripped into my blood at their own rate. The nurse controlling the infusion stayed with me for the first fifteen minutes of my transplant. He took my obs every five minutes and monitored me for any reactions. What he was looking for was any changes to me, whether that was going red in the face, breathlessness, or a fever.

The chlorphenamine made me feel sleepy, which was a very common side effect. Mum was on FaceTime to Dad and Kristy while I was having my transplant. I was falling asleep very quickly and decided that, for the history books, I had to take a quick picture while my cells were being infused. I was out cold for most of my transplant, sleeping all the way through it. The nurse was shocked by my ability to sleep at a ninety-degree angle, but really, I was just so tired I couldn't be bothered to recline my bed! I usually find it difficult sleeping when being watched by Mum, a nurse, and an observing student nurse, and I'd try my best to stay awake. I don't know what was in that antihistamine, but it knocked me out!

After the fifteen minutes was up, the nurse and the student nurse left the room. They made it clear to Mum to watch me for any changes or, if I suddenly felt unwell, to press the buzzer to notify them. My transplant would take about an hour in total, and the student nurses or healthcare assistants would come in to take my obs and check on me every fifteen minutes until then and for a little while afterwards.

I felt absolutely fine when the final drop of stem cells entered my body. Everything was fine for the remainder of the day, too. It wasn't too bad at all! Immediately after my transplant, I was woken up by the sudden urge to urinate, and I didn't feel dizzy or lightheaded in the hours after transplant like Bristol had told me to expect five years ago.

Of course, I was happy that after such a traumatic year, my transplant had finally happened. And while it was a massive milestone and the one that would ultimately give me a third chance of life, I didn't celebrate it as such. I do see April 22nd, 2022 as my new birthday. But I think I was so disheartened by my relapse, that I didn't want to celebrate the way I did after my first transplant.

My first transplant was the final hurdle of my first battle, but this time, I knew that the chemotherapy on Days 3 and 4 were still on the horizon, which meant I wasn't done just yet. For the rest of the day, I was quite sleepy and didn't do much. Unlike my Day 0 in 2016, which was very eventful, my Day 0 in 2022 only really involved my transplant, and it was quite a boring day.

Saturday 23rd April 2022 (Day 1). I was still feeling well Day 1 post-transplant. In fact, Mum and I were actually worried that I was still feeling so well. Even though I feared the upcoming fevers, we were told to expect it after transplant, and the fact that things weren't going as expected made us feel anxious. The doctors and nurses, on the other hand, were pleased that there were no fevers, which made me think that maybe the expected immediate effects were not necessary for transplant to be a success.

My temperature did rise a little, reaching 37.6°, which was above the standard range of 36.5° to 37.5°, but not enough to be considered a fever. This required no paracetamol, and it went down on its own. Perhaps it was because I had to have a unit of blood on this day, and whenever I had blood transfusions, my temperature always raised a little.

Sunday 24th April 2022 (Day 2). On Sunday, I suddenly began to feel very shivery. I had spiked my first fever of my transplant! With it came relief, because things were going exactly to plan, but this feeling was undoubtedly outweighed by fear. And I was right to fear it because I ended up becoming very sick.

On Days 2 to 4, my body experienced cytokine release syndrome: literally a war inside my body as my own cells and the donor cells attacked each other. This was the cause of severely high fevers. With the temperatures came out of control diarrhoea and nausea and vomiting. The next few days were going to be hell!

Even though the fevers were expected, because I was neutropenic and had received chemotherapy, the necessary checks had to be done to make sure it wasn't an infection. This entire period was treated as an infection, even though the doctors were pretty sure it was cytokine release syndrome. It was better to be safe than sorry and was still important to check the source of the fevers.

I was placed on the IV antibiotic, tazocin, which had the ability to hit most parts of the body to kill an infection if there was one. To best treat the potential infection, however, the source had to be found. The nurses took blood cultures, both through my line and peripherally, from my arm. I also had lots of ECGs done to monitor my heart. I was due for a chest X-ray, and radiographers came to the ward with a portable X-ray machine for me to have at bedside, but the nurses turned them away because I was so sick that there was no way I would have been able to even manage it.

Monday 25ᵗʰ April 2022 (Day 3). Going into Monday, my fevers were getting much worse, reaching as high as 39.8°. The fevers were difficult to manage. Paracetamol was good at reducing my fevers, but to prevent overdose, I had to space my doses out. It usually lasted three or four hours while cooling my body down, but it wore off very quickly, and as soon as it wore off, my temperature reached crazy levels. Fevers were very uncomfortable because the body's way of cooling down is to make you shake and shiver uncontrollably, which is known as a rigor. When rigoring, even though your body temperature is burning hot, you feel super cold and need to wrap yourself in lots of blankets, which the hospital strongly advised against. In fact, when rigoring, the nurses make you take your blankets off!

Rigoring is interesting because while the body is trying to cool you down, it's also trying to make you hotter. By causing you to shiver uncontrollably, it is cooling you down to encourage you to warm up. The body's way of killing the infection is to raise your temperature as high as it can go so the infection cannot survive such harsh conditions, which is why a fever is a sign of infection. It is amazing how the human body works!

The rules of paracetamol doses were that I could take it every four hours, up to four times a day. But the problem with that was that I could only have it for sixteen hours of a twenty-four-hour day, leaving eight hours with nothing to control my temperature. Therefore, the nurses only wanted to give me paracetamol every six hours to space it out. Understandably, they didn't want me shivering for two hours, so they prescribed a drug called pepadin. This didn't bring down my temperature but stopped the rigoring and made me feel more comfortable. It was quite a strong drug, I could only have twice a day, with doses twelve hours apart, although it wore off after a few hours. As a result, for a lot of my day, I was left shivering uncontrollably!

I received the chemotherapy, cyclophosphamide, on this day. Like my conditioning phase, it consisted of a 1000 ml dose. By this point, I was seeing a doctor morning, lunchtime, afternoon, and evening, just to keep an eye on me. When the evening doctor arrived, he told me that, although the necessary checks were being done for an infection, as expected, this was most likely as a result of the transplant. During the doctor's visit, I was wrapped in blankets, shivering uncontrollably. He told me that while he understood I was feeling rough, I'd need to take some layers off and put the fan on in my room. He said that I needed to hold it out a little bit longer and the fevers usually began to settle twenty-four hours after the first dose of chemo.

The fevers weren't the only issue. Nausea was also a problem, and by this point, I was throwing up every so often. I hadn't had anything to eat or drink on this day and sometimes I didn't throw anything up, I just gagged into a sick bowl. Sometimes it was bile, but I don't think I ever threw up any food or drink.

Another problem was diarrhoea. This was severe diarrhoea, and I was having to go at least every hour, perhaps even every half hour. Because I was losing fluids from the diarrhoea, and I hadn't had anything to drink, I needed to be topped up with IV fluids constantly. IV fluids generally took about eight hours to go through my line, and as soon as one bag of fluid was finished, the nurses put up another! For someone who wasn't eating or drinking, my weight was somehow on the increase, from 68 kg to 71 kg! This was because of the fluids!

The fluids were becoming an issue, and the doctors became concerned that they were giving me too much. This was evident by my weight gain and also the fact that my face and legs had quite a bit of swelling. I was even worried that the ferocious groin from a couple of months ago had regenerated! Luckily, when the doctor had a look, she couldn't find anything, but she did say that the groin and scrotum were common places for the body to store excess fluid, which may have been a reason why things weren't feeling their usual selves down below.

To get rid of the excess fluid, I was given a diuretic medication through my line to make me urinate. This stuff worked like dynamite! Almost immediately, I felt the urge to go to the toilet. I was urinating every five minutes and producing greater amounts, perhaps half a urine bottle per urination, the norm being maybe over a quarter of a bottle. It was pain having to drag my drip machine to the bathroom back and forth. It probably would have made sense to just stay in the bathroom, but of course the nurses decided to give me a diuretic when my machine was out of charge! I had to give my machine charging boosts after every visit to the toilet. And I couldn't even urinate in a bottle at bedside to save having to go back and forth, as I had to do it sitting down because standing up would have caused an accident the other end. The diuretic and my severely loose bowels meant that fluid gushed like waterfalls at both ends. Thankfully, the medication was fast-acting and was out of my system within an hour and a half, but I hoped I would never need it again. It didn't help having super high fevers, and all you want to do when you feel so sick is stay in bed!

Monday night was a horrible one. I genuinely believed that I was coming to the end of my life.

"I'm dying!" I said to Mum.

My fever was very high, and because my bowels were so loose, I had to do everything I could to avoid defecating the bed again. I never dared lock the bathroom door while in hospital just because I knew how rapidly my health could change at the flick of a switch, and this time I'm glad I didn't. I managed to walk to the toilet okay, but as soon as I sat down and emptied my bowels for the thousandth time that night, I shouted to Mum, "Sick bowl!" Mum came in to find me sat on the toilet seat, with my trousers down, my bum making loud rumbling sounds as diarrhoea exploded all over the toilet bowl. I made throwing-up actions into the sick bowl, like something was coming out, but nothing came up. The gagging seemed to have put massive strain on me, and with sweat pouring down my face like a waterfall, I began to black out, and as the room spun, I passed out. Still sat on the toilet, my head was caught by the nearby sink, where I rested for a few minutes. Alarmed, Mum pressed the button to notify the nurse, who entered the bathroom to check on me. I had managed to recover from the blacking out once the nurse got there, but because of what had happened, a close eye needed to be kept on me. I was so embarrassed having my mum and a nurse watch me sat on the toilet while my bottom was making angry rumbling sounds, splattering diarrhoea everywhere.

"Have you had anything to eat today?" asked the nurse.

"No," I said.

"That's the problem. Have you had anything to drink today?"

"No," I said.

"That's the problem."

I wasn't allowed any privacy as being left alone without a nurse would be very dangerous. Therefore, I had to face wiping my bum in front of both my mum and the nurse, which I found highly embarrassing. Once I was done, I washed my hands and the nurse escorted me back to my bed. I was able to walk, but I had lost all feeling in my feet and felt as if I was floating rather than walking, needing my drip stand to keep me balanced.

The nurse said she would get the night doctor to examine me, but they never arrived. It was a rough night, involving frequent trips to the bathroom, but they were nowhere near the level of me almost collapsing in the bathroom. It was going to be a struggle, but I did not want a repeat of this, so I decided that despite my nausea, I was going to force myself to eat and drink something the next day.

Tuesday 26th April 2022 (Day 4). I finished treatment on Day 4, with another dose of cyclophosphamide. I was relieved that after such a horrible year, I had finally reached the milestone of finishing treatment! Now I could focus on recovery. It was such a shame that I was feeling so unwell that I wasn't able to celebrate this milestone.

Fearing a repeat of the previous night, I decided that I needed to increase my efforts to eat and drink. Unlike all the previous rounds of chemo, this time, drinking was more of a problem than eating. Dehydration was easily solved by IV fluids but getting nutrients in was more problematic. There was no way I was going down the tube route, and I understood that TPN was an absolute last resort. I couldn't manage much, but a cereal bar and yoghurt for breakfast seemed to go down well. I usually skipped lunch and had a mid-afternoon snack instead, then depending on how well I felt, I'd decide what I would have for dinner from the ward menu, which was a challenge.

Being a transplant patient, Mum and I asked the doctor if I was allowed takeaways, since there was a Burger King downstairs. She said that places like Burger King were generally safe, and they were good to consume when blood counts were coming up. My counts were going in the opposite direction. She said it was most likely fine, but she'd check with the dietician. The dietician agreed that Burger King was completely fine as long as we were 100% sure that it was cooked fresh. In Bristol, takeaways would have been a no-go, but in the last six years, the policy on the neutropenic diet had changed. Burger King was something I could actually stomach, and I did have it regularly, sometimes having it twice in a day!

The doctor from the previous day was correct. The fevers seemed to settle twenty-four hours after the first dose of chemotherapy. I may have had one or two on this day, but I noticed how, rather than being present constantly, they were more sporadic until they disappeared completely.

This, however, could not be said for the diarrhoea. If anything, my trips to the toilet seemed to be on the increase. The constant wiping and the irritation from the diarrhoea made my bottom very sore, and going to the toilet every thirty to forty-five minutes was extremely painful. On the night of Tuesday, and going into the early hours of Wednesday, I had made many trips to the toilet. Because I was attached to three different machines at once to keep me stable, the pressure on my line was heavy, and I was feeling so unwell that I didn't have the energy to be dragging my drip stand to the toilet.Mum, who was staying with me, was getting fed up with my constant need for help and her inability to sleep with the beeping machines every time I unplugged them. To solve this, the nurse gave me a commode so I could empty my bowels at bedside. This was much more convenient for me as I could just jump out of bed and relieve myself, but it didn't help Mum as she had to keep getting up to pass me the loo roll and urine bottles! The night was rough with sickness being a problem, in addition to the diarrhoea. I randomly woke up in the middle of the night violently gagging but did not have enough in my stomach to throw anything up other than a small amount of bile.

Wednesday 27th April 2022 (Day 5). On Day 5, I started two immunosuppressant medications. These worked by suppressing my own immune system to prevent my cells from rejecting the donor cells, helping engraftment and also to help prevent severe GvHD. My immunosuppressants were mycophenolate mofetil and tacrolimus. I'd had mycophenolate in Bristol, but they referred to it as MMF, and it wasn't until I researched this that I found out it was the same drug. I'd also had tacrolimus in Bristol, which was the alternative to cyclosporin, the immunosuppressant I'd initially had but was found to be allergic to.

The amount of tacrolimus changed almost every day until doctors were able to get the dosage right. You may remember from my first transplant, I had to have blood tests to check my tacrolimus levels. Too high meant that there was a chance of toxicity and too low meant that I wasn't getting enough of the medication for it to be effective.

It is also worth mentioning that, while in Bristol, I received my immunosuppressants via my line, but at Addenbrooke's my immunosuppressants were taken in tablet form. Therefore, this time I didn't have to worry about the sticky tacrolimus medication causing high tacrolimus levels when blood was taken through my line.

Also on Day 5, I started another medication. Unfortunately, it was another injection: G-CSF. By this point I was getting fed up with injections, with the blood-clot preventing injection, dalteparin, causing me great pain. Once my unsupported platelet count was below 30, I could stop this injection, but as soon as that one was stopped, they gave me another one! For the previous few days following my conditioning and transplant, my blood cells seemed to be going down very slowly, and one day showed a very slight increase. But by Day 5, my counts were flat, and I needed the G-CSF to stimulate the growth of white blood cells in my body to help the donor cells engraft.

My appetite was on the increase by now, although it wasn't great. I still couldn't drink very much because of my nausea. I was baffled how I could eat well but was completely put off by drinks, the opposite of my previous chemo rounds. IV fluids were the doctors' answer to this, but I was still gaining weight. The swelling was visible in my face and ankles. The doctors' solution was to give me that dynamite diuretic again, and it worked! As soon as it went through my line, I felt the urge to urinate. One trip to the toilet took four urine bottles before I could return back to my bed, and they were often filled over half full and my urine was as clear as water! Over one hour, I produced thirteen urine bottles, all neatly set out in lines on the floor by the bathroom wall, shocking the healthcare assistant.

"You've set a record!" she said, carrying all the bottles to the weighing scales.

When she returned, she said there was 2 kg of urine that I'd been able to produce in the hour, and she asked me to step on the scales. It was actually more, as I managed to go from the 71 kg mark to 68 kg! I wish losing weight was always that easy!

Thursday 28th April 2022 (Day 6). I woke up on the Thursday morning feeling much better and brighter. Even the ward doctor doing the ward rounds noticed an improvement in how I was looking. I actually felt like having breakfast, rather than having to force something down myself, and I managed to keep an improved appetite all throughout the day. In even better news, while the sickness was still there, it was in the background, and I didn't throw up again throughout the entire course of my transplant. And in even better news that that, rather than opening my bowels six times an hour, I was going only six times a day! My stools were becoming more formed, and while still soft, they were no longer watery or dark green in colour.

The doctors decided to give me a day free from IV fluids to give me more of a chance to drink orally. My belief was that I was so overloaded with fluids that I couldn't manage any more without wetting myself 24/7. I was able to drink much more than I had the previous few days, but at only one litre, I was only managing half of what my intake should have been, and I was back on IV fluids the next day.

I hoped that the worst of transplant was over, and Dr. U seemed to think this when he was doing the ward rounds. He told me that while he wasn't happy that I had been so unwell, it was actually a good thing as it showed that the cells were doing their job. Overall, the doctors and nurses were happy with my progress, and everything was going as planned and expected.

With the worst being over, I did my best to build my energy and even started planning my dissertation for university! Even though I made good progress on that day, perhaps I overdid it, as for the next few days I did little to nothing, having to take regular naps in the afternoon to regain my energy.

Friday 29th April to Friday 6th May (Day 7 to Day 14). Now that the worst was over, all the days stuck in my isolation room merged into one and not a lot happened.

I wasn't extremely unwell, but I wasn't well enough to the point where I was able to occupy myself and keep busy. My daily routine was not eventful at all. I had difficulty getting back to sleep after my 6:00am obs and blood test, so I usually scrolled on my phone or tried to get some time with my eyes shut until 8:00am. Sometimes I was able to sleep really well, and I wouldn't wake up until I received my daily morning visit from the healthcare assistant, who came to weigh my urine bottles and to check to see if I needed anything.

Breakfast was usually around 8:30 to 9:00am, and what I ate varied. Mum would sometimes go down to Marks & Spencer downstairs in the concourse and get me a croissant, or I'd have a cereal bar and yoghurt, and later on, Coco Pops from the ward was a very popular choice. After having breakfast and having my morning medicines, which, to prevent nausea, I often spread throughout the morning, I'd usually scroll on my phone more or watch YouTube. I liked to watch a lot of daytime TV too. Mum usually did work from her laptop in my hospital room throughout the mornings and when I was asleep.

Depending on my appetite or how late I had breakfast, I'd either skip lunch or order something from the ward. I didn't enjoy the food from the ward much, and all I could really stomach was toast, jacket potatoes, and pizza. For a few days during my stay, Mum was actually staying in a hostel, which she preferred as she didn't have to beat other parents to the only parents' bathroom on the ward to shower. As I was well enough and the worst seemed to be over, Mum thought it was safe to leave me by myself at night-time. Having the hostel was also a huge advantage, as Mum was able to go over there at lunch and dinner time and cook me a meal if there was something I was craving. The neutropenic diet rule change was a blessing!

After lunch, my day just involved more daytime TV, watching game shows. Mum usually watched them with me too once she stopped working. There really wasn't much more to my days other than having something for dinner, then watching *EastEnders*, and Mum and I spent our evenings before bed getting through my *SpongeBob SquarePants* DVDs.

I should mention that Thursdays were a little bit different. I'd often receive a visit from a lady who offered all patients a foot massage and would cut their nails. I had met her in January, but because I was on and off the ward, I'd only had a few foot massages, and it wasn't until I was a transplant patient that they became a lot more regular. I looked forward to my weekly foot massages, and my feet felt amazing afterwards! It was also good to have someone different to talk to, and I usually spoke to the foot massage lady about politics and which movies or TV shows I was watching to keep busy.

Healthwise, a week or so after my final dose of chemotherapy, passing urine began to become very painful. I was also producing less amounts of urine and was not going as often as usual. I provided a urine sample for the nurses, and the result came back negative for bugs. The good thing was that I had avoided an infection! However, my blood test results showed that my kidneys were not functioning properly. The doctor reassured me that this was very mild and it was most likely because of the cyclophosphamide. To cure my problem, I was required to drink as much as possible, and I was hooked up to IV fluids for eight hours a day. I was baffled by the fact that I was constantly attached to fluids all day but needed nothing at night. Even though I spent most of my days in bed, wouldn't it have made more sense to give me overnight fluids when I would be sleeping anyway and not trying to move around my room? Eventually, the fluids stopped once I was discharged, but the pain when urinating didn't disappear completely. On a good day, when I drank plenty of fluids, urinating wasn't much of a problem.

Another issue I had been suffering from was nausea. After suffering from cytokine release syndrome, I was able to eat small amounts, but strangely, drinking was still a challenge. I was rarely vomiting; it was just the sick feeling that remained with me. I could be sick, but I hated feeling sick. None of my anti-sickness medication seemed to be working, and the only drug I could think of that I knew would work was dexamethasone, the steroid that had made me feel so well during Round 2. When I looked at my transplant protocol sheet, it stated that I had to refrain from taking any steroids such as dexamethasone during transplant.

To manage my nausea, the ward doctor referred me to the palliative team. This almost gave Mum a heart attack! Palliative care is end of life care, which aims to treat the symptoms of a disease rather than the disease itself in order to make life as comfortable as possible. The doctor reassured Mum that it was nothing to worry about and I wasn't coming to the end of my life – the palliative doctors just had better experience in managing nausea and vomiting, especially when all the options recommended by the haematology team had been exhausted with little success. I met the palliative consultant, who recommended a few alternative options. She said that she would look at the anti-sickness medications I was on and see if there were others available or if I could potentially try a different combination of drugs. She also suggested IV anti-sickness, which would be attached to me like a pump, and I could push a button whenever I felt I needed a dose. Luckily, my nausea seemed to have settled by the time the palliative doctors could come to a clear plan of action, and I ended up not needing their support.

On Day 13, after my white blood cell count had been stuck on the 0.0 mark for a week, it increased to 0.1, with my neutrophils reaching 0.04! The ward doctor doing the rounds that morning told me that this could possibly be a sign of engraftment, but we would have to see. Later that day, Dr. U said that this was just a flicker at the moment, a potential sign of engraftment, but still too early to determine whether I had engrafted. My counts were expected to still be flat by this point, but it was just a matter of waiting and seeing which way my counts went.

With the help of the G-CSF injections I was having, my neutrophils suddenly increased to 0.45 the next day, Day 14. The nurses had told me a couple of nights prior to this that they were really happy with my progress and said my discharge would be soon, but it was by this point that I realised that I was very near the finish line. Dr. U surprised Mum and I by popping his head round my door to tell me the news that if my bloods the next day were all good, I'd possibly be allowed out of my room. He told me to look out for any rashes over the next couple of weeks in case I had GvHD, which the doctors would then be able to deal with.

The visiting rule had changed at the hospital in my last couple of days there. Previously, it had been just Mum and I, with the rule being only one named visitor per admission due to Covid. Now, the policy had changed, and I was allowed two people to visit me at a time, and it didn't have to be the same two people per admission. I was delighted to hear the news, and Dad began to visit Mum and I in the evenings, often for Burger King. What was annoying though was that I had gone through almost my entire second cancer battle with just one named visitor, and then as soon as I was done and almost ready to escape the ward for good, they changed the visiting rule! I am very grateful for Mum, who stayed with me consistently for the five months I was ill. It was clear that she often needed a break, and for the psychological wellbeing of both of us, it would have been good to see some other familiar faces during that very difficult time. I guess I'd rather see people at home than the hospital, but that doesn't change the fact that the previous five or six months had been a very lonely and depressing time for the two of us.

In my final two days on the ward, even though I had been receiving G-CSF injections for a week and a half, it was only by this point that the side effects were beginning to kick in. I thankfully avoided them during Round 2, but the back pain was awful from Round 1. And Round 3's pain was intensified! It was so painful! I'd be fine anywhere from a few minutes to a few hours, and then all of a sudden, my back would start throbbing, like something constantly jabbing my spine. It was excruciatingly painful, and I describe it as a mild bone marrow aspiration pain. It wasn't just my back. Like a bone marrow aspiration, the G-CSF caused an effect that felt like an aching, pulling feeling. My walking was quite weak for a few days. Paracetamol dulled the pain slightly but not for long, and on my last night on the ward, I was up until 3:00am, in so much pain that I couldn't sleep! The nurse gave me morphine, which put me to sleep but didn't help the pain, as when I woke up to go to the toilet the constant throbbing was agonising.

The pain was usually worse after getting up and walking. The nurse told me that perhaps walking around would help me, rather than being stuck in bed all day. When I gave it a try and, in fact, every time I returned from the toilet, my back would suffer a terrible sharp, shooting pain, which first shot through my spine and then my heart. I'm sure my heart stopped beating for three seconds every time it happened, and sometimes I found myself clutching my chest in pain.

There was still uncertainty about when I would be coming home. Dr. U said that it would potentially be the weekend of Saturday 7th and Sunday 8th May but discharging transplant patients on the weekend was not ideal due to the complexity of checking medications. Because we didn't know, Mum went home on the Friday night, ready to come back by Saturday afternoon. However, I knew that I was being discharged soon because I was told, if not by the weekend, I'd be home by Monday, provided everything continued to go well.

Saturday 7th May 2022 (Day 15). I was woken super early on Saturday morning as soon as the night shift nurses handed over to the day shift. The weekend doctor liked to get the C9 ward rounds done early so she could get them out of the way and do C10, the much larger adult haematology ward, afterwards.

She told me that the plan was to get me discharged that day. I had never been more excited! While it wasn't ideal to be discharged on the weekend, I was going to for three reasons.

Firstly, and most importantly, my neutrophils had reached over 0.5, at 1.69, so it was considered safe. Secondly, there was a massive waiting list for transplants and the ward was stretched for beds, so they needed me out of my room as quickly as possible. Thirdly, I was very keen to go home, and I think the doctors and nurses were feeling the pressure to get me out. Dr. U had said the day before that being discharged by Day 15 was early for my kind of transplant and they were expecting at least another week of isolation.

The doctor asked if I had any other concerns. My back was still as painful as ever. She said that I needed to hold out a little longer because the back pain was a sign that the G-CSF was working and stimulating my bone marrow. Therefore, while it was extremely painful, my bone marrow was at least doing the right thing, and it wasn't worth stopping the injection for back pain.

The day was mostly uneventful. I was so bored the entire day, and as Mum and Dad had decided to go home the night before, all I really did was try to catch up on the sleep I had missed the previous night due to the pain. I spent most of the day not only super bored but also feeling groggy and dehydrated with a sore throat. My back was throbbing, and I was still experiencing the really sharp pain in my heart, which coincided with the back pain.

Shortly following my lunchtime medications and injections that day, the nurse asked me when my parents would be arriving. The next occupant for my room had already arrived and there was a rush to get moved out so they could clean my room and let the next patient in. The ward really *was* tight for beds.

Mum and Dad arrived at 2:15pm. They took their time arriving as I hadn't told them about the pressure that we were under to leave. They had brought lunch and were shocked that the discharge process was going so quick, thinking they could take their time, as from previous discharges, we were often left waiting hours. We quickly gobbled up all our lunch before we started packing. Thankfully, having learnt our lesson from accumulating clutter in Bristol, we had decided to pack lightly prior to my admission, and most of our belongings were still in their bags and boxes to make them easy to move. Moving out didn't take too long, and we were out by about 3:00pm.

Even though there was a rush to get me out of my room for cleaning, my discharge papers and medicines were not completed. There was no time to enjoy or process being out of my room for the first time in over three weeks. The pressure to get out of Side Room 1 was all we were focused on. In fact, I didn't even realise I was out of isolation until I was home!

As soon as we vacated my room, the cleaners were in. The nurse then directed us to one of the quiet rooms on the ward. I had sat in one of the quiet rooms before, but I had never been in this one, so it was a new experience. It was very comfy with sofas and bean bags. We waited for about an hour until the nurse went down to the pharmacy to collect my medicines and go through my discharge information.

I knew I was on a lot of medication, but I didn't realise just *how* many medicines I was taking. From previous discharges, a nurse would bring my medicines in a bag and go through them. This time, the nurse had to bring an entire trolley into the quiet room!

Just in case you're interested, here is the listed medication I was taking once I was discharged for the final time: acyclovir, ciprofloxacin, posaconazole, nozinan, ursodexoycholic acid, mycophenolate mofetil (MMF), tacrolimus, ondansetron, chlorphenamine maleate, loperamide, Peptac, omeprazole, magnesium aspartate, granulocyte-colony stimulating factor (G-CSF), and Co-Trimoxazole Forte (to start on May 23rd, 2022).

This was a lot of medicine, and it was very important that I stuck to the discharge information provided and took the exact doses at the exact time. Even though my neutrophils were above 1.5, and I was no longer considered neutropenic, it was still necessary to continue the G-CSF until my box of injections ran out. This meant five days of having to inject myself and deal with the terrible back pain! Even though my neutrophils were above 0.5, I was advised to continue taking the prophylaxis antibiotic, ciprofloxacin, until the doctor instructed me to stop. The anti-sickness tablets, ondansetron and nozinan, started off as being regularly scheduled, but once the nausea settled, I was allowed to move them to the as and when needed pile. It was Day 15, and provided there was no evidence of GvHD, by Day 35, I would be able to stop taking the immunosuppressant, MMF, which would take me one step closer to freedom. Tacrolimus needed to continue until it was deemed safe to stop by the doctor. My magnesium levels were low, so I was given a sachet of magnesium powder, which could be dissolved in water to drink. This tasted foul, and having to have two sachets two times a day made me feel quite nauseous. I was going to be on posaconazole, a drug that is useful for fighting fungal infections, for at least the next couple of months, and I was going to have to take acyclovir, the anti-viral medication, for at least the next year. Because taking so many tablets can take a damaging toll on the liver, I had to take even more tablets to combat this: ursodexoycholic acid. All the remaining medications were to be taken on an 'as and when needed' basis. I was also given all my previous medications that I was no longer taking, such as oramorph, folic acid, and dexamethasone, in case the doctor re-prescribed them, in which case I'd be all stocked up at home.

After going through the medication checklist, the nurse then went through the advice of what to do and what not to do at home. I needed to stick to a clean diet as much as possible, but these rules had changed since my transplant in Bristol. If I ate out or ordered a takeaway, I needed to be 100% sure that the food was cooked fresh. I also was not allowed any raw vegetables, and any I did eat needed to be well-cooked. I was not allowed to be around anyone with a cough or cold, and I needed to avoid crowded places as much as possible. Any visitors needed to ensure that they had tested negative for Covid, and it was advisable that they wore a mask when around me.

It was really hard to follow these rules in the hospital. Once I was given the go-ahead to go home, which was roughly around 4:00pm, as soon as we left the ward and entered the lifts, they were crowded! For someone with my levels of haemoglobin, there was no way I'd be able to go down nine flights of stairs. The good thing was that it was a Saturday, so most of the shops in the concourse were closed, meaning it was less crowded with people.

I stepped outside the front doors of Addenbrooke's and breathed my first breath of fresh air in twenty-one days with a sigh of relief.

I had done it again, I thought. *I've reached the end!*

Chapter 20

Overcoming Obstacles

My first 100 days post-transplant from May 7th, 2022, to August 1st, 2022

Coming home from Bristol felt like a massive celebration, finally celebrating the end of a traumatic time. Returning home from Addenbrooke's felt a bit different, though. It was like I had only been away for a few weeks and I was just coming home from a regular stay in hospital. It was the end, but it didn't feel like a special moment like Bristol did. I'm unsure why that is.

I had managed to grow a beard and keep hold of my hair when in my isolation room. Starting as soon as I was discharged home, my hair began to fall out rapidly. I went to bed one night, only to wake up the next morning with my beard completely gone. It took a few days for my hair to fall out, but it was going fast. First to go was the hair on the back of my head, so I couldn't see the difference all that much. It wasn't until Mum showed me a photo of the massive bald patch, which took up half of the back of my head, that I realised how much had fallen overnight.

More and more hair kept falling. It was embarrassing going into the day unit, with hair covering my neck and shoulders, which made me very itchy. I left hair trails. You knew where I had been because there would be a pile of hair around the chair that I was sat on!

My hair was getting thinner, and I had lost hair in every place imaginable. My chest, arm, and leg hair, which had stayed with me after previous rounds of chemo, were falling out. I even lost my eyebrows and eyelashes, something that had never happened to me before in all my rounds of chemo.

By Wednesday 11th May, all that was left of my hair was a tiny mohawk at the top of my head. Dad shaved it off for me, which was very easy to do as it was going to fall anyway. The remaining strands of hair on my head eventually fell out over the next few days, and by the weekend I was completely bald, looking how I'd looked in Bristol.

While I was proud of my bald look after my first transplant, and embraced it thinking I looked cool, my confidence the second time round wasn't as strong. I didn't really like showing off my bald head, and I have very few photos of what I looked like. In fact, I only have one or two photos of my bald head. The hat came back as part of my personal fashion. I preferred to hide what the chemo had done to my hair. It's strange because less than a year before, I had written a blog for the Teenage Cancer Trust on hair loss, inspiring people to embrace their new look. Ironically, I ended up taking the opposite of my own advice.

***

The early days of being home, up until Day 35, involved visits to the Ward C9 day unit twice a week. My Tuesday appointments just involved visits to the day unit for blood tests and dressing changes and anything else needed to be done, such as any IV supplements, which would be infused through my line on that day. My Friday appointments consisted of a blood test in the day unit, then I went down to the haematology and oncology outpatients clinic to have my weekly appointment with either my consultant or the BMT clinical fellow.

My tacrolimus levels were still monitored and would

continue to be until I stopped taking the medication. When I was at the hospital, I wasn't allowed to take my morning dose of tacrolimus until I'd had my blood test. A high tacrolimus level, generally regarded somewhere above 15, had the potential to cause toxicity to my body, so it was important to alter my doses if need be. The doctors preferred my level to be between 5 and 10. By this point, however, I was pretty much at a stable level and my doses changed very little.

I think everyone on C9 was surprised that I had been discharged so quick. I remember Rosie coming into the day unit on one of the days I was in just to catch up with all the patients. When she spoke to me, she asked what day I was on.

"Were you Day 28?"

"No, I was Day 15," I said.

"Day 15?" Rosie said, shocked.

"Day 15!" came an echo from another transplant patient sitting opposite.

That didn't mean I didn't have problems. Things weren't going too smoothly for me. One problem I was suffering from was a deficiency in magnesium. Normal magnesium levels are above 0.70. At their lowest, my magnesium levels were 0.48. If they were below 0.50, I had to have IV magnesium. As you might remember from my reaction back in August 2016, I was allergic to it. Usually, IV magnesium took two hours to be infused, but due to my allergy, I had to have it infused in double that time. I had to go into the day unit, have my blood test and dressing changed, wait for the results, and then wait for a doctor to prescribe the magnesium. By the time all that was over, it wasn't until around 2:00pm that I actually received my magnesium, then added four hours onto that to wait for it to go through. Sometimes I didn't leave the ward until about 6:30pm!

I was taking magnesium supplements at home too. I was

given a powder sachet called magnesium aspartate when I was discharged. To begin with, I needed to take two sachets three times a day. The sachets could be mixed with water, orange juice, or tea and really did not taste very nice. I had to drink it immediately, meaning I couldn't just sip it throughout the day. The magnesium supplements did not help my nausea, something I suffered with on and off in my early days of discharge.

I went at least a week of not needing oral magnesium supplements after my sachets ran out. This was probably because I was having IV magnesium so often. With my levels still low though, I was then prescribed some magnesium supplements in tablet form. The tablets were a lot more manageable than the sachets but still a pain to take. I needed to take two tablets three times a day, but the tablets were massive. We were given a tablet cutter, which could cut down the size of the tablets. This made eight ordinary tablets per dose. They were chewable, so I could have just chewed and swallowed the whole tablet, but I usually just ended up getting magnesium stuck in my teeth, and they tasted horrible, so my only chance of absorbing them was from swallowing eight tablets at a time, combined with the other medications I was taking.

I was soon becoming an expert in tablet taking, and instead of taking my medications one by one, I was very good at swallowing three or four tablets in one sip of water!

In my Friday 20th May (Day 28) consultation with Dr. U, my magnesium levels were still low. Dr. U said that the body absorbed the magnesium aspartate sachets better than the tablets and moved me back on to them instead. This time it was only one sachet three times a day, which improved the taste as the solution wouldn't be as strong. It still took a bit of getting used to.

Also, on Friday 20th May, I had my first chimerism test of my second transplant, which the doctors preferred to have done around Day 30. As you'll remember from my first transplant, the chimerism test checks the amount of donor cells in my blood compared to my own cells. According to Greek mythology, the Chimera was a creature with the head of a lion, the body of a goat, and a tail of a serpent. When used in medicine, it essentially means two different people living in one body. It was hoped that my chimerism would be 100%. However, Dr. U assured Mum and I that, with the type of transplant I'd had, it would be okay if it wasn't quite 100% yet. Because my blood type was O+ and Dad's was B+, engraftment of the red blood cells would take longer than it would have done if he was the same blood type. By this point, I was still anaemic, and my haemoglobin was averaging at about 102 to 104 for a couple of weeks, below the standard range of 135 to 172. Therefore, my red blood cells were still trying to engraft, and once they had, my blood type would change, and it would be expected that my chimerism would be 100%. The test took a couple of weeks to come back.

Another issue I was suffering from was my bowels. My bowel movements were really unpredictable, but I was going more than usual. Before my relapse in December, I was probably going about three or four times a day. This seemed excessive in itself, but my bowels hadn't recovered after my first transplant, and I was never the same again afterwards. After my second transplant, things got much worse. My bowel movements were difficult to describe. My stools were never solid but alternated between watery and mushy. The amount of times I went in a day changed, anywhere from five to ten times a day! Sometimes it looked like I wasn't digesting my food properly, as I could see exactly what I had eaten when it came back up in the toilet. Something really wasn't right.

The BMT clinical fellow, the doctor who I saw in clinic when Dr. U wasn't available, said that unstable bowel movements were to be expected post-transplant. It was always difficult to describe my bowels to the doctor. They always wanted to know if my condition had worsened or improved, but the problem was that they were so unpredictable. When I told the doctor that my stools were becoming more formed or I was going less frequently, as soon as I returned home from the hospital, it would be the complete reverse of what I'd told them an hour before. My bowel movements were frequently up and down, and it was impossible to give an accurate account of what was going on just because of how frequently they changed.

To solve my bowel problems, I was required to take three different medications. Before I could take any medication to relieve my symptoms, though, I had to bring in a few stool samples to take to the lab. I tested negative for C. diff, which the doctors were most concerned about, and I was also negative for all other infections, so I was given the go-ahead to take the prescribed medicines. I took only one of these medications at any one time, but some were not as successful as others, and I had to keep switching. The first medication I was prescribed was something called loperamide. Loperamide was good at resolving my excessive bowel movements, but the problem was that having only taken two tablets I seemed to become constipated on them, which was the opposite end of the extreme. Next was buscupan, which, while I'll admit I often forgot to take, when I did remember, didn't seem to have much effect. The third medication I tried was budesonide, which was more effective than the other two. It managed to reduce the number of times I was going to about three times a day.

By Day 35, I had reached another milestone. As I was showing no active signs of Graft vs Host Disease, it was deemed safe to come off my immunosuppressant, MMF. Even though I was still taking my other immunosuppressant, tacrolimus, this was a sign that things were going in the right direction, and it was a step closer to freedom. Also, by Day 35, the tacrolimus levels in my blood were a bit high and there was a chance that it was causing toxicity to my body. Dr. U was surprised that I was feeling so well, because people with a tacrolimus level that high often find it very difficult to cope. Previously, I was taking 1 mg of tacrolimus every morning and 1 mg every night. To lower my blood to a safer level, I continued with my 1 mg dose in the morning, but every other evening I would alternate between a 1 mg and a 0.5 mg dose.

I also asked Dr. U about when I'd be allowed to start getting out and about again. I had already started doing this, but I was very careful about where I went and tried to meet people outside as much as I could, but I wanted to know when I'd be able to return to normal. Dr. U suggested that I lived like it was the Covid lockdown, which included limiting the amount of people I met and making sure I met them outside. And, if possible, it was best if I wore a mask and got people to do lateral flow Covid tests before seeing me. He also said that it was important to look after my psychological wellbeing too, so it was good for me to be seeing people, but I needed to be careful as my immune system was going to be weak for a very long time.

***

After reducing my immunosuppressants, problems began to arise. My bowel problems were continuing to be on and off, and I had become quite itchy in my lower body, just above the waistband of my trousers, and my groin. My back, flanks, and my face had been particularly itchy too.

"I think you have a bit of Graft vs. Host Disease," concluded Dr. U after he had finished typing his notes in my weekly check-up with him on Friday 10th June (Day 48).

In the appointment, Dr. U checked me over for any other rashes on my skin. He seemed to be able to detect a rash on my back but described it as "almost invisible". There was a bit of redness on my neck, and I was particularly itchy behind my ears. Considering that a rash is the most common symptom of GvHD, and there had been disturbance in my bowels for quite a while, it seemed to all of us that a bit of mild GvHD was the case.

Just to refresh on what GvHD is, it is where my donor cells (the graft) perceive my body's cells (the host) as foreign and begin attacking them. Having a bit of GvHD is a good thing as it can produce the Graft vs. Leukaemia effect, where the new cells attack the leukaemia cells that not even the most powerful microscopes can detect. In fact, when I watched a YouTube video presentation on bone marrow transplantations by Dr. G, he found that 50% of BMT patients who did not get GvHD actually ended up relapsing, showing that there was an association between GvHD and the GvL effect. This was likely the reason why I relapsed, as I didn't get GvHD the first time round.

Doctors will often tell you that they hope for GvL in transplant patients without causing too much toxicity as a result of GvHD. That's why they try to prevent GvHD with immunosuppression as much as they can. What happens in GvHD is that the donor cells might have engrafted, but they are still not used to being in a new body, so while they attack the bad cells, they start attacking the good cells, which, in my case, was my skin and bowels. So having GvHD is a mix of good and bad. There is the struggle of finding a balance of completely eradicating the leukaemia and causing toxicity to the body.

The way to treat GvHD is through increased immunosuppression, which essentially suppresses the power of your own immune system to prevent the need of the donor cells to fight against it. Since my GvHD was only mild, and I had discontinued taking MMF and reduced my tacrolimus dose only a couple of weeks earlier, Dr. U did not really want to do this. He suggested trying to treat it symptomatically instead, so we treated the symptoms instead of the cause. I was given a number of creams to help my rash. Instead of using regular shower gel, I now used Dermol cream as a soap substitute. For my rash, in areas such as my back and my flanks, I was prescribed a steroid cream called Eumovate. Unfortunately, long-term use of Eumovate had a chance of thinning the skin, so for the more sensitive areas of my body where I was affected by the rash, such as my groin and face, I used hydrocortisone. The key to managing my rash was to keep my body as moist as possible, so I was prescribed Diprobase to moisturise regularly. I used Dermol cream whenever I showered, often once a day, and moisturised with Diprobase after my shower. Eumovate and hydrocortisone had to be applied twice a day. I found it quite time-consuming and tiring applying all these different creams every day, and it took about an hour every day to apply the right creams in the right places at the right time!

The next week, in my Friday 17th June (Day 55) consultation with Dr. U, my GvHD had worsened. My rash had spread to my arms and legs and also to the area of my Hickman line, where it was impossible to apply cream. The rash was also more visible, with my waist and upper arms bright red, and I had light red blotchy marks on my forearms, hands, abdomen, and back. Redness on my face and neck kept coming and going.

I was then moved to the Grade II category of GvHD, which is considered moderate GvHD, with more than 50% of my skin affected and still some disturbance to my bowels. There are four grades of GvHD. Grade I is mild, Grade II is moderate, and Grade III is severe. Grade IV can be considered life-threatening. Interestingly, the higher the grade, the lower your relapse rate, which I assume is because severe GvHD causes a greater GvL effect.

Because my GvHD had got worse, the doctor formulated a new plan of action. While it was good that I had got a bit of GvHD, it was now time to dampen things down before things got too out of control. We would continue treating it symptomatically, but the Eumovate I had been applying twice a day was discontinued, and in its place, I had to apply a stronger steroid cream called Dermovate. Unfortunately, we also had to go down the immunosuppressant route. I was prescribed a steroid called prednisolone, which involved having to take eight tablets every morning. Dr. U was hopeful that the steroid, which acted as immunosuppressants, would settle my rash, and I would begin to come down on them within a month. Even though it was hopeful that I'd be on them for the short-term, I had to look out for potential side effects. These included weight gain, particularly in the face and upper body, the thinning of my skin, and muscle loss. I was allowed the occasional cake, but it was important that I kept away from sugar as much as possible, particularly sugary drinks.

The doctor also asked me if I had been on holiday to anywhere exotic lately. My eosinophils, a type of white blood cell, came up as abnormally high on my blood test. The standard range for eosinophils is 0.02 to 0.50, but mine were

1.43. Dr. U just wondered because you only seem to have high eosinophils if you've been somewhere exotic and caught a certain parasitic infection. Dad and I were a bit puzzled because I had not left the country in two years. It was only after we listed the countries we had visited when Dr. U told us that there was usually an association with high eosinophils and GvHD! That was a relief, and I was glad that I had not picked up any parasites! He said that even if I did, the treatment wouldn't be too bad and would just involve a course of worm tablets, but it was unlikely to come to that. My eosinophils did indeed come down the next week, within the normal range at 0.05.

Regarding my bowels, Dr. U decided to book me in for a flexible sigmoidoscopy at the endoscopy department. Even though I was seeing some improvement with the medication I had been taking, we both agreed that something still wasn't quite right. The flexible sigmoidoscopy would be able to take a sample of my bowel and see whether there was any GvHD going on down there. However, waiting lists for these types of procedures were quite long, and even though one would be booked, it was likely that it would be booked weeks down the line. If I was seeing further improvement with the medication, then an endoscopy might not have been necessary, but it was something to be booked just so I had the slot if needed.

***

My flexible sigmoidoscopy was booked for Monday 27th June, but I ended up having to cancel. Covid-19 had struck again!

On Tuesday 21st June, I began feeling shortness of breath, but I tested negative on my lateral flow Covid test. Being a transplant patient, I wasn't going out for the rest of the week, so I didn't feel the need to use any more tests until I left the house.

My symptoms hadn't improved by Friday 24th June, and in fact, I had developed a cough and thought I was suffering from a really bad cold. My breathlessness was improving but I was still having trouble breathing, particularly when trying to sleep at night. I didn't want to enter the hospital with Covid symptoms, so I took a lateral flow test on Friday morning, and there was a very strong second line, which clearly indicated a positive test result. *Great,* I thought. *Back to Room H for me.*

Mum called Ward C9 as I was due in the day unit for a blood and dressing change before my clinic appointment in haematology and oncology outpatients. The ward clerk said that I wasn't allowed to attend my appointment there, and instead I was booked in for the isolation room. Room H was no longer Room H. It was still in the same location, and I had to meet a nurse at the back of the radiotherapy department, but there were now multiple isolation rooms. The isolation clinic was also renamed the James Watson Suite. I don't know who James Watson was, but I would not want my name to be associated with Room H!

The isolation clinic had somewhat improved since my many visits there in February. First of all, probably the best thing about having to attend the isolation clinic was that it gave us free parking, which Mum loved.

An improvement was that this time, I was only left waiting outside the door for half an hour, and at least I wasn't standing outside in the pouring rain with an electronic drip machine! I wasn't seeing a nurse from C9; the nurses from the oncology outpatients department took responsibility for the isolation patients from now on. The nurse had actually spotted me a lot earlier but was, for some reason, expecting me to arrive in an ambulance, so she didn't realise it was me who was waiting to be let in.

The nurse took my bloods and changed my dressing. The weather had been really hot recently, and I was noticing that my line dressings weren't lasting seven days anymore, and in fact, my line seemed to become unlooped after only two or three days. Dad used to change my dressings in 2016 when he had to, so he had some experience, and I asked the nurse if I could take some spare dressings with me, which she allowed. I was then sent home.

I thought that would be everything, but when I returned home, I received a call from Jo. She said that the hospital had found out by accident that I had tested positive for Covid and no one had informed them. I said I told Ward C9, who told me that they would let clinic know, and that I was told my appointment with the doctor would most likely get moved to a telephone appointment. I thought that was enough information provided, but Jo said that no one had told them and that if something like this happened again, I needed to make use of the haematology helpline. The doctors and nurses were in a state of panic about what needed to be done. I was Day 62 post-transplant, meaning I was in the most vulnerable patient category. I may have been feeling fine, but I had a very real possibility of becoming seriously ill with the virus.

Jo was not happy that I had been sent home without seeing anyone and that no PCR swab had been done to get full confirmation of my positive Covid result. She said that I needed to be referred to receive anti-viral medication at West Suffolk Hospital as quickly as possible and it was an emergency. Jo began making emails and phone calls behind the scenes while I waited to hear from the doctor and for the news regarding my anti-viral treatment.

At about 4:00pm, I received a phone call from Dr. U. I

would have seen him in clinic that day, and he had actually tried to find me in the isolation room, expecting my appointment to be face-to-face, not realising I had been sent home. He wanted to know more about how I was feeling with Covid and told me that while he thought I'd be fine, I needed to get my anti-viral treatment as soon as possible. He remembered the trouble I had gone through to get anti-viral treatments the first time round, when I was referred from Ipswich to Bury to Bristol, back to Ipswich, only for Cambridge to reject me in the end. The doctor said that if I was denied the treatment this time round, I needed to ask the anti-viral team to give him a call on his mobile. My doctors and nurses really wanted me to have this treatment, but I was feeling absolutely fine!

Regarding everything else in the consultation, everything was fine. I noticed that my neutrophils had gone up a bit, well above the normal range. Dr. U said that this was nothing to worry about and was as a result of the prednisolone that I was taking for my GvHD. White blood cells cling to the blood vessels, but for some reason, steroids cause them to fall into the bloodstream. Therefore, I still had the same amount of my white blood cells in my body, and my bone marrow wasn't being overactive, they were just showing up more in my blood. I told the doctor that my GvHD had mostly cleared up, but there was still a bit of a rash, to which he replied that I should keep going with the creams and my steroid doses. Hopefully, when I'd get reviewed in clinic face-to-face the next week, we would be able to think about weaning me off the steroids.

Back to my Covid treatment, Dr. U reiterated that it was important that I had it. He told me that as it was a Friday, everything would be closing for the weekend so there was a bit of a rush. I was told to give it another hour, and if I heard nothing from the anti-viral team, I needed to call the haematology helpline and Jo to chase it up.

I called the haematology helpline an hour later as I had heard nothing. I was sick from Covid and just wanted to rest. It was so annoying having to make phone call after phone call tracking the medication down! I was feeling ill from the virus but my symptoms were nowhere near severe, and I just wanted to be left alone. When ordinary people get Covid, they're allowed to rest. I just get constant phone calls because of my vulnerability, and I found myself getting very stressed and worked up about it! The helpline nurse agreed with me that I needed to get the medication soon but didn't know what she was supposed to do about it. For something that was such an emergency, they didn't make the process easy. I thought this treatment was more hassle than it was worth. I was going to be absolutely fine!

It was about 6:00pm when I finally heard from the Covid Medicine Delivery Unit (CMDU) at West Suffolk Hospital in Bury St. Edmunds. I spoke to the doctor, who wanted to know how many days post-transplant I was and wanted to know every single medication I was taking. He said that I was eligible for treatment but as it was now officially the weekend and they were closing their department, they didn't know when I'd hear from them.

"You will have to come to West Suffolk Hospital to spend a couple of hours with us for an anti-viral injection. You will get a phone call either later today, tomorrow, or the next day. Thank you, bye."

If it was that much of an emergency, then why did they close their department on the weekends?

The weekend passed and I still had not heard anything. My Covid symptoms had improved massively though. I was struggling to get rid of the remaining snot in my nose, as this bout with Covid had also affected my nose, but my cough and shortness of breath had cleared. In fact, I even managed a two hour walk in the woods!

On Monday morning, I received a call from the CMDU at West Suffolk. They made it seem as if it was my choice whether I wanted the antibody treatment or not. Since I had been feeling so much better, and also remembering my first battle with Covid when I was denied the treatment because my symptoms were improving, I thought I'd pass on the treatment. Once again, if it was that urgent, they would have told me to come in, not giving me the option. Anyway, I was home alone and had no one to take me to the hospital that day, so that was also a deciding factor.

I had made a huge mistake though, and when Jo asked if I had received my treatment over the weekend, she was not happy with my response. First of all, she said that rather than Monday, I should have had it at the weekend, so she was quite unhappy about that. Also, she said that even if my symptoms had improved, there were cases where patients thought they were improving and said no to the treatment but ended up becoming very sick. Therefore, she phoned the CMDU and got me referred back straight away to receive my anti-viral medication as soon as possible. Dr. U eventually gave the CMDU a call to tell them that it was essential that I had the treatment.

On Monday evening, I received a phone call from the same doctor who had called me Friday evening. I could tell he wasn't happy with me for messing the department around, but I was only doing what I thought was right. I find it very difficult under pressure, and because I had very little information about what this treatment was and had been let down the first time I had caught Covid, I genuinely believed it was more hassle than it was worth and would have preferred to risk becoming ill with the virus. To improve the system, I think all vulnerable patients should be given an information sheet with all potential options and the important details regarding anti-viral treatment for Covid, rather than having to phone lots of different numbers and useless people to track down medicine you know nothing about.

"We tried to get hold of you, but you didn't come in for your treatment today. You are in our most vulnerable category of patients, so we will aim for you to be our first patient tomorrow. Thank you, bye," said the doctor.

I tried to ask what this medication was and what it involved, but he put the phone down on me as soon as I tried to speak. I don't think he was happy that I had unintentionally got the CMDU in trouble with a potential complaint!

I attended the CMDU at West Suffolk Hospital on Tuesday 28th June at 10:00am. Because I was going to be spending the morning on a Covid ward, of course I wouldn't be allowed to have anyone with me, and I had to find the department myself. It was quite easy as I could access it from outside. I rang the doorbell and the receptionist let me in. I didn't have to say my name; she knew who I was as she had been expecting me.

The CMDU was very modern, and I'm guessing it had been built very recently to accommodate the fairly new virus. The technology, such as the obs machine, was so much more advanced than Addenbrooke's. Ward C9 was still using manual blood pressure machines or the same electronic machines as Ward C2 had used in 2016, but the CMDU's looked like iPads!

The receptionist warned me that I would be staying on a bay with other Covid-positive patients. She assured me that I'd be as safe as possible and that there would be barriers put up. Hearing the coughs and the breathing from some of these patients, I did wonder whether the receptionist thought I really needed to be there! I looked well, just casually walking into my bedspace with my backpack, and sat on the chair. The other patients looked like they were on their last breath and sounded like they were dying! Most of them were elderly women who snored really loud. There was one woman in her thirties, who was having trouble because her daughter had got kicked off the school bus, and since she was in hospital, she couldn't get her daughter to school. It was quite interesting hearing that conversation. I was the only nineteen-year-old male on the bay. I was questioning to what I extent I really needed the treatment, but the nurses were really welcoming.

The nurse sat me down and said she would be with me shortly to take my obs. Quickly after, I met the doctor, who wanted to know my allergies. Because I was under Addenbrooke's and not West Suffolk, my details had not been transferred. I explained that I was allergic to ciclosporin, ambisome, and magnesium sulphate, and described my symptoms, but the doctor wasn't overly concerned. After the doctor visited, a phlebotomist arrived to put a cannula in me. I hate cannulas! She was very quick, and it seemed to be a running theme on the CMDU that the phlebotomists were the best because I was constantly hearing praise about them. She was very good!

Once my cannula was in, the nurse did a set of obs just to check that everything was generally good. She then explained the procedure. This would be an ordinary half an hour IV infusion through a cannula, as I'd had many times. The drug was called sotrovimab, and its purpose was to help my body create antibodies against Covid to reduce my chance of hospitalisation or death from the virus. Covid anti-viral drugs had been found to be very effective in reducing hospitalisations for the vulnerable, and for vulnerable patients like myself, it was the protocol for me to receive anti-viral medication whether it was felt it was needed or not. Obs were going to be every fifteen minutes while the sotrovimab was being infused, then I needed to sit and wait for an hour to be observed, then once that hour was up, I had to have a final set of obs before being discharged. The regular obs was to check for any potential reactions, as if I felt out of the ordinary then the infusion would have to be stopped.

I was absolutely fine during the infusion and just sat there, preparing for my meeting with the Teenage Cancer Trust the next day. I got in touch with the charity again, wanting to write a piece related to my relapse and ways of coping. I spent my two hours in the CMDU department obsessively scribbling away in my notebook, trying to formulate my story in as few words as possible. It was pretty much an entire summary of Chapter 13 from this book. Writing with a cannula in your right arm is quite painful, but I wasn't going to waste valuable time!

I was back testing negative for Covid a couple of days after my visit to the CMDU, and while it took a few days to get rid of my excess snot, I did feel a little bit of improvement with the anti-viral drug. My lungs felt clearer and fresher, and I was no longer coughing up any green mucus. Maybe it was worth having the medicine after all, despite the hassle!

***

On Friday 1st July (Day 69), I still had to attend the isolation clinic. Although I had been testing negative at home, the hospital had no proof of this, so I had to stay isolated. I also saw Dr. U face-to-face, though he had to be in full PPE before he could enter the room.

Dr. U congratulated me on finally getting my Covid anti-viral medication! He said he understood why I initially said no, and a lot of people would have done the same, which made me feel better. However, he did say that regardless of what I would have said, he wanted me to have the treatment anyway because there was a chance I'd become very sick with the virus, as Jo had warned me about over the telephone after I initially rejected the medicine.

He was a little disappointed to hear that I was struggling to keep on top of my creams for my GvHD but said that he understood that it was a tiring process. Looking at my arms and the side of my body, he could definitely tell that the prednisolone was working, and therefore my GvHD was moved back from Grade II to Grade I. The doctor decided to wean me off my steroids. I had been taking eight tablets once a day, but from Saturday I would take six for a week. If all continued to go well, starting Saturdays I would go down to four, then two, then one. Although undecided, I may have had to have five alternate days of taking one steroid tablet, just to give me a softer landing. Everything GvHD-wise was going in the right direction, although he asked that I start to get back into my creams more seriously as sometimes lowering the steroid dose can cause the rash to come back.

I was slightly concerned about my platelet levels from my blood tests the previous week. I was noticing that they were going down. My platelets were 120 on this day, which was below the normal range of 150 to 370. Dr. U wasn't too concerned and told me not to jump to any conclusions just yet. He said that there was an association between thrombocytopenia and GvHD, and also, I was taking Co-Trimoxazole Forte, which was known for suppressing blood counts. We were just going to have to keep an eye on it, and I was due for a bone marrow biopsy at the end of the month anyway for my 100-day restaging, where we hoped for a complete remission.

***

On Friday 8th July (Day 76), I was still attending the isolation clinic. This was because the hospital still had no proof that I was negative for Covid, even though I had been testing negative at home for a week. They finally did a PCR swab on me on this day, and the test came back negative! I would be allowed on Ward C9 for bloods and dressing changes the next week!

I saw Dr. U in the isolation clinic again. Once again, I was concerned about my worsening thrombocytopenia as my platelets had fallen to 96. Dr. U still wasn't really concerned though, just reiterating what he had said the week before. He was pleased to hear that I had my bone marrow biopsy booked on the Ward C9 day unit for Thursday 28th July anyway, so if there was anything to worry about then this would pick it up.

He was pleased to hear that my GvHD had further improved and that I was beginning to put my creams on more seriously and regularly. The go ahead was given to further reduce my steroid tablets, and I was from then on to take four prednisolone tablets a day for the next week.

Dr. U also saw the piece that I had written for the Teenage Cancer Trust in my meeting with them the previous week. The piece hadn't been published yet as there was no plan for it at the moment, with it being so long that the charity was working out potential ways they could split it into multiple projects. But they always shared their stories with the hospital first, and Dr. U got to read it. He congratulated me and said that I write well. He said that he remembered very well the absolutely horrible consultation of December 17th, 2021, but he was glad to see me out on the other side, and we had evidence that my new immune system was working and doing its job. This was the first time that I had told him about my book, and he said that it would be very helpful for people going through something similar.

The plan of action was to just continue as I had been, which involved being weaned off my steroids and keeping to the doses of my previous medications, including the tacrolimus. Carrying on just seemed to be the way to go. When he asked if I had any questions, I did have a couple.

First of all, I noticed my magnesium was well within the normal range of 0.70 to 1. My magnesium levels the previous week were 0.81. Dr. U said that if my levels were 0.75 that day, then I'd be able to decrease my oral supplement dose from two sachets a day to one. My test results that day showed that my magnesium was 0.83, and I was able to reduce my magnesium dose!

And most importantly, I noticed that my haemoglobin was coming up. The standard range is 135 to 172, and I noticed that the previous week mine was 131. On Friday 8th July, my haemoglobin officially reached 137, which meant I was no longer anaemic. My ten-month battle with anaemia had finally come to an end. I didn't actually realise that I had been anaemic since October 2021, as it had been so mild and I was feeling so well that the doctors were not really concerned (they were just worried about my steady white blood cell decline). Still, for someone who was so anaemic, I surprised myself when realising I had managed to go two months averaging 15,000 to 20,000 steps a day, travelling to university, and doing so much overtime at work! Then, of course, when I started chemotherapy, my red blood cells declined as expected but never recovered to the standard range as they are the slowest blood cells to recover. Therefore, I had gone ten straight months of having low amounts of oxygen in my blood, and finally the struggle was over!

In fact, I was starting to get out and about a lot more, and I had been managing to go on lots of long walks. I found that having a long walk the day before my daily blood tests boosted my haemoglobin.

I asked Dr. U, since I was no longer anaemic, if I could resume driving lessons. His concern wasn't so much my energy levels, just more about my immune system and me being in close proximity with someone who could potentially have Covid. But he also understood that he didn't want to restrict me so much that it affected my psychological well-being. So, he reluctantly gave me the go-ahead to resume my driving lessons, which meant that the first of my three post-transplant goals were complete. He made it clear that I needed to try to avoid Covid at all costs, so if I was going to relearn to drive, I'd have to wear a mask, drive with the windows open, and use lots of alcohol gel.

My second post-transplant goal was to finish Year 2 of university with a 1st. The day before, I had submitted my final assignment for the year, for which I needed to achieve a mid-2:1 just to scrape the 70% needed for a 1st. I just had to hope that my results later in the month would achieve this and I'd be on my way to achieving Goal 2!

I did want to ask Dr. U about the removal of my Hickman line. Removing my line would also ensure Goal 3 of returning to work. Because September was my ultimate goal for returning to work, I decided to hold off on asking the doctor about my line. I got the feeling he was very reluctant about letting me drive again, and I didn't want to appear too pushy!

***

On Monday 11th July, I was sat at home, having a normal day, until I received a call from the receptionist at the haematology and oncology outpatients department. The receptionist informed me that I had been booked in for a flexible sigmoidoscopy at the endoscopy department for the next day, Tuesday 12th July, for 2:20pm. I was supposed to have this a few weeks ago but catching Covid meant that it had to be postponed. The receptionist told me that as it was such short notice, she was guessing it was 'urgent', and I didn't get much choice whether I'd be able to make the date or not – I had to do it.

She told me that there was prep for the procedure and asked if I could make it into hospital that day to pick it up for the procedure the next day. I was home alone as both my parents and Kristy were at work, which meant there was no way I could get down to Addenbrooke's. The receptionist said that a courier would bring my prep instead, saving me a journey.

I almost missed the courier because he arrived during my afternoon nap. While it was so much easier receiving medications via post and not having to stand in the pharmacy for hours, I was annoyed by how I had to constantly sign for these medications. Most of the time when they arrived, I was not in or it was so early in the morning that I was asleep, and they had gone before I realised there was a knock at the door! Thankfully, I realised the courier was stood outside the door and I was able to collect my prep.

The prep was brutal! For the procedure to be most effective, it is important to ensure the bowels are completely empty, hence the purpose of the prep. Firstly, you're usually given seven days to prepare for a flexible sigmoidoscopy. I was given twenty-four hours. In these seven days, you're supposed to stop medication used to control diarrhoea. I had been taking budesonide to control my frequent bowel movements, and it had actually been working, reducing the number of times I was going to about two to three times a day. Unaware of the next day's procedure, I had taken my budesonide on the Monday morning.

Next, to prepare for the procedure, I had to change my diet. Thinking it was a normal day, I was looking forward to what I could make myself for lunch. Then, the receptionist called and sprung upon me the news that I needed a procedure. I was disappointed to be restricted on a diet of biscuits and white bread for the Monday morning. After a light lunch on Monday, I was then forbidden to consume anything other than clear fluids until after my procedure on Tuesday afternoon. I was told on the appointment letter that I had to expect to be in the endoscopy department for up to four hours, which meant I potentially wouldn't eat again until roughly 7:00pm on Tuesday evening. That wasn't going to be easy!

If the prep sounds nasty already, it gets worse. After surviving the rest of the day on nothing but water, at 7:00pm on Monday evening, I had to consume 500 ml of Plenvu solution. Plenvu was a laxative. This worked by turning the stools in my bowels into water to flush and cleanse the bowel, ensuring an empty bowel for the procedure. The solution was mango flavoured, but it still had a thick, salty, medicine taste to it, which made it very unpleasant to drink. Consuming 500 ml of it in thirty minutes was very difficult to do.

The laxative solution took a while to go through my system, and I didn't have my first bowel movement until about two hours later at 9:00pm. But then, it really started to hit me, and the laxatives worked like dynamite! I was constantly on the toilet seat. I emptied my bowels and flushed the toilet three times in just one visit to the bathroom! I hardly got any sleep that night, and I even had to sleep downstairs in the living room just because it was the closest room to the toilet. While the laxatives hadn't completely exited my system, my bowel movements became less frequent by about 3:00am, and I enjoyed about three hours of sleep.

Three hours of sleep was all I got because the intensive prep still wasn't complete! If my bowels had not been torn apart by the 500 ml of laxatives the night before, it was time to consume another 500 ml! This time the Plenvu was fruit punch flavoured. I still hadn't recovered from the laxatives from the night before, and now, a further 500 ml over half an hour had entered into my system.

Tuesday morning was absolutely brutal. I hadn't had anything to eat, only consuming clear fluids, as the prep required, and I was feeling very sick as a result of the laxative solution. It didn't help that the UK was in the middle of a heatwave either! I was emptying my bowels every half an hour. I was going so powerfully that my bowels could have flushed the toilet! This, combined with constant wiping, made my bum very sore. While it was not as bad as chemotherapy, it definitely brought back some memories!

By about 12:00pm, while the laxatives still hadn't left my system, I was opening my bowels less frequently, as had happened at 3:00am that morning. By this point, my stools were no longer brown; they were as clear as water. The laxatives had really done its job at bowel cleansing.

My appointment was at 2:20pm, and as I needed to be there half an hour before my appointment, an hour drive plus traffic meant that I needed to leave for the hospital by 12:30pm. The journey, while not as bad as I thought it would be, was still uncomfortable, and I was suffering from stomach cramps. Luckily, my newly acquired disabled parking space meant that Mum and I could park easily and I could arrive at the endoscopy department and use their toilet as soon as possible.

I thought I was smart and knew where I was going. On the appointment letter, I saw 'Level 3 Outpatients'. Being a regular in the ultrasound department when I'd had my giant groin swelling, I thought I was an expert on the hospital's third floor and thought I could find the endoscopy department easily. I ended up taking Mum and I the complete wrong way and, about to have an accident at any moment, we ended up walking to the complete opposite end of the hospital to where the department was!

After an entire lap around the hospital, I finally arrived at the endoscopy department. Mum wasn't allowed to accompany me for this procedure, so she had to go to concourse to have lunch while I attended my appointment alone. I couldn't wait to get checked in at the front desk so I could go into the waiting room and find a bathroom as soon as possible. But the endoscopy department was quick, and I got called into a room before I even had the chance to sit down!

I met a nurse who went over the procedure with me. A flexible sigmoidoscopy would involve sticking a camera up my back passage. What they were looking for was any abnormalities, particularly trying to diagnose GvHD of the bowel. They were also going to cut off a couple samples of my bowel to test in the lab, which could investigate whether I had GvHD of the gut or not. I then went through the consent forms with the nurse, who warned me of the risks. The only risk was a bit of bleeding afterwards, and it was a relatively safe procedure, although I was warned that it would be quite uncomfortable.

I told the nurse that I was desperate for the toilet and that the prep had really messed me up. She told me not to worry because I was about to be directed into a room that had a toilet.

The nurse took me to a room for me to get changed into a hospital gown for my procedure.

Once again, the endoscopy department was quick! I was relieving myself in the bathroom when the nurse spoke to me through the door to see if I was okay. To be honest, I wasn't, as my frequent bowel movements had made my bum very sore and the toilet tissue was covered in blood. The nurse said that they were ready for me. I hadn't even had a chance to sit in the waiting room – I was very impressed! *I might not be here for four hours*, I thought.

As soon as I came out of the bathroom, another nurse greeted me. She told me that the patient scheduled before me was not ready, so they had pushed my appointment forward to get me seen sooner. I was very happy! The nurse walked with me to the room where the procedure would take place. I said that I still hadn't recovered from the prep and thought I needed to go to the toilet to empty my bowels again.

"Don't worry, we have a machine that will suck everything up. You won't have an accident," she reassured me.

I arrived in the treatment room, where I met the surgeon and another nurse. The second nurse showed me how to use the gas and air, which was always offered to me during my bone marrow biopsies. Gas and air are used to calm yourself during a procedure, although I had never used it. She made me take a deep breath into a tube to make sure it was working properly. She recommended that I not use too much of it and only breathe into it when needed.

The surgeon then asked me to lie on my left side and lift my knees up to my abdomen. He asked me to lower my underpants.

"Just examining your rectum," he said as he began to feel the area.

Then, with hardly any warning, he stuck what felt like a massive stick up my rectum. It was the camera. I think the cold ultrasound jelly was on it. It felt like a massive ultrasound stick getting inserted into my back passage. It was very uncomfortable. I didn't know how far he was sticking the camera up me, but I felt a terrible pain in my abdomen, almost as if it was being torn apart. The feeling was a combination of cramping and having something being poked around in my tummy.

I was relieved when the surgeon said, "We've gone as far as we need to go."

He began the process of removing the camera, and my body soon returned to a more comfortable feeling.

I was then shocked when he said, "Other side!"

He stuck the camera far into my bowel again, and the abdominal pain was excruciating!

I guess I should have been breathing in my gas and air, as recommended by one of the accompanying nurses. But the surgeons and nurses were so fascinated by their newly working HD camera and the images they were finding of my bowel on the TV monitor that I actually ended up watching the TV with them! It was so fascinating to see the inside of my body in colour and in HD! My bowels looked very fascinating, and I wasn't sure if I was intrigued or disgusted to see the clear fluid from the laxatives being sucked out. I did notice that my bowels seemed to have a red rash on them.

"Wow, I love what I'm picking up with my new HD camera!" said the surgeon, almost doing a little bit of a dance while I had a super massive camera shoved into my bum.

"We need music in here!" said the nurse.

They were all so excited about what they were finding. It seems as if every doctor or surgeon had some fascination with my procedures. I remembered the biopsy on my groin on February 18th, 2022.

"Right, all done," said the surgeon. "Bowels are okay, a bit red. We have a sample, and we will see what the results are and if your problems are caused by GvHD."

I was wheeled to recovery by the two accompanying nurses. Because I wasn't sedated during the procedure, I was allowed to go home as soon as my obs were done and a nurse had returned with my report for the procedure. My obs were fine and the nurse offered me a hot drink, which I kindly declined. I was just desperate to get out of the department.

The nurse went through my discharge notes with me. She said that my bowels were abnormally red, which could be attributed to diet, stress, medication, or something else. Whether it was a result of GvHD would take three to five weeks to come back from the lab, and I was told that Dr. U would be the one that would inform me of the results. She then gave me permission to get changed out of my hospital gown and into my normal clothes, and then I could get up and leave as soon as I was ready.

Mum was very surprised to see me out of my surgery so quickly, both of us expecting four hours. I was in the endoscopy department for an hour and a half maximum. I was very impressed by how quickly I was seen!

I was so happy to be able to treat myself to a massive meal as soon as I got home, where I ate a plate of chicken wings. The next day, I treated myself to a massive Chinese takeaway with my friends. Unfortunately, the laxatives took a while to exit my system and I still had pretty bad diarrhoea by the time of my Friday 15th July consultation with Dr. U.

***

On Friday 15th July (Day 83), I was finally back on the Ward C9 day unit for blood tests and a dressing change after having to spend three weeks in the isolation clinic. You could have a bone marrow transplant and recover fully by the time the hospital lets you be free of Covid!

Following my visit to C9, I was back down to the main clinic in the haematology and oncology outpatients department, where Mum and I saw Dr. U.

I hadn't been feeling well for a few days. Overall, I was just in a low and deflated mood as a result of the steroids. They hadn't just affected me mentally, but physically too. Because of my relapse in December, I had now been extra cautious when viewing my full blood count, and I was often terrified to receive my results. If one number was too high or too low, I would automatically panic. Unlike the aftermath of my first diagnosis, I had a lot of anxiety over my health after my relapse.

I went into the appointment with the idea that I was going to receive bad news, and to begin with, I thought that that was the way it was going.

Dr. U observed his computer with my blood results and said, "Have we sorted out a date for your bone marrow biopsy yet?"

He noted that my platelets had dropped again, to 80. My thrombocytopenia was worsening. Once again, he said that it was just something to keep an eye on. He reassured me not to jump to any conclusions as he was aware that I was taking Co-Trimoxazole Forte, which is known for suppressing blood counts. He told me that after a transplant, it was normal to have things like this happen, and as I was having a bone marrow biopsy soon anyway, it would be investigated. I was slightly reassured by what he had to say, but I did have my reservations just because we thought that my mysterious neutropenia from

October to December 2021 could be resolved, but it ended up being something very serious. It was just proof of how much anxiety my relapse had caused me.

Another issue with my bloods was that Dr. U noticed that I had macrocytosis, which is where red blood cells are larger than average. Once again, they discovered this while trying to work out why I was neutropenic the previous year. While macrocytosis isn't a medical condition in itself, having it can be a sign of an underlying blood condition, which in my case happened to be leukaemia the previous year. The doctor put this down to likely being a folate or vitamin B12 deficiency, and he booked these to be tested on that day's blood test. When my results came through on MyChart at 6:00pm, it was confirmed that I was deficient in these.

I was also having problems with my skin. I had grown spots on my face, upper arms, and back. I originally thought this was acne caused by the steroids, but Dr. U said it looked a lot like something else and it was actually a mild bacterial infection. I also noticed that I was experiencing pain in my toes, and it turned out that both of my big toes were infected. The doctor assured me that these types of infections were also very common. I was prescribed an antibacterial steroid cream for my spots and an antibiotic, called flucloxacillin, for my toes.

Once all these issues were out of the way, my consultation with the doctor was actually a lot more positive. He once again told me to not jump to any conclusions regarding my bloods, considering my neutrophils were normal. He was also glad to see an improvement in my skin GvHD-wise and gave me the go ahead to continue weaning my steroids down to only two tablets a day. He also said that my magnesium was sustaining itself on just one supplement sachet a day, and in fact, I could think about coming off the supplements completely but keeping them stored away just in case I needed them in the future.

I had developed a lump on the back of my neck, which Dr. U told me was a result of the steroids and was not anything to worry about. He said that the steroids would change my body shape, but once I was off them for good, I would reverse back to normal. Mum was also concerned about my mood as I had been feeling low and quite short-tempered. The doctor said that it could have been the steroids as they are known to affect mood, but in general it was completely normal for someone to feel that way after a transplant. He said I just needed to go easy on myself, and while it was completely normal, it didn't mean that I didn't need help and that if my mood worsened I needed to let the hospital know.

Overall, what the doctor had to say was very good news, despite my terrible feeling about that day's consultation.

On a finishing note, I did ask him when I could think about getting my Hickman line removed. Dr. U said that I would still be having blood tests once a week, so it depended on how good my veins were for bleeding. He said that I should have my bloods taken peripherally for my appointment the next week, and if there were no problems, he'd get my specialist nurse, Jo, to book me in for a Hickman line removal! I was hopeful I'd pass my trial!

***

Friday 22nd July 2022 (Day 90). I attended Ward C9 for my weekly dressing change and blood test. I asked the nurse to take my bloods peripherally, as requested by Dr. U the previous week, and I ended up passing the vein test! I hoped that this would mean the doctor would give me the go ahead to get my

Hickman line removed!

Following my appointment on C9, and a quick stop to Costa in the hospital concourse, it was straight to the haematology and oncology outpatients department. As soon as I signed in, I was called in straight away to have my obs taken. For some reason, my blood pressure was on the high side. The nurse wrote my blood pressure down on a piece of paper and told me to show the doctor and ask her about it in the consultation.

After waiting for a while in the waiting room, we were called in by the doctor. It was a new doctor we saw. She was the BMT clinical fellow and referred to herself as the 'random Australian'. Mum and I liked the random Australian as she was a very reassuring and supportive doctor, who went through all our concerns with us.

Firstly, I showed the doctor the piece of paper with my blood pressure on. The random Australian said that she had been getting pieces of paper with high blood pressures on all day, and by the looks of it, she had a collection of them on her desk. She told me not to worry, as 140/91 wasn't actually as alarming as it may seem, though the preferred range for blood pressure should be about 120/80. The reason for my high blood pressure was probably as a result of the immunosuppressant medication I was taking, as it is known to increase blood pressure. Also, it probably didn't help that one of the hospital lifts were out of order and I had to climb nine flights of stairs to get to my C9 appointment earlier that day. I was also very stressed about my appointment, due to my concerns about my ongoing thrombocytopenia and my upcoming bone marrow aspiration, scheduled for Thursday 28th July. Exercise and stress can contribute to high blood pressure.

The random Australian then did a thorough examination,

making sure I was doing well health-wise. My heart and lungs sounded fine, and my mouth looked healthy. She noticed I had a few spots on my arms, which I had been prescribed creams for the previous week. On the whole, she was very happy that my GvHD seemed to have cleared up, and she gave me the go ahead to wean my steroid dose down to one tablet (5 mg) once a day for the next seven days. My toe infection still hadn't cleared up, even with the seven-day course of the antibiotic, flucloxacillin, so my course was extended to a full ten days, in the hope that there would be some improvement. Overall, I looked very well, and the doctor was very impressed with my progress.

Unfortunately, the doctor had not received my blood test results, but was concerned that if there was something that I needed, she didn't want me to go home only to be called back in. Therefore, she told me to pick up my medications from the pharmacy, get some food or drink, and go for a walk, then return to the waiting room when Mum and I were ready. She'd then catch us in there and speak to me about my blood test results once she had received them.

Mum and I waited about forty-five minutes in the pharmacy and ate some cake outside before returning to the waiting room at roughly 11:30am. The random Australian spotted us and discussed my blood test results back in the consultation room.

The doctor wasn't concerned at all. She knew that I was worried about my platelet counts, so she addressed this first. The bad news was that my platelets had indeed dropped again. They were now 67, down from the previous week's 80.

The random Australian reassured me that this was okay though. While she strongly advised against me going skydiving or riding horses anytime soon, she said at 67, she'd let me have surgery if I needed it. When platelet counts go below 150, thrombocytopenia is split into mild (100-150), moderate (50-100), and severe (0-50). While my platelets were dropping, they were still in the same range as the previous week, and as blood tests are taken as samples, there was a possibility that another blood test sample could have picked up a higher number of platelets. While it was a low level, 67 was still a safe count. I was told that the doctors really start to worry when the platelet count reaches 20. Therefore, for now, my thrombocytopenia was just something to keep an eye on.

In terms of explaining what the thrombocytopenia could be, she once again reiterated what Dr. U had said about me taking Co-Trimoxazole Forte, which was known to suppress blood counts. She also repeated what Dr. U had said about there being an association between GvHD and thrombocytopenia. I also learned another interesting fact, which could be attributed to thrombocytopenia: viral infections. When looking at my previous blood test results, the random Australian noted that my platelets were 152 before Covid, and the fall of my platelets coincided with my infection. She told me that even in healthy people, viral infections lower the platelets to levels even lower than mine currently were. The only reason why healthy people don't panic as much as leukaemia patients is because they don't realise that they're suffering from thrombocytopenia as their bloods aren't checked weekly like mine. Since I was a BMT patient, there was a possibility that my bone marrow was struggling to bounce back up and make a recovery. All three of these reasons could potentially have been working in combination to destroy my platelet cells.

To further reassure me, the random Australian reviewed the rest of my bloods. Firstly, I was her only patient that day who had a healthy kidney function. My neutrophils were completely normal at 3.33, although I did note that for a while, my white blood cells had been on the lower side. My battle with anaemia had come to an end a couple of weeks before, but it was now back, with my haemoglobin being 133. This wasn't exactly a bad thing though and was more of a fluctuation rather than a sign that my haemoglobin was in decline. My red blood cell count was still low, but they still hadn't recovered from all the chemotherapy I had endured. Therefore, my thrombocytopenia was the only real concern from my blood tests, and the doctor wasn't even concerned about that, rather she just wanted to keep it under review.

My platelets would potentially stand in my way on one issue though. I asked the random Australian if she would approve the removal of my Hickman line. She seemed a bit reluctant. There was a two-week waiting list for my line to be removed, as it couldn't be removed on the ward like a PICC, because a Hickman line is more central in the body. If I had my Hickman line removed on this day, it would be fine. But because of the downward trend of my platelets, in two weeks' time, it may not have been considered safe to have my line removed due to my risk of excessive bleeding and internal bleeding. Also, if my platelets reached lower than 10, then it'd be best to keep my line in, in case I became dependent on platelet transfusions. The doctor made a deal with me that she would book me in for a Hickman line removal in two weeks, but I needed to understand that this might not happen and there was a possibility that it would have to be pushed back. Usually, I would have celebrated the news that my line was potentially getting removed, but I had a feeling that my line removal wouldn't happen. At least I had passed my vein test earlier that day, so I knew I was capable of surviving needles.

The random Australian then moved onto the topic of my upcoming bone marrow biopsy. She told me what they were actually looking for when doing the biopsy. Firstly, they wanted to make sure that all of my leukaemia was gone, and they did this by looking for any remaining leukaemia cells under the microscope. These results would take up to forty-eight hours to come back. They would also put my bone marrow sample in a machine to check for minimal residual disease (MRD), where they hoped I'd be MRD negative. This test usually took about a couple of weeks to receive the results. If I was MRD positive, this meant there was still leukaemia hiding in my bone marrow that not even the most powerful microscopes could detect, and my chances of relapse would be considerably high. In this case, they'd think about giving me something called a donor lymphocyte infusion, which would essentially involve giving me more of Dad's stem cells to help my new immune system recognise a cancer cell and attack it. Speaking of topping me up with Dad's stem cells, there was also a chance they would have to do it anyway. The bone marrow biopsy would also carry out a chimerism test. Although this is often carried out through blood tests, which had shown my blood as 100% donor cells on Day 30, the bone marrow is more sensitive to this type of test. Therefore, to ensure that I was as much of my dad, and not me, as possible, there was a chance I would need a top-up of Dad's stem cells if my chimerism wasn't high enough.

Of course, because of my thrombocytopenia, Thursday's bone marrow biopsy would investigate this too. The random Australian told me that the cells in the bone marrow that produced platelets were called megakaryocytes. If there were a sufficient number of megakaryocytes in my bone marrow, then there would be less reason to worry as it would show that the bone marrow was trying to produce platelets and something could be done to stimulate their growth. However, if there was not a sufficient number of megakaryocytes, then the doctors would have to look into this.

On the whole, the random Australian reassured me that all was still going well. She could tell there was something still on my mind and that I wasn't 100% reassured, and she tried to get me to open up. I think I just had my reservations about everything just because of what had happened with my neutrophil decline the previous year. I was initially told not to worry, but I'd ended up becoming very sick, and I did fear that the leukaemia was making a comeback. I was definitely growing more anxious, and my relapse had definitely affected me mentally. Quite often I was very stressed, depressed, and worried about everything, and my bone marrow biopsy had been on my mind for weeks.

She told me that was completely understandable, and the anxiety of my 100-day bone marrow aspiration was always going to be there. The random Australian was a fan of distractions and told me to watch lots of shows on Netflix over the coming days to take my mind off the upcoming biopsy. Though, having just moved from Australia, she admitted that she hadn't seen many British shows so was having trouble recommending any. She made it clear how important it was that I didn't catch Covid again before my biopsy, as that would delay it. Because I was worried, it was important that I got my biopsy out of the way as soon as possible so I didn't have to worry about it for much longer. I was therefore advised to stay at home as much as possible for the next week, although she understood that the whole purpose of my transplant was to enjoy my life. She said that had Covid not existed, I would have been approaching a much more normal stage in my transplant journey by now.

Mum also asked if I would require future bone marrow biopsies after my 100-day one. The doctor said that this was consultant driven. While I shouldn't expect to have bone marrow aspirations every three months, some consultants liked to carry them out at twelve months. It depended on the consultant's opinion, and it would ultimately be Dr. U who would make that decision for me in the future, though the 100-day restaging biopsy was mandatory. I found this interesting, as back in 2016, I was told that the leukaemia was most likely gone after my transplant and a biopsy at any point after was unnecessary.

The random Australian was very helpful and said that if I had any more questions or concerns to just email Jo, who would notify her to give me a call. She further emphasised that I was still doing well and wished me luck for my bone marrow the next Thursday. Following the consultation, I was allowed home and returned to the car park, ready to go.

As soon as I got in the car, Mum received a call from Jo. She wanted me to return to Ward C9!

No, I thought, *I was so close to escaping!*

Jo was following up on my blood tests the previous week, which had found my Vitamin B12 deficiency. My Vitamin B12 levels were found to be very low. The standard range for B12 is between 211 and 911, but my level was 150. Jo said that the doctors believed that the reason why my bloods were dropping was because my Vitamin B12 was low, and in fact, there was an association between B12 deficiency and thrombocytopenia, neutropenia, and anaemia. Articles online suggest that a B12 deficiency is known to mimic leukaemia, and also, when diagnosing leukaemia, it is important to rule out a B12 deficiency first. It had been established that my platelets were very low, and while still in the normal range, it was also clear that my white blood cells and red blood cells had been on the decline.

I should also mention that symptoms of a B12 deficiency include depression, irritability, diarrhoea, difficulty walking and moving around, and pins and needles. All of these symptoms I had been experiencing for quite some time. Was fixing my B12 deficiency the answer to my problems?

I got out of the car, and it was off to C9. I required a B12 injection that afternoon, then I'd have to return to the Ward C9 day unit the following Monday and Thursday (the same day as my biopsy) for another injection. This was in addition to my Friday clinic appointment. This meant that I was now having to attend the hospital three days a week, which was a set-back for me, but I was hoping this would only be temporary.

The injections would hopefully boost my B12 levels to help my platelets increase and stop my red and white blood cells from dropping. It would also hopefully bring the surface area of my red blood cells back to the standard range, fixing the macrocytosis, as discussed the previous week with Dr. U, as there was a common association between this and B12 and folate deficiencies.

Because of the short notice, the ward hadn't stocked any B12, so I had to wait in the day unit for quite a while until my injection was collected from the pharmacy. Rosie gave me my injection on C9 as she had been helping out in the day unit. It went into my arm muscle, very similar to the flu jab. The colour of the injection was red, so I was told not to worry about it if it looked like I was bleeding if the injection leaked. Rosie also said that there were hardly any side effects to the injection, so there wasn't much to worry about, although if I did suddenly feel unwell then I needed to call the haematology helpline. After that, I was allowed out of the ward and was actually allowed to go home! We had arrived at the hospital early at 8:30am, expecting to be out quickly due to my early appointments, but didn't get home until 3:30pm!

***

Thursday 28th July 2022 (Day 96). I arrived on the Ward C9 day unit at 11:00am for my bone marrow biopsy. Prior to my biopsy, I had my bloods taken. There was quite a wait for my biopsy, and I received my blood test results before going. There seemed to be a glimmer of hope that the Vitamin B12 injections were working when, on the day of my bone marrow biopsy (Day 96), my platelets were 62. This was still a decline but not as big of a decline as I was used to every week.

After a wait of roughly an hour and a half, the ward doctor called me to the treatment room. This was my ninth bone marrow biopsy and the fourth I'd had while awake. Two doctors (the ward doctor and the haematology registrar) would carry out the procedure, while a nurse accompanied me for support.

The procedure would involve a bone marrow aspiration, where they took a liquid sample of my bone marrow from my hip, which would then be looked at under the microscope. This was what I was used to. Another procedure, called the trephine biopsy, was going to be carried out. This was done in my December 2021 biopsy, but the procedure wasn't really explained to me. It should have been done after my first round of chemotherapy, but because I'd had that nasty groin infection, the doctors didn't want to cause more pain to me than was necessary, so they'd just stuck to the aspiration biopsy. The trephine biopsy involved taking out a sample of my solid bone, with my bone marrow attached to it, which could then be looked at under the microscope to check for leukaemia cells.

I laid down on the bed in the foetal position as required. I pulled my shirt up and my trousers down, while lying on my side with my knees tucked as close to my chest as possible. A nurse kept hold of my leg and arm for support and said that if the pain became unbearable, I could squeeze her hand.

"Would you like to check if the gas and air is working?" asked the ward doctor.

"I've never really used it," I replied.

"Wow, okay," said the doctor, a bit surprised and taken aback.

Supervised by the haematology registrar, the ward doctor began to press down hard on the potential areas of my back where she could stick the needle. Once they had worked out where they were going to go, they injected my back with the anaesthetic needle. This was always the most painful part of the procedure as I felt the sharp needle pain in my bone. The doctor then waited a while to let the anaesthetic kick in and then proceeded to press down on my back in multiple areas to check whether I could feel the area.

Once it was clear that my back was numbed, the doctor then attempted to stick the needle in my back to retrieve the liquid sample of my bone marrow. Unfortunately, my bone marrow was dry and crusty and was being very stubborn. They couldn't get a lot out as a sample.

The haematology doctor took over from the ward doctor and repeated the anaesthetic procedure, having to choose a different location on my back.

"I remember the last time I did your biopsy you had that nasty infection in your groin, and you were limping into the treatment room," said the haematology registrar. "Has that all healed now?"

"Haha, yeah," I said.

I loved how almost six months later my groin infection was still well-remembered by even the doctors I didn't see that often. My infection really was the most famous thing on the ward at the time.

After the anaesthetic procedure was repeated and my back was numb, the doctor was able to retrieve the liquid sample of my bone marrow. It hurt a little bit, but surprisingly not as bad as my past biopsies. I think that having had nine biopsies, I was getting used to it. Even the pulling sensation on my legs, while still there, was not as painful as I was used to. In fact, I went the entire procedure completely calm and reactionless.

Once the aspiration had been completed, it was time for the trephine. This hurt a little bit but not as bad as I was expecting. Because I was facing the wall and couldn't see what the doctors were doing, I didn't know the exact procedure. What I could feel, though, was a twisting feeling, almost as if the doctor was scraping away at my bone in circular rotations.

This was the least painful bone marrow biopsy I'd had in my lifetime, yet probably one of the longest. I'd say it took roughly half an hour. The doctor said that everything was good from their end and said to leave the dressing dry for the rest of the day and the next day, and by the weekend it should be fine to peel off. I was worried about my platelets and potential prolonged bleeding. The doctor said that 62 was actually a good platelet count, and you can do bone marrow biopsies with single-figure platelet levels, which I found very interesting!

I was free to recover in my own time, and I think I surprised all the doctors and nurses when I just got straight out of my bed and put my shoes back on, ready to go. The nurse was very surprised.

"You were as cool as a cucumber!"

"I'm used to it," I said as I tied my shoelaces.

The nurse said that in the bone marrow biopsies she had previously accompanied patients for, it was the most traumatising experience for them, and she didn't understand how I had gone through all that hardly feeling any pain. I didn't deny that the biopsies were painful, but I guess I'd had so many that I knew what the procedure involved, and perhaps I was just immune to pain in that area. That could be a completely made-up theory, but even getting dressings removed during line dressing changes didn't hurt anymore, even with chest hair.

I thanked the nurse for her support, and she wished me luck for the results. The first, and scariest, result would take forty-eight hours to come back, and the rest a couple of weeks. I exited the room, completely pain free and walking normally. I did feel a bit of pain over the next couple of days as the anaesthetic wore off and my back was a bit sore, but not to the extent that the previous biopsies had brought me.

***

Friday 29th July 2022 (Day 97). I was seen by the BMT clinical fellow in my Friday consultation in clinic with the doctor.

The previous day, I was encouraged by the slightly slower decline of my platelets and thought that the Vitamin B12 injections were doing the trick in at least stabilising my counts. However, my platelets unfortunately declined to 53 from 62 in one day. I became very panicked by this as I was beginning to get very close to the severe thrombocytopenia stage.

The doctor didn't seem too concerned though. She reiterated what the random Australian had said the previous week and mentioned how platelets drop after a Covid infection, sometimes to even lower levels in healthy people. She said that they had done the bone marrow biopsy now anyway, so if there was anything concerning, she'd let me know. The main results of my biopsy were still pending, but the doctor said that she would call me either the following Monday or Tuesday with the results.

Plans for my Hickman line to be removed were cancelled. Unfortunately, my platelet count was just way too low. The doctor said that preferably, for a Hickman line removal, they liked platelets to be above 80. At 53 and declining, they didn't really want to cause me unnecessary bleeding and therefore my line had to remain for a little while longer. I was a bit deflated and depressed by this, as my big plans for my recovery and the summer most likely wouldn't be happening.

Even though my bone marrow biopsy results weren't back, the results of my flexible sigmoidoscopy were. Despite disturbance to my bowels, the procedure found no evidence of GvHD. The doctor wanted me to take this as good news, and in a way, I did. But the problem was that this left me with more questions than answers, as it didn't explain why my bowels were red. The doctor ordered some stool sample pots for me to take when I was next in clinic, which would then be looked at to investigate my ongoing bowel problems.

Finally, the rest of my blood counts were still on the lower side, despite my completed course of B12 injections. Although my blood counts hadn't made the best recovery, I was stocked up on Vitamin B12, proving the injections had worked. The standard range for B12 is 211 to 911, and mine were >2000. Now that my B12 deficiency was fixed, it was time to work on my folate deficiency. The doctor advised me to start eating more green leafy vegetables to get more folic acid absorbed into my body and eventually prescribed me folic acid supplements later in the week, which I received via post. I was also once again deficient in magnesium, which I was told to expect for as long as I was taking tacrolimus. Therefore, I was unfortunately put back on the nasty magnesium sachets, which I had to dissolve in water and take every morning and evening.

***

Monday 1st August 2022 (Day 100). I spent the entire weekend worrying about my bone marrow biopsy results. The doctors were telling me not to worry about them and didn't seem too concerned about my platelet issue. I think I didn't want to appear too complacent, as I had assured everyone that I was well in December 2021, and look where I ended up. Having been through what I'd been through, particularly declining cells, it only made sense that I'd fear a relapse.

The BMT clinical fellow woke me when I received a call during my afternoon nap, at 3:00pm. At first, the doctor almost gave me a heart attack.

"So, I have your bone marrow results here, and the sample wasn't great ..."

"Okay ..." I said.

My heart sank, and I was about to burst into tears. *I was right*, I thought, *the leukaemia is still there!*

"You know, the actual sample that they took wasn't great. There wasn't much to see," continued the doctor.

"Oh ..." I said as I gave a sigh of relief.

"The sample found that there were no myeloid blasts present in the bone marrow, and therefore you're still in remission, so that's something to be happy about," said the doctor.

"Oh, that's great!" I replied.

The doctor said that the rest of the results would be available over the next few weeks and would be discussed in my Friday clinic appointments. The aspirate was described as a suboptimal sample, which meant that it wasn't the best quality, however, the doctor said that she would ask the bone marrow team to investigate the platelet issue as there were still no answers on this. Although the aspirate sample wasn't of the greatest quality, the trephine sample was good, and the doctors awaited the results of this.

Mum and Dad were at work, and I told them that whether it was good news or bad news, I would only tell them about my results in person, once they'd got home. My parents' phone number was still under my medical details, though, and the doctor called Mum's number first. Therefore, Mum knew that I was getting a call from the doctor, and she couldn't concentrate until she knew what my results were. Sharing my good news was reduced to a simple message on the family group chat, stating that I was still in remission. As a result, my Day 100 news didn't seem as special.

The haematology registrar who had carried out my bone marrow biopsy asked if I had any plans to celebrate Day 100. The Day 100 milestone is very important for transplant patients as the first 100 days are generally considered as the most challenging stage of recovery post-transplant. I told the registrar that I hadn't really thought about it. I think I was so nervous about the bone marrow biopsy results, and was so sure that they'd be bad news, that I didn't want to celebrate anything. The good news of being in remission on the 100-cell count was enough of a highlight for my Day 100 that the day didn't require much celebration.

I was still nervous about receiving my MRD result and

finding out the cause of my platelet issue, but so far, so good. At least I had received good news on the scariest of the tests.

Chapter 21

One Step Forward, Two Steps Back

My progress and setbacks after my Day 100 milestone

Friday 5ᵗʰ August 2022 (Day 104). I was back in clinic for my Friday appointment with the doctor, where I saw the BMT clinical fellow.

Firstly, my platelet decline seemed to have stopped! The previous week, they were 53, and now they were 57! The doctor told me that they would take a while to reach their normal level, but an increase by 4 was a good sign that the decline had stopped. The doctor put this down to almost certainly being as a result of my Covid infection, and now my platelets were on the recovery.

However, I was a bit concerned about the rest of my blood counts. My anaemia had returned, as my haemoglobin had managed to reach 137 a few weeks previously, but now it was 123. My white blood cells were 3.9, the lowest value in the standard range. If they dropped any lower, I'd have leukopenia, which is the term for low white blood cells and was what I was suffering from in late 2021 when I was re-diagnosed with leukaemia. Most important was my neutrophil count, at 2.85. This was an entirely normal neutrophil count, and anything above 1.5 is good. But I was alarmed by this because, while I was still in the standard range and understood that neutrophils fluctuated (like all blood counts do), I had never reached this low, unless I was on chemotherapy. Despite fluctuations, I knew my neutrophils had always been between 3 and 6, yet in recent weeks, they had been declining in the 3 range and had now reached into the 2 range. To me, this seemed clear that my neutrophils were declining, and automatically, the first thing in my head was that the leukaemia was returning.

The doctor wasn't concerned though. I was still fixing my folate deficiency by taking my folic acid supplements daily. The clinical fellow said that when Vitamin B12 and folate levels are low, everything in the blood goes down. It was something we were working on, and hopefully in time, I'd see an improvement in my blood counts. My fears were definitely psychological, and because of everything that had happened in 2021, seeing abnormal blood counts made me assume the worst in everything. I spent a lot of time living in constant fear, and when doctors attributed a problem to something else, I always attributed it to leukaemia.

I had spent several weeks being tapered off my steroids, which had been treating me for GvHD. I was now taking 5 mg of prednisolone once a day, which was only one tablet compared to the eight (40 mg) I was originally taking. Now that I was no longer showing evidence of GvHD, evident by me showing no signs of a rash and also by my flexible sigmoidoscopy results, the doctor gave the approval to allow me to stop taking my steroids, starting the following day. I was now steroid-free! But the visible effects were clear, having gained lots of weight and having the face of a hamster!

I handed in my stool samples quickly before leaving the clinic. At about 8:00pm that evening, I received a call from another haematology doctor. He asked me how my bowels were, then explained his reason for asking. In my lifetime, I'd had so many antibiotics that not only had they killed the bad bugs in my body, but they'd also killed the good bugs, and therefore I had picked up a nasty infection called C.diff. I'd had this infection before, as you'll be aware from earlier in this book. I needed to stop some medications: omeprazole, which I took to reduce stomach acid, and budesonide, which I took for diarrhoea. And because nothing about the human body makes sense, to cure an infection caused by too many antibiotics, I was going to be treated with a ten-day course of the antibiotic, vancomycin.

As it was the weekend, it made getting my hands on the antibiotics very difficult. The doctor said that he'd get my medication couriered out and told me to chase it up if it hadn't arrived by Sunday. It never arrived on Sunday, but I received a call from the BMT clinical fellow the next day, who told me that it should be arriving that day. It didn't, but I thought I'd leave it until Tuesday to see if it arrived then. It still didn't. I emailed my nurse, Jo, on Wednesday to ask about my medicine, who got back to me on Thursday to tell me that pharmacy was looking into it. I didn't hear any more, and by my next Friday clinic appointment, I was still without my antibiotics! I had been suffering from stomach cramps, watery diarrhoea, and had been opening my bowels more frequently – I desperately needed my antibiotics!

***

Friday 12th August 2022 (Day 111). I had my blood test and dressing change done in the Ward C9 day unit, as was the norm. When I arrived in clinic and showed myself at reception and answered the relevant questions, the receptionist had to telephone a colleague to ask what they were going to do with me. I was puzzled by this, as I had always just signed in and gone straight to weight room for obs before sitting in the waiting room and waiting for the doctor.

I then realised that I had C. diff, and I was supposed to be kept isolated from the other patients in the waiting room. What I didn't understand was why they allowed me to be on C9 as normal, yet I couldn't sit in the waiting room. Anyhow, the receptionist directed me to the weight room, where I had my temperature, height, and weight taken, then the healthcare assistant directed Mum and I to one of the consultation rooms, where I'd wait for the doctor there instead.

It was a short wait before Dr. U entered the room. I hadn't seen him for a while.

Firstly, he went over C. diff again and thought that it was this that was causing my frequent bowel movements. He explained the ten-day course of antibiotics and wasn't too happy that I still hadn't received them when I was initially told they'd arrive by Sunday. He ordered some more vancomycin for me to pick up at the hospital pharmacy.

There was a lot of focus on my skin in this consultation. I had been off the steroids for a week now, and unfortunately there was another flare up of my GvHD. My rash was visible on my arms, my flanks, hands, feet, and in my upper legs around my groin. Dr. U said that this was a little flare up, and it wasn't worth putting me back on the steroids just yet. It was important that I just kept up with my recipe of creams. I was applying a cream called Fucidin H for the spots that had been growing on my face and skin, but I was told to stop this to use a lotion, called clindamycin, instead. I was told to continue applying Dermovate to the affected areas of my skin and continue using hydrocortisone in the more delicate areas of my body where the rash was present. I was also told to continue using Dermol as a soap substitute to shower with and was encouraged to keep my body as moist as possible by applying Diprobase on most areas of my body. Hopefully, the creams would be enough to manage my flare up and putting me back on steroids would not be necessary, and the doctor was hopeful that within the next one or two weeks they'd be able to taper me off my immunosuppressant medication, tacrolimus. As long as my GvHD remained, though, I'd have to stay on tacrolimus.

Dr. U had reviewed my blood counts before coming to see me, and he said that the Vitamin B12 and folate supplements had been doing the trick after all. In fact, we were beginning to see my previously declining blood counts come back up. My platelets were now 74! The increase in my platelets led to the doctor giving his approval for the removal of my Hickman line and wrote on my notes to book its removal! My white blood cells, while still on the lower side, were on the increase from the previous week at 4.4, up from 3.9. Most surprising of all were my red blood cells. The standard range for red blood cells is 4.30–5.75, and mine were 4.34. This was the first blood test I'd had since September 2020 where my red blood cells were in the standard range! Even better, my haemoglobin shot right up, from 123 the previous week to 138 this week, meaning I was no longer anaemic again! This could definitely be attributed to the folic acid supplements, as their aim is to help the body produce healthy red blood cells.

However, there had also been a few issues that I'd been suffering from. Firstly, I'd had difficulty walking for quite some time as I was suffering from leg pain. The pain could be anywhere from minor to causing me slight disturbance, to severe, where I could hardly get out of bed and had to phone the haematology helpline, on the verge of going to A&E. I was also suffering from headaches, sore throats, and earaches.

Even worse, I was abnormally tired, needing constant naps, and finding that walking up the stairs was really difficult. I also found that I was struggling to sleep at night.

Dr. U attributed this to coming off the steroids. Firstly, the leg pain could be due to the effects of the steroids themselves, as they are known to cause muscle loss. Also, having come off the steroids, my body had to relearn how to make its own steroids, and perhaps the process was just a bit slow, and my body was suffering as a result. With time, I was expected to get better but was told not to be put off by that answer, and if things were getting worse, I needed to let the hospital know. Just because I was feeling so tired that I couldn't get up the stairs, didn't mean I should stop trying, and Dr. U continued to encourage me to get out and about and improve my strength.

Regarding my tiredness and inability to sleep, Dr. U asked how my mood had been recently. I'd been better. Mum and a few other members of my family had been suspecting that I was depressed for quite a while, as I was always tired, irritable, couldn't sleep, and had lost passion for most things. All my days really consisted of was sitting at home doing nothing, and I think the lonely feeling, and the thought that I'd gone through a bone marrow transplant only to live a life like I was, was getting to me. I'd gone through a bone marrow transplant and received very few benefits to my life. All I wanted was my life back. Dr. U, as the TYA lead haematology consultant, had obviously looked after a lot of patients the same age as me, and he said it was always around the Day 100 mark that patients would begin to process what had happened to them now that the most difficult part of the journey was mostly over. Perhaps all this time I was struggling to process what had happened to me. I was referred to the TYA counsellor, who got in touch to organise a meeting on September 8th, 2022. Despite never actually needing it, I'd found counselling very helpful during my days as a paediatric, so I thought I'd take up the offer and give it a go as part of my recovery.

***

Friday 19th August 2022 (Day 119). In my clinic appointment with the BMT clinical fellow on Day 119, I received the rest of my bone marrow biopsy results.

Chimerism tests are most commonly done via a peripheral blood test, which checks what percentage of the blood are donor cells. The bone marrow is a bit more sensitive, so my biopsy also looked at how much of my bone marrow was made up of donor cells. The good news was that my bone marrow was 100% donor cells, reflecting my blood tests!

I still hadn't received my MRD result, which I questioned. In fact, even though I was told that an MRD test had been done in my few previous biopsies, I'd never received any results, as you may have noticed from Part III of this book. MRD was such a big thing during my first battle, but the doctors never really brought it up after I relapsed. Perhaps it was because the second time round, I was going to have a bone marrow transplant regardless of the result, whereas the first time we had hope that a transplant would not be necessary, and therefore there was less need to monitor the tiny traces of leukaemia after my relapse.

The clinical fellow explained to me that the doctors were not so concerned about MRD with me. When I relapsed, the bone marrow biopsy also investigates a number of gene mutations, which are an indicator of prognosis. One of the genes is known as the NPM1 gene, and when this gene mutates, it is associated with a poor prognosis for AML. Thankfully, my

NPM1 gene had not mutated, leaving less concern for my MRD result. I do not fully understand what the gene mutations mean or how they affect MRD, but I took the doctor's word for it and was reassured. She also told me that since my bone marrow was 100% donor cells, and I was suffering from GvHD, any minimal residual disease was likely being taken care of by the donor cells.

GvHD was still an absolute pain to live with though! The previous week was a mild flare up, but by the time I was in clinic that Friday, my rash was arguably worse than my first onset of GvHD. It had spread across my back, down my entire legs, and was particularly very itchy on my feet. I had a few blotches of a rash on my flanks, arms, and chest. My hands had also suffered quite a bit, with an on and off rash, which at times could get very itchy. The doctor decided to continue to hold off on steroids for the time being and instead encouraged me to keep using my creams. I was doing very well with my creams, continuing to apply Dermovate, although she told me I needed to abandon the hydrocortisone as it was not powerful enough to combat my rash. The doctors really wanted to think about tapering me off my immunosuppressant medication, tacrolimus, but once again, they preferred that my rash settled before going ahead with it, so I was to be stuck on the same dose of tacrolimus.

The doctor said that as I seemed to have new complaints every week, I'd have to stay on weekly appointments. I found that comment quite funny because it was true! Having said that, I was desperate to return to normal life. My driving lessons were going well, and I had my test booked for November 23rd, 2022. I also received my final grade for Year 2 of university. I had averaged the entire year with a 1st. I managed to scrape the required 70% by 0.09%! Post-transplant goals #1 and #2 had been achieved!

That left post-transplant goal #3 – returning to work. My goal was to be back by the end of September, which may have sounded slightly unrealistic due to the fact that it is advised that transplant patients wait at least six months before going back. I knew what was right for me though, and my reasoning for wanting to return so soon was more for mental reasons rather than physical reasons. Even though I knew I'd be weaker, I was sure I could begin a phased return of a few hours a week to ease myself in, which would then also help my psychological well-being of finally regaining some normality. Sitting at home all day was really getting to me!

The doctor didn't really give me a straight answer. At first, she said I needed to be off tacrolimus before I could think about returning to work. I was a bit disheartened by that, so I decided to use my negotiating skills. She was put more at ease when I said that I could make adaptions to ensure I wore a mask and that I didn't need to interact with too many people at work. She was also relieved to hear that I wasn't working with children and that I only worked one or two days a week, which would limit my exposure to potential infections. I think we settled on thinking about a phased return once my Hickman line was removed, which I was very happy about. The doctor said she would speak to Dr. U about it and I would find out soon.

Regarding my Hickman line, it looked likely that it was going to be removed very soon! My blood test results were seemingly improving, reaching 93 on this day. This was above the 80 required by the haematology doctor to refer me for the removal, and she got my nurse, Jo, to book my line removal for the next Friday!

***

Friday 26th August 2022 (Day 126). It would have been my sixth transplant anniversary birthday had I not relapsed the previous December. Usually, August 26th would have been full of celebrations, but now it was just an ordinary day, one I will never celebrate again. It was still an important day to look back on though, and even though my first transplant did ultimately fail, the five years it gave me was worth it!

The doctor told me that cord transplants (the type of transplant I'd had in Bristol) do not have T-cells, so they are immature baby cells building a completely new immune system. This makes GvHD less likely, and also their immaturity means that they're less likely to recognise a cancerous cell. My French cells were definitely a lot easier on me, and the doctors were hopeful that my more aggressive Salvadorian cells, which did contain T-cells, were causing any remaining disease great harm, even if they were harming the rest of my body through GvHD.

It was an early start at the hospital as it was going to be an eventful day. I made it to the Ward C9 day unit, just in time for 8:30am. The nurses on C9 had been desperate to find out when my line would be removed, I think because they hated having to do dressing changes and also because my line removal was so overdue that they couldn't believe I still had it. Whenever I hadn't seen a nurse for a long time, they'd always get their needles out to take a peripheral blood test, until I'd tell them that my line was still in! I told the nurses that my line was getting removed that afternoon, and they were happier than I was! I was very excited to get it removed. Because I didn't require a dressing change due to my Hickman line's imminent removal, the C9 process was quick, and I was out of the day unit very quickly.

After a quick stop to Costa Coffee for a hot chocolate,

I was back in the haematology and oncology outpatients department for my clinical appointment. I saw the locum haematology consultant in what had to be the quickest consultation I'd ever had. I saw him in Room H, which surprised me. Now that Covid patients had their own clinic, Room H was back to being a normal consultation room. I had hardly any new complaints, just the GvHD, with my rash being more or less the same as the previous week. He took a picture of my rash to upload it to my records to make a comparison with the progress and reiterated what the doctor the previous week had said about tapering me off my immunosuppressants. Unfortunately, I couldn't be weaned off them just yet because my rash needed to settle.

The doctor was pleased to hear that my Hickman line was getting removed later that day. He was able to give the go-ahead for the removal as my platelets had increased to 123, which was great news! He said I'd be reviewed in clinic the next week.

Following a wait in pharmacy for some more Dermovate, it was straight to the Vascular Access Unit at the hospital to have my Hickman line removed! After a short wait in the waiting room, I was called into a bedspace. I was welcomed by the same practitioner who inserted my PICC line in December 2021. I don't know if she recognised me, but I remembered her positivity when I told her about my relapse, so it felt so good to tell her that my Hickman line was being removed because I no longer needed it! The same practitioner was the one who would remove my line.

She went over the procedure with me. As I've mentioned it many times, you'll be aware that as an adult, I had to face my surgeries and procedures while being awake. My line removal as a paediatric was under general anaesthetic, but my line removal as an adult would be under local anaesthetic. She then went to explain the risks of the procedure. The risks included bleeding, which would mean that I'd have to apply pressure under my collarbone to stop the bleeding. I also needed to watch out for infection, which could show as redness or pain around the line removal area. Regarding the procedure itself, I also needed to be aware that the line could snap during the procedure, in which case I'd have to be admitted to the hospital for a day to get a team to fish the piece of plastic out of my arteries. The practitioner handed me a hospital gown for me to change into, and then after a very short wait, I was in the surgery room.

After going through all the necessary checks to make sure I was who I said I was, and that I was clear what procedure I was having, the practitioner and accompanying nurse made me lay down on the hospital bed. The nurse took my obs to ensure I was feeling well and had a final look at my records to make sure my bloods were good enough to have the procedure done.

The most painful bit was the anaesthetic needle, and I could feel the practitioner inject my line site with a few needles to really numb the area. She waited a while to let the local anaesthetic kick in before she pricked me with a needle a few times to check whether I felt anything. Luckily, I didn't feel anything, and the rest of the procedure was actually pain-free! The practitioner proceeded to then make an incision into my artery to pull the Hickman line out of the area where it had been sitting near my heart. The line was officially out of my artery, but it was still inserted under my chest skin, above the bone. The practitioner pulled the line out of the hole in my chest (this is the hole you can see where the line is looped under the dressing) and removed it. The area where my line had previously come out was able to heal itself, but where the incision into the artery was made, I required a number of stitches. These stitches were dissolvable, and I wouldn't notice them. A dressing was put on my wound, and I was told to be careful and keep it dry for the next three or four days, then I was officially free! I now had two matching scars – one on my right from January 2017 and one on my left from August 2022.

The procedure didn't take long at all, although recovery took a while as the practitioner said I was a bit of a bleeder and was struggling to stop the bleeding. I was curious about my platelet levels. I knew that they were at a good enough level to have the procedure, but I still understood that they were low. The practitioner said that my platelets were fine, and in fact they only needed to be above 40 for a Hickman line removal. If that was the case, I could have had my line removed a lot sooner than I did! This left me confused over whether my platelets needed to be 80 or 40, and if I remember correctly, the random Australian would have let me have my line removed at 67! Different doctors and departments require different things, and I've realised that it is very difficult to determine right or wrong answers when it comes to medicine. A lot of it is opinion-based.

After the procedure, I was helped back up from the bed and told to wait back in my bedspace for ten minutes. The bleeding had mostly stopped but the practitioner wanted to change my dressing before I left. I was given a couple of spare dressings in case I continued to bleed over the weekend. Once I left the department, I was still bleeding, and I regretted wearing a white shirt that day! I applied pressure above my collarbone as was required, and by the next day most of the bleeding had pretty much stopped, although there were a few drops of blood over the weekend.

I was finally line free, and what a time it was for me to have it out! I looked forward to celebrating my birthday weekend!

***

Saturday 27th August to Monday 29th August 2022. I decided to give myself a birthday weekend, as I felt like I deserved it after the terrible and chaotic year it had been. Making it to fourteen was difficult enough, and no one told me that reaching twenty years old would be even harder! My birthday was such an important milestone, and I planned the perfect weekend to ensure I could have just one weekend of my year that would go well! I was very selective over who I spent my birthday with, and I made sure I tried to make time for my friends, family, and loved ones. Unfortunately, it didn't come without its challenges, and some of my birthday didn't go fully to plan, but everyone did their best to make my weekend special.

I spent the Saturday with my family. Me, Mum, Dad, Kristy, and her boyfriend, Bogdan, all had a lovely day at Newmarket races. Kristy and Bogdan were the most successful, winning around £30. I took home about £9. After our family afternoon, the five of us returned to Stowmarket, where we all went out for Chinese food, joined by Grandma, Auntie Karen, Uncle John, cousin Jade and her husband Pete, and Uncle James. My meal was delicious, and the Chinese restaurant did an amazing job at making it my birthday party, with my birthday cake and candles afterwards. It was a lovely family meal as we were all together once again, and it was so nice to be able to spend time with my family who had supported me so much during my difficult time.

The Saturday night, however, things began to go downhill. My legs began to seriously hurt to the point where I could hardly walk, and I had an absolutely awful flare up of my GvHD, which made my face very red and my entire body itchy. I got no sleep that night and I woke up feeling very unwell. One perfect weekend was all I wanted, and I couldn't even get that! I was supposed to be seeing my mates in Norwich on the Sunday to celebrate my birthday with them, but having to survive the day on only two hours sleep, there was no way I could face it. The birthday boy had to cancel his own celebrations, which left me very upset.

It wasn't completely the end of the world on Sunday though as my friends were supportive and were able to come over to my house in the evening instead. We had a nice buffet and a Mario Kart night instead, which was fun! I wasn't able to see all my friends due to the change in timings of the day and location, and also due to illness, but I appreciated Ryan, Clare, and Will coming over to spend the evening with me. It was a really nice evening, and although not the original plan, I was thankful that my birthday celebrations were being kept alive throughout the weekend!

Because of my delayed Hickman line removal, my platelet issue, and immunosuppressant situation over the summer, Edinburgh with Lauren, which was the original plan in my list of reasons to live, was unfortunately off the cards for my birthday. We decided to postpone it instead, perhaps to January 2023 to celebrate two years as best friends. She still wanted to make my actual birthday, on Monday 29th August, special though, and she had been planning a surprise day for me. Even those plans had changed due to the weather, transport issues, and the fact that she had a bad feeling about my health. And those bad feelings were true, because my Sunday night was even worse than my Saturday, and once again my legs were hurting so bad, and my rash was so itchy to the point that I was on the verge of calling the haematology helpline on the morning of my birthday! I did everything I could to bring myself together to make sure I was there to celebrate my birthday the way I wanted, and I had only really recovered with half an hour to spare before seeing her, fearing that I'd have to cancel.

While I told her absolutely nothing about what was going on with me, Lauren's bad feelings made her change things last minute, and a quieter day was planned instead. I still had a really nice surprise day! She treated me to a three-course meal and made my dessert special by bringing in candles and singing 'Happy Birthday' to me. We then spent the rest of the day at her house, talking about pretty much everything going on in our lives, and then once my legs had recovered fully for the day (which they seemed to do), we went for a walk around the fields in her village before my legs started hurting again and we had to turn back.

I had a lovely birthday, and even though I wasn't able to do all the plans I'd wanted to do, I still really appreciate what everyone did to make my weekend special. Everyone I spent my birthday with meant so much to me because of everything they had done when I was undergoing treatment, and I was so glad that I had dedicated a weekend to spend time with as many of my loved ones as possible.

That being said, I was left slightly depressed by my birthday. Having been through what I'd been through, I couldn't help but have thoughts that it would be my last birthday. My health had changed quite a few of my plans, and I think I had put too much pressure on myself to have the perfect weekend because I wanted to live like I knew I was dying. Throughout the weekend, I found myself getting very emotional because, as dramatic as it sounds, I did question whether I'd see August 29th, 2023. As I said though, I ended up enjoying my birthday and by no means was it the disaster I was fearing when my health took a turn for the worse.

***

Thursday 1st September 2022 (Day 132). From September, some of my clinic appointments were moved to Thursdays as Dr. U moved to a Thursday clinic. When not seeing my consultant, I'd still be reviewed by one of the BMT clinical fellows in the Friday clinic. Appointments were to remain weekly for the time being.

My day at the hospital began on Ward C9, as was the norm. I wasn't spending all that much time on Ward C9 now, especially as my line was out. It was good to catch up with the nurses, who I had seen a lot of during my hospital stays, so I always liked going through the C9 process first rather than having my bloods taken in clinic. Attending just involved showing up for a blood test, although now they were done peripherally, which meant the return of needles. I'm used to needles though, so I was fine with it. My line had been out for just under a week by this point, and the previous day I had enjoyed my first proper shower in months!

Shortly after my C9 appointment, I was back in clinic with Dr. U. We had a catch up about my health in general.

I was still suffering from my leg pain, which I had suffered in July and August, and had recently had a terrible episode over my birthday weekend. The doctor had previously attributed it to coming off the steroids, but since my pain was on and off, he didn't think this was the case anymore. Tacrolimus could also have been a potential cause for the pain, but he was unsure. Because of the inconsistencies with my pain – at times it was both legs, one leg, in just one knee, or my shins – and because it was very sporadic, from severe at the point of calling the helpline to mild discomfort when walking, Dr. U just wanted to keep an eye on it. Mum told him that pain medicine, such as paracetamol and ibuprofen, wasn't touching the pain, and he said that while I could take medication such as morphine, he'd rather know what the cause of the pain was before prescribing something like that. If my pain continued to be sporadic, he advised that I kept an eye on it, but he would book an MRI scan if things worsened in the coming weeks.

I also told him about my GvHD flare ups over the weekend. I wondered if the flare ups could be caused by stress because I was very stressed about making sure my birthday weekend was perfect. He said that my rash could have possibly flared up due to stress, but once again was unsure. However my rash looked over the weekend, Dr. U was really pleased with how my skin was looking during this consultation. It was a bit dry, and he encouraged me to continue applying moisturising cream, but on the whole, my GvHD had dampened down quite a bit thanks to the topical steroid cream, Dermovate. It looked like I had avoided having to take oral steroids again, which I was happy about because I was still recovering from the effects of them. My face was still swollen like a bullfrog.

Because of how well my skin was looking, Dr. U questioned whether I really needed a steroid cream as strong as Dermovate, so he put me back on Eumovate. This was the cream I had started on when my GvHD had first appeared back in June. Being on Eumovate would be more of a preventative measure for my rash, to ensure that my skin was still getting exposure to steroids but not as much. If my rash did flare up again, then I was encouraged to continue applying Dermovate to the affected areas.

With my rash somewhat settled for now, Dr. U began outlining the plan to take me off my immunosuppressant medication. This was great news! Tapering me off my tacrolimus would be a slow process, taking around six weeks. I would be weaned off very slowly, and depending on my GvHD symptoms, there was a chance that I'd have to slowly increase and decrease my doses each week, rather than have a straightforward steady decline. But it was hoped that I'd be off immunosuppressants by mid-October.

I asked about returning to work once I was off my tacrolimus. Dr. U said that it was still a bit early to be thinking about going back, but also understood for psychological reasons that it was good to be getting out and about. His concern was me catching Covid, so he wanted to know how many people I would be interacting with, and he was also worried about my type of job potentially causing irritation to my skin. He said to leave it at least another month and see how things would go from there. Despite his reluctance, he said I could start thinking about going back but to make sure work understood that I couldn't be too definite about things and would need to have back up ready in case I did have to take more time off than expected. My goal for September may have been a bit too ambitious, and October was still a bit early, but I believed that it was possible for me to return by the end of October. My new goal was set!

***

Throughout the rest of September, I attended my weekly clinic appointments as normal, while also trying to continue with everyday life as best as I could.

I did end up attending one counselling session, had a bit of a break, and then got back into it. My main problem was the frustration I felt that I'd gone through a transplant only to live a life very different to what I'd lived during my five-year remission period. The counsellor helped me understand things better and provided me with a new outlook. Counselling also helped to get my emotions out to someone whose job it was to listen, as I'm not the most comfortable about opening up to family and friends.

My GvHD continued to be an on and off struggle of flare ups, and weaning me off my tacrolimus was an up and down process, not the smooth six weeks, which Dr. U had warned me about. Instead of tapering my tacrolimus every week as planned, I averaged every two weeks of making the next step in lowering my dosage. The Dermovate cream was very effective in fading my rash. GvHD continues to be a pain to live with, but I have managed it well.

***

Going into October, my blood counts remained fine, and despite my GvHD, my health complaints in my weekly appointments were getting less and less. However, a week into October, I began to feel very unwell, suffering from headaches, loss of appetite, and feeling cold and tired. A rash had also formed all over my body, which looked different to a GvHD flare up. My fatigue was severe, and I recall sleeping for nineteen hours one day!

On Friday 14th October, I attended my clinic appointment as planned. After having my bloods taken, I went to the room where my height, weight, and temperature would be recorded. The healthcare assistant told me that my temperature was 38°. I knew I was unwell, but this came as quite a shock. Of course, the main concern was Covid, and I was asked to isolate from other patients to avoid passing on any potential infection. I didn't have Covid.

I saw the BMT clinical fellow, who told me that as I had a fever, the BMT protocol stated that I had to be admitted to hospital. I had escaped Ward C9 for five months, but unfortunately, I was going to make a comeback as an inpatient! The doctor's concern was meningitis, however, when the haematology consultant came to have a look at my rash, he was certain that it wasn't that. He did agree that my rash didn't look like GvHD, and with my other symptoms, he was sure that there had to be a viral infection going on. While he thought it was an infection, it was important to rule things out regarding leukaemia. Because I was displaying symptoms such as headaches, the consultant wanted me to have a CT scan to make sure the leukaemia hadn't spread to the brain. He also mentioned a lumbar puncture to me, where they would inject chemo into my spine just as a precaution, if leukaemia was the cause of my problems (which looked unlikely as my blood counts were good). I'd had these as a paediatric, and they were extremely painful, so I am glad that I eventually ended up not needing to have one. I took a Covid test in preparation for my admission, then I was back on Ward C9 for a cannula insertion in preparation for my CT scan.

The CT scan was slightly different to the ones I'd had in the past. The dye that they'd usually inject wasn't necessary for my brain scan as they were able to produce good enough images without it. I was relieved when the doctor told me that nothing concerning came back on the results, although he noticed that my brain was smaller than the average person's, though he didn't think there was much to be concerned about. It was clear that I was suffering from an infection and the headaches were linked to it, but what was the infection?

I was settled on Ward C9 by the evening. I had my own room – Room 3, which was my favourite! Four haematology doctors looked at my rash, three of whom had no clue what it was. One suggested hand, foot, and mouth disease. The Ward C9 doctor had a look and thought my rash looked very similar to chickenpox. I received a visit from the dermatology registrar, who had no clue what my rash was but took pictures of it to show to her consultant and said she would revisit me after the weekend.

My CRP levels remained at a normal level, so doctors were more inclined to believe that I was suffering from a viral, rather than bacterial, infection. However, I had to be treated in line with the protocol, so I had IV meropenem, an antibiotic, twice a day while staying on the ward. While I was still spiking fevers, which stayed roughly around the 37.9° to 38.1° mark, I'd require blood cultures every forty-eight hours to check for any bacterial growths. Because I was no longer recovering from chemotherapy and I visibly had a rash, I managed to avoid the other protocol measures, such as an ECG and chest X-ray. Also, to tackle anything viral, the anti-viral medication that I had been taking as tablets for months, acyclovir, was changed to IV, which I had infused through my cannula twice a day.

My rash still remained a mystery. Antibody tests for hand, foot, and mouth disease, measles, rubella, and chickenpox all came back negative. One haematology consultant was sure that I was suffering from a virus, but another believed I was suffering from a GvHD flare up. Dr. U came to visit me on Thursday 20th October (I was supposed to see him in clinic that day), and he came up with a compromise. He thought that I was suffering from a viral infection which had then caused a flare up of my GvHD.

On Wednesday 19th October, the dermatologist carried out a skin biopsy on my arm. This involved injecting anaesthetic into my arm and then cutting out a sample from one of the lesions of my rash. It didn't hurt at all, except for the initial anaesthetic needle, and I was left with a couple of stitches on my arm afterwards, which would dissolve in the shower. The results took a while to come back, and I was discharged before receiving them. Regarding treatment, the dermatologist recommended Dermovate, which I had been using for my GvHD, and a moisturising cream called 50:50.

Adapting to hospital life again was difficult, made harder by the fact that I no longer had a line. Even though I was no longer receiving cancer treatment, the standard procedure of the ward still applied to me. I was required to have blood tests every morning at 6:00am, and I did not like being woken up at that time to be stabbed by needles (they couldn't take blood out of my cannula). It didn't help that my veins had been hit quite badly throughout the year and taking bloods from them was now near impossible. One morning, I was stabbed six times! As I was still spiking fevers, blood cultures were required every forty-eight hours, and special blood tests were required to find the source of my infection. Also, my cannula had to be changed every two days, so that meant more needles. And if that wasn't bad enough, as I was an inactive patient in hospital, I required a daily blood-thinner injection, dalteparin, at 5:00pm. I did not miss that from my days as a cancer patient! The result of all of these needles were two severely bruised arms.

There were positives though. It was nice to catch up with my old nurses and healthcare assistants, some of whom I hadn't spoken to in months. I had good political discussions with the consultant on the ward rounds, who was as passionate about politics as I am. His ideology was in line with New Labour, so he and his team of junior doctors would always ridicule me for being a Tory when he did the ward rounds in January earlier in the year.

It was also nice having two visitors, instead of the one named visitor, a rule had taken up most of my time in hospital that year. I stayed by myself at night, despite having my own room, but Mum and Dad would drive up to Cambridge to visit me every day. I only liked having breakfast from the ward as I could not stomach the microwave meals. An advantage of having my parents visit me every day was that they always brought in food for me that I enjoyed!

It was probably one of my better hospital stays, but I did get fed up and wanted to go home as soon as possible. The constant tests and being poked and prodded with needles were getting to me, and I'd just had enough. The Dermovate was effective in fading my rash, and as the week went by, my viral symptoms began to improve. Fevers had settled by Wednesday, and I was thankfully discharged from Ward C9 by Friday 21st October 2022, after what I hope was my last ever stay there.

***

My first clinic appointment after discharge resulted in good news! My blood counts were looking really good, and I was feeling really well. Perhaps a stay in hospital was what I needed! The consultant allowed me to continue my tacrolimus tapering, giving me more responsibility to slowly go down on the doses by myself, guided by a chart, rather than having to be given the go ahead by a doctor. By this point, my appointments were still weekly, but he gave me a trial to have a week off from the hospital, hoping that my appointments would soon go down to every fortnight.

Before my hospital stay, I was in contact with work about returning. The haematology doctors wanted me to be completely off my tacrolimus before going back to work, but my goal of returning in October remained in my mind. My first counselling session had changed my outlook on my recovery, and I decided that returning to work was best for me. The cause of my depressed feelings was sitting at home doing nothing while I knew all my family and friends were out living their lives. I wanted my life back, whether I was immunosuppressed or not. I agreed with work that I'd be back by Sunday 30th October, whether I was still on tacrolimus or not.

And I did return to work on that Sunday! The plan was to start with just a couple of hours a week, as my type of job was quite tiring and physical, then slowly increase my hours back to my original contract as and when I felt well enough. I did well on my first day back, only feeling slightly more exhausted than usual. My co-workers were surprised to see me back as they didn't know I was coming in that day!

I lasted two weeks back at work before I was off sick again. I was able to get my tacrolimus down to just Monday, Wednesday, and Friday doses. Only another couple of weeks and I would have been off the medication completely! But unfortunately, it appeared I was tapered off the medication too quickly, and by Friday 11th November, my rash had flared up everywhere. I should mention that my skin biopsy from when I was hospitalised did come back as GvHD, and my GvHD was now showing in different characteristics. Some areas remained a red, continuous, itchy rash. Other areas were nasty blisters. Painful blisters appeared on the palms of my hands and fingertips. I was suffering again from GvHD of the gut, as diarrhoea was once again becoming a problem. GvHD of the mouth was a new symptom as I had lost all my tastebuds, all food had a dry consistency, and my lips were very red, sore, and crusty. My face was also very red, like I had been badly sunburnt. The worst symptom, however, had to be on my feet. My feet were dark red, with heavy dry skin, on the verge of turning purple. They were extremely itchy and sore, and walking became extremely difficult.

The consultant was very concerned by this and put me on 80 mg of steroids straight away, and I was called back to be reviewed on Ward C9 the following Monday, 14th November. Despite little improvement, I was sent home, and Dr. U made a special request to see me in clinic on Thursday 17th November, cancelling my weekly Friday appointment.

What Dr. U was worried about was my steroid dependency. If my GvHD was going to be a long-term thing, the doctors didn't want me managing it with steroids forever due to the side effects I had experienced previously. As of writing, I am still on them but am in the process of weaning. Tacrolimus is a steroid-saving drug, and my dose was increased by quite a bit. This meant that my progress of tapering since September had been for nothing, and I am back where I started in order to keep the drug at a therapeutic level to keep my GvHD under control.

I also had to sign consent forms for an alternative treatment called extracorporeal photopheresis (ECP). This would involve me going to the hospital every fortnight for two consecutive days to begin with, where I would be hooked up to a machine, which would separate my white blood cells from the rest of my blood. A medication would then be added to my bloodstream, and my white blood cells would be exposed to ultraviolet light to let the medication work. Unfortunately, as I was now deemed to have chronic rather than acute GvHD, it was very likely that I'd have to put up with the condition on and off for many more months or years, or maybe even the rest of my life. ECP is not effective straight away, and it is likely to take at least twelve to twenty-four weeks to work, with the average response rate being nine months. Because it's quite an exhausting treatment being attached to a machine, and requires good veins, there is a chance I may need another PICC line inserted in the near future. Unfortunately, it is looking likely that a lot of my 2023 will be spent attached to a machine, and hospital visits will increase rather than decrease. I intend for the final version of this book to be completed by the time I've started my ECP, which will commence at the end of November 2022. Therefore, it's unknown what the future holds.

Despite being back only two weeks, I did make it back to work, and I can say that post-transplant goal #3 has been completed. Therefore, I have found the appropriate place to end this book. My life is not the same, and I don't think it ever will be. I am exhausted most of the time and battling the absolute pain that is GvHD, which has created lasting visible damage on my body, not to mention the mental effects that my second bout with leukaemia has caused. Although I am not as optimistic about this comeback as I was about my first, I have at least shown that I've achieved the steps to begin my second comeback, and that is something to be proud of.

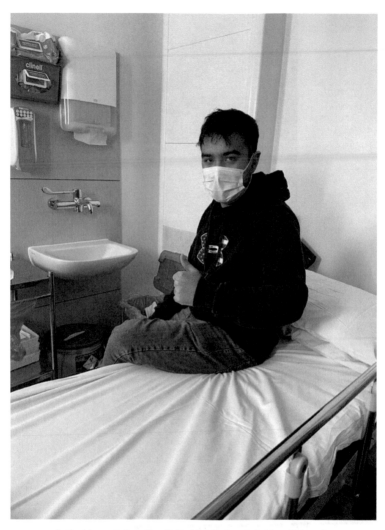

In the Haematology Day Unit at Addenbrooke's Hospital ready
for my first bone marrow biopsy in over five years, December 9th
2021. On December 17th 2021, I received the results which found
my bone marrow to be crammed with 68% leukaemia blasts.

My last night of normality with my best friend, Lauren, on December 19th 2021. Despite everything, our friendship continued to grow and to this day, the Conservative Connection is stronger than ever.

Mum and I with all of my belongings, waiting to be let into Ward C9 for the first time as an inpatient, December 22nd 2021. Mum helped me unpack and settle into my bedspace before she left later that evening.

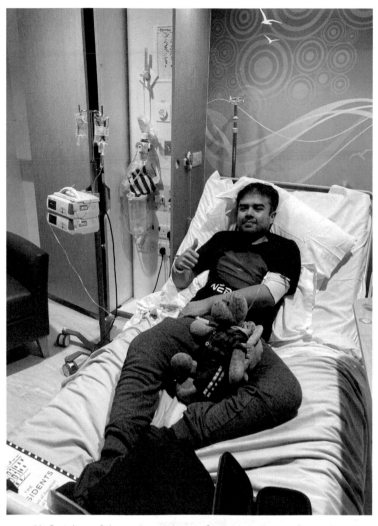

My first dose of chemotherapy in over five and a half years, December 23rd 2021. I'm ready to put the leukaemia back in remission!

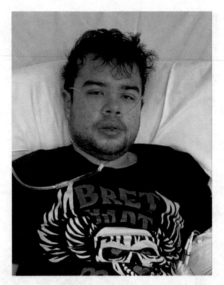

After spending the Christmas period on intensive chemotherapy and with an infection, my condition worsens on December 27th 2021.

Me after my haircut at home, January 13th 2022. I really liked the bald head with a beard style.

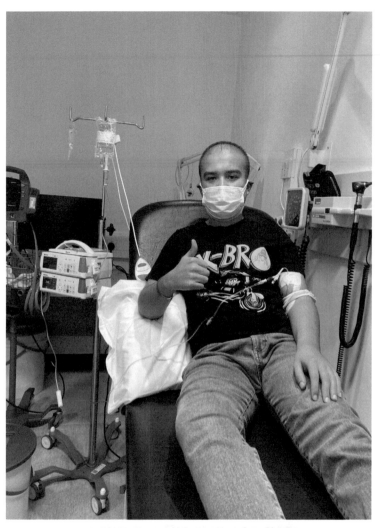

Round 2 of chemotherapy begins, February 28th 2022. My never-ending bout with Covid-19 meant that I had to receive my infusion in Addenbrooke's Hospital's isolation room, the dreaded Room H.

At Elsworth House, attached
to the CADD pump, March 1st
2022. I was attached to the CADD
pump for five days straight.

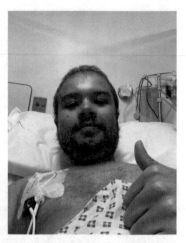

Waiting in recovery after
the insertion of my second
Hickman line, April 5th 2022.

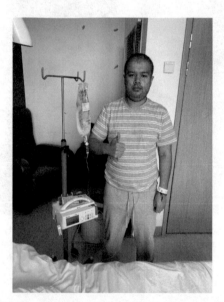

The conditioning phase of my second bone marrow transplant begins,
April 15th 2022. I am shocked by the size of the chemotherapy drug,
cyclophosphamide. I'd had my first dose of fludarabine earlier that morning.

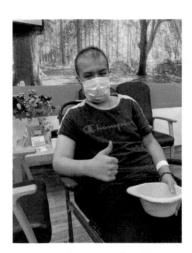

Falling asleep in my wheelchair
following my morning dose of
radiotherapy, April 20th 2022.

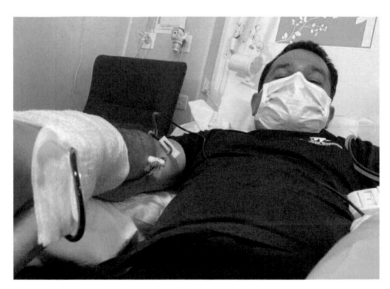

Dad donates his stem cells, April 21st 2022. This was the best photo
he could get as he had to stay still for over four hours. The cells were
supposed to be transplanted to me the same day, but a delay in
processing them meant that Transplant Day was pushed back.

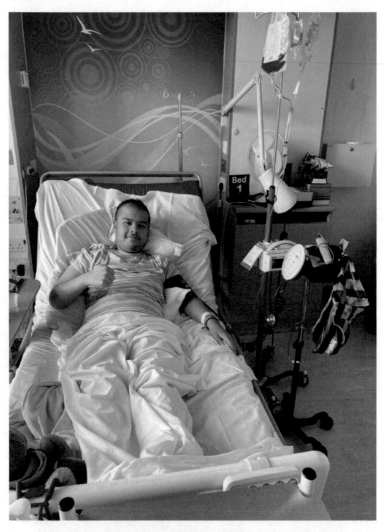

My second bone marrow transplant, April 22nd 2022. Due to Covid-19, only Mum could be present, though we FaceTimed Dad and Kristy. The antihistamine drugs that I was given beforehand made me very tired so I had to take a quick photo with the cells before falling asleep.

I make my grand entrance through the house as I am discharged from hospital, May 7th 2022.

'Never Give Up!' Me after receiving my bone marrow biopsy results on Day 100, August 1st 2022.

Family Chinese birthday celebration – Uncle James, Pete, Auntie Karen, Grandma, Uncle John, Bogdan, Kristy, Dad, me, Mum and Jade, August 27th 2022. This was the first time the whole family had been together for a while.

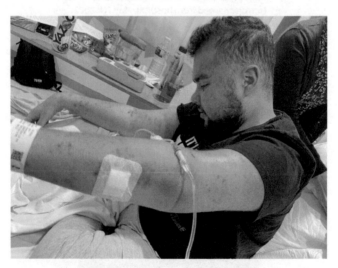

Me after my skin biopsy, October 19th 2022. I was hospitalised for a suspected infection, but the results a few weeks later came back as GvHD.

Back to work, October 30th 2022. All three of my post-transplant goals are now complete.

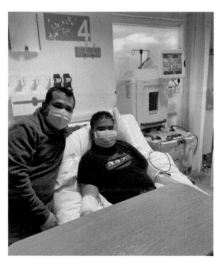

Dad and I while I receive my first ECP treatment, November 30th 2022.

Epilogue

Five years in remission seemed like a good place to end this book. As you can imagine, when I relapsed in December 2021 and Part III of this book was born, I was left unsure as to where this book would end.

I didn't want to wait another five years, because, as the events of December 2021 have shown, I don't know where in life I will be then. Also, I have already proven that it is possible to live a good life and make a good comeback after treatment, and I'm not sure if it is really necessary to write about it all over again. People told me to publish what I already had and just write a second book dedicated to my second journey with leukaemia. I didn't really want to do that because I wanted to tell my entire leukaemia journey in one volume, like a single journey from start to finish. Even though this has increased the length of this book significantly, seeing the whole journey as one makes it feel more complete.

But the thing with cancer journeys is that they never end. Even at five years in remission, you still have hospital appointments and are making progress each time. Sometimes it goes the opposite direction and relapse hits you out of nowhere. Cancer creates a life of uncertainty. There are good times and there are bad times, but you can never predict what will happen. I thought I was safe at five years, but clearly, I wasn't.

This book intended to have a happy ending, but now it's an uncertain one. I'm doing well, and I fully intend on finishing with a happy ending. But December 2021 showed that life can throw curveballs, and I don't know what will happen in my life now. I've decided that the best place to finish my book is once all three of my post-transplant goals have been achieved. At least then, that has shown that I have had the ability to return to a somewhat normal life again!

I wrote this book for a number of reasons.

The first reason I wrote it, of course, was to share my experiences, which could be used as a tool by other patients and their families going through something similar, to help them. As I wrote in my introduction, I hope that in this book there is something for every cancer patient. All cancer journeys are different, but I hope that there is a lot here that is relatable.

The second reason is to educate the general reader, who may or may not have been affected by cancer. Before my diagnosis in 2016, I knew very little about it, and in fact, I thought it was the cancer itself and not the treatment that caused hair loss! I became fascinated with haematology following my December 2021 relapse, and I hope that my story, while of course quite depressing in some areas, is fascinating, interesting, and enjoyable to the reader.

In this book, I also wanted to provide hope and positivity to those going through something similar. Unfortunately, not everyone will make it, and many patients, particularly in my days as a paediatric, sadly did not make it. I hope this book doesn't make cancer out to be 100% positive, because it is not. It is traumatic for patients and families and causes a lot of psychological and physical distress. But in this book, I try to pick out the positives and show that cancer isn't 100% doom and gloom either. You can get through it and will get through it if you fight hard, never give up, and maintain good faith! My determination and the army of people that I had behind me is what got me through my two leukaemia battles. Hope and positivity are the key to survival.

There have been advantages of having cancer too. How many people can say that they've had a wish granted by Make a Wish? Although I'll never forget what cancer has taken away from me, I'll never forget what it has given me. I've been able to undertake a number of opportunities as a result of my diagnoses, and it has given me nothing but courage, strength, and determination to continue to live my life to the absolute fullest.

My two battles with Acute Myeloid Leukaemia and my two bone marrow transplants have changed how I am perceived in society. I will always be in the 'vulnerable' category. The global pandemic has added pressures to this. I was amongst the first group to receive the Covid-19 vaccine; I had mine in February 2021. I'm sure getting Covid will always be a worry to the hospital should I continue to keep catching it.

I feel that for the rest of my life, I will constantly be on edge. Any cold or cough brings fear that the leukaemia is back. Any dizziness or unusual feeling causes anxiety. Any lump or bump that appears on my body will always cause fear. I do get the occasional lump come up from time to time, and with my clinical history, it is highly important that I get it checked. Mum used to (and still does) worry about it more than I do, though with my 2021 relapse, my fears have increased a lot.

I think my fear of relapse has something to do with being an adult too, which means I've been increasingly involved in my own care. As a paediatric, I was kept away from most of the blood test results. You may notice that Part III of this book is a lot more technical than Part I, and that's because I had so much more knowledge about my second battle with regards to my care. Nowadays, after every clinic appointment, I anxiously await my blood test results to come through on MyChart at 6:00pm. I never had that as a child. As briefly mentioned in Chapter 20, having an abnormal result automatically puts fears and anxiety in my head. I'm sure I was having abnormal results post-transplant as a paediatric too, but because I wasn't informed, it was only a problem if a doctor mentioned it. Now I'm an adult, I have access to my own information, which can leave me worrying for weeks. I'm not sure if it's a good or bad thing. I definitely would have liked more information as a paediatric, considering I was thirteen and capable of understanding the seriousness of my illness. But as I've noticed as an adult, I've been left traumatised by my second battle with leukaemia and viewing my blood test results causes stress and anxiety.

In the long-term, my two battles with leukaemia have had a lasting impact on me. The thought of relapsing again does terrify me. Of course, I feared it the first time. But I knew that if I relapsed the first time, then something could be done. Now that I've had AML twice and have had the maximum number of transplants that is considered safe and can be funded, I have lost my safety net. I often say that it feels like having a gun attached to your head 24/7. I have to live my life knowing that at some point in the future, I have a 50% chance of the trigger being pulled. Unfortunately, it's something beyond my control.

Sometimes I reflect too much on the negatives of my cancer journey. I feel I focus too much on the negative 50% and not the positive 50%. There's a 50% chance that I am set up for life. For two bone marrow transplants, I have made a miraculous recovery, and the fact that I am so keen and energetic to return to normal life should be a sign that I can live my life to the fullest, whether I have one year, five years, twenty years, or eighty years left to live! One thing that my first battle with leukaemia didn't do, though my second did, was give me the kick up the backside to live my life. As soon as the restrictions on myself regarding my immune system begin to ease, I will go back to work, finish my degree, and spend lots of time with my family and friends. There are so many places I want to go with so many people! I have a lot of ambitions in life, and if anything, the challenges that I have faced have encouraged me to pursue them further! Life is short, and I've realised I need to live it to the fullest.

I believe that having a difficult life makes you a better person, and even though leukaemia has been a torturous disease to have to put up with for a third of my life, I wouldn't change any of it. I've had a turbulent few years, but it is that that makes me proud to do the things I do each day. Completing a year at university is a challenge in itself but facing the challenges of cancer treatment at the same time only makes me prouder to have got through it. I haven't had the easiest life, but I have been able to turn my negatives into a positive. I have written a book on my AML, and I have shared my story with charities. It has to happen to somebody, and I've fully accepted that. I can use my experiences to the best of my ability to not only better myself but also help others going through something similar. The 'normal' life I wish for, and have always wished for, will only make me prouder once I've achieved it, because I know what I've been through to get there. Ultimately, I've learned to never take my life for granted because you don't know how long you've got it for.

I want to finish with a few thankyous. There are lots of people – both groups and individuals – who have collaborated in different ways, but all make my journey. Doctors, nurses, specialist nurses, dieticians, healthcare assistants, cooks, cleaners, counsellors, support workers, surgeons, radiographers, and many more hospital staff have all been responsible for why I am continuing to function well on the health side of things. Hospital teachers, play specialists, music therapists, and our hospital friends all helped me and my family function on the social side of hospital life. Extended family, friends, workplaces, and community nurses all made sure that things ran well back at home. Tutors and teachers did everything to ensure that my recovery and catching-up process ran as smoothly as possible. Charities ensured that they gave me everything they could to give me the best life possible during and after treatment. All of these, whether the effort was big or small, had combined to make sure I lived not only as comfortably, but also as enjoyably as possible during a traumatic time. I will never forget what everyone did to ensure this.

I would like to start by thanking all the doctors and nurses that cared for me under all three hospitals that I was treated under. My story began at West Suffolk Hospital in Bury St. Edmunds, and if it wasn't for the Rainbow Ward and them finding out what was wrong with me to begin with, my journey never would have got started! In my final days as a paediatric, they were very good to me during clinic appointments.

I would also like to thank the Bristol Royal Hospital for Children, where I had my first bone marrow transplant as a paediatric. The BRHC, particularly the care of Ward 34 and Day Beds, allowed me to enjoy five years of remission once I had finished treatment, and the care that I received there was absolutely amazing up until I was discharged.

Of course, the hospital I have to thank the most is Addenbrooke's Hospital in Cambridge. Ward C2 and the Paediatric Day Unit undertook the bulk of my care in 2016, where I had three rounds of chemotherapy, and Ward C9 undertook the entirety of my care from 2021 to 2022 when I relapsed. I had my second bone marrow transplant there, and there is absolutely no chance I'd be alive today if it wasn't for Addenbrooke's. They are amazing!

There are too many nurses for me to thank personally as I met many across my journey, but I am very thankful to those who made a personal impact on me. I appreciate every nurse who ever took care of me during my time in hospital, who worked around the clock to ensure I received my medications, blood tests, and any other medical procedures.

It is hard to personally thank the doctors, as getting permission to use their names in this book has been a very difficult process as they can move hospitals quite frequently. However, every doctor, both registrars and consultants, across all three hospitals that cared for me did their utmost to ensure I was cared for and well looked after. I'd like to personally thank my paediatric haematology consultants at Addenbrooke's, Dr. A and Dr. M, my BMT consultant in Bristol, Dr. G, and my current haematology consultant, Dr. U, who I am still under the amazing care of today. These four doctors have been responsible for my care over the past six years, and if it wasn't for them, I'd be in a very different place right now!

I'd also like to thank my specialist nurses. Amanda at Addenbrooke's was very good to my family and I when under paediatric care, writing letters to help out with school and work problems. We really appreciated Chris, at the BRHC, who helped my family and I settle into Bristol and continued to care for us throughout my stay. Jo, my current haematology specialist nurse at Addenbrooke's, has been very good to us and was particularly supportive during my mysterious neutropenia in late 2021, and I'd like to thank her for continuing to care for me to this day and being very good at replying to emails and getting my many issues sorted. I'd also like to thank Rosie, my TYA specialist nurse, who was very supportive of Mum and I during my stay on Ward C9 and was, and still is, always a text away if I needed anything, whether it was health-related or just for a general chat. I praise Rosie for all her support during my never-ending battle with Covid, and it was really good for me to have an assigned nurse who took care of me during such a difficult time.

I would like to thank all other hospital staff from across all three hospitals. Once again, there are too many to personally thank. Thank you to the healthcare assistants, who came to visit me every morning to ask if I needed anything, visited me every four hours to take my dreaded obs, and for being people I could just have a general chat to. I may show slight dissatisfaction with dieticians throughout this book, but I accept that the dieticians were doing their job and really cared about my health, and for that I am grateful that they always did what they thought was in my best interest. I'd like to thank the cooks and housekeepers for visiting me regularly throughout my hospital stays to make sure I wasn't going hungry and the cleaners who ensured my hospital rooms and bedspaces were always clean. There are so many hospital staff members to thank, whether they were ward clerks, receptionists, music therapists, counsellors, radiographers, pharmacists, radiologists, practitioners, phlebotomists, cardiologists, chaplains, or support workers, and there were many more amazing people who contributed to making sure I received the best care and support.

I'd like to thank the teachers at the Bristol Royal Hospital for Children and Addenbrooke's Hospital. Of course, a special mention has to go to Denise, who I worked really well with during my stay at Addenbrooke's, and I hope one day she finds this book and sees how well I am doing. Thank you also to Jackie, my home tutor, who I worked really well with and who ensured my return to school process was as smooth as possible. I'd like to thank Stowmarket High School, who were so supportive of me during my catching-up process, GCSEs, and my A-Levels, ultimately getting me to where I am today. I personally want to thank my teachers: Miss Smith, a very supportive head of year, who was able to adjust my awkward timetable to help me work the best I could; Mrs Arnold, who kindly gave up her Friday lunchtimes in Year 11 just to catch me up on the GCSE English content I had missed in the first half of Year 10; Mrs Dolby, my Year 11 French teacher, who was very supportive of me and worked very hard to get me the best grade possible; and Ms Relf, who supported me throughout both GCSE and A-Level history, enabling me to be where I am today to study the subject I love. And going into my 2021 battle, I'd like to thank all of my lecturers at the University of Suffolk for being flexible with my assignment deadlines and types of assignments to allow me to stay in the same year as my classmates. I am particularly grateful for my personal tutor, Scott, who met up with me on Microsoft Teams every Thursday at 4:00pm to discuss any of my concerns, worries, or anything university-related. Going through treatment and doing a degree would have been very difficult if I didn't have Scott's support.

I would like to thank all of my friends, both then and now. Special mentions go to Fin, who was absolutely amazing during my treatment for 2016, and I would like to congratulate him on all the fundraising he did. Fin did everything he could to support me, texting me as often as possible, and any time I was home, he took the opportunity to visit me. When I was in hospital, he'd often travel hours by train and then bus to come see me.

Everything Fin did meant a lot to me during my treatment, and it upsets me that we hardly talk anymore, but it is always good to hear from him from time to time. Although I never speak to Zoe now, she was also very good and supportive of me during my first time in hospital, and I am very glad that we got back in contact in September 2022. Fin and Zoe were absolutely amazing friends who allowed me to return to somewhat normality every time they came to visit me.

My other special mention goes to my best friend, Lauren, who was, and still is, absolutely amazing to me. She stayed by my side through everything during my 2021 to 2022 journey and, due to Covid and my weakened immune system, was the only person I saw outside of my family from December to April. She never stopped believing in me, even when I had doubts about undergoing treatment, and was always there for me. I appreciate everything she did when I was diagnosed for the second time: the box she made me when I went into hospital, the FaceTimes, and the positive voice messages. I enjoyed the quality time we spent together when I was home, which made me feel 'normal' again, including the many Chinese takeaways and movie nights we had. She was the only reason why I kept on with university, a decision and a promise that I am so glad that I made and kept. My frequent absence affected her a lot, both personally and university-related, and she had many hardships along the way, and I am so proud of how she overcame everything, often by herself. I am happy that we were able to complete our second year of university together.

Of course, it would be wrong not to acknowledge how amazing all my friends have been to me. I am so appreciative of my friendship group – Ryan, Skye, Alfie, Clare, and Will – who all put their differences aside to unite when first hearing eant a lot to us! Make a Wish gave me probably the best experience of my life so far, and I am so proud to have said that I've had my own wish granted. Glasgow was amazing, and the Make a Wish charity did everything they could to make my three days there special, where I made many memories! Make a Wish is a truly wonderful organisation! I am thankful for the Liam Fairhurst Foundation, which provided me with a gift of £500 when I relapsed, just to treat myself and make me smile over Christmas! And, of course, the Teenage Cancer Trust has been, and still is, absolutely amazing. I am grateful for their support after my initial treatment. I particularly enjoyed the Find Your Sense of Tumour residential. Little did I know that three and a half years later, I'd end up being taken care of on one of their wards and have to receive my second bone marrow transplant there. Without a doubt, I wouldn't be alive today if it wasn't for the Teenage Cancer Trust, their amazing units, nurses, and support workers. It is a pleasure to be able to write blogs and share my story with them on their website, and I hope to work on many projects with them in the future!

Of course, I have to say a massive thank you to my 2016 transplant donor. It upsets me that I don't know who they are, but wherever they are, I will forever be grateful for their kindness in donating their stem cells to give me a second chance of life. Even though my first transplant ultimately failed, it prolonged my life by another five years. It may not have reached the long-term remission we hoped for, but those five years were worth it! I still hope that one day I get to visit France to meet the person who was technically my 'twin sister' for five years!

I'm proud of my scars, which Dad says are like bullet wounds. It shows that I fought a battle and won. But I only did the frontline fighting. My two battles are just the tip of

my news in December 2021. I appreciate them messaging me regularly to check I was okay, their cards, and their joint presents that they all contributed to get me at Christmas and Easter to give me the most enjoyable time in hospital as possible. They may not realise but they have been absolutely amazing in helping my recovery as I have begun to see more people, and they are completely understanding of anything I can and can't do due to my health restrictions.

And I can't forget my best mate, Liam, who no doubt had a tough time at school in 2016 when his friend disappeared for months. What I went through resulted in hardship for him, and I'll always appreciate how he sacrificed his own social life just so I didn't feel replaced when I returned to school. To this day, he remains one of my very closest and most loyal friends.

Special mentions also have to go to my extended family. I'd particularly like to thank Auntie Karen and Uncle John, who visited Mum and I every week while I was in hospital in 2016. We appreciated their time and their help with getting shopping for us. Even though Covid made visiting non-existent in 2021 and 2022, Auntie Karen still kept in regular contact and sent me cards and gifts. I'd also like to thank Grandma, who once again kept in regular contact with me during both my battles with leukaemia, and I praise her for all her hard work with her fundraising for charities, such as the Teenage Cancer Trust and Anthony Nolan. I'd also like to thank my cousin, Jade, who regularly surprised me with gifts during the lonelier 2022 days when visiting was restricted, and I also appreciate the efforts she took to look after Kristy during my treatment in 2016.

Family friends also played a very important role in looking after my family and I. Firstly, I'd like to thank my neighbour, Sharon, who helped my family out at home in

2016 by supporting Kristy and cooking us meals. I'm also appreciative of her effort in organising my first transplant birthday party, where we raised money for the charity DKMS. I'd also like to thank all other family friends who contributed in some way in 2016 and from 2021 to 2022 to help things run smoothly at home when my parents were away, whether that was Dad's co-workers cooking my parents meals, family friends inviting Kristy over for dinner, or our neighbours helping to feed the cats.

It's also important not to forget the Krutke family, especially Lorna, and all the other parents on the wards that Mum eventually became friends with. Lorna kept Mum sane during the days of Bristol, when both Jacob and I were undergoing our transplants, and Lorna remained a massive support to Mum throughout my relapse, regularly meeting her for coffee in the hospital concourse. We are grateful to have made such good friends, and we appreciate Lorna setting up the GoFundMe page to support my family when I relapsed.

All my appreciation goes out to every member of my 'Jake's Leukaemia Fight' Facebook page, who have stayed with me to track my progress and offer words of encouragement. I am truly grateful for all my friends, family, co-workers, family friends, and the supportive people on my group that I have never met, who have stayed with me to track my progress from December 2021 to now. I plan on 'Jake's Leukaemia Fight' being a long-term thing, where I will post updates on my hopefully improving health over the years.

I would also like to thank the workplaces of both of my parents. Dad was so lucky to be able to take so much time off when he looked after me in 2016. His work was also very kind to me by making me two hampers full of sweets and games when I first became ill. Mum's work, Glasswells, was equally supportive, allowing her to work remotely with a l̶ m̶ allowing her to be more flexible with her time and ̶ e̶ off when needed, both in 2016 and from 2021 to 2̶ t̶ company has also been very good to me, understan̶ t̶ need to take time off.

It is important that I acknowledge all the chariti̶ supported me in some way throughout both my ̶ journeys and my time in remission. Thank you to the̶ Children's Trust, a charity that was undoubtedly̶ helpful to my family as soon as I was first diagnosed ̶ leukaemia, providing brilliant services, such as Acorn Ho̶ to accommodate my parents while I was staying in hospit̶ Thank you to the Callum Pites Smile Charity – the first chari̶ that I, personally, was able to benefit from – who were kin̶ enough to provide me with a £500 PC World voucher. It was̶ that gift card that enabled me to buy the laptop I began writing this book on. Thank you to CLIC Sargent, now known as Young Lives vs Cancer, whose support in Bristol was outstanding in providing my family and I a place to stay at Sam's House. Thank you to my Young Lives vs Cancer social worker, Kathy, who supported me throughout both my cancer journeys. I was very surprised when she remembered who I was when my case was reopened in 2021! Kathy helped me with my referrals and paperwork for my disability allowance, PIP forms, and grants to support my parents. Thank you to Supershoes; I am very grateful to own two pairs of amazing Supershoes, which are proudly displayed on my shelf! Thank you to Henry's Holiday Help, which I am saddened to hear has since shut down; it was a very important charity to my family and I during my first cancer battle. The yearly Christmas parties, the Christmas gifts for my entire family, and of course the £1000 grant towards our holiday in New York the iceberg. There was something keeping me stable. My parents were the ones who suffered the most and had to work very hard, struggling with their work in addition to having the burden of taking care of me, all the while having another child at home. Yes, we all had to travel to and live in Bristol and Cambridge regularly, but who was paying for it? Yes, we all did food shopping every day, but who was paying for it? Yes, I had many medicines to take when an outpatient, but who was ensuring I was taking them? Who could afford all this time off work? Particularly as a paediatric, their responsibilities on the ward included making my bed, helping me get washed and dressed, and keeping me company, and these responsibilities were increased as an outpatient when they drove me to appointments and managed my medicines, as well as having to make the difficult judgements of whether to send me back to the hospital in the times I was struggling. Mum and Dad suffered the most, helplessly having to watch their son fight two battles, which at times felt unwinnable, and I am forever thankful for what they did for me and what they did to keep the family together, and I am very sorry for what I put them through.

My 2021 relapse was even harder as Covid meant we were a divided family, but I am so appreciative of Mum for consistently being there for me on the ward and in the hospital to look after me and keep me company. Mum and I spent every day together during those very difficult days. I will forever be grateful for Dad, who gave me my third chance of life by donating his stem cells for my second bone marrow transplant, and all the work he did to keep things running smoothly at home and to keep Mum and I afloat with supplies at the hospital. I am proud of Kristy, and equally apologetic to her, for keeping going, even through the absence of her parents, who she needed most. I am glad that after a few years of struggling with her own problems, she has got through them and is now studying Biomedicine at the University of East Anglia in Norwich, a lot of which has been inspired by my transplants and my journey with Acute Myeloid Leukaemia.

My family were always there for me, from holding the sick bowl while I was sick, to being there for me when I was mentally at my lowest, and to ensuring that I was well-informed of what was going on regarding my condition. And for that, it is my family who I will forever credit for my survival.

Family photo in Newmarket, August 27th 2022.

my news in December 2021. I appreciate them messaging me regularly to check I was okay, their cards, and their joint presents that they all contributed to get me at Christmas and Easter to give me the most enjoyable time in hospital as possible. They may not realise but they have been absolutely amazing in helping my recovery as I have begun to see more people, and they are completely understanding of anything I can and can't do due to my health restrictions.

And I can't forget my best mate, Liam, who no doubt had a tough time at school in 2016 when his friend disappeared for months. What I went through resulted in hardship for him, and I'll always appreciate how he sacrificed his own social life just so I didn't feel replaced when I returned to school. To this day, he remains one of my very closest and most loyal friends.

Special mentions also have to go to my extended family. I'd particularly like to thank Auntie Karen and Uncle John, who visited Mum and I every week while I was in hospital in 2016. We appreciated their time and their help with getting shopping for us. Even though Covid made visiting non-existent in 2021 and 2022, Auntie Karen still kept in regular contact and sent me cards and gifts. I'd also like to thank Grandma, who once again kept in regular contact with me during both my battles with leukaemia, and I praise her for all her hard work with her fundraising for charities, such as the Teenage Cancer Trust and Anthony Nolan. I'd also like to thank my cousin, Jade, who regularly surprised me with gifts during the lonelier 2022 days when visiting was restricted, and I also appreciate the efforts she took to look after Kristy during my treatment in 2016.

Family friends also played a very important role in looking after my family and I. Firstly, I'd like to thank my neighbour, Sharon, who helped my family out at home in

2016 by supporting Kristy and cooking us meals. I'm also appreciative of her effort in organising my first transplant birthday party, where we raised money for the charity DKMS. I'd also like to thank all other family friends who contributed in some way in 2016 and from 2021 to 2022 to help things run smoothly at home when my parents were away, whether that was Dad's co-workers cooking my parents meals, family friends inviting Kristy over for dinner, or our neighbours helping to feed the cats.

It's also important not to forget the Krutke family, especially Lorna, and all the other parents on the wards that Mum eventually became friends with. Lorna kept Mum sane during the days of Bristol, when both Jacob and I were undergoing our transplants, and Lorna remained a massive support to Mum throughout my relapse, regularly meeting her for coffee in the hospital concourse. We are grateful to have made such good friends, and we appreciate Lorna setting up the GoFundMe page to support my family when I relapsed.

All my appreciation goes out to every member of my 'Jake's Leukaemia Fight' Facebook page, who have stayed with me to track my progress and offer words of encouragement. I am truly grateful for all my friends, family, co-workers, family friends, and the supportive people on my group that I have never met, who have stayed with me to track my progress from December 2021 to now. I plan on 'Jake's Leukaemia Fight' being a long-term thing, where I will post updates on my hopefully improving health over the years.

I would also like to thank the workplaces of both of my parents. Dad was so lucky to be able to take so much time off when he looked after me in 2016. His work was also very kind to me by making me two hampers full of sweets and games when I first became ill. Mum's work, Glasswells, was equally supportive, allowing her to work remotely with a laptop and allowing her to be more flexible with her time and take time off when needed, both in 2016 and from 2021 to 2022. The company has also been very good to me, understanding my need to take time off.

It is important that I acknowledge all the charities who supported me in some way throughout both my cancer journeys and my time in remission. Thank you to the Sick Children's Trust, a charity that was undoubtedly very helpful to my family as soon as I was first diagnosed with leukaemia, providing brilliant services, such as Acorn House to accommodate my parents while I was staying in hospital. Thank you to the Callum Pites Smile Charity – the first charity that I, personally, was able to benefit from – who were kind enough to provide me with a £500 PC World voucher. It was that gift card that enabled me to buy the laptop I began writing this book on. Thank you to CLIC Sargent, now known as Young Lives vs Cancer, whose support in Bristol was outstanding in providing my family and I a place to stay at Sam's House. Thank you to my Young Lives vs Cancer social worker, Kathy, who supported me throughout both my cancer journeys. I was very surprised when she remembered who I was when my case was reopened in 2021! Kathy helped me with my referrals and paperwork for my disability allowance, PIP forms, and grants to support my parents. Thank you to Supershoes; I am very grateful to own two pairs of amazing Supershoes, which are proudly displayed on my shelf! Thank you to Henry's Holiday Help, which I am saddened to hear has since shut down; it was a very important charity to my family and I during my first cancer battle. The yearly Christmas parties, the Christmas gifts for my entire family, and of course the £1000 grant towards our holiday in New York meant a lot to us! Make a Wish gave me probably the best experience of my life so far, and I am so proud to have said that I've had my own wish granted. Glasgow was amazing, and the Make a Wish charity did everything they could to make my three days there special, where I made many memories! Make a Wish is a truly wonderful organisation! I am thankful for the Liam Fairhurst Foundation, which provided me with a gift of £500 when I relapsed, just to treat myself and make me smile over Christmas! And, of course, the Teenage Cancer Trust has been, and still is, absolutely amazing. I am grateful for their support after my initial treatment. I particularly enjoyed the Find Your Sense of Tumour residential. Little did I know that three and a half years later, I'd end up being taken care of on one of their wards and have to receive my second bone marrow transplant there. Without a doubt, I wouldn't be alive today if it wasn't for the Teenage Cancer Trust, their amazing units, nurses, and support workers. It is a pleasure to be able to write blogs and share my story with them on their website, and I hope to work on many projects with them in the future!

Of course, I have to say a massive thank you to my 2016 transplant donor. It upsets me that I don't know who they are, but wherever they are, I will forever be grateful for their kindness in donating their stem cells to give me a second chance of life. Even though my first transplant ultimately failed, it prolonged my life by another five years. It may not have reached the long-term remission we hoped for, but those five years were worth it! I still hope that one day I get to visit France to meet the person who was technically my 'twin sister' for five years!

I'm proud of my scars, which Dad says are like bullet wounds. It shows that I fought a battle and won. But I only did the frontline fighting. My two battles are just the tip of the iceberg. There was something keeping me stable. My parents were the ones who suffered the most and had to work very hard, struggling with their work in addition to having the burden of taking care of me, all the while having another child at home. Yes, we all had to travel to and live in Bristol and Cambridge regularly, but who was paying for it? Yes, we all did food shopping every day, but who was paying for it? Yes, I had many medicines to take when an outpatient, but who was ensuring I was taking them? Who could afford all this time off work? Particularly as a paediatric, their responsibilities on the ward included making my bed, helping me get washed and dressed, and keeping me company, and these responsibilities were increased as an outpatient when they drove me to appointments and managed my medicines, as well as having to make the difficult judgements of whether to send me back to the hospital in the times I was struggling. Mum and Dad suffered the most, helplessly having to watch their son fight two battles, which at times felt unwinnable, and I am forever thankful for what they did for me and what they did to keep the family together, and I am very sorry for what I put them through.

My 2021 relapse was even harder as Covid meant we were a divided family, but I am so appreciative of Mum for consistently being there for me on the ward and in the hospital to look after me and keep me company. Mum and I spent every day together during those very difficult days. I will forever be grateful for Dad, who gave me my third chance of life by donating his stem cells for my second bone marrow transplant, and all the work he did to keep things running smoothly at home and to keep Mum and I afloat with supplies at the hospital. I am proud of Kristy, and equally apologetic to her, for keeping going, even through the absence of her parents, who she needed most. I am glad that after a few years of struggling with her own problems, she has got through them and is now studying Biomedicine at the University of East Anglia in Norwich, a lot of which has been inspired by my transplants and my journey with Acute Myeloid Leukaemia.

My family were always there for me, from holding the sick bowl while I was sick, to being there for me when I was mentally at my lowest, and to ensuring that I was well-informed of what was going on regarding my condition. And for that, it is my family who I will forever credit for my survival.

Family photo in Newmarket, August 27th 2022.